Cruising the Caribbean

Cruising the Caribbean

U.S. Influence and Intervention in the Twentieth Century

Ronald Fernandez

Common Courage Press   Monroe, ME 04951

Library of Congress Cataloging-in-Publication Data

Fernandez, Ronald.
Cruising the Caribbean: U.S. Influence and Intervention
in the Twentieth Century / Ronald Fernandez
p.   cm.

Includes bibliographical references and index.
ISBN 1-56751-036-1—ISBN 1-56751-037-X (pbk.)
1. Caribbean Area—Foreign relations—United States.
2. United States—Foreign relations—Caribbean area.
3. Decision-making—United States.
4. Decision-making—Moral and ethical aspects.
I. Title. F2178.U6F49 1994b
327.730729—dc20   94-8365 CIP

Common Courage Press
P.O. Box 702
Monroe, ME 04951
207-525-0900
Fax: 207-525-3068

First Printing

With love, this book is dedicated to
Benjamin Harrison Fernandez

Acknowledgments

I owe a true debt of gratitude to June Wellwood, Steven Cauffman, and Kiyomi Kutsuzawa at Central Connecticut State University. They managed to happily and efficiently fill numerous requests for books and articles via interlibrary loan. Thank you.

Karen Beyard and George Clark provided great assistance and enormous encouragement throughout this long project. Burt Baldwin read and criticized the entire manuscript. He helped a great deal.

I was again lucky enough to work with the staff and resources of the Connecticut State Library. This a superb facility, managed by a group of exceedingly capable and friendly librarians. My thanks to Julie Schwartz, Al Palko, Nancy Peluso, Steve Kwasnik, Joy Floyd, Susan Harris, and Doreen Di Bonis.

The U.S. system of presidential libraries is a remarkable resource for scholars. My thanks and gratitude to Dennis Bilger at the Truman Library, Jim Leyerzapf at Eisenhower, Leesa Tobin at Ford, Martin Elzy at Carter, Regina Greenwell at Johnson, Dale Miller at Hoover, and the staffs at the Kennedy and Roosevelt libraries, as well as the staff at the Nixon Project in Virginia. Thanks, too, to the staffs at the National Archives and the Navy Library in Washington. D.C.

Brenda Harrison was my partner at a number of presidential libraries. More important, this book would not exist without her.

Hartford, Connecticut
June, 1994

Contents

Introduction

This book was prompted by two questions: Why do intelligent men and women sometimes pursue inconsistent or contradictory foreign policies; and why do decent people sometime pursue cruel political, economic, and military strategies?

The answers to these questions involve cultural beliefs, values, and practices. Policymakers often see, not reality but their culturally inspired version of it.

Cruising the Caribbean is thus a study of the cultural beliefs, values, and practices of America's twentieth century policymakers. My focus is on the taken-for-granted assumptions which shape the contours of a century of American thinking. My aim is to comprehend how a president like Woodrow Wilson could be committed to democratic values and nevertheless use Marines to impose three military dictatorships (in Haiti, the Dominican Republic, and the Virgin Islands) within two years.

The Caribbean is a region in which the foreign consequences of American culture are most clearly revealed. Islands like Grenada and Hispaniola are generally so poor, small, weak, and outside the mainstream of world consciousness that mitigating factors, for example, world opinion, rarely deter U.S. policymakers. Thus, presidents from Roosevelt to Reagan had a free hand in the Caribbean, and their actions show the foreign consequences of U.S. culture when it operates without restraints.

Americans see themselves in positive terms. Through two hundred years of history the American people have allegedly helped others to pursue the political and economic values which make the United States such a remarkable country. The argument of this book is that, at least in the Caribbean, *we are not who we think we are.* The goals and consequences of U.S. Caribbean policy have had little to do with the dominant and quite positive assessments of American culture, and even less to do with the ideals championed by the revolutionaries who, in 1776, sought to start the world all over again.

The goal of this book is to look at the cultural sources of U.S. Caribbean policy. If we are not who we think we are, then the bridge between one century and another is a perfect place to begin the reevaluation that could exchange empathy for ethnocentrism, idealism for expediency, and hope for the desperation that drives people to embark on the perilous voyage from Haiti to Guantanamo, from Cuba to Miami, from the Dominican Republic to Puerto Rico, or from Jamaica to the sugar fields of Florida.

Supreme Hypocrisy

"If we pass this amendment against Cuba we advertise to the rest of the world what supreme hypocrites are in control in Washington. I would rejoice to see Cuba peacefully annexed to the United States but I am not willing to steal it."

—Congressman Williams of Illinois,
March 1, 1901[1]

Unhand that woman. Let Cuba go. Or, "law or no law," Senator George Gray would revenge the "violated womanhood, childhood, and motherhood" of the Cuban people.

Speaking in support of President William McKinley's (April 6, 1898) war message, Senator Gray said his colleagues should think of themselves as good neighbors. Next door lived "a villainous and cruel neighbor who every day choked his wife and starved and maltreated his children." For "days and weeks" the good neighbor, in the name of law, listened to the screams and endured the pain of the helpless woman and children. He tried to restrain himself, but, overwhelmed by the horror at his door, the good neighbor finally took the law into his own hands. "He entered the residence of his neighbor, took him by the throat, and said, 'take your hand off that woman and let these children go.'"[2]

Senator Gray said the rest of the neighborhood applauded the courage of their forceful friend. All saw the wisdom and morality of armed intervention. But if "our neighbors in the family of nations" failed to see the necessity of illegal action, then the problem was theirs. Our neighbors will applaud, and, "if they do not, God help them and the civilization they represent."

A colleague interrupted Senator Gray. What if, after we invaded Cuba, and made her independent, our neighbor had the temerity to form a government which, in our estimation, was unjust? Would we recognize such a government? If not, would we again invade to assure a government that comes within our approval?

Senator Gray never hesitated. The United States had to take care that Cubans formed a government "under our supervision and care and tutelage." They would take what we gave them and be grateful because all Cubans knew the United States "did not mean to forever exercise a protectorate" over the island; and every Cuban also understood that the United States of America had "no selfish considerations." All we wanted to do was "set up a republican government" and "we would retire and leave the Cubans to conduct better housekeeping than was ever conducted under Spanish rule or Spanish protectorate."[3]

Senator Gray meant what he said. Indeed, any man who spoke of "sucking the tyrant-hating milk from New England's hardy breasts" could hardly be accused of hypocrisy. Unless, of course, you were one of the senator's, and the president's, opponents; hypocrisy then became the charge of the hour. The opposition argued that the president's war message violated not only a pledge to the Cuban people, but a pledge to the democratic principles that made the United States such a unique and successful experiment.

Washington, Hancock, Lafayette, Von Stuben and De Kalb—before this debate was over, these "immortal adventurers" would appear in the Congressional Record as witnesses to the alleged suppression of the inalienable right of the Cuban people to self-determination. Suddenly—and often quite eloquently—a battle about Cuba and the Caribbean became a battle about the meaning of the United States of America.

The president refused to recognize the Cuban revolutionary government. He argued that "such recognition is not due to a revolted dependency until the danger of its being subjugated by the parent state has entirely passed away." McKinley claimed that if we recognized their government "our conduct would be subject to the approval or disapproval of such government. We would be required to submit to its direction and to assume to it the mere relation of a friendly ally."[4]

Critics argued that the president's first problem was his secretary of state. On February 28, 1896, then-Senator John Sherman had not only championed the cause of the Cuban revolution, he had argued that it was absolutely untrue that the Cubans had no organized government. "Sir, much to my surprise...they have gone through all the formulae of self-government as fully and completely as the people of the United States did at the beginning of the Revolution." To Sherman, Congress had no choice but to recognize the Cuban revolutionary government, and the independence of the Cuban nation.[5]

An ardent supporter of Sherman's suggestion was Senator Henry Cabot Lodge. He said the Cubans had endured "a year of desperate and successful fighting against heavy odds." The United States should recognize the independence of Cuba because it was "reasonable and proper," and because Lodge had no doubt that "the American people would sustain [a recognition of independence] without a dissenting voice and that the civilized world would applaud."[6]

Lodge was right. The Congressional Record indicates that his pro-independence speech was greeted by "manifestations of applause in the galleries." By April of 1898, however, Lodge had changed his mind and John Sherman, now secretary of state, was in charge of a department that refused to recognize a government that, according to Senator Sherman, was as legitimate as the one officered by George Washington and assisted by the Marquis de Lafayette.

The Marquis assumed center stage when critics focused, not on political contradiction, but on the "sinister influences" that mocked America's commitment to democratic principles. Senator David Turpie of Indiana asked what would have happened if the French had refused to leave after Britain accepted the harsh reality of defeat? What if they had stayed in the United States until the establishment of a government that met with the approval of the French king and the French government?[7]

Turpie said the founding fathers would have fought another seven years if the French had had the audacity to suggest imposing their will on a now free American people. It would have been immoral for the French to do any such thing in 1783; and it would be immoral in April of 1898 if Congress, following the president, refused to recognize "the great, overshadowing, outlying fact in this whole transaction"—the existence of the Cuban Republic.

"Where in the history of the world," asked Senator Turpie, "has there been an instance when a free de facto government in arms had been suppressed by a friend and ally for any cause, [or] had been supplanted by a friend and ally for any other form of government?"[8] Turpie said never, and then introduced the issue of the Spanish-Cuban war debt.

Before its birth as a nation, Cuba, thanks to the Spanish, already owed $300,000,000 to mostly European creditors. The United States, if it took over the island, could become responsible for the resolution of this debt. To Turpie that was a grave and unthinkable possibility. So, in addition to his principled rejection of the president's message, Turpie added a practical element. Recognize the Cubans because that is the right thing to do, and because we don't want to be Europe's Caribbean debt collector.

President McKinley had his defenders. Indiana's other senator, Charles Fairbanks, sounded a theme that cut through these debates when he stressed America's goodness. We wanted nothing. We were indisputably a fine people who simply had no choice. "We must intervene for and in the name of humanity. No higher motive can actuate any government."[9]

Nevertheless, the senator's colleagues refused to support the president. In the House of Representatives, vigorous arm twisting had produced the resolution McKinley desired. In the Senate, the Democrat

13

Turpie joined forces with the Republican Joseph Foraker to produce an amendment "that the people of the island of Cuba are, and of right ought to be, free and independent, and the Government of the United States hereby recognizes the Republic of Cuba as the true and lawful government of the island."

This amendment passed by a vote of fifty-one to thirty-seven.[10] McKinley was in trouble, and, so too, the Cubans, because in an attempt to settle its war resolution differences, the House-Senate conference committee could scrap political principle. Cuba's fate, now in the hands of Congress and the president, depended on the answers given to these particular questions: Was the United States going to act like a Great Power, or, like a Great Example? If a Great Example, would it perform this service by forcing others to adopt its system of government, language, and culture?

These questions dominated the 1898 debate about the independence of Cuba. Congress' answers reveal a great deal, not only about our policy in the Caribbean but about the overall thrust of American foreign policy. As one scholar put it to Congress in 1973, "to me the Caribbean is a laboratory. I think the world tends to see it to some extent as a kind of laboratory or showcase in which the American policy is exhibited."[11]

In no other part of the world do U.S. policy makers act so freely, and, as the 1898 debates are meant to suggest, are their decisions so at odds with the ideals championed by Washington and Hancock, Paine and Jefferson.

Jefferson became part of the congressional

14

debate as soon as the Senate discussed the results of its consultations with the House of Representatives. In private McKinley had threatened to veto any resolution which recognized the government recognized (in 1896) by his secretary of state. Therefore, the Senate put political peace ahead of political principle. As Joseph Foraker told his colleagues, "when we went into conference, although it was not because I changed my mind about it, but in order that we might have harmony and unity of action with respect to this important matter, we did promptly agree to abandon the Turpie amendment...."[12]

There was one condition. The conference committee must restore the words "are and" to the first lines of the war resolution, which would now read "that the people of the island of Cuba are and of right ought to be free and independent."

Any compromise was impossible. If the United States did not recognize the independence of the Cuban people, it contradicted the position taken by virtually every American political leader. To Foraker, all Americans agreed that, by its barbarous conduct, Spain had forfeited its sovereignty over Cuba. Thus, "if there be no sovereignty of Spain in that island, surely the people of that island are free and independent, and it seems to us absolutely unjustifiable upon principle that we should fail to recognize the independence of the people of that island."[13]

Senator George Hoar of Massachusetts disagreed with Foraker. Erase the "are and" and simply indicate that they ought to be free. Otherwise you imply that "in fact they are not free."

Foraker's response was a dagger: "It is the language of the Declaration of Independence!" In writing the proposed amendment Joseph Foraker had copied the words of Thomas Jefferson, and he seemed surprised when Hoar refused to endorse what any American agreed was a miraculous document.

Hoar expressed no reservations about Jefferson or the Declaration of Independence. His reluctance stemmed from applying American principles to the Cuban people. Using "are and" might imply recognition of Cuba, and, since recognition meant a limitation on U.S. power, and U.S. political, economic, and military options, it was impossible to accord legitimacy to the revolutionary forces.

Senator Roger Mills now took the floor. Whatever his motives, the Texas Democrat quickly turned the debate into a memorable battle about God and natural law. "Mr. President, it seems to me that the criticism upon the language 'are and of right ought to be free' is a hundred years too late." Did Senator Hoar and his supporters deny the "self-evident" fact that all men are created equal? And, if they truly accepted this "orthodox faith" of the American people, how could they draw a distinction between ourselves and the Cubans? "Is not Cuba in the same position now that the Continental Congress was in 1776?"

Senator Mills then recruited another soldier for the Cuban army; God was on the island's side. "My friends, the fathers who settled these colonies maintained that freedom was the gift of God." It was a natural right which no person could democratically deny unless "he was willing to turn his back on the history of his own country...[I] insist that we will not abandon our creed, even in this supreme moment."[14]

Supreme Hypocrisy

Several senators shouted, "Vote! Vote!" They
wanted instant action, but in such a charged
atmosphere, and in a Senate where informed and
elegant debate was still the order of the legislative
day, silence was out of the question. John W. Daniel
of Virginia argued that the House of Representatives
wanted a resolution that "erased" all recognitions of
Cuban freedom. Charles Allen of Nebraska not only
refused to compromise, he refused to engage in any
more conferences; recognize the independence of
the Republic of Cuba and let the House of Representatives explain their peculiar position to the people
of the United States.[15]

Ultimately compromise won, and principle partially lost. During the war resolution debates a suggestion made by Henry Teller of Colorado was added
to the Senate's list of demands; under all and any
circumstances, the United States "explicitly dis-
claimed any intention or disposition" to exercise
sovereignty or control over Cuba and its people. We
would intervene only for the purposes of "pacifica-
tion" and, that done, we would "leave the government and control of the island" to the Cuban people.

Teller's disclaimer became point four of the
Senate's (and House's) ultimate war resolution. The
words "are and" also remained in the document, but
instead of any recognition of the Cuba revolutionary
government, or the unconditional independence of
the Cuban people, the U.S. voiced a desire that the
Cubans are and ought to be free and independent.

McKinley expressed "great satisfaction" with this
final resolution. He had requested that "our conduct"
not be subject to the prior approval or disapproval of
anyone and the Senate's new resolution gave him

what amounted to carte blanche. Even though Cuba's representatives had told both the president and the congressional leadership that Cuba did *not* want the United States to intervene with soldiers,[16] McKinley could use the U.S. army if he saw fit.

The president was smiling. Many senators were not. The day after the resolution passed, Butler of North Carolina expressed surprise when, after a close study of Cuban and American revolutionary government, he concluded that Cuba's organization "is vastly superior to the one we had at the time." Senator Foraker agreed and stressed that "it never occurred to me that if we were to recognize the independence of the people of Cuba, we would deny recognition to that political organization under the direction and control of which that independence had been achieved."[17] Stop "cavilling," said Foraker. We did "our duty" to the Cubans when we tried to recognize their legitimate government. Given our gallant fight, no one could blame us for surrendering.

We lost and so did the Cubans. Two weeks later, the president privately summarized his strategy: "While we are conducting war and until its conclusion we must keep all we can get. When the war is over we must keep what we want."[18]

Cuba and Puerto Rico

Cuba's flag has white and blue stripes flanked by a white star in a *red* triangle, and Puerto Rico's flag has red and white stripes flanked by a white star in a *blue* triangle. Each flag is, of course, unique. Never be forced to explain to a patriotic Cuban or Puerto Rican how you missed such an obvious difference! Their striking similarity nevertheless suggests two important facts: both Cuba and Puerto Rico have their national roots in Spanish colonialism and in the struggle to confront that colonialism.

Because Cubans and Puerto Ricans shared a common enemy, victory in Congress offered William McKinley a number of alternatives. He could interpret Congress' war resolution in a liberating manner (the Cubans and Puerto Ricans had a "natural, God given" right to be free), or he could decide to act like an imperialist and "subject peoples to the primary advantage of rulers who operate from an outside power center."[19]

In Puerto Rico the United States soon established a government that one of its creators called an "autocracy." The beauty of the Puerto Rican system, William Willoughby argued, was that "it had an administration of its governmental affairs that was similar in all respects to that of old [i.e, pre WWI] Germany." The Puerto Rican government was also based on that of the British colonies, but the island's colonial government squared the circle: In the name of democracy, it created an apparatus that "to a large extent took the whole control over the manner in which the actual administration of affairs shall be exercised out of the hands of the people itself."[20]

How, in the name of democracy, establish autocracy? And why use British colonialism as a partial model for the United States' Puerto Rican government? In the Crown colonies of Jamaica and Trinidad, and in the "unincorporated" territory called Puerto Rico, the key political arm had the same name, the Executive Council. This body ruled with autocratic force, and it was legitimate in Puerto

Rico only because the United States of America practiced a form of "good colonialism."[21]

Puerto Rico, for example, was the first unincorporated territory in U.S. history. From Louisiana (1803) to Arizona (1848) to Hawaii (1898), all lands purchased or conquered by the United States were promised eventual statehood. Thus, even in the Pacific, Hawaii was an incorporated part of the United States.

Puerto Rico was the first of the former Spanish colonies to have its fate determined by Congress. Sentiment was against offering these new possessions (*i.e*, Puerto Rico, the Philippines and Guam) any equal place in the Union. To underline their unique status, Puerto Ricans were even forbidden to call their non-voting representative in Congress a delegate. That was the special label reserved for representatives of Americans-in-waiting. Puerto Ricans would call their emissaries "resident commissioners" because, as the U.S. Supreme Court noted in 1901, "whilst in an international sense Puerto Rico was not a foreign country, since it was subject to the sovereignty of and owned by the United States, it was foreign to the United States in a domestic sense, because the island had not been incorporated into the United States, but was merely appurtenant thereto as a possession."[22]

Translation: Puerto Rico was an international nothing. Someday Congress might or might not decide its permanent legal status, but, while islanders waited, William Taft helped write a 1902 book, *Opportunities in the Colonies and Cuba*[23]—that clarified the island's de facto status: Puerto Rico was a colony. Men like William Howard Taft openly confronted that undemocratic fact because they understood the difference between good and bad colonialism. The bad sought only to exploit others, but the good colonialist "held another people under control because they were, in the judgement of the power which governs their territory, not capable of self-rule."[24]

Recall Senator Gray and the violated childhood of Cuba, or scan the political cartoons of the period. Cuba and Puerto Rico are invariably children, woman or little girls in need of protection. They require U.S. assistance because, as Senator Perkins of Georgia told his colleagues on April 2, 1900: "The people of a country cannot, like Aaron's rod, blossom and bear fruit in twenty-four hours." It took a "thousand years" for the Anglo-Saxons to develop self-government and, while he put no thousand year perspective on Puerto Rico's tutelage, Perkins, and a number of his colleagues, stressed that, given their terrible Spanish heritage, "the transition of a government of despotism to democracy would be a slow process....[G]eneration after generation must first be educated in the school of civil and religious liberty before they can fully appreciate the benefits they may enjoy under a republican form of government."[25]

Today U.S. culture makes a distinction between developed and underdeveloped nations. In 1900 the everyday concepts used to compare countries lacked our contemporary subtlety, our frustrating attempts to achieve objectivity. In 1900, many congressmen and senators simply made a distinction between us and them, between civilization and barbarity. Speaking in the House of Representatives in 1901, Congressman Scudder of New York said that Cuba before our intervention "was like having an open cesspool opposite one's front door." The Spanish naturally bore principal responsibility for this human horror, but Congress also had to understand an elemental fact: "The Cubans did not want those [i.e, sanitary] improvements; they did not want to be clean and healthy." They had the temerity to oppose the "American innovations as so many assaults upon their traditional privileges and freedoms."

Why? Congressman Scudder said "the Cubans preferred the old way of doing things. They liked smells; and they had a fondness for dirt."[26]

Scudder was crass even by Congress' then prejudiced standards. But his arguments, 'the Cubans like dirt,' help to explain the ability of so many American leaders to remain oblivious to the natural law issues raised in the debates about Cuba and its revolutionary government. If the United States was civilized and "they" were barbaric, incapable or black, then creating an autocracy in the name of democracy was *not* contradictory. These people needed our help. They were, as William Taft told the Cubans, our "wards,"[27] and we could disregard their inalienable rights because, at their primitive stage of civilization, they had no inalienable rights.

The roots of good colonialism lay in two sets of cultural assumptions which conceived of the Caribbean and its peoples in negative terms. First was racism. Half of all slaves that were brought to the "New World" found themselves prisoners in the Caribbean.[28] Five million black Africans labored in a small set of islands situated just below one of the world's most powerful and prejudiced nations. Even

Cuba's staunch defenders made distinctions among Cubans. For example, Congressman Sparkman of Florida said that the Cubans, "or those of them belonging to the white race," were in fact capable of self-government. Thus it was easy to dismiss an entire geographic region because, as one senator lectured his colleagues on Puerto Rico, "bananas constituted 75% of their total [food] consumption."[29]

Second, added to the prejudice based on color was a bias against Spain because of the Spanish lust for carnage and plunder. As if using the slave's machete, the Spanish had swathed their way through the New World, leaving a terrible record of death and destruction. Their easy defeat in the war proved that the Spanish were a declining people. Spain, said Henry Cabot Lodge, was "medieval, cruel, and dying." Whatever greatness it had was a thing of the past. Lodge contended that the Cubans, Puerto Ricans and Dominicans were the colonial children, "largely mongrels" said one congressman, of a bloodthirsty bunch of evolution's rejects.[30]

Despite evolution, the United States still had an historical obligation to act as a Great Example for the rest of the world. Call it mission, manifest destiny, or cultural conceit, by the turn of the twentieth century many Americans accepted that the "founding fathers" had in fact begun the world all over again. Perpetual youth, opportunity, liberty, equality, natural resources, freedom, ingenuity—our national character contained so many splendid traits that, added up, the total was Wilson's law, "Whatever America touches she makes holy."[31]

In 1898, Washington's leaders passionately believed in Wilson's law; they made policy by looking in a mirror sparkling from a hundred years of great-ness and, liking what they saw, U.S. politicians decided to bless Cuba, Puerto Rico, Haiti, and the Dominican Republic with a necessary dose of Ameri-canism. In Puerto Rico, islanders received a spelling lesson. Puerto became Porto for the men in charge of America's new possession. So, until 1932, islanders had to misspell the name of their own country in all federal documents. On a Spanish speaking island, English became the medium of instruction in the school system. How children who could not speak English would learn anything from teachers who could also not speak English was an interesting question, but irrelevant if Americanization was an unquestioned end in itself.

America's sense of exceptionalism was a dis-tinctive addition to traditional colonialism. Other nations also thought of themselves as superior (no Grenadian or Jamaican would ever call the British self-effacing), but only the United States was the heavenly appointed missionary of democracy and development. Thus, the U.S. brand of colonialism was especially acceptable because its citizens were uniquely qualified. As Sumner Welles would later write about the Americans in the Dominican Republic, destiny "thrust" the role of educator and civilizer on the United States. We were the best in the world, and if, as Welles himself noted, conceit often bred "a patronizing sense of superiority," that was a small price to pay for the benefits of American civilization.[32]

Racism and exceptionalism were different sides of the same coin; heads or tails the islanders became wards of their developmental guardians.

However, the Caribbean was also subjected to a set of assumptions that allowed the United States to act like a Great Power. Force was the operative means and, in sharp contrast to the civilized justifications used to explain "good colonialism," here the primary explanation was self-interest, openly enforced by the barrel of a marine's gun or the cannon of an Admiral's cruiser.

A special people had special license. As early as the conquest of New Orleans and Florida, congressmen stressed the nation's unquestionable right to all the adjoining coastal territory because "nature had intended it for our own benefit." Present at the creation, America's representatives knew that God's intent was to reserve certain geographical areas for the American people. President Thomas Jefferson, expanding his revolutionary proclamations, said that "our geographical peculiarities may call for *a different code of natural law* to govern relations with other nations from that which the conditions of Europe have given rise to there."

Since natural law was a uniform factor, Jefferson's exception to the rule was rooted in the exceptional qualities and extraordinary privileges of the United States and its citizens. Americans had a right to the continent, a right to security, and, especially in the Caribbean, a right to exclude anyone they considered dangerous. As Senator Gouverneur Morris instructed his colleagues in 1808, "No nation has a right to give to another a dangerous neighbor without her consent."[33]

In December of 1823, President James Monroe codified these beliefs in the doctrine that bears his name. Historians have long debated the doctrine's exact meaning and intent but few disagree that this bold assertion of American rights stated a case of the United States vs. Europe, *not* of the United States vs. Latin America.[34] Monroe banned future colonization by any European powers of the American continents; he banned any attempts to extend Europe's political system to any part of either continent; and he banned any attempts by any European power to oppress or control any Latin American nation which had declared its independence or had that independence recognized by the United States of America.

By 1898, the Monroe Doctrine was a taken-for-granted assumption of many U.S. policymakers. As one Congressman told his colleagues during the debates about Puerto Rico, "It would be hard to find a citizen of the United States who would give up that Monroe Doctrine."[35] From Cuba to the Virgin Islands to Trinidad, European nations controlled most of the Caribbean islands. Political trouble could thus equal American intervention.

Speaking for all Americans, Horace Chilton of Texas argued, on February 4, 1899, that "neither by war, purchase, voluntary cessation, vote of the people, nor in any conceivable way shall a single foot of new territory upon this hemisphere be added to European dominion." This was a traditional, if extreme, interpretation of the Monroe Doctrine but Chilton broke new ground when he used Monroe to justify expropriation of any lands the United States desired. "Yet we will take Porto Rico and we reserve the right to take Haiti or Brazil or Cuba or any other part of North or South America when we think proper to do so."[36]

American policymakers artfully twisted the

Monroe Doctrine into a variety of shapes, and, especially in the Caribbean, it became the Great Power justification for a century of "invited" interference and intervention. As Secretary of State Lansing later wrote, "in its advocacy of the Monroe Doctrine the United States considers its own interests. The integrity of other American nations is an incident, not an end."[37]

With these four sets of assumptions (that is racism, hatred of the Spanish, America's mission, and the rights that came with the Monroe Doctrine), a majority of American political leaders embraced a set of beliefs that their contemporary critics called "supreme hypocrisy." As a Great Example, the United States had the obligation to help its less than civilized Caribbean neighbors. As a Great Power, the United States had the right to treat the Caribbean as an extension of Florida.

Time, circumstance, Congress, and a president's personality all helped dictate which set of assumptions would dominate a particular Caribbean issue, but whether in politics or the economy, the well being of the island nations was always incidental and never the primary aim of America's Caribbean policies.

In November of 1940, Charles Taussig submitted a long report to President Franklin Roosevelt. Acting on the president's request, Taussig had just completed an intensive investigation of social and economic conditions in the British West Indies. His detailed summary contained the information Roosevelt requested. In related documents, however, Taussig could not resist an overall assessment of the

Caribbean. "Perhaps nowhere in the world do we find in more concentrated form all the end products of human greed, stupidity and cruelty than in this archipelago."[38]

Taussig was right. But instead of countering four hundred years of European colonialism, when the United States entered the Caribbean in the twentieth century, it studiously followed the examples set by the British, the French, the Dutch, and the Danes.

At the turn of the century, the Caribbean islands all shared a number of basic characteristics. First, none of the European powers ever tried to produce what Haitians, Cubans, or Grenadians needed. These islands were export economies (long before the phrase became fashionable) because they always produced only what others needed. In 1900, sugar was the most well-known of these export commodities, but coffee was king when the United States conquered Puerto Rico, and bananas were a key money maker in late nineteenth century Jamaica.[39]

Along with crops, working conditions also varied from island to island. In Haiti, masters placed tin masks over their slaves' faces to prevent them from eating even a morsel of sugar cane.[40] The constant factor was the monopolization of scarce lands to produce what others might, or might not, need.

Second, in an archipelago dominated by outsiders, trade never meant a calculated exchange of goods and services. National interest was an alien idea in the Caribbean because its trade revolved around the exportation of everything that was produced and the importation of everything that was needed. It was often more expensive to live on lower wages (or no wages) in the Caribbean than to live on higher wages in Great Britain or France.

Finally, the profits which the colonial powers derived from the Caribbean always went in the same direction as the sugar, coffee, tobacco, spices, or bananas. Nobody reinvested in the interest of Puerto Ricans or Barbadians because in Puerto Rico the profits returned to Spain, and in Barbados sugar created so much wealth for the British that this 250-square-mile island sometimes produced more profits than all the mainland colonies combine. As William Pitt once said in the opening words of a speech in the British House of Commons, "Sugar, sugar, sugar, sugar, Mr. Speaker."[41]

Pitt sought to emphasize the power of the sugar lobby in British politics but, by calling attention to its strength, he also underlined its weakness. By definition, every Caribbean economy and every colonial planter was inherently vulnerable because their well-being depended on access to the home market. Metropolitan markets were the lifeblood of all Caribbean societies, and if access to those markets was closed or restricted, the Caribbean faced economic ruin. One reason Jamaica turned to bananas in the second half of the nineteenth century was a change in London's policies. In a battle with other parts of the British Empire, West Indian sugar lost (in 1846) the tariff protection it had so long enjoyed, and, in a freer world market, the Caribbean could not compete.[42]

In a free market, neither could the United States. By 1898, sugar had already enjoyed a hundred years of government protection, and, to further cut reliance on outside sources of supply, the United States Department of Agriculture used the 1890s to

29

create a new type of sugar industry. Like a group of evangelical preachers, federal officials crisscrossed the midwest to broadcast the beauties of beet sugar. In Idaho, Kansas, Iowa, Minnesota and Michigan, officials induced farmers to grow the beets at a subsidized price and then helped to fund the factories that, with more government assistance, would sell the already subsidized sugar.[43]

While these subsidies became institutionalized in a free enterprise system, the contradiction never publicly bothered the recipients of sugar beet sweeteners. Growers took the money, championed the survival of the fittest, and built seven new beet sugar factories in 1898 and fourteen new facilities in 1899.[44]

When the United States took over Cuba and Puerto Rico, Caribbean sugar already had government subsidized competition in well-established as well as new sugar production. A cautious investor might have shied away from producing sugar in the Caribbean but, because one part of the federal government was working against the other, in Cuba and Puerto Rico senators and congressmen eagerly assisted growers when they sought access to the American market.

The American growers started out with the same vulnerabilities as their British counterparts in Barbados and Jamaica; that was, of course, the grower's risk and the islanders' tragedy. However, the ultimate responsibility for these economies must be laid at the door of the federal government in general, and its colonial representatives in particular. If, as in Puerto Rico, American officials stressed that they had all the power in their hands, then, with total power, comes complete responsibility. An official cannot reasonably claim one without the other.[45]

In 1900, Puerto Rico was a colony and Cuba, a protectorate. In each country, Americans exploring the possibilities for sugar sought open and guaranteed access to the metropolitan market, but given their different statuses, the rules of entry differed for each island.

Puerto Rico belonged to the United States, and while some called it a colony, others a possession, and still others a territory, investors felt secure once Congress passed the Foraker Act in 1900. Primarily because they had no voting representation in Congress, islanders would pay no federal taxes. For two years Congress would collect a fifteen percent tariff on the island's exports; after that it was free trade forever. And, in a thorough if thoughtless (for the Puerto Ricans) transformation of the tax system, an economics professor from Baltimore, Jacob Hollander, made it easy for outsiders to buy up Puerto Rico's best lands.[46]

The Spanish had taxed the income earned by a particular farm. Professor Hollander taxed the value of the farm's acreage, which was standard operating procedure on the mainland and a green light to the Americans in Puerto Rico because, as Secretary of War Root told the president as early as 1899, "the principal difficulty now in the island of Porto Rico is that the transfer of the island from Spain to the United States has not resulted in an increase in prosperity but in the reverse."[47]

Puerto Ricans were broke. Right after the war the Spanish imposed tariffs on the island's exports; that immediately sealed off King Coffee's principal world market, and, because the United States took two years to decide Puerto Rico's fate, Washington continued the coffee tariffs in place at the beginning of Cuba's war for independence. For two years some of the finest coffee in the world sat rotting on the docks. When colonial officials approved Jacob Hollander's tax system, many Puerto Ricans found that the only way to pay property taxes was to sell one parcel of their land to retain control of the rest. Others, in bankruptcy, simply lost the lands which were promptly auctioned off to Americans who incorporated in Boston, Connecticut, and New Jersey.[48]

By 1901, sugar already accounted for 55% of Puerto Rico's exports; the 1897 figure was 22%. Americans had quickly transformed the economy but not without a fight from those beet men in Idaho and Michigan. One provision of the Foraker Act stipulated that no island farm could contain more than five hundred acres; the idea was to limit competition from Puerto Rican growers, but since the law was never enforced by the island's American *and* Puerto Rican officials, Boston investors worried about the five hundred acre limitation as much as they worried about their native city's "blue laws."[49]

The real stumbling block to the development of the Puerto Rican sugar economy was a congressional prohibition on refined sugar. None was permitted to enter the United States. One group of Americans fought with another. So, with the prohibition on refined produce, Congress gave the owners of companies like South Porto Rico Sugar (based in New Jersey) an added incentive to send their profits home. Puerto Rico was allowed to be only one part of a one crop economy, and islanders always worked part time because of sugar growing's "dead time." Six months out of any year workers had nothing to do and no chance of employment in a refining factory because Congress refused to permit the downstream jobs that came with self-sustaining economic development.

From 1900 on, Puerto Rico was politically unincorporated, economically dependent, and its twentieth century labor force was born already disadvantaged because substantial unemployment was built into the fabric of the mainland-dominated sugar and tobacco industries.

As a potentially independent nation, Cuba had a chance to avoid Puerto Rico's fate. While the conventional wisdom argues that Americans instantly dominated Cuba's sugar industry, the island's economy was, from 1898 to 1901, still up for grabs. Size alone (Cuba is thirteen times bigger than Puerto Rico) meant that it would take some time, and enormous amounts of capital, to buy up the island. English and Spanish investors also competed with the Americans and, in Cuba, an element of democratic principle still determined political and economic policy. The Foraker Act allowed Puerto Rico's administrators to grant all the concessions they desired, but in Cuba, that same law forbid the occupation authorities to grant business concessions. Foraker wanted to avoid a permanent occupation of Cuba, and his hesitation forced investors to do the same thing. Millions did go into Cuban sugar (and railroads, tobacco, and electrical installations), but many sugar growers hesitated until the federal government guaranteed both political control of the island and preferential access to the American marketplace.[50]

CRUISING THE CARIBBEAN

Platt Amendment

Secretary of War Elihu Root lobbied for the Platt Amendment because the occupation of Cuba was not only a burden, it was expensive. Five hunded thousand dollars a month to keep U.S. forces on the island and what did Washington have to show for it? Like the Puerto Ricans, the ungrateful Cubans bitterly complained about the absence of democratic rights. By January of 1901, immediate evacuation became the administration's watchword, if the United States obtained the political, military, and economic prerogatives which were its war-given right.

As commander of the U.S. forces in Cuba, General Leonard Wood had coveted Guantanamo Bay for two years. He and the navy meant to have it at all costs, but the Cubans refused to consider such a possibility. To the Cubans, selling or leasing land to the United States violated the island's independence. The United States faced a real dilemma. How could it convince the Cubans to concede the rights they had refused to concede?[51]

Blackmail was the answer. The exact nature of the extortion was yet to be determined, but as early as January of 1901, the Senate Committee on Relations With Cuba had drafted eight demands as a condition for eliminating the United States bothersome occupation. Rights to a naval base stood near the top of the Senate's list; in fact, Guantanamo came in second, just behind ultimate political control of Cuba's political future.[52]Root and his congressional associates worried about the right timing. The first months of 1901 saw the Cubans eagerly writing their own constitution. Should the United

States submit its list of demands after they finished and installed their own government, or should the United States act at once?

Root favored immediate action because "Congress has so tied the hands of the president by its [Teller] resolution that, unless the Cubans themselves can be induced to do voluntarily whatever we think they ought to do...the president must either abandon American interests...or engage in a controversy with the Cubans...."[53]

To avoid a controversy after the Cubans were in control, Root decided to create one before they were in control. Along with Congress, the Cuban constitutional convention received the administration's demands in the form of the Platt Amendment because, as Senator Orville Platt of Connecticut stressed, waiting until the Cubans had a constitution and a government in place, and risked surrendering "any right to be heard as to what relations shall be," we risked having to be "content with nothing at all."[54]

To do nothing was never an American option. Setting a precedent that would be followed in Puerto Rico in 1952 and in the Virgin Islands in 1980, the government of the United States of America sent the Cuban people a constitutional ultimatum.

History calls that "ultimatum"[55] the Platt Amendment. In an attempt to shepherd it through Congress, Orville Platt attached his amendment to the army's annual appropriation bill. He hoped to get "practical unanimity" from his colleagues but instead received a stern lecture on proper congressional procedure, and U.S. obligations to the Cuban and American people.

Toward the end of his long speech, Senator Morgan of Alabama asked if any of his colleagues had read the Cuban constitution. Morgan had never seen the document, and his colleagues, silent after his question, also had apparently failed to read or see it, "yet we are proposing grave amendments to their constitution in the shape of an ordinance or proposition to be carried into their constitution after they have made it, after they have signed it, and, I suppose, after they have adjourned."[56]

Those grave amendments included the United States' right to intervene for the preservation of Cuba's independence; the right to partially control the amount of Cuba's public debt; the right to prevent Cuba from entering into treaties which impaired or tended to impair the island's independence; the right, primarily in order to "maintain the independence of Cuba and the people thereof," to maintain American naval bases in Cuba; and—here is the blackmail clause—the right to determine at some later date, sovereignty over the Isle of Pines. This roughly 50x20 mile island lay south of Cuba. Even though Secretary of War Root later admitted that "the Isle of Pines was and had been for centuries a part of Cuba...and that it is not and never has been territory of the United States," in the 1901 Platt Amendment its sovereignty was suddenly negotiable, if only because the Cubans adamantly refused to accept Congress' demands.[57]

Senator Morgan understood Cuba's reluctance to submit to the Platt ultimatum. The United States got "unlimited authority, not terminable according to this agreement by any lapse of time, an authority that stands forever." To Morgan, it was a piece of

36

"arrant hypocrisy" to make these demands on the Cuban people. To leave the United States with an endless right to intervene "was to compel Cuba at once to subordinate herself at all times to...our ideas of what she ought to do. Can any man imagine a more absurd position that the Congress of the United States could possibly place itself in than that which is on these papers. I would be ashamed."[58]

The United States gave its word. "We pledged ourselves to that course [Cuban independence] and tonight we are violating every one of those pledges we made to the people of Cuba and to the world and we are bringing disgrace on the name of the American people." Only a blind man could fail to see what Congress was doing; or, as the English put it, "that they should take who have the power, and they should keep who can."

The U.S. had the power, and Cuba did not. That was the essence of the Platt Amendment and, according to Pettus, "it is disgrace that we are bringing upon the American name; and if we have any spark of love of country in our bosoms we ought to keep that name untarnished at home and abroad."[59]

These sentiments fell on deaf ears. The senators listened politely and then voted as the administration desired. In the House, critics also called the amendment everything from "supreme hypocrisy" to a "blot" on the American democratic system, but, in the House, supporters found justification in the blessings of American involvement. Grosvenor of Ohio, after admitting that the Platt Amendment was an "ultimatum," argued that "no act of injustice has been done to the people of Cuba." Americans had, after all, fortified their harbors, eliminated their diseases, sup-

37

pressed their insurrections, set in motion the wheels of commerce, and, in fact, "eradicated the evil conditions that have existed in that island for so long."[60]

In less than four years Americans had eliminated the problems of four centuries. We recognized and applauded our achievements, but the Cubans did not. Congressman Scudder of New York, who had read the Cuban constitution, was amazed that the document "made no mention of the obligations due from the islanders to the United States for their emancipation from Spanish rule, but, on the contrary, ignores the subject, while Cuban politicians who are now in control do not hesitate to give out the most violent expressions of hatred for the United States and our people."

Hatred for America was a fact of occupation life. As Scudder stressed in the 1901 ceremonies celebrating the beginning of their 1895 struggle against Spain, "the occasion brought out in the public speeches to large assemblages the sentiments of the popular leaders showing the bitterest animosity toward this country." The Cubans staged "vigorous protests" against the proposal to submit their constitution for our approval, and they denounced the idea of granting the United States any naval bases.[61]

In Puerto Rico, islanders were making similar complaints and publishing them in the Congressional Record. An open-minded Congress might have questioned its actions and authority. Instead, Scudder criticized the Cuban constitution's grant of universal suffrage and then explained his reasoning. That constitution "vests the political power in the hands of an ignorant and thriftless population, composed largely of negroes, in view of which fact the prospects of peace and prosperity for the newly enfranchised island would be poor were the United States to abandon Cuba at this time," and "whether the Cubans will accept or repel these amendments is of more interest than importance...they will be insisted on by this country. The Cubans will do well to accept them, for if they do not voluntarily agree to them they will be required involuntarily to conform to them. This Republic is done with nonsense."[62]

As Congressman Grosvenor suggested in public and General Leonard Wood and Howard Taft wrote in private,[63] men like Scudder had serious support and, except for the notions of power, the "good colonialism" of men like Grosvenor, Wood, and Scudder were the principal justification for the Cuban protectorate. We were their guardians, they were our wards, and, whether for power or principle, we would force them to do as we saw fit.

The Cubans said no. Fully a month after McKinley signed the Platt Amendment, on March 1, 1901, the "agitators" and "radicals" who worried General Wood refused to accept what Congress had passed. Article Three, the U.S. right to intervene to protect Cuban independence, proved to be the principal stumbling block, but the Cubans still resisted the base agreement, and they wanted concessions on trade. Wood promised to support special tariff exemptions for Cuban sugar. Secretary Root, frustrated by the Cubans "ingratitude," took the time to explain that Article Three did not give the United States the right to interfere or meddle in the affairs of the Cuban government; and, as its ace in the hole, the United States continually refused to decide the final fate of the Isle of Pines.[64]

As Senator McCormick of Illinois assured his congressional colleagues in 1925, "I think the administration withheld formal decision as to sovereignty over the Isle of Pines and compelled Cuba to do so in order to better bargain with Cuba for a naval base...I think our government was making ready to drive a hard bargain with Cuba for the greatest naval base in the Caribbean."[65]

Senator McCormick was right. Washington played hardball; and the Cubans, sensing a choice between no sovereignty or limited sovereignty, decided to compromise. As an appendix, the Platt ultimatum was added to their already written constitution in June of 1901. The U.S. now had the "right" to intervene, but, since this was an option to be used with great reluctance, the U.S. negotiators played their Isle of Pines cards with great skill and no principle.

Even after "accepting" the Platt ultimatum, the stubborn Cubans refused to concede the four bases that the navy's enlarged vision quickly deemed "absolutely essential." In negotiations, Cuban leaders refused to consider a base near Havana, and they refused to allow an outright purchase of the two (if you were talking to a Cuban) or four (if you were talking to an American admiral) bases.

In Washington, U.S. officials began to pressure the Cubans. Before General Wood turned over the Cuban government to the Cuban people in the spring of 1902, he was, wrote Secretary of War Root, to make certain they added a new paragraph to the already written documents: "It is understood...that the present government of the Isle of Pines will continue as a de facto government, pending the settlement of said island by treaty."[66]

40

Meanwhile, President Roosevelt continued to negotiate about the possibilities of free trade but on the question of the bases, he was adamant. In October of 1902, he told Secretary of State Hay that, "whatever is done about reciprocity, the naval stations are to be ceded and in the near future...The question itself is not a matter open to discussion by the Cubans. It is already contained in their constitution and no discussion concerning it will be entertained."[67]

The Cubans, remembering that the Platt Amendment was an American ultimatum, wanted to continue talking. Roosevelt, angrier than ever, now offered this suggestion to his secretary of state, "What do you think of this? Would it not be a good plan to put our troops thus peaceably on the lands we intend to take as coaling stations."[68]

Troops never arrived in this manner because, as H.G. Squiers, America's negotiator in Havana, said, "the anxiety of the Cuban Government to settle the status of this island makes the time very opportune for such settlement in connection with the question of coaling and naval stations."[69]

On February 23, 1903, the United States made two separate agreements. The navy got its bases in one treaty. Guantanamo came under U.S. control for 99 years at a lease rate of $2000 a year, and the Cubans got the Isle of Pines in another. In the second article of the Cuban treaty the tradeoff was made explicit: "This relinquishment, on the part of the United States of America, of claim of title to the said Isle of Pines is in consideration of the grants of coaling and naval stations in the island of Cuba heretofore made to the United States of America by the Republic of Cuba."[70]

41

That seemed pretty clear, except to the Americans who had bought up large parts of the Isle of Pines as soon as the war ended. In 1899 many midwesterners started new lives in *their* Isle because, as they saw it, an assistant secretary of war had assured them the island belonged to the United States. Actually G.D. Meiklejohn was far more equivocal than the American settlers later claimed. He had written that the Isle of Pines was "a part of our territory" but he also indicated that it was "attached to the division of Cuba for governmental purposes," and, any question of "homesteading" laws had to await congressional action.

Meiklejohn wrote that letter on January 15, 1900. Settlers later said it was their government seal of approval but, in truth, even a month after reading the Meikeljohn letter, a Mr. E.C. Harrington, who had just purchased 160 acres of the Isle of Pines, asked the U.S. attorney general if "it is United States territory...and if so will I be protected in locating on this unsurveyed land or not?" Another fellow, writing to Secretary of War Root on January 31, 1901, precisely and succinctly stated the issue: "Dear Sir: Is the Isle of Pines United States as Porto Rico is United States or is it Cuba? Cordially yours, William O. McDowell."[71]

In scores of responses to scores of letters, Secretary of War Root instructed his subordinates to make the same response; the Isle of Pines was "at present" subject to the jurisdiction of the military forces of the United States. Its ultimate destiny, however, was not a matter for the war department to settle. Jurisdiction over the Isle of Pines was a "political question," to be determined by Congress.[72]

42

Congress had seven months to pass the treaties and, while the base agreement went through at once, Congress refused to act on the Isle of Pines. When Rear Admiral Albert S. Barker formally accepted control over Guantanamo Bay on December 10, 1903, no high-ranking Cuban dignitary dared show up at the ceremonies. The Cuban people were upset over the concession of the bases and over Congress' refusal to abide by the terms of the agreement. The Cubans had kept their word. What about the Americans?[73]

In Congress, Senator Foraker told his colleagues that while the treaties were "not legally binding on the United States without ratification by the Senate, yet it is morally binding, and equity and justice would seem to require that without respect to whether the United States has a good title to the Isle of Pines the Treaty should be signed." Remember, Foraker counseled, a failure to sign the treaty could cause Cuba to "abrogate and annul" our base rights. Since the Cubans had no power, "whether this [their refusal] would give us any serious trouble or not is immaterial. It would put the United States in the attitude of having failed to perform its part of a moral obligation after value therefore had been fully received."[74]

Foraker wrote those words in February of 1906. The U.S. was already two years late on fulfilling its moral obligations. While the Cubans waited, U.S troops took over the island. In September of 1906, the United States once again militarily occupied Cuba.

Meanwhile, Congress, even after a 1907 U.S. Supreme Court decision indicated that Cuba held sovereignty over the Isle of Pines, refused to abide by the terms of the agreement. It was 1925 before the Senate fulfilled what Foraker called its "moral obligations" and, in the meantime, the United States had twice militarily intervened in Cuba, and, from a naval ship docked off its coast, General Enoch Crowder helped rewrite Cuba's constitution beginning in 1919.

Americans seemed oblivious to their own contradictions and their own history. When, on March 17, 1960, members of the Eisenhower administration discussed the fate of Guantanamo in then "top secret" sessions of the National Security Council, Secretary of State Herter ended a long discussion with President Eisenhower in this fashion: "Our treaty rights to the base were as clear as a bell."[75]

Cartels

Industrialization is both a blessing and a challenge. The mechanized and efficient production of goods and services makes more available for everyone. However, a country or corporation that produces more goods than its own markets can consume is confronted with an elemental problem of the twentieth century: overproduction.

Nations and corporations often react to the problem of overproduction in a similar fashion; they try to control the market. Nations do with it with tariffs and quotas, and corporations do it with cartels.[76] The sugar trust was a fact of early twentieth century American life. Combinations also existed in steel, aluminum, rubber, and chemicals, and the first time General Electric and Westinghouse were found guilty of controlling the light bulb market was in 1911. They had also tried to eliminate new production by effectively controlling any competitor's access to glass.[77]

Using laws like the Sherman Antitrust Act, the U.S. government tried to help control the free market, for the benefit of its citizens, while corporations tried to control the government and, through it, their markets. In such an economic system, and in a society so heavily dependent on sugar, Cuba's problem was that it controlled neither the American government nor its corporations. Indeed, once Cuba signed its reciprocity treaty with the United States in 1903, its fate was tied to forces that were outside of its own control.

When the House Ways and Means Committee began to debate, in 1902, the trade consequences of the Platt ultimatum, Cuba found powerful allies in the Americans who owned, or wanted to own, sugar plantations in Cuba. The accurate argument of those who sponsored trade preferences for Cuba was that men like President Roosevelt had promised such "assistance"; and, given Washington's political protectorate of the island, the United States had an economic obligation to assure Cuba's prosperity and stability.

Opponents were well organized. When cane growers linked arms with the government-subsidized producers of sugar beets, *and* with those who opposed the sugar trust, the reciprocity treaty looked like a nightmare for American refiners. Advocates wanted a sharply reduced tariff on raw sugar but the beet people first helped limit that reduction to 20% of the regular tariff and, in a slap at the refiners, successfully attached a provision reducing the tariff on refined sugar.

45

The tariff reduction would help Cuba to create a more self-sustaining economy but the last thing the refiners wanted was more competition. Thus, in 1902, the refiners used their capital resources to buy the producers and refiners of sugar beets. Within months virtually all production and refining was controlled by groups like the Havermeyer interests. The trade bill came in with the 20% tariff reduction on raw sugar, no preferences for refined sugar, and, as a way to gain more support in both countries, Cuba agreed to substantial tariff preferences for American imports.[78]

The government the Cubans could not control was at least partially controlled by a cartel that also had no interest in a self-sustaining Cuban economy. Men like Havermeyer and Hershey wanted to assure themselves of a cheap and dependable source of a raw material. If they could, they would use Cuba and the U.S. government to serve their purposes. To the extent the Havermeyer and the Hershey bought up Cuba in the same way they bought up the sugar beet interests, Cuba added to its loss of government control, any meaningful control of the corporations that were the lifeblood of its economy. Profits would follow sugar to the mainland, while, as in Puerto Rico, Cubans would have to find some way to use six months of sugar-institutionalized dead time.

Why would Cubans accept such a deal? Before and after the war, Cubans had already lost significant control of their own productive resources. Spaniards had a substantial stake in the Cuban economy, and so too the British and American interests who before and after the war invested heavily in Cuban real estate. Add to this the self-interest of

46

many Cubans, the impoverished state of the island's economy, and the import interests, also heavily Spanish, that wanted to take advantage of the trade agreement's sharply reduced tariffs on American imports, and the sum total is a substantial amount of island support for the trade bill.[79]

Primary responsibility for this marriage of economies rests on the American presidents, senators, and congressmen who found the trade bill an effective way to assure Cuba's peace and prosperity. In sugar and tobacco, in exports and imports, Cuba was, from 1903, a creature of the United States, a society with no control of the foreign forces that controlled its economic future.

Captain Christmas

Buy one person and American culture called it slavery. Buy 25,000 and the United States called it manifest destiny. As William McKinley put it to Captain Walter Christmas in late 1899, the president had always considered it "natural and right" that the United States buy the Virgin Islands. They had "been on the market" for a long time and McKinley was ready to consider an offer.

Captain Christmas, an entrepreneur, and possibly a scoundrel, explained to the president that the King of Denmark "would never allow his colonies to be on the market." It was "out of harmony" with the dignity of a great country to sell land and people as if they were commodities. But Denmark would consider putting the islands under America's control, funds would change hands, and, most important of all, Captain Walter Christmas would receive a ten percent commission on the sale of the Virgin

Islands and its inhabitants.[80]

For the next two and a half years, Captain Christmas crisscrossed the Atlantic to sell the islands and obtain his anticipated six figure commission. Ultimately, Christmas caused a national scandal by falsely accusing President McKinley's brother of being a part of his commission scheme, but even when the U.S. Department of State emphatically denied Captain Christmas' allegations, it stressed that "this country wished to buy and Denmark wished to sell. Nobody had to come here to persuade anybody that the United States ought to own the islands in question, and nobody had to go to Copenhagen to convince the government there that it ought to get rid of the islands."[81]

McKinley was right. The islands were *on* the world market; and the United States was *in* the market for new colonies and possessions. In 1902, the negotiations for the Virgin Islands never came to a satisfactory conclusion, but, as the islanders waited for a future president to do what was "natural and right," other parts of the Caribbean began to occupy America's attention. In the Dominican Republic an American company controlled the island's customs houses, and, even after America's representative told the president that the island's creditors were "merciless, blood-sucking money sharks," the United States still found itself deep in Dominican waters, acting as an advocate for the sharks. It was a strange policy, in the United States called the Roosevelt Corollary to the Monroe Doctrine.

Merciless,
Blood-Sucking
Money Sharks

"I would rather see that [U.S.] flag lowered and trampled upon than used as a pirate's ensign and raised, not as an emblem of honor, but as an instrument of terror and oppression to the helpless and enfeebled races of mankind."
—Senator Rayner of Maryland, January 8, 1906

His first name was Edward Hertzberg, his second Edward Hartmont. Using the first, Hertzberg went bankrupt in Paris, in 1867, as a German; he then fled to England, changed his name, and claimed no particular nationality. Years later, Edward Hartmont would express surprise when he heard of Edward Hertzberg's two year French jail sentence.

Using either name, Hartmont sold foreign bonds; mines were a particular interest, but appropriately enough, fertilizer was Hartmont's first concern in the Dominican Republic. Guano deposits attracted investors, and the island government requested a loan. Hartmont arranged an offering in London in 1869, but, when the public refused to buy, he and his associates filed incomplete and false statements to the stock exchange. At prices ranging from 64% to

71% of the bond's value, Hartmont "unloaded" the issue to the British public.[1]

Based on a total loan of *no* predetermined amount, Hartmont promised, after taking a commission of £100,000, to give £320,000 to the Dominican Republic. However, only £38,000 ever changed hands, and, after sixteen years of litigation, the island received a bill for Hartmont's fraud. £757,000 was owed to European investors.[2]

Nobody expected the Dominicans to pay that amount, and in 1888, the island government agreed to pay £142,869 of the Hartmont debt to an Amsterdam banking house. In return the republic received portions of a *new* £770,000 bond issue. This loan was guaranteed by a right to control the island's principal source of income, its customs houses.

In 1888, Amsterdam bankers began to collect the Dominican revenues that first paid off British bondholders. Unfortunately, one large loan quickly led to another, money was misplaced in transactions (£77,521 of the 1888 loan disappeared), salesmen exacted gigantic commissions, and the Dominicans often dipped into the customs revenues.

All bonds sunk into default in 1892 and the Dutch, seconded by their English, French, Belgian, and American bondholders, tried to sell their Dominican debt to the United States. The State Department refused to consider such a proposal, but interested in ending 23 years of thievery in the Caribbean, it induced a group of Wall Street attorneys to form the Santo Domingo Improvement Company in 1892. Incorporated in New Jersey, the Improvement Company quickly became one of the most controversial enterprises in Dominican history.[3]

During its first nine years of operation, the Improvement Company arranged a series of international loans. Contemporary critics charged usury, but while each of its many bond issues did charge (what President Roosevelt's advisor later called) "excessive rates" of interest, the generally accepted justification for the processing fees, commissions, and high interest rates was risk. Doing business in the Caribbean made any banker nervous, so, to compensate for high-stakes gambling, bankers were obviously entitled to a greater return on their investment. To assure payment, the American bankers not only demanded control of the customs houses, they demanded that in the event of default, the governments of the bondholders (Holland, Belgium, England, France and the United States) would provide the forceful assistance needed to collect all monies owed to outsiders.[4]

Critics stressed the contradiction that an international safety net would eliminate justification for the high interest rates. Nevertheless, in this and other transactions (in 1897 Improvement Company officials charged off 9 percent of a £600,000 loan to "expenses and commissions") the United States government supported loans every bit as controversial as the work of Edward Hertzberg Hartmont. Dominicans once again complained, but the United States argued that "the industrial-creditor nations had the right and duty to police underdeveloped areas." Peace, prosperity and stability depended on the actions of the civilized powers, so countries like the United States never analyzed their own inconsistencies. The Dominican Republic certainly had its share of corrupt politicians and unethical bankers, but what if the American bankers were greedy beyond belief? Did the United States guarantee all loans, no matter how outrageous the interest and commissions? And, as in its Cuban and Puerto Rican sugar policies, how did a free enterprise, *laissez faire* system reasonably justify government "guarantees" for its entrepreneurs?

The Dominicans answered these questions in 1900; they tried to oust the Improvement Company. Long and contentious negotiations provided more money for a strapped island government but the Improvement Company not only placed its own interests first, it lied to the Dominican and U.S. governments.

The new agreement stipulated that the French and Belgian creditors, who held fully two-thirds of the bonded debt, had to agree to the new contract. Judge John T. Abbott assured the Dominicans that the foreign bondholders had done so, but, far from agreeing to the new contract, the Belgian bondholders expressed outrage. Holding most of the debt, they were also asked to make most of the short-term (no interest for three years) and long-term sacrifices. Meanwhile, the Improvement Company received its monies, commissions, and other assorted "internal debt" payments.

Once the lie became public, the Dominican government asked the Improvement Company to stop using customs receipts to pay off the debt. Judge Abbott, not a man to be bothered by the Belgian denial, still claimed that he had their full support, and that he thus had the right to collect and distribute the Dominican government's funds. The standoff ended when, in January of 1901, the Dominican government issued a decree forbidding the Improvement

Company to continue collecting customs revenues.[5]

Using all the contacts and resources at their disposal, Abbott and his colleagues "made their presence very much felt in the State Department." They wanted Washington to support them because they wanted first claim on Dominican revenues. They also wanted to avoid using their international guarantees because Abbott and his colleagues now doubted that, given its commitment to the Monroe Doctrine, any American administration would sanction a solution that included European control of Caribbean finances.[6]

Secretary of State Hay offered Washington's assistance. America's Dominican minister later noted, "when, as was usually the case, a foreign claim was backed by the vigorous representations of a diplomatic representative, who took his countryman's word and whose representations and demands were given prompt attention on account of the presence of a war vessel, it is clear that a Dominican government could do nothing but accept the amount and terms insisted upon by the foreign creditor."[7]

Ambassador William Powell used strong language to demand a settlement favorable to the Improvement Company, and despite being aware of the charges against Abbott and his associates, Powell never mentioned the Improvement Company's exorbitant commissions, or its low priority attitude toward the interests of two-thirds of the bondholders.[8]

The Dominicans struggled once again to avoid their impossible position; they were, as the American minister noted, "practically at the mercy of their creditors."[9] After agreeing to arbitrate claims with the Improvement Company, the Dominican representative sailed to Paris, came to terms with the French and Belgian bondholders (many were Catholics who thought they had invested in bonds for the Dominican religious order) and submitted the two agreements to the Dominican Congress.

That body quickly approved the European agreement but refused to countenance any arbitration settlement with the American Improvement Company. President Roosevelt's advisor later stressed that the Dominican Republic, like so many other Latin American nations, had learned at least two lessons by "mournful experience." "Imperfect financial records and mediocre representation work a fatal handicap in arbitration proceedings; and the foreign creditors...are certain to get the best of the controversy."[10]

Judge Abbott had adamantly "refused to furnish a full and detailed account of the Improvement Company's dealings with the Republic." This infuriated the Dominicans who, as Abbott openly admitted, were presented a bill which included "partly duplicated" claims, charges for profits on deals that were never consummated, and additional charges of $764,000 for "expenses" on the 1897 loan that saw only 8 percent of the funds go to the Dominican government. Most outrageous of all to the Dominicans, the Improvement Company's bill included substantial payments for the Edward Hertzberg/Hartmont loan of 1869.[11]

U.S. officials "demanded" that the Dominicans accept arbitration. They refused to do so. Betting that they would be outfoxed by the company's lawyers and, lacking their own records *or* any documentation from the Improvement Company, the Dominicans settled for the lesser of two evils. "The agreed compensation was, to say the least, liberal,"[12] but the Dominicans nevertheless consented to give the company $4.5 million as a final settlement of its claims. That agreement was signed on January 31, 1903, but again at the insistence of the State Department, the Dominicans were forced to submit the agreement to an arbitration board of two Americans and one Dominican. The board would determine the interest rate on the $4.5 million, the security the Dominicans needed to supply, and the date and amount of the installment payments the Dominicans would make.[13]

The arbitration board began to deliberate in late 1903. At this point the United States had no intention of protecting, much less annexing the Dominican Republic. On the contrary, all diplomatic efforts on behalf of the Improvement Company added up to "normal" advocacy work for U.S. citizens doing business abroad.[14]

American policy changed after the Venezuelan Blockade of 1902. Money was again the issue, but this time, instead of diplomatic threats, the British and German governments (cheered on by the Italians) resorted to force. Because the Venezuelan government refused to pay its foreign debts, the Europeans powers, with President Roosevelt's consent, blockaded Venezuela's coasts in December of 1902. Two Venezuelan gunboats were sunk, and aided by their warships' cannons, European soldiers had actually taken a fort in the Western Hemisphere. This was a terrible precedent in its own right, but Navy officials worried about the sinister long-term intentions of the British and Germans. The Kaiser wanted a strategic outpost in the Caribbean and, given America's recent commitment to the Panama Canal, any foreign control of islands near the isthmus was out of the question. Using the tiny Puerto Rican island of Culebra, the United States prepared a colonial base of operations, just in case war broke out.[15]

Arbitration replaced war in this particular controversy, but the threat of European control of Caribbean and Latin American customs houses moved Roosevelt to reconsider American policy. U.S. support of European governments who were forcefully supporting their citizens could lead to long-term, or even worse, permanent, *new* European involvement in the Western Hemisphere. By definition (of the Monroe Doctrine), that was out of the question. Also unthinkable was a German demand for preferential treatment. Like the Santo Domingo Improvement Company, the Germans refused to sign any agreement that put them second or third in line to receive principal and interest payments. So, one lesson drawn from the Venezuelan controversy was that the government who showed up first got first rights to all available resources.[16]

Meanwhile, in the Dominican Republic, the harbor at Santo Domingo City proved to be a magnet for foreign warships. Political revolution in the island nation created so much havoc that competing political factions held, or threatened to hold, the customs houses pledged to a bevy of foreign creditors. French, Belgian, German, American and Italian interests all wanted their piece of the quickly disappearing pie. The Dominicans, quite conscious of what had happened in Cuba and Puerto Rico, tried to hold on to their sovereignty by making the

Americans an offer they could not refuse. In return for leases to coveted coaling stations in Samana and Manzanillo Bays, the United States would pay off the Dominican Republic's debt. In one bold stroke, most foreigners would leave the Dominican Republic and, instead of the pittance received by the Cubans for Guantanomo, the Dominicans would use America's millions to rid themselves of both Edward Hartmont and his successor, the Santo Domingo Improvement Company.[17]

This Dominican daydream could became reality only under one condition; Theodore Roosevelt had to accept the deal. He asked a group of his advisors to study the Dominican situation. What should our policy be? What were our options and responsibilities in what was a chaotic political and economic situation?

Francis Loomis represented the State Department. Along with naval officials, he visited the island and quickly summed up the situation. "The country is largely in the grasp of desperately selfish irresponsible political brigands. Many of these guerrilla leaders are little better than savages as far as their ideas of property rights and the rights of those weaker than themselves are concerned."[18]

Loomis did not suggest annexation or military intervention. He countered the Dominican lease proposal with one of his own; the only way to keep the "savages" at bay was to remove the cause of their fighting. Take over the customs houses and you would control the ultimate goal of all political efforts, and the finances that kept soldiers in the field. Loomis told his superiors, the Dominicans never fought over ideology. Their "bloody civil wars" occurred only because of "shameless sordid struggles for the privileges of controlling customs and disposing of their revenues."[19]

Loomis counseled rejection of the Dominican lease proposal; the president accepted his advice; and to avoid political troubles at home, President Roosevelt hinted that the Dominicans should return to the United States after the November, 1904, presidential elections. In the meantime, the Dominicans might avoid anarchy if they used the good offices of two trusted American advisors; Commander Alfred Dillingham and America's new Dominican minister, Thomas Dawson.

Dillingham and Dawson devised a proposal which, as in Puerto Rico, used English colonialism as its role model. They studied British imperial policy in Egypt, and, admiring the success achieved there, tried to do the same in the Caribbean.

One problem was President Morales. Once the American elections were over, Dawson received instructions (on December 30, 1904) to "discreetly but earnestly" ask the Dominicans to request our takeover of their customs houses. This tactic—requesting a request—would be used by U.S. administrations throughout the twentieth century. It was a device that, from President Morales in 1905 to Sir Paul Scoon (in Grenada) in 1983, met with a substantial degree of Caribbean resistance.

On January 2, 1905, Dawson told his superiors that Morales appeared "almost ready" to ask for our assistance but, "given the deeply grounded prejudice against any sort of American intervention existing among some of his supporters," Morales hesitated. While the Dominican president clearly understood that, if not the Americans, the French, Belgians, Italians, or Germans, would use force in the Dominican Republic, the legislators Dawson called "malcontents" refused to surrender any portion of the island's sovereignty. And, even more ominous for the United States, the Dominican constitution required that all treaties be submitted to Congress. That body could easily reject the proposed treaty. Therefore, Morales and Dawson devised a way to circumvent both the Dominican Constitution and the Dominican Congress. They would present legislators with a *fait accompli* and station Captain Dillingham and the marines nearby. As Dawson's biographer put it, he was "willing to use the Naval Force for more than mere 'moral effect' if it were necessary to accomplish the transfer of the customhouses."[20]

By January 20, 1905, the Dominicans finally saw "they had no alternative." The Dominicans signed an agreement which gave 5 percent of their customs revenues to the American debt collectors and 4 percent to the Dominican government. Dawson reluctantly agreed to a clause that guaranteed the territorial integrity of the Republic. Dominican opinion was "unanimous on this subject" and the Dominican negotiators had "left no doubt" they would break off negotiations without such a clause,[21] but beyond that, the Egyptian precedent took hold in the Caribbean. Dominicans could no longer change their system of duties and taxes without the consent of the American government; any surplus would go to the debtors if the Americans said so; and the agreement also stipulated that the Dominicans had to pay the salaries of the American customs officials who were using Dominican funds to pay off the Santo Domingo Improvement Company and the bondholders of Edward Hertzberg/Hartmont.

In Washington, officials listened closely to Judge Abbott and his Wall Street associates. Only a week after the agreement was completed the State Department instructed its subordinates to provide some money for the Dominican government but under no circumstances "interfere with the rights of the Improvement Company."[22]

Minister Dawson was tired. "Nobody knew how much the Dominican government owed." For six months Dawson had been working "continuously" but still had no idea how much money was owed or how much of what was owed was legitimate debt.[23]

Nevertheless, he assured his superiors that, barring another unexpected revolution, nobody would interfere with the rights of the Improvement Company. They would begin to receive the $4.5 million already promised. "I have slowly come to the conclusion that it is impossible to ignore or overcome the dislike of the Improvement Company and all persons connected with it....This hatred...has been exacerbated by the bitter controversies which have continually gone on during the last five years....[It] was hopeless to try to persuade the president and cabinet on this point."[24]

Dawson wrote those lines on February 13, 1905. Two days later, Theodore Roosevelt transmitted the Dominican agreement to the United States Senate. History calls this speech the Roosevelt Corollary to the Monroe Doctrine. But, as the president promised "absolute equity" for all concerned, the "hated" Improvement Company was already collecting its usurious earnings. How did Roosevelt plan to assure stability on a foundation of fraud, usury, and hatred? What were his motives?

One aim was to assure that Americans were first in line in any debt-collection agreement. Roosevelt stressed that, while some of the debts were properly contracted, "others were without question improper or exorbitant, constituting claims which should never be paid in full and perhaps only to the extent of a very small portion of their nominal value."[25] How these claims would be settled was a matter for economists and other specialists. "Absolute equity" was guaranteed but senators had to understand the government's decision; the president chose intervention because of the United States' obvious obligation "to protect the contracts and concessions of its citizens."[26]

Months later, in congressional debate, Senator Lodge explained Roosevelt's intent: Without the agreement "we would be relegated to a secondary place in the payment of debts, and, moreover, we should have to join with other nations...Instead of doing it ourselves on our own terms, we should join with other countries and have them do it."[27]

Judge Abbott and his colleagues naturally applauded this position. They had lobbied effectively because of their political connections *and* because the president was quite sensitive about any precedent which potentially damaged U.S. interests.

A second Roosevelt motive was fear of European intervention in the Dominican Republic. Along with the Improvement Company, French, Belgian and Italian interests were also pressing their claims. "Those who profit by the Monroe Doctrine must accept certain responsibilities along with the rights it confers," so Roosevelt agreed to protect the Dominican Republic. Like McKinley in Cuba, he had not the "slightest desire" for territory, but the Platt Amendment, "that most wise measure of international statesmanship," did set a precedent. Foreigners were to be kept out of the Caribbean, and that gave the United States the opportunity to "safeguard" a country like the Dominican Republic "against molestation in the interest of mere speculators."[28]

The Corollary joined conflicting interests. Europe was prevented from any new, long term involvement in the Western Hemisphere and the United States was free to protect and develop its neighbors. As the president assured the Senate, "the advantages that will come to us are indirect, but nevertheless great, for it is supremely to our interest that all the communities south of us should be or become prosperous and stable, and therefore not merely in name, but in fact independent and self-governing."[29]

The president's speech was not specific. How did he plan to assure prosperity in a nation now pledged to give 55 percent of its principal revenue to foreign debtors? How would he develop self-government in a nation that needed American approval to raise its taxes or protect its native producers? What was he going to do if government examiners discovered that Americans held substantial portions of the improper and exorbitant debt? Would United States institutionalize injustice if found?

If the president had no answers to these questions, his many critics did. A special session of Congress produced no agreement, so, despite approval by the Senate Foreign Relations Committee, the Dominican treaty never came to a vote. In February and March of 1905, the president had no chance of obtaining the two-thirds majority required by the U.S Constitution.

On the island, Dawson faced chaos. The Dominican minister had appeared in Dawson's office, pleading that "he could no longer stand the strain and that he contemplated resigning." He wanted Dawson to take responsibility for the customs house receipts but the minister first explained that was impossible until the Senate ratified the treaty, and, in any event, "I could not agree to anything that would affect the rights acquired under the Improvement Company award...."[30]

Dawson did agree to take a new proposal to the foreign creditors. Instead of giving 55 percent of the customs revenues to the debtors, the new plan suggested that "the revenues of all the ports be deposited in New York, and held as a trust fund until the convention is ratified or rejected." The Europeans immediately and "unconditionally" accepted this plan; the stumbling block was the Improvement Company. Because he thought his State Department superiors would disagree, Dawson was reluctant to infringe on the revenues earmarked for Abbott and his colleagues, who, alone among the creditors, refused to put their funds in trust. Another stalemate seemed to be on the horizon when the president stepped in and forcefully pushed the "trust fund" proposition. The Improvement Company withdrew its objections, the president agreed to wait for ratification until the next regular session of Congress, and he sent a Johns Hopkins professor to examine finances that were as confusing to a professor as they were to a minister.

Jacob Hollander was "considered one of the most eminent economists in the United States" and had reformed Puerto Rico's tax system at the request of the State Department. As Minister Dawson later told Congress, Hollander "had a great reputation through the West Indies on account of that [Porto Rico] work" and he was hired as "special commissioner" to prepare a report for the president.[31]

Hollander stayed in the Dominican Republic for ,six months, and, on October 1, 1905 he submitted a report to the president. It is excruciatingly difficult to read. Hollander had to pile detail on top of numbers, but his book is essential for any just assessment of the debtor's claims. The special commissioner echoed the president when he noted that we had a responsibility never to allow the Dominicans "to relapse, slowly but surely, into social and moral barbarism." Hollander not only supported the president, he emphasized that justice demanded holding the Improvement Company "to a detailed financial accounting." Even Hollander had not seen their books so "it would be to the last degree unfortunate" if the Improvement Company was "uniquely exempt from the scrutiny to which it is proposed to subject every other item of the aggregate debt."[32]

State Department officials closely examined Hollander's book, and the Senate the treaty and the policies that produced it. Twelve months after the agreement was signed, Roosevelt was still on the defensive as senators opened fire in debates that consistently contained three wonderful elements: humor, substance, and an accurate appraisal of the dilemma.

Merciless, Blood-Sucking Money Sharks

Speaking on January 8, 1906, Senator Rayner of Maryland blasted the president because "we must realize that this new Monroe Doctrine is strictly a financial doctrine." Citing the details of the 1869 Hartmont loan, Rayner said, "On the one side Belgium's invincible armada; on the other, the converted scows and rowboats of the lamented Morales....[T]he battle cry of the British Navy had been 'England expects every man to do his duty;' this battle cry shall be 'Belgium expects every man to collect his money'."[33]

Rayner had "carefully looked over the various provisions of the Constitution" and, despite his search, found "no clause that empowered this government to act as a receiver for any other government." Perhaps "the printer omitted it from the original proof sheet of the Constitution" but, barring that, it seemed that Roosevelt wanted to act as "a trustee for all the uncivilized nations on earth." Arguably this was a good idea but what about the new expenses in personnel? "We will evidently have to provide a new portfolio to be known as the "department of foreign receiverships" and a new secretary to be known as "secretary of foreign bankruptcy." This fellow would have a great deal to do because, "from Yucatan to Tierra del Fuego," many nations verged on bankruptcy. Did we mean to help everyone? How long would the receiverships last? And, "are we not trying to accomplish too much in a brief period? Are we not venturing beyond our limits as a world power and intruding officiously into affairs that do not possibly concern us?"[34]

Rayner concluded with this argument: While the Monroe Doctrine applied when republican institutions were threatened, the president forgot that European nations taking over customs houses threatened nothing except perhaps their own sanity. The United States would never teach other nations to be self-reliant by forcing them to be dependent on us. It was dangerous to argue, as did Senator Beveridge of Indiana, "that we will not renounce our part in the mission of our race—trustee, under God, of the civilization of the world...thanksgiving to Almighty God that he has marked us as his chosen people, henceforth to lead in the regeneration of the world."

Rayner scoffed at such conceit. He was willing to match religious fervor with anyone in the Senate, but he assured Beveridge that he would find "no such decree as this enrolled in the chancery of heaven." Nor would he find any such decree or authority in the "Magna Charta" of the American people. "This government is not a foreign missionary society or an institution for the feeble minded." The Constitution gave the president no authority to take over customs houses and no authority to decide the proper and improper debts of others. To do what Roosevelt wanted was to use the American flag as a "pirate's ensign" and, along with Edward Hartmont, tarnish the civilizations we sought to protect.[35]

Two weeks after Rayner's salvo, the president's supporters echoed some of his critic's sentiments. One after another, senators underlined the moral problem of "enforcing the collection of the indebtedness, the greater part of which cannot be regarded as honest." Spooner of Wisconsin admitted that only the presence of our warships allowed American officials to peacefully collect the customs house revenues, but, unlike Senator Rayner, the president's supporters reasoned that taking the customs houses was the lesser of two evils. Constitutionally, it was hard to find support for the president's position, but the nation had no Caribbean alternative.[36]

Henry Cabot Lodge said of Cuba, "We made her make those limitations [the Platt Amendment] a part of her Constitution." That "saved us from the annexation of Cuba," and the president's moves in the Dominican Republic would save us from annexing that "feeble and helpless" nation. To Lodge, it was a simple choice; "In order to avoid the complications growing out of the taking of customs houses by a foreign government it is infinitely better to take possession of them and administer them ourselves."[37]

Principle partially won the day in these spirited debates. Congress refused to countenance a situation in which the United States of America accepted responsibility for the Dominican Republic's debts. That made no constitutional sense. But the Senate would look the other way, and ratify the treaty if the president found a subterfuge to avoid legal and national responsibility for doing what he had already done. As a State Department official later noted, it was a backroom deal, "hardly more than a matter of form."[38]

Secretary of State Root rehired Jacob Hollander. He was the only man with a true grasp of the Dominican Republic's tangled finances. He later explained his position in House hearings, "I was rendering a service, the success of which absolutely depended upon the withholding of any specific definition as to whom I was acting for."[39] Hollander admitted that he was working for both the State Department and the Dominican government, but, if he told anyone he was an employee of Washington that would nullify Root's deal with the Senate. If he told anyone he was working for the Dominican Republic, that would nullify the guarantee all creditors now demanded: Washington in charge of the customs houses.

Hollander worked for no one and everyone. He and the State Department put nothing in writing ,and his verbal instructions were always deniable. In this way "at times I was the agent of the State Department and the next day I was the financial agent of the Dominican Republic; when I was effecting settlement with a creditor I was the financial agent of the Dominican Republic; when I was endeavoring to communicate the desires of the State Department to the Dominican representative I was the agent of the United States."[40]

Did the Dominicans know what was going on? Hollander "felt quite sure in my own mind that they knew" but to tell them was to admit that he was indeed a representative of the United States government. The truth had no public place in these negotiations. Nothing was real except the obligations of the Dominican people to the Santo Domingo Improvement Company.

In his report to the president, Hollander said it would be "to the last degree unfortunate" if the Improvement Company's claims were not subjected to the same scrutiny as all others. However, in his role as negotiator, Hollander never checked the company's books. In fact, it was the threat of a check that moved the company to finally accept a 10 percent reduction in its claim. Initially, Judge Abbott and his colleagues had refused the reduction, but, waving a carrot of payment in cash, the State Department also wielded the stick of potential scrutiny. The Improvement Company settled for 90 percent of its $4.5 million claim in cash.[41]

The other creditors lacked State Department support. Some of the European creditors received only 50 percent of their claims and the Dominican creditors found their bill slashed to 10 percent of the total. "We put in the knife deeply there," said Hollander, and he explained why: "The Dominican Government drew up a plan of settlement which, as far as the foreign creditors were concerned, required the consent of the creditors, because they had their Governments to back them, but as far as the domestic creditors were concerned the Dominican Government exercised its sovereign power and said: These we are prepared to adjust on such and such a basis."[42]

The final irony of this bizarre corollary is that the Dominican government used the little power at its disposal to virtually eliminate the debt of its own citizens. Meanwhile, Professor Hollander, who worked for no one, got paid by everyone. He took $1,000 a month and expenses from the State Department and, once he formally resigned that position, received a $100,000 payment from the Dominicans "for services rendered and to be rendered." Asked by a suspicious congressman, "how long is that service to continue, one year or ten years?" Hollander responded, "To eternity, sir, if I live and the Dominican government requires it."[43]

Hollander died. The agreement did not. Signed in July of 1907 and ratified by the legislatures of both nations, the Convention formally institutional- ized injustice. By using Hollander to carry out his wishes, President Roosevelt substituted pure expe- diency for "absolute equity." The Improvement Company got its money, and the Dominicans got a treaty that linked them to the United States, not for eternity but until they paid all their foreign debt.

Roosevelt had established an open-ended com- mitment to the Dominican Republic. If their system broke down, the United States had a legal and moral obligation to assure payment of dishonest debt. In Washington, no one knew if the commit- ment included military intervention. The policy was so unclear that any action was possible. For exam- ple, when Dominican President Rafael Trujillo informed President Harry Truman that he had paid off the debt on July 21, 1947, Trujillo himself had seen presidents do everything from intervening in the Dominican Republic to disregarding, not only Trujillo's murders but his embezzlement of the money required to pay the debt.[44]

A clear consequence of the treaty was the United States' direct involvement in the well-being of the Dominican economy. As Senator Lodge stressed in debate, "Mr. President, if we take this ground, and we always have taken it, then the responsibility goes with it."[45] In theory, responsibility meant "a reason- able degree of order"; in practice it meant one gov- ernment overseeing another so that both could regu- late their free market economies.

U.S. officials began to help reform, and then transform, the Dominican Republic's tariff struc- ture. Everything was geared "to getting revenue and making a showing for the foreign receivership."[46]

70

The island allowed all the American imports it could handle, and, in a move that still determines the island's economic destiny, the United States helped Dominicans produce more sugar than they or their export markets could ever consume.

Sugar was a mainstay of the Dominican economy long before the Roosevelt treaty was signed. Between 1882 and 1908 the island witnessed a dizzying increase in the amount of land devoted to mechanized sugar plantations. By the time the Americans arrived, a mere seven central plantations already controlled close to 200,000 acres of sugar lands. The receivership substantially increased the island's trade with the United States; it helped reform the land title laws in a way that allowed Americans to easily buy lands that were once communal properties; and, most important of all, it opened the island to the sugar trust that also controlled Cuban and Puerto Rican sugar.[47]

The problem for the the Dominican Republic was that it quickly became the weakest of America's Caribbean suppliers. Even Cuba had more political clout than the Dominican Republic. The treaty tied the island's sugar economy to that of the United States, and Washington linked the island's well-being to Congress' willingness to import foreign sugar. As Felipe J. Vicini told Congress in 1982, only ten percent of world sugar is sold on the free market, but the Dominican Republic sold 80 percent of its produce in that tiny free market. "We are more dependent on the volatile sugar market than any other sugar producing nation."[48]

What was true in 1982 had also been true in 1911. Since the goal of the new customs legislation

71

was to make a "show for the receivership," the long term consequences of American policy were either neglected or disregarded. President Roosevelt boasted that the customs treaty "would prove literally invaluable in pointing out the way for introducing peace and order in the Caribbean and its borders."[49] His subordinates considered the treaty a design for good government and Woodrow Wilson would use it as a model when he sought, in 1914, to assist the hapless Haitians.

In Cuba, Puerto Rico, and the Dominican Republic perpetual economic problems only proved the islanders inability to compete with the civilized nations; and the "malcontents" who complained about U.S. colonialism—*e.g*, in Puerto Rico in 1909—were the ungrateful children who failed to appreciate the blessings of Americanization.

It was the era of the Big Stick; a stick used to club the Spanish speaking Caribbean into submission, while, in the British West Indies, Jamaicans and Barbadians used their sticks and shovels to dig the Panama Canal.

Gold and Silver Payrolls

In Jamaica and Barbados, poverty produced a desperation so great that the Caribbean citizens of one empire built a canal continuously celebrated by another. In New York and California, Minnesota and Maine, magazines and newspapers published the feature stories that applauded America's engineering wizardry. The path between the seas underlined not only the genius of George W. Goethals and his talented staff, but the genius of the civilization that sent them into the Caribbean wilderness.[50]

Merciless, Blood-Sucking Money Sharks

Meanwhile, for the Jamaicans and Barbadians who helped build the canal, engineering excellence meant extraordinary effort. Hire anyone who can "make the dirt fly," said President Roosevelt, so American recruiters found more than 100,000 Caribbean islanders eager to avoid the dead time that was sugar's certain legacy. Only the best and strongest men received the jobs ("any who looked too old, too young, or too feeble were told to leave"[51]) which, in the name of progress, stripped societies of their most able-bodied and ambitious citizens.

From Panama, Jamaican and Barbadian laborers remitted money to families without a father. While one segment of the Caribbean stayed home, the other worked on an engineering project that underlined the islander's dilemma and civilization's shame.

Racism received little publicity in the countless articles celebrating American genius, but in Panama, George Goethals and his predecessors established payrolls of gold and silver. On the gold list were "white Americans" receiving $75 a month or more; "white Americans" receiving less than $75 a month; Panamanians receiving more than $75 a month; and, finally, "other whites" holding jobs for which no white Americans could be found.

The silver payroll was simple; it included the roughly 80 percent of the labor force not covered above.[52] Those other persons, black Jamaicans and Barbadians in particular, received substantially less money than their white counterparts but, adding taxation to racism, Goethals made his black workers pay to educate the children of his white workers. Financing all Panama Canal zone schools was a tax on the labor of silver payroll employees; Jamaicans (among others) thus paid for the institutions that a Caribbean or Panamanian youngster could never attend.

It was a perverse but, by 1908, institutionalized part of the Canal's rigorously segregated life. Gold employees enjoyed everything from free housing to free medical care; silver employees paid for their inferior housing, and, instead of the liberal leaves and vacations given to their gold colleagues, they lived in communities set apart by Jim Crow color lines. As one worker later noted, "life was some sort of semislavery."[53]

In theory that semislavery ended when the work did; but, in the Caribbean, that semislavery became an institutionalized part of island life. Migration to the Panama Canal may have been the most massive early twentieth century movement of the Caribbean peoples; what it unquestionably signals is an exodus that continues to this moment. Accepting exploitation to avoid starvation, Haitians and Dominicans search today for what their West Indian predecessors also never found at home, i.e., work.[54]

With Great Britain, the United States must assume a substantial share of the responsibility for the century-long Caribbean exodus. In Cuba, Puerto Rico, and the Dominican Republic, no American administration ever attempted to create self-sustaining economies. Indeed, in a studied imitation of his predecessor, William Howard Taft used Dollar Diplomacy in Haiti to support Americans who were every bit as controversial as the men who ran the Santo Domingo Improvement Company.

Dollar Diplomacy

In Santo Domingo it was the customs houses. In Haiti it was bananas. Americans loved them so much that in 1909, James McDonald convinced Haitian officials that bananas were a form of stalked, green gold. McDonald agreed to build a railroad for the Haitian government, and for each kilometer of main line built, he was to issue $20,000 worth of bonds, at 6 percent interest. The Haitian government agreed to guarantee these bonds, but, since it lacked the funds necessary to do so, the Haitians signed a companion contract with McDonald. He would receive generous leases on valuable Haitian land, plus a fifteen year exclusive right to any banana exported from Haiti. With the export duty levied on every stalk of green gold the Haitian customs collectors would count up their take and pay for the railroad with McDonald's bananas.[55]

McDonald never grew, much less picked, a banana. The Haitians were left with a debt they could never pay, and New York's National City Bank was left with a $500,000 loan to the very persuasive Mr. McDonald. He had "built" the railroad using New York money which was guaranteed by $878,000 of Haitian bonds which were guaranteed by the now non-existent bananas. Most of the bonds had been sold in France, and, once again, foreign investors lined up in the Caribbean to collect their principal and interest.[56]

For nearly a century, France had treated its former Haitian colony as a cash cow. By the time of the banana fiasco the principal Haitian bank was the Banque National d'Haiti. Controlled by French investors, the bank acted as fiscal agent for the

Haitian government, and, along with Haitian officials, French bankers often made sudden withdrawals from the Banque's always nearly empty coffers. It was such a splendid situation for thieves that, long before the Duvaliers took power in 1957, a cynic could accurately call Haiti a "kleptocracy."[57]

Germans bankers also competed with the French to overcharge the Haitians. In 1910, political unrest compounded problems caused by the absence of funds and bananas, and Haitians came to the United States. With luck they would find there the funds needed to help satisfy their native and foreign schools of merciless, blood-sucking money sharks.

The Haitians came at the right time. In charge of the State Department was Philander Knox, a man who disliked sentiment and Latin Americans.[58] Knox was a nose-to-the-grindstone diplomat who shared the racial prejudices of his time but never the nation's penchant for "grandiloquent sentimentality." That was a "national foible," a disease that, as it involved us in good works, neglected an elemental rule of serious foreign policy: Charity began at home.[59]

To Knox and his associates the relation of government to foreign investment was rooted in common sense and power. Power guaranteed that the government would fulfill all obligations to the investors it sponsored. Common sense dictated that the government got involved only when it could achieve economic or political advantage. Perhaps the United States needed new military bases, or wanted to nourish ties "with other great powers," or wanted to "strengthen influence in spheres where it ought to predominate over any other foreign influence on account of reasons of fundamental policy, like the Monroe Doctrine."[60] Knox saw no contradiction in using the government to underwrite loans and investments, and he and his assistant argued that, "by urging on the investors to lend themselves as instrumentalities of foreign policy, the government clothed those investors with rights to protection of especial dignity."[61]

Negotiating with the Haitians, American bankers demanded control of the customs houses. Knox refused, so the Haitians found themselves forced to negotiate with German and French bankers. The Americans, who had bet $500,000 on bananas, feared that foreigners would control the customs houses. National City Bank might thus be third in line to receive its money, so it now lobbied to retain a position it had already rejected. An American official summed it up to his superiors in Washington, "the American eagle and the German wolf were quarreling over the carcass of a lamb," or, as the official added, "a black sheep."[62]

Somebody was going to slaughter the Haitians, and the only issue was who. Knox's dollar diplomacy argued that a German proposal for multinational control of the customs houses must be rejected. The 65 million franc loan offered by a French-German consortium smacked of usury. Since the Haitians would receive only 72 percent of the money, Knox and his colleagues argued that these terms were unthinkable. Moreover, they failed to protect American investors, and they promised the prospect of future European intervention in Haiti.[63]

Knox demanded, and was assured of, American

involvement in any reorganization of Haiti's national bank. In the new loan, American interests now controlled 20 percent of Haiti's national bank. Knox had made it clear that the U.S. meant to have a forceful say in Haitian affairs, but, in the process, the Haitians received a loan which Knox had formerly called unjust. In the new transaction, Haiti received $9.4 million of a $13 million loan. Since that translated into the same 72 percent formerly rejected by the State Department, it was hard to see how the State Department had helped the Haitians. But, as Assistant Secretary of State Huntington Wilson later stressed, helping others was never the intent of dollar diplomacy. In fact, a diplomat "defrauded" his country if he ever sought anything other than the political and economic advantage of the American taxpayer and the American nation.[64]

Haiti was forced to meet the interest on McDonald's railroad bonds by using its own revenues. Then, after the advent of dollar diplomacy, not only did McDonald retain his concession, the Haitian nation had to borrow money to continue paying for a railroad which still lacked tracks. McDonald, "extremely unpopular" because he did not keep his word, now compounded his and the State Department's problems by siding with a corrupt and ruthless Haitian dictator, Antoine Simon.

To build the railroad McDonald needed land, which (with the support of the government) he cavalierly took from people in the northern half of the country. McDonald claimed rights granted by his railroad concession, but Haitians, enraged by losing both their houses and their land, soon backed rebels eager to overthrow the Simon government. There was a summary execution of all resisters, including the slaughter of a youngster who, before he was put to death, had his arms and legs chopped off.[65]

While the State Department complained, the political situation was out of control. When northern rebels burned property belonging to the railroad, the Haitian government asked Washington to back its ruthless tactics. Warships arrived, but Knox and his associates understood they were backing a loser. McDonald, however, was linked to the government; indeed, he gave officials the dynamite needed to blow up the rebel village of Capotille.[66]

With his opponents shouting a battle-cry of "Down With McDonald," the Simon government fell in August of 1911. One dictator followed another, while, at the State Department, officials decided to produce change by becoming more involved in Haiti's affairs. Although the Dominican Republic was on the verge of exploding,[67] Knox and his associates never lost faith in the Dominican/Egyptian/British model as a means to stability in Haiti. National City Bank's man on the spot had suggested American control of the customs houses, and, like Theodore Roosevelt in 1904, Philander Knox said that if the Haitians asked, the United States might say yes.

As National City's troubleshooter in Port-au-Prince, Roger Farnham was an artist, a banker every bit as adept as Edward Hartmont. Farnham first visted Haiti in June of 1911 and had no trouble making friends with the German representatives who had recently swindled Antoine Simon. To hear Farnham tell it, Haiti's president had purchased an antiquated ship for $16,000. German officers brought it as far as Puerto Rico when they suddenly discovered the need for another $100,000 payment. Simon agreed to pay $75,000 for delivery, but, as Farnham later explained, "before turning it over to the Government the German officers stuffed waste into certain parts of the machinery." They then filled the boilers with salt water and charged the government another $10,000 in cash to be deposited on the German ship, to tow the useless vessel to Port-au-Prince.[68]

Farnham said the Simon government eventually paid $600,000 for the sabotaged ship. He thought the Haitians were fools but said little about the Germans who swindled them. This was business in Haiti, and Roger Farnham knew how to do business, especially with the State Department. What Farnham did was try to assure National City's railroad investment by creating fear of another insurrection in Haiti. Blacks were about to overthrow the government of Simon's light skinned successors. The only alternative to more death and destruction was American control of the customs houses and American reorganization of the Haitian army.[69]

Knox hesitated because the Haitians never asked for a customs receivership and because French and German interests wanted partial control of any American control of Haitian monies. The result was more interim financing and more constuction of a railroad that eventually put the State Department in a difficult position.

By June of 1912, McDonald demanded payment for the first section of completed work. Because of engineering problems, officias refused to pay anything. McDonald had repositioned one of the promised stations near a swamp, and in the summer, the swamp became a river. Everyone in Haiti knew that this section of the country always flooded, so McDonald positioned the station which serviced Port-au-Prince in a location that could only be reached by the boats purchased from the Germans. Inspectors also stressed that, even without the water, only the boldest traveler would use the tracks because the most untrained eye could see they were "wavy." Not a roller coaster, but nevertheless so out of kilter that no engineer would dare travel more than twenty miles an hour on such "grossly substandard" support. As the American manager of the Haitian National Bank put it to the United States minister, "the Haitians had been cheated."[70]

In Washington, officials ordered the American minister to tell the Haitians to pay for the "completed" work. As in the Dominican Republic, principle made way for expediency. Since the Haitian government refused to guarantee the additional railroad bonds which the bankers were selling in Europe, both the railroad and National City Bank could lose everything. Already neck deep in the Haitian swamp, Knox refused to drown. It was easier to force the Haitians to pay for the road and hope that, somehow, the next section of track would be flat rather than wavy, safe rather than dangerous.[71]

In August of 1912, the dictator who overthrew Simon was blown up in the presidential palace. His successor, Tancrede Auguste, took office with the support of the American minister. Because Auguste was "a strong man and pro-American," the State Department exchanged recognition of the new government for recognition of McDonald's satisfactory work. Four days after the U.S. gave him a green light, Auguste agreed to accept the railroad's work.

National City's investment was secure but Roger Farnham still had his doubts about the Haitian people. As he later explained to Congress, "I know that in the construction of this railroad in Haiti, where we had them as laborers, the American foreman, who had previously been on railroad construction in Mexico and all up and down South America and in the United States told me—and I saw myself too—that they reckoned four Haitians were necessary to do the work of one Irish track hand."

When asked to explain why this was so, Farnham had a ready explanation: "They [the Haitians] were very weak and they had no food."[72]

American Motives

In April of 1912, Secretary of State Philander Knox visited Cuba, full of pride because the Panama Canal was nearly finished and full of advice because no one could doubt "the purity of motive" which had always characterized America's Caribbean policies. "As I [Knox] said in Panama, intelligent consideration of the relations between the United States to the other American Republics makes it clear that our policies have been without a trace of sinister motive or design, craving neither sovereignty nor territory."[73]

Was Knox serious? Was the architect of dollar diplomacy, a policy proudly rooted in self-interest, really convinced that his motives were pure, his nation's record "consistent and unblemished?"

Either Knox was a hypocrite, or the sense of exceptionalism and self-righteousness which motivated American policymakers acted as a mental shield to the world that was actually there. Intelligent men pursued stupid, ruthless, and undemocratic policies because objective reality had little to do with their assessment of Caribbean life.

When Knox spoke in Cuba, the United States Supreme Court (on April 8, 1908) had indicated that "all the world knew the Isle of Pines was an integral part of Cuba."[74] No one could doubt Cuba's legitimate sovereignty except the Senate which refused to pass the treaty which was part of the 1903 Guantanomo transaction. Knox boastfully noted that "good faith is a thing that proves itself by deeds, not words. Our deeds in respect to the Cuban people are before you. Look to them for fresh assurance—if there be any doubting Thomas who thinks he needs it."[75]

Cubans listened as the secretary promised "a new era of even greater prosperity and progress." Then, in May of 1912, the country exploded in a "race war" that baffled American policymakers. As the American minister put it to Knox, "I cannot go further than to say that it would seem evident that the present movement is organized and directed by some unknown interest, it being highly improbable that the negroes at the head of the Independent Colored Party would be capable of engineering a movement on this scale."[76]

The American minister wrote those lines in Havana. Racism blocked any just assessment of the abilities of Afro-Cubans, and, even more importantly, it blocked out the social and economic sources of the widespread resort to arms. Since 1898, Afro-Cubans had received few positions of power; valiantly, and in large numbers they had fought in the war for independence but they never lived in a Cuba free of the racism that came with Spanish authority. In 1907, Afro-Cubans formed the Partido Independiente de Color. It enjoyed a measure of success, but early efforts at organizing Oriente province, the principal site of the 1912 resort to arms, failed. The people were so indifferent that the new party failed to secure even the small number of signatures required to appear on the ballot.[77]

By 1912, however, the Independiente party found the Afro-Cubans of Oriente eager to receive their message. Part of the about-face was caused by the government; in 1910, it had banned political organization along racial lines so, by 1912, "Cuban politics had polarized around the issue of race." Skin color suddenly mattered because the many black citizens of Oriente found that, as in Puerto Rico and the Dominican Republic, U.S. intervention and investment meant widespread loss of land. An American sociologist then in Cuba noted, "the sugar companies purchased land from the peasants where the land could show a title, but where titles were in question—as so many of them were—recourse was had in the courts."[78]

Illiteracy never helped anyone in a court battle, and for those citizens who could read and write, the handicap was money. The companies hired the best lawyers and if those lawyers failed to discover loopholes in the law, they resorted to bribery. One way or another peasants lost. By 1912, those predominantly black citizens resorted to arms. In Oriente, where the best lands were now in the hands of the sugar companies, the "most common insurgent gesture" was the destruction of sugar property. None of the principal estates near Guantanomo escaped damage, and all over the province the railroads used to haul sugar discovered that citizens despised their purpose. Tracks, bridges, stations—everything went up in smoke as peasants finally found a way to vent the frustrations that had been simmering for nearly a decade.[79]

In Washington, Secretary Knox responded to the disturbances with dispatch and decisiveness. The marines had already landed four companies, to be followed by "four large war vessels," and, if that proved insufficient incentive for the Cuban government to act, Knox told his minister that "you will vigorously impress upon the president of Cuba that a continued failure on the part of his government to adequately protect life and property will inevitably compel this government to intervene in Cuba under and in response to its treaty rights and obligations."[80]

Since the Americans had just ended a 1906 intervention in 1909, the Cubans got the point. They ruthlessly ended the revolt by ending the lives of more than 3,000 Afro-Cubans.

In Washington, "unknown interests" may have caused the revolt, but swift action ended it. Nothing seemed capable of moving American policymakers to question their beliefs, values, and practices. Indeed, Knox and his colleagues still remained steadfast when the supposedly docile Puerto Ricans stopped asking to be Americans. The Unionists (the dominant Puerto Rican party) suggested independence as the island's ultimate alternative, and the Americans' only response was to charge ingratitude.[81]

In Puerto Rico, a decade of persistent complaints about American rule had reached its peak in 1909. Using the only power at its disposal, the only elected body in Puerto Rican politics—the House of

Delegates—refused to pass the 1909 budget. Islanders hoped to catch the attention of the American people but the only thing they caught was the wrath of President Taft. He reminded Puerto Ricans they were the United States' "favored daughter"; thus, ten years of complaining about the lack of self-government reflected, not only a surprising degree of ingratitude, but "an indication that we have gone somewhat too fast in the extension of political power to them for their own good."[82]

Taft suggested that Congress pass a law which stipulated that, in the event that Puerto Rico ever again refused to pass a budget, last year's budget went into effect. In congressional debate that ranks with the most open manifestation of racism ever published in the Congressional Record, representatives tried to remind Puerto Ricans of their twelve year "joy ride" on the merry-go-round of American life. But, as Congressman Rucker of Colorado reminded his colleagues, what could you expect from people that made distinctions no one else could see. In Puerto Rico to inspect conditions, Rucker had watched a woman point out an upper and a lower class youngster. But, to the congressman, "both boys were hatless and shoeless, and begging alike on the street, and both as black as the ace of spades." [Laughter][83]

Hate was still a congressional joke in 1909. The ingratitude of the Puerto Ricans a taken-for-granted assumption of congressional debate. Rucker told his colleagues, "the history of recent events conclusively shows that if all the atoms of gratitude they have in their souls were poured into a humming bird's quill, and with a blast furnace blown into the eye of a mosquito, it is my unqualified judgement that eye would not bat."[84]

Congress' response to Rucker's comments was "loud applause." That response is clearly marked in the Congressional Record. Missing, however, is the reaction of Puerto Rico's resident commissioner. In 1909, he quietly listened to hours of unrestrained contempt for his people; in 1910, he eloquently defended his people when Congress yet again refused to grant self-government;[85] and in 1912, he reluctantly followed suit when his Unionist party decided that Congress' hate for the Puerto Ricans barred any possibility of statehood. Islanders, if they ever meant to achieve the self-government promised in 1898, might have to become an independent republic. What alternative did the Americans leave?[86]

Neither President Taft nor Secretary Knox got a chance to answer that question in 1912. After more than a decade of Republican rule, Washington was about to make way for a president who labeled his program "the New Freedom." That slogan could be interpreted in many ways. In Puerto Rico, Cuba, Haiti, and the Dominican Republic, Caribbean citizens impatiently waited for the Democrats response to a region in turmoil.

"The old order changeth" said President Woodrow Wilson, as he assured all Americans that, "I don't care how benevolent the master is going to be, I will not live under a master. That is not what America was created for."[87]

Popes, Plebiscites, and Possessions

"We were all imbued with the fact that we were trustees of a huge estate [Haiti] that belonged to minors."
—General Smedley Butler, Congress, 1921[1]

Secretary of War Lindley Garrison said he had "never been there" and knew "very little" about Puerto Rico but he nevertheless proposed a plan to make islanders U.S. citizens against their will. To Garrison the issue was justice; not only was there "no sentiment whatever" that Puerto Rico be independent, but, "there is no suggestion that it should not be connected with the United States for all time, and that we should not in the fullest measure be responsible for it...."[2]

Islanders disagreed. In 1913 the dominant Unionist Party had formally removed statehood from its list of possible status alternatives; and this year (1914) the "agitation" for outright independence had gained such a foothold in the Puerto Rican mind that islanders apparently assumed they were free to determine their own destiny. Garrison argued it was both unwise and irresponsible to foster such an idea. Garrison said the Puerto Ricans had to understand an elemental fact: "We [the Wilson administration] feel that Porto Rico, being a possession of the United States, to be governmentally included in the United States should be, as I have said before, officered and manned and run by citizens of the United States."

Garrison stressed that the U.S. citizens did not have to come from the mainland. Islanders would do also, but only if Puerto Rico remained a territory "with a small 't'." The Wilson administration objected to an outright grant of citizenship to all islanders. If you did that, "then the laws you enact here would apply there; whereas it is desireable, *as you may see from all the bills which have ever been presented*, that such shall not be the case." [Emphasis added.] Puerto Rico was and would remain "for all time" an unincorporated territory of the United States. "It shall be legislated for as a body politic, in a different situation from a Territory with a capital 'T' or a state."[3]

Garrison said to fix a time in the future when islanders "acquiesced"; give them six months or a year and then, when Puerto Ricans "easily and freely" selected or rejected a new nationality, Congress was off the statehood hook.

The Secretary of War asked "...if there is a great body of people down there who wish to have all the benefits of the protection of our flag and do not want to assume any burden. If that is true, I particularly would like to know that."

Congressman William Jones (Chair of the House Committee on Insular Affairs) was less sympathetic. He stressed that the principal reason Congress wanted to make islanders citizens was to end the agitation for independence. "Porto Rico is to remain permanently a possession of the United States."[4]

Puerto Ricans, however, refused to accept second class citizenship. Resident commissioner Luis Muñoz Rivera made that clear in his passionate testimony during the House hearings. And, two weeks after Muõz's testimony, islanders sent Congress an extraordinary message. In a statement "unanimously approved" by the only elected officials in the island's territorial government, Puerto Ricans said, "[W]e firmly and loyally maintain our opposition to being declared, in defiance of our express wish or without our express consent, citizens of any country whatsoever other than our own beloved soil that God has given us an inalienable gift and incoercible right."

Islanders reminded Congress and President Wilson that "any government not based on consent of the governed is a tyranny."[5]

In these hearings, the Wilson administration defined the meaning of "New Freedom" for the Caribbean and its peoples. Real Americans might not have to live under a "benevolent master," but the Puerto Rican did. And, if they refused small 't' citizenship, Puerto Rico and its people could face the future Woodrow Wilson had already mapped out for Haiti and the Dominican Republic. Once again those nations were up in arms and once again an American administration decided to base its policy on the Roosevelt Corollary to the Monroe Doctrine.

But, this time, the Corollary was overloaded with such a heavy cargo of inconsistency and self-interest that the United States created two "benevolent dictatorships" on the same island. As Senator Pomerene of Nevada later explained to his colleagues, "...the [Wilson] policy was one of cruelty."[6]

Hispaniola

Woodrow Wilson often lied to himself. He would proudly proclaim an American ideal, disregard it, and then dismiss anyone who questioned his commitment to truth, justice, and democracy.[7]

In Mobile, Alabama, President Wilson delivered (on October 27, 1913) a famous speech in which he championed the rights of Latin American nations. For decades, bankers had "driven harder bargains with them in the matter of loans than any other peoples in the world." In fact, "interest has been exacted of them that was not exacted of anybody else, because the risk was said to be greater; and then securities were taken that destroyed the risk—an admirable arrangement for those who were forcing the terms."[8]

Was the president talking about the Dominican Republic? Or Haiti? He never said so. But he did stress that he sympathized with the Latin American nations whose rights and freedom had been compromised by outside interference. That would never happen under Woodrow Wilson, a president who emphasized the absolute priority of "human rights, national integrity and opportunity as against material interests."

The fascinating thing about this idealistic speech is that it bore no relation to policies then being actively pursued by the Wilson administration. In Haiti, for example, Roger Farnham and his colleagues told the island's leaders (on March 24, 1913) that the second section of the railroad had been completed. Would the government please issue the bonds required by its contracts with McDonald, Farnham, and National City Bank?

The Haitians said no. The State Department noted, "with much justification" a team of engineers found the second section of road as poorly constructed as the first. The tracks were unfit for trains and, once again, the railroad had positioned stations in "extremely unsatisfactory" locations. The Haitians refused to be cheated twice, and they so informed Roger Farnham and his associates.[9]

Farnham called in the State Department, which supported his position, and instructed Assistant Secretary of State John Osborne to convince the Haitians to accept the faulty railroad. The Haitians were thus "persuaded" to pay high interest for a useless system that had the determined and powerful support of the United States government.

The Haitians accepted the second section of railroad on July 21, 1913. In October, the president promised to forever avoid government backed usury, and in December his secretary of state helped Farnham and his colleagues place Haitian money on an American naval vessel and deposit it in New York.

Haiti's political situation was chaotic, and money, necessary to pay the troops, was in short supply. Against the wishes of the State Department, the Haitians issued new currency while, at the National Bank, American officials feared a raid on their coffers. They wanted Secretary Bryan to send a warship to collect the Haitian's gold before the Haitians did.

Bryan not only agreed, he lied to the Haitians. He assured them the U.S. had no intention of overseeing their fiscal affairs as he simultaneously instructed the U.S. Minister to devise a plan to take Haiti's gold. At one o'clock every afternoon Port-au-

Prince closed up shop. This was the perfect time to commandeer the money so "eight men [who were marines] armed with stout canes and concealed revolvers" entered the bank, loaded the gold onto a waiting cart, and drove it through Port-au-Prince's deserted streets. "Strolling" the sidewalks were more out of uniform marines, also carrying "stout canes," who would presumably keep any suspicious natives at bay. When the wagon reached the dock, the money was placed on the U.S warship *Machias*, taken to New York, and, thanks to Roger Farnham, deposited in the vaults of National City Bank.[10]

The outraged Haitians thought Bryan was a hypocrite. He and President Wilson said one thing in Mobile and did another in Port-au-Prince. The French manager of the bank, who presumably took a long nap during the robbery, had to go into hiding. In Washington the Haitian minister asked why, if the bank had formerly opposed gold outflows because of the war in Europe, was this one justified? And how had the American government dared use marines and a warship to contradict the bank's own policy?[11]

Publicly and privately Bryan gave the same answer; for the Haitian's own good. He told the minister that Haiti's political unrest (rebel troops were in fact massing in the North) proved the wisdom of America's action. In New York the money was safe; in Port-au-Prince it could be robbed.

In a confidential letter (dated January 7, 1915) to President Wilson, Bryan explained his motives and actions. The situation in Haiti was "still embarrassing and we have apparently made no progress." Insurrection in the North threatened the new president, but for the United States, "the important matter of interest is the bank." While it was a French institution "the stock was largely owned by Americans." They had asked for Washington's help, and even though Bryan "did not like the idea of forcible interference on business grounds," he had already done this by sending the *Machias*. The money was safe but Bryan reminded the president that "I believe that there will be no peace and progress in Haiti until we reach some such arrangement as we have in Santo Domingo, and, as you remember, we have proposed that to them but have not felt like compelling acceptance of the plan."[12]

What did the president want to do? "How far do you think we ought to go in forcing the bank's views and interests?" Bryan saw an opportunity in the revolution to give the United States a chance "to propose a plan similar to the one adopted in Santo Domingo." To be effective, Americans would have to take over Haiti's customs houses, and "the success of this Government's efforts in Santo Domingo would, it seems to me, suggest the application of the same methods to Haiti whenever the time is ripe."[13]

Bryan wanted to use the Dominican model to pacify Haiti while the republic was itself in the throes of a year-long political revolution. In September of 1913, to stop the war, Bryan sent two pointed messages to Horacio Vasquez: Washington would not recognize his government and, if he did not agree to American mediation, Vasquez would receive none of his own government's money (the 45 percent from the 1907 agreement) from the American controlled customs houses.

Vasquez surrendered, but more fighting seemed certain when, in December of 1913, an American guarantee of fair local elections resulted in "flagrant fraud" by the side Washington supported. Bryan disregarded the fraud and agreed to an increase in the Dominican debt *if* islanders gave the United States power to control the customs houses, all other government expenses, and the planning and execution of the national budget.

The Dominicans agreed to that proposal in early 1914, but, when the president in charge allowed the dateline for promised elections to pass, the revolution broke out with more intensity than ever. In July of 1914, Washington issued the "Wilson Plan." Stressing that the United States "desired nothing for itself," Wilson and Bryan publicly "warned everyone concerned that it is absolutely imperative that the present hostilities should cease and that all concerned should disperse to their several homes...."[14]

Under American-imposed rules, Juan Jimenez won the election in October of 1914, but his chief rival was appointed secretary of war. That meant Desiderio Arias controlled the armed forces at the very moment a wave of anti-Americanism spread through the Dominican Congress. President Jimenez could be fatally compromised if the Americans continued to provide their unwanted support.[15]

To Bryan, the only way to control the islanders was to increase the level of American authority. The United States wanted "to prove its sincere and disinterested friendship," and needed to "fulfill its responsibilities as the friend to whom in such crises as the present all the world looks to guide San Domingo out of its difficulties."[16]

A week after Bryan wrote his dollar diplomacy letter ("the important matter is the bank"), he acted on the president's joint instructions for Hispaniola. As of January 12, 1915, "no more revolutions would be permitted." Anyone who made trouble would be "put out of the country," and the United States "would furnish whatever force was necessary to help the president maintain order."[17]

In Haiti, the situation was equally tense. Acting on the president's suggestion, Bryan decided to send the Haitians the same troubleshooter who arranged the peace in the Dominican Republic. With orders to plan a presidential election, John Franklin Fort went to Haiti in early 1915. He soon received a copy of the treaty Bryan wanted the Haitians to sign. If they refused to do so, Fort's job was to "secure the necessary concessions to enable us to give stability there as we do in Santo Domingo."[18]

In exchange for the recognition President Guillaume Sam desired, the United States would obtain control of Mole St. Nicholas. This bay, located in northern Haiti, was a potential prize for the Europeans then at war on the western front. Wilson had already decided "that it should not be permitted to fall into the hands of other foreign governments or foreign capitalists," One part of the recognition package was control of a bay that was ominously close to both Guantanamo and the United States.

The second part of the recognition package was control of the Haitian government as a means to the dominance of American business interests. Bryan told the president that "as long as the government is under French or German influence American interests are going to be discriminated against there as they are discriminated against now." However, the American interests were willing to remain in Haiti and even purchase a controlling interest in the Haitian National Bank. It would become a National City subsidiary if "this government takes the steps necessary to protect them, and their idea seems to be that no protection would be sufficient that does not include a control of the customs houses."[19]

But what about the human rights and national integrity Wilson had so eloquently championed? If the issues were usury and thievery, Roger Farnham and National City were responsible for a railroad with "wavy" tracks that led to stations in a swamp.

Bryan and Wilson avoided their own inconsistencies by relying on two assumptions of U.S. culture. One was that Americans were not foreigners. The Haitians or the Dominicans might think so, but, since the Caribbean was an American lake, how could U.S. citizens be foreigners?

The second assumption was the inherent legitimacy of "good colonialism." Bryan told the president that, if the United States agreed to "insist on more active supervision in the [Haitian] government," the two remaining questions were "time and method." Any revolutionary situation was a good time. As to method, Bryan proposed Dutch colonial policy in Java and British Imperial policy in India. Why India was a better model than the Egyptian model used by Theodore Roosevelt in 1905 was an issue Bryan never raised. The Republican and Democratic *cultural constant* was the use of British colonialism as a model for American policy.[20]

The Haitians had to present an opportunity, and any pretext would do. No one, however, predicted an opening as gruesomely appropriate as the fall of Guillaume Sam. With his opponent, Rosalvo Bobo, threatening the capital in June of 1915, Sam had considered U.S. support. Haitian officials would provide a public relations front for American control of the customs houses while Sam obtained the "guaranteed" support of the United States against all domestic enemies.[21]

However, control of the customs houses "had been violently opposed by the Haitian people for a number of years and even at the present time" (July of 1915).[22] Sam's opponents already charged that he was a tool of the Americans.

Sam decided to fight. He used the paper money printed in defiance of U.S. wishes to raise a new army, which, in a surprise offensive, managed to produce a stalemate. By late June, Sam had control of Port-au-Prince, the enemy had control of the countryside, and, cruising the Caribbean was Admiral William Caperton.

On July 2, 1915, the admiral had his assistant hand-deliver a letter to both sides informing them that he felt compelled "to insist that no fighting whatever take place in the town of Cape Haitien." The Admiral's edict was based on a simple principle; his job was to "protect the lives and property of American and other foreign citizens." In the last 58 years no foreigner had ever been killed but, to avoid a first time, Caperton outlawed the fighting that would surely endanger American and foreign lives and property.

To prove his neutrality Caperton suggested "that they fight on the plains outside of the city. I would recognize the man who won, and I would see that he afterwards took possession of the city but that he did so in an orderly manner. In other words, I did not wish to appear to be wanting to stop this revolution, or as taking any sides one way or the other."[23]

Caperton was an umpire. One senator asked him, "you were just establishing rules like those of the Marquis of Queensbury?" Caperton: "Yes sir."

The Haitians, however, refused to play by English rules. On July 27, 1915, a revolutionary group managed to storm the presidential palace. Sam, using a key always carried by every Haitian president, managed to escape through a door that led to the nearby French embassy. Just before his exit from the Haitian stage, Sam ordered the death of the many political prisoners held in the palace's jails.[24]

Tragically, Sam's soldiers followed orders. They went from cell to cell, shooting some and hacking others to a grisly death. A survivor (he feigned death) alerted the city to what had happened and, suddenly, an angry mob stood in front of the French embassy clamoring for Sam's head. When a French official reminded Haitians of the embassy's inviolability, the crowd dispersed, and even during a long night, no one stormed the embassy. Haitians may have refused to play by the Marquis of Queensbury's rules, but they always comprehended the threat to their independence posed by the admiral and warships.

Those warships provided the pretext for the American intervention. Seeing black smoke pouring from the stacks of Caperton's ships, the rumor quickly circulated that the Americans meant to land troops to protect the foreign legations.

Sam's opponents stormed the French embassy, dragged him outside, a crowd tore him to pieces, and in celebration of their revenge, citizens paraded through Cape Haitien flaunting various parts of

Sam's severed body.[25]

Watching from the deck of his ship was Admiral William Caperton. After a consultation with the French and British charge d'affaires, he decided to land troops "to prevent further rioting and for the protection of the lives and property of foreigners and to preserve order."[26]

The State Department seconded Caperton's decision with a very specific proviso: "That representatives of England and France be informed of this [the admiral's] intention—informed that their interests will be protected and that they be requested not to land." This would be a solely American operation, more ships and marines were on the way, and, "if more forces are absolutely necessary, wire immediately."

The admiral did just that. He wanted two more ships, and all the marines they could carry, as soon as possible. But, in the meantime, "landing force established in city." Slight resistance "easily overcome."[27]

The State Department could rest easy because the admiral was in command, and, if President Sam was in pieces, President Wilson was in Washington overseeing a military occupation that became a nightmare on the island and a joke at the White House. In Haiti, soldiers received, for the next four years, "little helpful guidance from Washington" as they established a "benevolent dictatorship." When Secretary of the Navy Josepheus Daniels came to cabinet meetings his colleagues would rise and shout, "Hail the King of Haiti."[28]

If Daniels was King, William Caperton was Prince Regent. He executed the navy's orders with such dispatch and efficiency that, within two weeks of establishing his position, he had already chosen Haiti's new president. America's candidate was Phillipe Dartiguenave, a senator who quickly grasped the new realities of island life. As Caperton put it, "Haiti must agree to any terms demanded by the United States."[29]

America's candidate had an opponent. Rosalvo Bobo not only controlled a substantial number of troops, he was "greatly beloved " in Haiti; he was also "intelligent, honest, and well meaning," a man who enjoyed so much support in Cape Haitien that the Navy feared his entrance into the city.[30]

Caperton devised a plan. He would circumvent the people by meeting Bobo on the warship *Washington*; that name alone would strike fear in Bobo's heart. Caperton had his assistant deliver the ultimatum to Bobo while, behind a door in an adjoining cabin, he listened to this exchange.

Captain Edward Beach asked if Bobo was a presidential candidate. Bobo responded, "Sir, I am more than a candidate. I am Chief of the Executive Power. I command an army in the north of Haiti which is now unopposed...The Haitian Presidency is already mine; the election is a mere formality."

Captain Beach, assured that Bobo was a patriot, informed him that "you are not a candidate for the Haitian presidency. And further, that instead of being a patriot, you are a menace and a curse to your country."

"Bobo jumped from his chair as if he had been lashed in the face." What did the captain mean? And why assault a commander-in-chief with such "intolerable insults?"

Captain Beach: "Sit down Dr. Bobo. Take it easy. You are not a candidate because the United States forbids....If the United States forbids you must realize you cannot be a candidate." Bobo, trying to deal with the captain's summary manner, then heard this addendum to the American ultimatum. "There is to be no more revolution ever in Haiti; no more presidents made by force....You are informed that you are a public enemy of the United States."

Captain Beach wrote that "it is hard to picture the effect upon this aspirant for presidential power. He sat cowering in his chair, his presence of mind gone. He gazed helplessly about, then wildly. *He was like a small schoolboy in the relentless grasp and power of a hard hearted master.*"[31] [Emphasis added.]

With Caperton listening nearby, Beach ordered that no more presidents be made by force, as he told a "beloved Haitian," on an American warship, that the United States "forbids" your candidacy. It was a forceful performance, carried out by soldiers, but backed, every step of the way, by America's new Secretary of State, Robert Lansing.

Monroe Doctrine

When William Jennings Bryan resigned in a principled dispute over President's Wilson's handling of the sinking of the *Lusitania*, Robert Lansing took charge of the State Department in July of 1915. His official portraits suggest a man of enormous self-confidence: grey hair, distinguished bearing, perfectly trimmed moustache, mandatory black suit and white shirt. In sharp contrast to Bryan and Wilson, this man avoided self-deception. He understood power, and he had no hesitation about using it. One of his first Caribbean responsibilities was to purchase the Virgin Islands. The Danish were hesitating, so Lansing "diplomatically" informed their minister of his options. He could sell the islands and get a decent price for them, or he could watch as America took them, and Denmark received nothing.[32]

In a long and detailed memo dated November 24, 1915, Lansing explained his "Caribbean Policy" to Woodrow Wilson. "I make no argument on the ground of benefit which would result to the people of these republics by the adoption of this policy....The argument based on humanitarian grounds does not appeal to me."[33]

Lansing stressed that his "essential idea was to prevent a condition which would menace the national interests of the United States." Forgetting Wilson's promises at Mobile, he noted that "the integrity of other American nations is an incident, not an end" of American policy. Granted "this may seem [a policy] based on selfishness alone" but "the author of the Monroe Doctrine had no higher or more generous motive in its declaration. To assert for it a nobler purpose is to proclaim a new doctrine."[34]

This statement marked one of the few times in the twentieth century that an American policy maker candidly defined America's Caribbean policies. Lansing's strategy would dominate because Woodrow Wilson was often bored by details[35] and consumed by America's possible participation in the Great War. The president happily let Lansing's views rule the Caribbean.

Lansing had three specific ideas. Take "control of the public revenues" out of the natives' hands;

make sure their governments were no longer dependent on foreign financiers for funds; and make sure their governments "possess a reliable and efficient military force sufficient to suppress any insurrection against the established authority."[36]

Intervention

Four days after Robert Lansing wrote his "Caribbean Policy" memo, the Dominicans received an ultimatum. Washington demanded that they expand the powers of the 1907 financial advisor; and that they disband their army, reorganize under American officials, and allow the commander of the Dominican forces to be an appointee of the president of the United States.[37]

Dominicans rejected Washington's demands. As the internal divisions institutionalized in 1914 once again came to a head, the United States closed the door to the treasury and refused to allow the customs receivership to give President Jiminez the money he needed to sustain a force equal to the one his opponents already had in the field. By May of 1916, the Dominican Congress threatened to impeach Jiminez. The Americans agreed to an intervention, but Jimenez refused to request U.S. troops. The U.S. minister stubbornly pleaded for an invitation to intervene, Jiminez said he only wanted arms, and the stalemate ended when the United States threatened to kill woman and children.

As President Jiminez's son later swore to Congress, "I wish to state that President Jiminez never requested nor approved nor consented to, nor was agreement made for, the American intervention." What happened was that Captain Crossley "sent a communication to the president one morning [May 3, 1916], stating categorically...that he needed to land forces to protect American interests." He planned to bring forces into the river, close to a nearby fort, "but, as on effecting the landing of the forces some shots might be fired...if the place from which the shot was fired could not be ascertained, the marines would have to fire at every living being— women, children, or aged persons. Those are the exact words of Captain Crossley."[38]

In Congress, representatives asked if anyone else was present when Crossley made these threats? Yes, a variety of Dominican secretaries, and the U.S. minister William Russell. He translated Crossley's English into Spanish, but, as Jiminez's testimony stressed, in either language the threat came through for what it was—the forceful policy of the Wilson administration.

On November 29, 1916, the United States government proclaimed a military occupation of the Dominican Republic. Since the Dominicans had violated the 1907 agreement by borrowing additional funds without permission, the United States came in to restore order. That neither the 1907 treaty nor international law authorized such an intervention was irrelevant to the proclamation. Elections were forbidden, sessions of the Dominican Congress suspended, the press censored (it became illegal "to criticize the Military Government with the intention to provoke disorder and revolt") and, in Washington, the Dominican minister who so "vehemently denounced" the proclamation "was replaced by a Dominican showing a greater understanding for the changed conditions."

Critics soon noted that "the Military Governor received no stated policy from the State Department or the Navy Department."[39] It seemed irrational to establish an occupation without a strategy, an intervention without an intention.

Rooted in the idealism of the administration and the culture, critics overlooked the realism of James Monroe and Robert Lansing. In the Dominican Republic, and in Haiti, soldiers might be allowed to act like dictators because the Monroe Doctrine was "based on selfishness alone." Its "essential idea was to prevent a condition which would menace the national interests of the United States."

In 1905 (in the Dominican Republic) and in 1911 (in Haiti) those interests were menaced by the possible involvement of outside governments in countries always "destined" to be under the mighty wing of the American eagle. By 1916, the Great War added a powerful incentive to "permanently" solve our Caribbean problems, but the threat of war in Europe was built on nearly one hundred years of resistence to European control over the Caribbean. In a dialectical relationship, one factor nourished the other, and, with Robert Lansing in charge, the result was two military governments "dictated by basic considerations of national safety."[40]

As Lansing told the president, sovereignty, equality and the Monroe Doctrine were incompatible: "The primacy of one nation, though possessing the superior physical might to maintain it, is out of harmony with the principle of the equality of nations which underlies Panamericanism, however just or altruistic the primate might be."[41]

Virgin Islands

Even after the Captain Christmas fiasco of 1902, the United States never lost interest in the Danish West Indies. American minister Maurice Egan always had a scheme in mind, but the reluctance of the Danes was so great that it sometimes reached bizarre proportions. In 1908 the Danish minister seriously proposed this plan: the United States would transfer sovereignty over an important Phillipine island to Germany, Germany would give Slesvig-Holsteing back to the Danes, and they in turn would give Greenland to the United States. All this, according to Minister Egan, "to avoid our purchase of the Danish West Indies by the gift to our country of the whole of Greenland."[42]

One reason for the Danish reluctance was American racism. Egan said the "most awkward question constantly put to me at court and in society was, 'But why do you lynch the black men?'" The Danes thought Americans were barbaric; they thought "that lynching is to the Americans of North America what bullfights are to those of South America."[43]

While Egan tried to dispel such notions, the Danes never tired of stressing their concern for the 25,000 black men and woman who inhabited the Virgin Islands. Egan wrote to Secretary of State Lansing that the Danish minister still wanted assurances about the negro population. Egan offered those assurances but also told the Danes "it seemed to me that we understood the character of the colored people and the way of making them content better than the Europeans."[44]

In November of 1915, Lansing threatened to

take the islands by force, and the Danes, looking at examples like Cuba and Haiti, soon agreed to sell for $25,000,000. In the end, they acceded to virtually every American demand, full citizenship, submitting the question of the sale to a vote of the inhabitants, and exemption from U.S. customs duties. All these sections of the treaty were omitted as the United States copied portions of its 1898 Treaty with the Spanish. As Lansing explained to the president, all concerned agreed that the Virgin Islands "should belong to the United States." They were ours by virtue of the Monroe Doctrine; and we followed the treaties of 1898 because experience showed they were a reliable guide to the transfer of island properties.[45]

But, "what will it be?" asked Congressman J. William Ragsdale of South Carolina. We could apply the U.S. Constitution to the islands if it suited our purposes, but, instead of doing that, the State Department specifically exempted the islands from the legislation relevant in many of our other territories. Why?

Lansing explained "that this was a precautionary measure." They were an "unorganized territory" in which the Constitution did and did not apply. But, "what will it be?"

"Just a possession of the United States," answered the secretary of state. "It is exactly like the Phillipines and the other possessions."[46]

Lansing referred to the "Insular Cases," a series of Supreme Court decisions which gave Congress the right to discriminate between incorporated and unincorporated territories. In Puerto Rico, for example, the Court said (in 1901) that it was legitimate to disregard U.S. Constitutional rights under certain circumstances because, "whilst in an international sense Puerto Rico was not a foreign country, since it was subject to the sovereignty of and was owned by the United States, it was foreign to the United States in a domestic sense, because the island had not been incorporated into the United States, but was merely appurtenant thereto as a possession."[47]

The Virgin Islands followed in Puerto Rico's unincorporated footsteps. Lansing was still trying to find a way to camouflage the island's actual political status. In the treaty, "these people" were theoretically citizens. However, to call them that was to implicitly promise incorporation, the right to be a state. So, Lansing and his associates "held them to be nationals, which was a new word intended to get around the word "subject."[48]

This word "subject" was foreign to America's political vocabulary but, on the eve of the nation's idealistic entrance into the Great War, it was banned. Nationals hid the colonial reality but nothing could hide Lansing's ignorance about the United States newest possession.

Could the secretary tell Congress about the ' various industries? "That is a subject we have not been able to study thoroughly," said Lansing.

Was the land owned by Denmark? Or by a "few whites?" "I do not know that I can give you the details on that: I do not know that we have it."

How about the harbors? Or the taxes? Or the way in which they were collected? Again Lansing said, "I do not know the details of that."[49]

What did the secretary know? He knew "that these islands, together with Puerto Rico, are of great importance in a strategic way, whether the strategy be military or commercial." Since he knew little about their commerce, Lansing stressed that the United States bought them for "largely" military reasons. They could be of use to the United States at some future date, and, in the meantime, the purchase guaranteed that they would never be controlled by any European power.

The Committee on Foreign Affairs agreed with the secretary's reasoning, but it did not want to spend any money on its new possession. Would the Secretary explain "how the $100,000 provided for in this bill will be expended?" Lansing indicated that this was a "precautionary measure," to be used only if the island's revenues failed to furnish the funds needed for the government. With luck those funds would materialize, but, in any event, the State Department would save money because the island would be ruled by soldiers who required no extra salary. "It is the president's idea to use the officers we have and not to appoint new officers at the present time—that is, until we have a more definite system of government there."[50]

The Virgin Islands would be ruled by a military government. As in Haiti and the Dominican Republic, soldiers would decide everything, but, in the Virgin Islands, there was no political or economic justification offered for the imposition of military rule. No revolution had occurred. No one had been injured. No monies allegedly borrowed. Instead, 25,000 people saw their rights disappear for $25,000,000.

In March of 1917, the Virgin Islands formally became a United States possession. Commanding the island was Rear Admiral James J. Oliver, a soldier who expressed concern about the islanders "low morality and high rate of malnutrition." The admiral decided that alcohol caused these problems, so, through his efforts, prohibition was brought to the island even before it became law in the United States.

The fact that this prohibition destroyed the island's principal industry, the manufacture of rum, never bothered the admiral. He saved his "nationals" from demon rum and underlined the early impact of American law in an unincorporated territory: it devastated the economy and maintained complete "racial" segregation in a black nation. Meanwhile, military governors were chosen in the following fashion: the president delegated the job to the assistant secretary of navy, who consulted with the director of naval operations, who consulted with the chief of the Bureau of Navigation, who found a captain who had visted the island two times, twenty years ago.[51]

Puerto Rico

By early 1917, Cuba was under the Platt Amendment and, along with the newly acquired Virgin Islands, Haiti and the Dominican Republic were ruled by soldiers. The only other issue was Puerto Rico, still eager for independence, and still rejecting American citizenship.

Congress first debated the newest version of the citizenship bill in May of 1916. Angered by complaints from the Puerto Ricans, Parker of New Jersey had been especially blunt: "Puerto Rico was our ward...our control over its territory absolute." Thus, since we could legally do as we pleased, now was the time to make the Puerto Ricans citizens because their "peculiar agitation" for independence had never ceased. As Representative Miller of Minnesota noted, the citizenship bill "means that the Congress of the United States says to the people of Porto Rico, once and for all, that they are part of the United States domain and will always remain there; that the agitation for independence in Porto Rico must come to a decided and a permanent end....If there is anything that you and I must be agreed upon, it is this: That Porto Rico will never go out from under the shadow of the Stars and Stripes."[52]

Other representatives emphasized Puerto Rico's ingratitude. Green of Iowa "disliked to say it" but he neverthless told his colleagues that the islanders "were raised by us so quickly from a depth of oppression...to a height of freedom enjoyed by few nations upon the globe that they are unable to appreciate the splendid bounty which had been conferred upon them....I am surprised at the ingratitude which seems to prevail among the leaders of the Philippines."

The Philipines? Green threw them in for good measure, yet he never questioned the "ingratitude" of islanders on different sides of the world. Perhaps there was something wrong with America's behavior? Perhaps the complaints of Muñoz from Puerto Rico and Quezon from the Philippines reflected an imperialism that spanned the globe?

That was inconceivable. As Congressman Miller of Minnesota noted, "We are going to give them citizenship. Ten years from now they are going to rise up and call us blessed for so doing. But we are not going to give everyone the right to vote (which the Puerto Ricans then had) and they are all going to rise up and bless us for doing that too."[53]

The blessing never came. Instead, Puerto Rican ingratitude acted as one of the roadblocks to congressional action. The citizenship bill stayed on hold through 1916 until, with war looming, and only Puerto Rico beset by "peculiar agitation," Congress passed the Jones Act in February of 1917. It gave Puerto Ricans American citizenship and, for the first time, an elected Senate as well as an elected House. But the governor now had veto power and, following the examples discovered by Secretary of State Bryan in Java and India, Puerto Rico got a financial advisor with even more power than the men controlling the customs houses in the Dominican Republic and Haiti. On April 1, 1917, Woodrow Wilson "welcomed the new (Puerto Rican) citizen, not as a stranger, but as one entering his father's house."[54]

Meanwhile, on June 19, 1917, American forces expelled Haitian legislators from their house. Its political name was the Haitian Constituent Assembly, and, "amid hisses and jeers, " General Smedley Butler dissolved the last vestige of Haitian self-rule. "What we wanted was clean little towns, with tidy thatch-roofed dwellings," said the general. But the Haitians refused to cooperate. So, soldiers used bayonets to expel them from the Assembly because "it was not desired to have a cabinet minister shot."[55]

Benevolent Dictatorships

Despite two years of trying, the American-sponsored Haitian president never convinced his colleagues to adopt the constitution written (as he later boasted) by Assistant Secretary of the Navy Franklin D. Roosevelt.[56] That constitution contained many controversial provisions. One was a proposal to permit foreigners to own Haitian land. In Washington, this change signalled an open market for the American investors eager to develop the island; in Haiti, foreign ownership spelled slavery and sugar. To alter the provision denying property rights to foreigners was to reinvite the exploitation that caused Haiti's war of independence.

The navy asked its commanders "to endeavor to accomplish end [acceptance of the Constitution] without the use of military force." An island full of "irresponsible agitators" forced the marines to brandish open bayonets, but, solving one problem, soldiers produced another: If Washington permitted a new election for the National Assembly voters "would return to it most probably the same members who were responsible for the utterly obstructive attitude of the Assembly."[57] Thus, a plebiscite became the way to circumvent Haiti's elected officials.

Colonel Alexander Williams, head of Haiti's gendarmerie, explained his problems. "The administrative system of Haiti was so nebulous that no uniformity of performance could be expected from the minor officials in the various parts of the Republic." Thanks to the occupation, Haiti's gendarmerie had not only been completely reformed, it was officered by marines who had learned to speak Creole. Thus, the gendarmerie would police the plebiscite, since the Haitian president "had no suggestions to make, because such things as a plebiscite was unknown in Haiti, and I had no suggestions to make, because I had never heard of one."[58]

Colonel Williams sent circular letters to each and every one of his officers, saying they would be supervising a plebiscite. He also told them "it was desirable that this constitution pass." In presenting their orders to the people, soldiers should stress that citizens could have valid objections to the constitution, but,"however they might dislike the constitution, it was better than no constitution at all....I do not remember how long before the plebiscite was held that these instructions were given, but there was a considerable time, ample time, to enable the gendarmerie officers to conduct this campaign, which was frankly pro-constitutional."[59]

On the day of the plebiscite, June 12, 1918, a widely publicized proclamation indicated that "any abstention from such a solemn occasion will be considered an unpatriotic act." Williams said "that the number of votes cast was ridiculous in comparison with the size of the electorate."[61]

Citizens who arrived at the voting places first saw a marine or a native member of the Haitian army. In most cases voters were simply handed a white ballot; this signified a yes vote. (Colored ballots were used because virtually no voters could read.) Pink ballots, a no vote, were available but to obtain one a citizen had to ask a marine to unwrap the package of tightly tied pink ballots.

The results of the balloting were 98,000 white and 700+ pink. Critics said the marines added the pink ballots for show, but Williams denied it. He later told Congress that "the plebiscite I considered in every phase...to be absolutely and entirely creditable to the gendarmerie. I am really very proud of the plebiscite."

The State Department had another opinion. Noting that the mentality of the peasants "has been variously estimated to be that of a child between six and ten years of age," department officials argued that the words "constitution" and "president" had no meaning to the "extremely primitive" Haitian people. The ballots "meant nothing" because, at one booth in Port-au-Prince, one man thought he was voting for a new head of state, another for a new Pope!

As the State Department assessed the situation, "the mentality of the peasant is so low" that efforts to educate the citizenry were "practically useless."[62] Then why try?

One aim was to provide legitimacy for a military government controlled by a president who had electrified the world (in January of 1918) with his Fourteen Points. The plebiscite served a clear political purpose. Only, however, if a new Caribbean policy now dictated military practice. In Haiti this never happened. In fact, since no one believed a vote of 98,000 to 700, the plebiscite proved nothing, *except* the ever widening disjunction between Washington and the soldiers who now ruled Haiti. Soldiers received more latitude than ever because of the administration's preoccupation with the Great War, the racist belief that the Haitians were "black children," and the cultural exceptionalism manifest in Robert Lansing's memo to the president. As one commander wrote after 18 months of the intervention "I have absolutely no knowledge as to the policy that our Government desires to follow in regard to Haiti."[63]

While soldiers waited for a policy to appear, they brutally suppressed a revolt of Haitian people, called cacos by the American soldiers. "A caco is a man in the field, a revolutionist, a bandit, or whatever you want to call him....They were the fellows fighting us. They were cacos and the rest of them were called just Haitians."

A special source of the so-called cacos' complaints was the military. To facilitate both commerce and the movement of troops in the event of social unrest, U.S. forces began a nationwide program of road building. Starting with three miles of good road in 1916, soldiers repaired some 470 miles of "highways" in two years.[64]

The program cost $205 a mile and the everlasting enmity of the Haitian people. Soldiers reinstituted an ancient and obsolete Haitian law, the *corvée*. At its best such a law required property owners to spend two or three days working on public roads as a means of paying their taxes. In Haiti, the *corvée* turned into a form of "military slavery." Citizens could pay a fee to exempt them from labor, but, as General Butler told Congress, "nobody had any money," so they were required to work.[65]

This requirement was fulfilled only if Haitian soldiers could find their frightened fellow citizens, or if they took the time to locate the people who actually had an obligation to provide labor. Soldiers were used because they were the only people the Americans could trust, and they were being trained by the occupation forces to provide internal security when the Americans eventually left.

As the American head of the gendarmerie explained it to Congress, the Haitians were hard to train. Citizens with an education refused to join because "the old Haitian police had enjoyed such a reputation that anyone who joined it practically announced his criminal tendencies." Since honest people refused to be part of the new gendarmerie,

Americans recruited their men from those with "criminal tendencies." As Colonel Williams told Congress, "our greatest problem in the organization of the gendarmerie was the gendarme. Our little experience with him had led us to believe that he was utterly indifferent to the value of human life; that he was prone to make the most of his police authority, and very liable to exceed it."[66]

American soldiers hoped to use discipline as a form of "regenerative" power, but in Haiti, Colonel Williams' men lacked discipline. They enforced the *corvée* by entering a town, and, instead of locating men who were eligible for service, they would go to a brickyard, empty it of personnel, and "thereby, of course, make it impossible to attend to the baking, or whatever you call it, of the bricks." If still short of men, the gendarmes might go to a harbor town, locate a boat's large crew, and then force every man into the road building program.

As word of widespread abuse reached him, Colonel Williams tried to create a sense of justice and accountability. When a man completed his service, he now received a card which proved that he was no longer eligible. When these fellows saw the gendarmes reappear in their vicinity, instead of fleeing with their neighbors, they would present their cards. Unfortunately, "the cards did more harm than good" because, "the gendarme's reasoning in that case was, "Well this is easy. I do not need to go any further. And he would take the man's card and tear it up and send him on to work."[67]

Eventually citizens fled whenever they saw a gendarme. That made finding labor even more difficult, so the gendarmes used more force. It was a terribly vicious circle in which the *corvée* acted to intensify the resistance which, by the time of the plebiscite, had moved the American forces to new levels of brutality.

For Colonel Williams and his commanders, Robert Lansing, and Woodrow Wilson, the buck stopped in Haiti. All officers of the gendarmerie were American; and even the occupation's supporters admitted they enjoyed an "almost complete domination" of the Haitian government and its financial resources. In an average month, 6 percent of Haiti's customs receipts went for government expenses, 75 percent went to pay off the country's debt, and the remainder went to the gendarmerie.[68]

Colonel Williams and his men used the money to comb the hills for cacos. In one drive through the north in late 1918, over seventeen hundred Haitians were killed, "the American casualties being negligible." Sometimes cacos lost their lives in a battle; just as often they were murdered by their captors. Commanders told subordinates to "soft-pedal" their reports while the phrase "bumping off" became popular. In one instance "men were marched out, required to stand by prepared graves, and shot. There was a general understanding that prisoners were not desired."[69]

Washington reacted to the slaughter when portions of a military report were published in mainland newspapers. Stories about "open season" on peasants and their homes demanded a response from Secretary of the Navy Josepheus Daniels. He lied. He denied seeing the report and then established a commission which, in late 1920, finally absolved the navy of "indiscriminate killing." Instead of widespread slaughter, the navy found only a small number of "isolated crimes"; the real truth was that America had restored "tranquility and security" to the Haitian people. Haitians had "welcomed the coming of our men"; they did not want us to leave; and who could blame them, when soldiers with "slender resources" had nevertheless managed to pacify a country which was finally paying off its international debts?[70]

Slaughter detracted attention from the financial impact of the occupation. Since its declaration of independence from France, Haiti's elite nourished itself on a series of taxes that starved Haiti's peasant majority. In 1881, import and export duties accounted for 98.2 percent of state income; in 1887 the entire government ran on taxes paid by the peasants, and, in 1909, more than 95 percent of government revenues came from multiple taxes on coffee—the peasants' principal crop.[71]

America paid off Haiti's foreign debt by continuing the practices of Haiti's worst leaders. Testifying before Congress, America's financial advisor said that "almost the entire revenues of the country are paid by the peasant class." In fact, "through the continuance of the present tariff exorbitant duties are being collected on some articles of plain necessity, while others of luxury pass almost untaxed."[72]

The existing duties "strangled the commerce of the country," but, since they were the only source of government revenues, and thus the only way to pay off the foreign debt, "no tariff reform can be undertaken until the existing pledges of specific revenues to the various debts are removed by the refunding of all those debts into one debt secured by the entire customs and internal revenue of the country."

When and if the United States found new foreign loans to pay off the old foreign loans, then it might be possible to tax the people in a just fashion. However, for the first four years of the occupation "no change of any importance" had occurred, and "no change" could occur because French and American lenders had pressured the State Department to place first priority on paying off Haiti's debt. McIlhenny stressed that even with 75 percent of the revenues earmarked for the debt, he *never* fulfilled America's contractual obligations. "The whole thing is this; if I were today to strictly apply the treaty...there would not be any money with which to maintain the Haitian government."[73]

Disregarding the treaty, McIlhenny gave some money to the Haitian government. The elite reacted with criticism and by passing a budget that gave them more of the peasants' money. McIlhenny rejected that budget in the summer of 1920 and, in August, he did to the Haitians what Taft wanted to do to the Puerto Ricans in 1909; McIlhenny simply cut off all government salaries. The financial advisor consulted no one before he stopped paying Haiti's president and every other government employee. However, the Americans collecting the customs revenues continued to receive their paychecks.[74]

McIlhenny eventually restored the Haitians salaries, but his hands were tied when it came to reallocating Haiti resources. He agreed that the State Department "was loaning money from Peru to China"; its complete unwillingness to loan funds to Haiti had "agitated my mind a great deal" but, as a functionary, McIlhenny never made policy. He only carried it out and in Haiti that meant continuing to pay off foreign loans with the sweat of the peasant's brow.[75]

The peasants suffered as American officials killed some, taxed the rest, and despised all with black skin. Under U.S. rule lighter skinned Haitians assumed more governmental positions than ever before because the racism from the north was transported to the south. Soldiers like Colonel Williams and civilians like John McIlhenny openly showed their preference for Haitians with lighter skin color. That created more tension in a corrupt elite and helped lay the groundwork for the racial ideologies of men like François Duvalier. The peasants' only solace was that the Americans seemed to be on an endless merry-go-round. As Representative Medill McCormick of Illinois noted, "we change chiefs of the Latin American bureau and chiefs of the gendarmerie of the Marine Corps as rapidly as the Haitians change presidents, do we not?" John McIlhenny answered that "It is, Mr. Chairman, the most disastrous thing for any continuity of administration."[76]

Robert Lansing's Caribbean policy never changed. He sought stability, and he got it. That the peasants also "got it" was an unintended result of the United States policy.

Dominican Republic

In the summer of 1919, Samuel Inman took "A Cruise With the Marines." He went to the Dominican Republic to report on the results of the U.S. military intervention, but, in a visit to the gigantic sugar operations of Central Romana, Inman discovered "a little bit of the United States set down in the tropics." For Romana's single employees, the company created a "splendid boarding club"; married couples lived in trim, new bungalows. For the children, Romana provided clean streets and a Boston school marm. She taught in English, and she taught in a facility closed to the people of the Dominican Republic. The "little bit of America" was for whites only because, as in its Puerto Rico facility, Romana maintained strict segregation. It reminded a person, said one visitor, of "the South and antebellum days."[77]

Since the occupation began, Romana (the Connecticut subsidiary of the New Jersey-based South Porto Rico Sugar) had been on a buying spree. Exact figures were not available, but one guess was it had tripled its holdings in three years. Romana owned a full hundred thousand acres of the Dominican Republic when Inman traveled with the marines in 1919. The land was divided into 100-acre plots, exact accounts detailed the fertility and yield of each subdivision, and, where the land proved unfit for cane, Romana had introduced "a fine herd of blooded cattle."[78]

Romana was a splendid facility, with a major problem. The Dominicans hated the company, and, even more, the occupation which allowed it to forever expand. Immediately after the occupation began, Romana asked the secretary of the navy for a special import permit for guns to protect its employees. It wanted the men who wielded those guns to be deputized by the occupation authorities.[79]

When Inman visited Romana over "200 Porto-Rican ex-policemen" patrolled everything from the sugar fields to the company store. Called "Guardas

Campestres," these men were subject to the laws set down by the occupation authorities; they were a public/private army that allowed the American commanders to reduce the number of marines who also were "on constant guard."[80]

Romana was a plantation and an armed camp. It quickly became a hated symbol of the occupation, and its security was best left to hired hands. In Quisqueya (the Dominican Republic's pre-Columbus name), American soldiers encountered their fiercest opposition to Robert Lansing's Caribbean policy. Between 1917 and 1921, the marines sent out no less than 5500 patrols to find and kill the Dominican resistance. However, marines came in contact with the resistance only 122 times. Long before Vietnam, American soldiers were in a guerilla war; and, as in the Far East forty years later, the U.S. occupiers complained of the difficulties encountered when marine instructors tried to leap over "the barrier of limited native intelligence."[81]

Lieutenant Edward Fellowes asked his commanders to have patience; outsiders "had no conception of the handicap under which an instructor works with these natives." As in Haiti, the best people refused to be associated with the army, which meant recruiters had to draw their men from the "scum of the island." These fellows had lived "their whole lives in some little hut built of thatched palm fronds," thoroughly satisfied to "live from day to day on the small earnings from their sickly crops of fruits and vegetables." Moreover, as in Cuba, the Dominicans liked dirt because "our greatest troubles arose at first from the natural aversion for soap and razor." Over time Lieutenant Fellowes did get

125

the natives to bathe, but he could do nothing about a more elemental fact—his recruits "were the most ignorant and crude specimens possible, as far as intelligence was concerned."[82]

Despite the Dominicans' obvious lack of natural abilities, Lieutenant Fellowes was under orders to create a group of native officers. Even after four years of military occupation and thousands of training hours, the overwhelming majority of Guardia officers were still American. In August of 1921 Lieutenant Fellowes used an abandoned agricultural experimental station to open Haina, the military school for Dominican officers.

The old Guardia had a terrible reputation; it "robbed and abused the peasantry" to such an extent that it lacked any legitimacy in Dominican eyes.[83] Lieutenant Fellowes' job was to create an officer corps capable of gaining the people's respect but, once again, the quality of the recruits limited any chance of success. Fellowes described them as the "thirty thieves"; they were the best the Dominican Republic had to offer, but even George, Fellowes "house boy" from the Virgin Islands, despaired of creating officers from a group that fought over a lost pillow! The first night of training, someone robbed another officer's pillow, and it turned into a question of "dignidad." Fellowes quickly settled the problem but lamented his task of creating officers from a group whose dignity "appears to be the dignity of a child playing grownup, and is soon discarded for some childish squabble or youthful frivolity."[84]

Over time Fellowes discovered an interesting fact; "As a general rule the degree of intelligence increased with the decrease of the ebony tinge." The blacker recruits were "simple minded giants," incapable of assuming any responsibility or initiative. So, Fellowes chose officers on the basis of their lighter complexion. "This rule worked out quite neatly"; indeed, from this first class of Haina officers Fellowes and his colleagues selected one Dominican thief for special attention. Rafael Leonidas Trujillo showed a marked degree of "ruthless efficiency"; he was an officer to watch if only because he used the marines as models for his personal as well as his military behavior. Trujillo later took to wearing pancake makeup to hide his "too dark" skin; sometimes it would melt in the sun, but Trujillo never forgot his marine training.[85]

In private, the marines admitted that many Dominicans "admired and respected" the native resistance. Villagers thought of the marines as "foreign intruders" so, in rounding up the opposition, marines actually needed to defeat two enemies—the "bandits" and the locals who supported them. One provocative tactic was the nine large-scale cordon operations in the bandit-infested provinces of Seibo and Macoris. In these drives, marines "swept inward, engaging any bandits they encountered and rounding up all suspicious persons [in practice every adult male] at a central collecting point." There, all men, innocent or guilty, bandit or law abiding citizen, were lined up, positioned under bright lights, and, instead of being sweated for information, "native informers" would identify the bandits mixed in among the people. The informers stood behind screens provided by the marines.

These tactics produced two results. One, the Dominican people complained so "vehemently" that marines agreed to stop hunting for bandits by rounding up every adult male in the infested provinces. Two, the level of banditry increased. The marines attributed this to the "depredations" caused by the Dominican resistance, while critics suggested it was the marines' depredations which caused the substantial increase in bandit activity during early 1922.[86]

Another cause of the unrest was the civilian practices of the American military authorities. Soldiers paid off the debt arrangements made by Jacob Hollander in 1907, and then created new debt for the republic without asking the Dominicans whether they wanted to spend money in the same manner as the marines. Besides the old and new debt, soldiers bought *American-made* goods in suspiciously large quantities. For the new school system devised by the marines, someone ordered $200,000 worth of desks and other school supplies. Dominicans said this was a complete waste of their money; soldiers responded by reminding them who ruled the republic.[87]

That rule assumed imperial proportions when soldiers put their new tariff into effect on January 1, 1920. Agricultural machinery, tools, cars, food, building materials—over 245 American items suddenly entered the Dominican Republic duty free, and another 700 items witnessed drastic reductions in import duties. At Central Romana, and at the other American dominated plantations, the tariff meant lower costs and lower wages. With the ability to buy American machinery duty free increased production was easier and, because imported food was now less expensive, employers cut wages to keep pace with the cuts in tariffs.

Meanwhile, native manufacturers found there was no way they could successfully compete with the American Goliath. In the Bible, David won; in real life, Dominicans were defeated. Producers of shoes and tanned leather discovered they could no longer compete in native markets. While the cheaper food helped those Dominicans who did not receive a reduction in wages, it had a terrible impact on local producers. Even coffee growers saw themselves threatened by cheap beans from Brazil.[88]

Dominicans protested, but as soldiers searched the nation for bandits, American firms made fabulous profits in everything from food to desks to sales commissions. W.R. Grace and Company, involved for years in Haiti's wavy railroad, moved over to the Dominican Republic as U.S. purchasing agent for the military government. With a better deal than today's Visa or Mastercard, Grace actually received a $10,000 commission for placing the $200,000 school supplies order. The company's commission was later reduced to 4 percent but Dominicans remained infuriated by a system that favored imports, and simultaneously paid mainlanders a commission to buy the American goods that put Dominicans out of work.[89]

It was an extraordinary system, made worse by the occupation's most monumental short and long term failure—the green light Washington gave to the American producers of sugar. By one conservative estimate U.S. investors increased their sugar holdings by 200 percent between 1915 and 1920. They bought property because (as in American-dominated Puerto Rico and Cuba) a revision of the land title laws facilitated the easy purchase of everything from communal to private holdings. They bought land because the Great War meant a great gap in the European production of sugar.[90]

Producers saw a new opportunity. Soldiers saw a way to develop the island. Dominicans saw their nation's economic fate militarily wedded to a commodity without a market.

The occupiers never asked what would happen when the war ended, and Europe began once again to grow substantial quantities of sugar beets. As in Cuba and Puerto Rico, only unrefined Dominican sugar entered the U.S. market. Where were the jobs tied to development? What was the future of Dominicans displaced by the new land and tariff laws? The occupiers never asked about the Haitians. Long before the occupation, Dominicans let Haitians cut their cane. It was a slavelike dependence, greatly exacerbated by the huge increase in sugar production. The occupiers never asked what would happen if Dominican producers were closed out of the American market. During the war years the United States bought roughly seventy percent of the island's sugar. What would happen when demand dropped? Would Dominicans receive the same tariff breaks enjoyed by the Cubans? And, if not, what would they do with their excess sugar?

Dominicans got a first answer to these questions in 1920. With sugar now accounting for an astonishing 423 percent greater rate of return than the next three exports *combined*, Washington broke its word to the Dominican people, soldiers apologized, and the Dominicans borrowed more money to make ends meet and pay off the $6.7 million still owed to the Santo Domingo Improvement Company and the other 1907 debtors.[91]

Dominicans complained bitterly about the tariff of 1920. They forecast the disaster that occurred, but the one saving grace was a promise made by officials in Washington; accept the new tariff and receive in return a reciprocal trade agreement with the U.S.

It never happened. Officials forgot the Cuban, Puerto Rican, Hawaiian, Philippine, Louisiana, and midwest sugar interests. None of these producers wanted more competition, so instead of the promised agreement, Dominicans received a letter from the State Department. It "sincerely regretted" breaking its word, but the Dominicans were out in the cold, left with a product Americans no longer wanted. Soon only 2 percent of the Republic's sugar came to the United States.[92]

Then the world sugar market collapsed in 1921. So did export earnings, as did the revenues required to pay off the 1907 debt. Sugar was more important than ever because the new tariff reduced the monies formerly obtained from imports. The occupation authorities had tried to replace portions of those lost revenues with a property tax, but, with sugar prices at an all-time low, and non-sugar Dominicans battered by duty free imports, property taxes "fell off to an alarming extent."

The horrors created by United States control of the Dominican Republic increased. Recall that the 1907 treaty mandated use of customs receipts to pay off the debt. In the banner years of the war, the customs receipts earned by the greatly increased sugar industry enabled the occupation authorities to pay off more of the debt than ever before. Officials bragged that they gave at least $1.2 million a year to pay off the principal of the 1907 debt.[93] After

131

America substantially closed its markets to the Dominican Republic in 1921 (amidst a world sugar crisis), the island nation found itself without a way to maintain either the military government, its own government, or principal and interest payments on the 1907 debt.

The State Department responded by giving the military authorities permission to increase the debt of the Dominican Republic. First in 1921 and then in 1922, the American military government obtained loans by helping to sell bonds that had a unique guarantee; all investors were assured, in writing, that "the issue of these bonds ($2.5 million in 1921, $6.7 million in 1922) has been approved by the United States government under the terms of the American Dominican convention of 1907 and by the U.S. military government of Santo Domingo."[94]

With that guarantee the United States promised investors that it would collect their money from the Dominican people, and substantially increased the length of an already seventeen-year-old receivership. These bonds were due in 1940, and Washington had thus agreed, without asking the Dominicans, to control both their customs and their debt level for yet another twenty years.

These new bonds established a vicious circle every bit as awful as the one in Haiti. On one side of Hispaniola, peasants paid the Americans (and the French) because the taxes on their exports and imports provided the principal funds required to pay off the foreign debt.

In the Dominican Republic, sugar exports provided the main source of customs revenues, so the new loans tied the island's economy to the production of a crop without a secure market. The new loans perpetuated dependence on sugar because sugar was the one major way to pay off the new loans which paid off the old loans which, all together, extended United States control of the Dominican Republic until 1942.

The Dominicans complained. In every international forum available, they let the world know about the consequences and injustices of the American military intervention. By 1922, that criticism had finally produced results. Congress openly debated whether to pull out of the Dominican Republic and Senator Borah of Idaho said that some of our actions equalled "sheer brutal despotism."[95]

But Congress was not willing to leave "until we can decently get out of that island," and islanders tried to fathom this kind of reasoning. Again quoting Senator Borah (on June 19, 1922): "It may be that we shall have to take possession of all the territory from here to the Panama Canal....I am not willing to subscribe to that doctrine as yet. But if we must carry out that policy, let us make it an announced policy; give those people a civil form of government and deal with them as we would deal with our own people, and not govern them by military power and through military force—wreck their governments and furnish them no government instead."[96]

Six years into two military occupations (the Virgin Islands were never discussed) and even Wilson's sharpest critics seemed resigned to America's difficult destiny. As in 1905 and 1916, the United States still had the right "to take possession of all the territory from here to the Panama Canal." However, this time we would take it the right way;

or, more accurately, whatever way Congress and Warren Harding decided to resolve the problems associated with protecting the Dominican Republic, Cuba, Puerto Rico, Haiti, and the (already forgotten) Virgin Islands.

Gangsters and
Good Neighbors

"...and the government was handed back to the citizens of Santo Domingo after a stewardship of about 12 years. We accomplished an excellent piece of constructive work and the world ought to thank us."
—Franklin D. Roosevelt, July 1928

"Can't you persuade Al Capone to offer him more money than he is making here to come to the United States as his instructor? That ought to attract Trujillo."
—Ambassador C. B. Curtis, April, 1930[1]

E. Montgomery Reilly, Enoch Crowder, and Sumner Welles: the first was a political hack, the second a distinguished general, and the third, a patrician public servant. They were remarkably different Americans; yet they all did the same thing. In a return to what President Harding called "normalcy," they reaffirmed the good colonialism ideal of U.S. culture.

As Governor of Puerto Rico, Reilly told President Harding (in November of 1921) about the "hold your administration has on these people." After four months in "Porto Rico," Reilly had helped sell 16,000 American flags, twelve times the sales of his predecessor. What did it matter if Reilly received a number of letters "telling me that if I did not leave the country in 48 hours I would be killed, and if I drove through the streets I would be murdered."[2]

It was a crazy time, both in the United States and in the Caribbean. As early as 1919, the State Department had decided to withdraw from Haiti and the Dominican Republic. Officials agreed that our attempts to impose democracy had been "unprofitable," while both at home and abroad, critics discussed the cruelties and contradictions of American policies.

Failure sometimes produces a desire for the truth. Confronted with mistakes, policy makers can accept responsibility for their behavior, analyze the ideological sources of their actions, and then walk into the future on the basis of a thoroughly reevaluated past.

This never happened in Congress nor in the administrations of Warren Harding or Calvin Coolidge. Senator Norris of Nebraska openly admitted that "our government was engaged from the beginning in a program of deception." Instead of helping the people of Haiti and the Dominican Republic, "the representatives of our government engaged in little political tricks that would disgrace the worst political machine in America."[3] Senator Borah of Idaho posed a query as valid in the 1990's as it was in the 1920's: "May I ask in all sincerity was any people in the world ever fitted for self-government under a military dictatorship?"[4]

Congress asked all the right questions. However, instead of allowing the facts to challenge the beliefs that shaped policy (racism, paternalism, or the Caribbean as an American lake), Congress helped set the tone for the rest of the twentieth century. Senators rooted their new policy in expediency and chaos control while they extolled the virtues of America and the deficiencies of the Caribbean. Senator Pomerene of Ohio said, "I have the most kindly feeling toward the Haitians and I am satisfied that with proper treatment they will become useful citizens of Haiti....They are the most generous people in the world when they are in possession of their faculties but when aroused and excited...." Anything could happen. The United States still needed to help the Haitians "organize a truly representative government."[5]

The alternative to the "we are civilized, they are not" dichotomy was to challenge the deepest assumptions of American political culture. Instead of the truth, Congress started to develop the strategies that would later be called the Good Neighbor Policy, the Alliance For Progress, and, most recently, the Caribbean Basin Initiative.

The new secretary of State was Charles Evans Hughes. He explained that the Monroe Doctrine had lost none of its validity. For the moment no European nation posed a threat to the Caribbean; but the future "held infinite possibilities" so "the Doctrine remains as an essential policy to be applied whenever any exigency may arise requiring its application."[6]

This sounded like Robert Lansing, and it was, with this qualification: "The declaration of our purpose to oppose what is inimical to our safety does not imply an attempt to establish a protectorate." The United States still had that right; and Washington would exercise it if circumstances warranted intervention. Hughes didn't want to because in Mexico, Cuba, Argentina, Chile, Ecuador, Nicaragua and Costa Rica diplomats protested our Caribbean policy. The ripple effects were so great that at the second Pan American Labor Congress of 1921, Samuel Gompers was on the wrong side of a labor walkout. Many Latin American delegates threatened to leave unless all representatives of American labor forwarded to the president of the United States their "unanimous opposition" to the military occupation of the Dominican Republic.[7]

Secretary Hughes based his Caribbean policy on a desire to avoid the negative diplomatic consequences of our military interventions. He accepted no responsibility for the economies of Cuba, Puerto Rico, Haiti, the Virgin Islands, or the Dominican Republic. He never challenged the cultural exceptionalism that produced what Senator Pomerene of Ohio called "cruelties of such a character as to make an American hang his head in shame."[8]

Hughes and Harding did the right thing for the wrong reason. They instructed their ambassadors and envoys to avoid interventions at all costs. Keep the marines out of the Caribbean, but never challenge the beliefs and values that made Puerto Ricans so eager to kill E. Montgomery Reilly.

Three Islands

Reilly was a monarchist, a man who told President Harding he meant to "rule" Puerto Rico. The president erased that word from Reilly's inaugural address (and wrote in "administer") but he had no problem with an admonition Reilly delivered in the strongest terms. The United States, said Reilly, "would be deeply distressed to see any feeling or growing sentiment on these islands toward any thought of independence....There is no sympathy or possible hope in the United States for independence for Porto Rico from any individual, or from any political party." Porto Rico would always be a part of the United States, and, stressing his fondness for flags, Reilly told the islanders listening to his address that "as long as Old Glory waves over the United States, it will wave over Porto Rico and will never be hauled down."

The Puerto Ricans were quiet on the outside, seething inside. In the 1920 elections, the Unionists, flying the banner of independence, had won one of the greatest political victories in the island's history. Thus, Reilly's speech was provocative and threatened to outrage even the most docile islander. After indicating that "I shall always have an extended hand and a sympathetic heart for every toiler on these islands" Reilly ended with this invitation: "All, all are welcome to come to me at any time, that I may be able to lift any burden, or assuage any sorrow."[9]

E. Montgomery Reilly became "King Monty." Newspapers received protest lctters addressed to "Darling Caesar" and some wanted a new section entitled "Letters to the Emperor." Reilly took the verbal assaults as a personal challenge. He refused to show the "white feather" and the president, despite protests from Puerto Rican and American officials, told his ambassador to seek a "tranquil" settlement "but we would not wish to bring it about by a surrender to those who have made the paths of government so difficult."[10]

Confronted with a governor who dismissed government workers committed to independence, the Unionist party removed that aim from its political platform. Islanders dissatisfied with this allegedly shameless surrender formed their own independence party, and, in the process, helped set the tone for the next thirty years.

In fact, when Pedro Albizu Campos began (in 1925) to suggest the need for a revolution, he pointed to the battle between King Monty and the Unionists. Islanders had voted for independence, but the Americans ridiculed the self-determination of the Puerto Rican people. Albizu made two bold suggestions: Never tolerate "any insolence" from an American president, and never forget that the only way to catch the Americans' attention was to produce "a grave crisis" in the colony.[11]

Reilly won the political battle, but his imperial attitude forced him to resign the governorship "for health reasons," in 1923. As Reilly told the president, "Porto Ricans, as all Continentals say, are children and change their attitudes almost daily." So, "when I struck as hard as I did it naturally caused a commotion, as I knew it would, but as they understand that I meant what I said fully, I do not believe we are going to have any further trouble."[12]

Reilly was a brute, but he had a president's support when he crushed the will of the Puerto Rican people, as did his successor, former Congressman Horace M. Towner. In February 1924, Towner told islanders that "the United States still has absolute control because in its legislation Congress can do anything it wants to....We retain absolute control. We are the governing power."[13]

The United States also governed Cuba. Harding

and Hughes sent a general who was the "genius of the draft." Enoch Crowder got ten million men to show up for military service. Combined with the experience he garnered in the 1906–1909 Cuban intervention, Crowder's skills made him an admirable candidate to reorganize Cuba's electoral laws. In 1919, the American government insisted that President Menocal invite Crowder to Cuba. The general came, he worked his administrative magic on the electoral law, and, at the State Department, it was a "forgone conclusion" that the Cubans would enact the law "substantially" as General Crowder had written it.[14]

With one crisis prevented, two others arose. First, the electoral losers accused the electoral winners of fraud. The liberals demanded the annulment of the election, but, after the State Department applied pressure, they agreed to use the remedies provided by the Crowder electoral law. Liberals dutifully filed their complaints and conservatives just as dutifully erected roadblocks. In Washington, officials agreed that "red tape and procrastination in the electoral boards" made it hard for the liberals to ever receive "fair treatment."[15]

The remedy proposed was to reassign America's "unofficial schoolmaster." Enoch Crowder would teach democracy to the Cubans by waving a sword and pointing it toward Hispaniola! In a breech of custom, the Cuban president was informed of Crowder's presence "without comment." The general would live on the battleship *Minnesota*, and would issue his directives from there. Complain as they might, the Cubans could deal with Crowder, or they could deal with the marines. The "choice" was theirs because Crowder explained that his mission "was to prevent the development of a situation where the United States would be compelled to take more drastic action."[16]

Crowder managed to get the electoral process moving, but, as he sorted out one crisis, the effects of the second threatened to undo even the fairest of elections. Sugar prices collapsed—22 cents a pound in the spring of 1920, four cents a pound by autumn, and so, too, the mills, families, and individuals who mortgaged their futures to the high price of sugar.[17]

Myth teaches that Americans monopolized Cuba's sugar as early as 1901. In reality it not only took 25 years for the Americans to "own" Cuba; the biggest and most consequential buying spree occurred between 1914 and 1925. Enoch Crowder saw the collapse of sugar as an opportunity for greater U.S. involvement, all modeled on the Roosevelt Corollary to the Monroe Doctrine.

In 1914, U.S. interests owned 38 percent of Cuba's sugar centrales and they produced 39 percent of Cuba's total sugar output. The figures for 1919 are 65 percent and 49 percent; and by 1924 U.S. interests controlled an astonishing 74 percent of Cuba's centrales and they produced fully 60 percent of Cuba's total production. By 1928, this last figure climbed to 75 percent of all Cuban production coming from American operations.[18]

Where did the sugar go? More than sixty percent of Cuba's sugar came to the United States, all theoretically benefiting from the 20 percent reduction in the tariff imposed on Cuban sugar. However, this benefit had effectively disappeared by the time Enoch Crowder took command in early 1921. Cuba got a 20 percent reduction in the tariff, but, with no foreign competition, the beneficiaries were U.S. refiners and U.S. consumers. Meanwhile, the Cuban producers not tied into the American marketplace through the sugar trust had to sell their produce (*i.e.*, the 40 percent that did not come to the United States) on the small and fiercely competitive free market.

By the time General Crowder took charge in 1921, the United States received the major benefit from the tariff reduction; mainly Cuban producers competed in the world's much smaller free market; and, all the while, U.S. growers and refiners were protected by the same federal government that was now going to make Cuba more dependent on the United States than ever before.

Estimates varied, but Cuba's expected budget deficit in 1921 was $46 million. Without a loan, say of $50 million, the economy could collapse, government employees would receive no salaries, and Crowder's worst nightmare would occur: The U.S. would be obliged to once again intervene in Cuba.

Crowder agreed to approve the loan offered by J.P. Morgan and Company, but before he agreed, the general asked the Cubans to reread Article Two of the Platt Amendment. This stipulated that Cuba "shall not assume or contract any public debt" unless the "ordinary revenues" of the island "adequately" funded the new obligations. Crowder said the ordinary revenues expected in 1922 did no such thing. The $50 million loan would, by the general's estimates, more than double the national debt. Before approval occurred, the Cubans had to accept some form of U.S. federal government supervision over their revenues.

After 17 years in the Dominican Republic and six in Haiti, the United States admitted failure. But, instead of reevaluating U.S. policy, Crowder, Hughes, and Harding followed two failures with a third. Cuba received the loan, and readers of the New York Times financial section read this advertisement for Cuban bonds: "Issued with the acquiescence of the United States Government under the provisions of the Treaty dated May 22, 1903."[19]

The United States thus avoided intervention by guaranteeing to supervise every aspect of Cuban administration for the next twenty years. Crowder began his "preventive and remedial" work on Cuban society by making "suggestions." Cubans had to reduce congressional expense accounts, reduce the civil service by 25 percent, reorganize the judiciary so that municipal judges would disappear, revamp the pension system, and, most important of all, every Cuban had to pay a sales tax which, under American supervision, was earmarked for the $50 million loan.[20]

Under the tax system approved and imposed by General Crowder, fully 49.4 percent of all revenues (in 1924–25) came from customs duties imposed on importers and on producer. of everything but sugar. Another 10.8 percent of revenues came from the Crowder sales tax imposed on all Cubans, and another 4.9 percent was earmarked to pay off another American-sponsored loan. Sugar producers paid less than 1 percent of their sales in taxes, and they contributed only 3.5 percent of the government's total revenues.[21]

This tax structure helped Americans buy more land from Cubans adversely affected by everything from the loss of their jobs to the world sugar depression. More importantly, this tax structure guaranteed, as in the Dominican Republic, a prolonged perpetuation of the status quo. Given the power of the sugar interests, the U.S. government guaranteed loans would be repaid only if this or a similar tax system remained in force. Instead of reducing Cuba's dependence on sugar, the nation became more dependent on this commodity than ever before, and more dependent on the United States than ever before.

Crowder, Hughes, and Harding created even greater institutionalized resistance to meaningful economic change.[22] After the debacles in Haiti and the Dominican Republic, America's Caribbean policy simply moved from one crisis to another. Thus, cartoons of the period show General Crowder wearing a sword and a firefighter's hat.[23]

The Cuban politicians denounced Crowder when they disregarded, after the loan was granted, his "Moralization Program." The general wanted changes in everything from President Zayas' cabinet to the structure of political patronage. Zayas, however, did as he pleased. By July of 1923, Crowder told Secretary of State Hughes "the prospects for a fair and honest election next year are steadily diminishing....The people argue, with some force, that as no relief against corrupt government can come through corrupt elections, and as the right of armed revolt against such a government has been denied them by the policy of the United States here and elsewhere in Latin America, the responsibility for the continuance of corrupt government here lies with the United States and that relief can come only through a much more aggressive attitude of our government."[24]

Crowder stated Cuba and America's dilemma. Secretary Hughes responded by washing his hands of the responsibilities the United States had just assumed. He told Crowder to curb his concern about the prospect of dishonest elections because the United States had now decided to let the Cubans work out their own problems. Intervention was out of the question. The result was a shotgun marriage of economic and political exploitation. The two forces joined hands when Gerado Machado won the Cuban presidency in a 1924 landslide. He carried every province except Pinar del Rio, and he won the hearts of the Americans when, prior to his inauguration, he told the Banker's Club of New York: "I wish to assure the businessmen present here...that they will have absolutes guarantees for their interests....The public forces...will lend to capital and the laborers every assistance to which they are entitled."[25]

When too many murders finally forced Machado from office in 1933, the sugar interests stayed, anxious to work with an ambitious sergeant named Fulgencio Batista and a public servant named Sumner Welles.

Sumner Welles possessed the supreme self-confidence produced by a patrician background, a Yale education, a friendship with men like Franklin Roosevelt, and a powerful job at the State Department when he was only 27-years-old. Sumner Welles wrote (in 1919) the first plan for United States withdrawal from the Dominican Republic. Islanders rejected that proposal but Welles never let that first failure challenge either his self-confidence or his ethnocentric view of U.S. Caribbean policy.[26]

Welles believed the Spanish-American War had made the United States "an empire." This was acceptable but problematic because "alien peoples on other planes of civilization" inhabited the islands now owned by the United States. To Welles, the Puerto Ricans and Filippinos "could never be amalgamated in that conglomerate but homogeneous mass" called America. Thus, "the role of the educator and of the civilizer was thrust upon the United States."[27]

Welles liked to teach so much he even lectured Howard Taft and Woodrow Wilson. They both were caught up in "the missionary spirit of the times." They failed because each practiced "a patronizing sense of superiority, which utterly ignored the possibility that another inheritance and other standards might possess their own excellence." Wilson was guilty of an "extraordinary paradox"; he wanted to "safeguard constitutional liberties throughout the world" yet he "dictated" the military occupation of the Dominican Republic.[28]

Welles knew what to do. The United States had the right to prevent the "noxious intervention" of any European power anywhere in the Caribbean. But, over and above this elemental right—*i.e.*, the Roosevelt Corollary was "unquestionably" a portion of "established" policy—the United States also had undefined rights and obligations because of the "unsettled condition" of certain Caribbean countries.

The occupations failed because they were "purely remedial"; they exercised American power by trying to "cure the disease after it had been contracted." The 1907 convention with the Dominican Republic was a lasting example of constructive statesmanship because "it removed the chief obstacle to the establishment of stable government in the Dominican Republic."[29]

Welles called the 1907 customs agreement a "sane policy of cooperation," and, in a distinction very similar to the one that his successors would use in the 1965 intervention in the Dominican Republic, Welles believed that Theodore Roosevelt's constructive policy was never an intervention.[30] That occurred when one nation interfered in the domestic affairs of another. Since paying off the loans or limiting the Dominican Republic's national debt was not purely domestic, intervention was never a proper label for such a policy. The term Welles preferred was "friendly cooperation."[31]

The distinction between intervention and cooperation is important for at least three reasons. First, as friend and aide to Franklin Roosevelt, Welles' views helped shape Caribbean policy for 25 years. As he told the British when they discussed the future of islands like Puerto Rico in 1943: "The basic concept used as the foundation for the [United Nations] trusteeship project is the concept that these people have not yet reached the stage of development at which they can make decisions themselves. The whole purpose of the trusteeship program is to help these people to make their own choice."[32]

Second, Welles reasoning reflects a twentieth century U. S. constant. As Thomas Mann (the career diplomat who held Welles' State Department position in the Kennedy and Johnson administrations) noted, "definitions of words like 'aggression' and 'intervention' are a signpost for the guilty and a trap for the innocent because a nation can take a definition and technically fit its actions within that definition."[33] In Welles' case, he called his behavior "cooperation" because the word "intervention" aroused the "suspicions, fears, and hatred to which the occupation gave rise throughout the American continent."[34]

Finally, Sumner Welles is important because he captained U.S. negotiations for what the Hoover administration would soon call an "amazing" agreement. "How this department ever saw fit to risk such a Convention I do not understand....I cannot hide the opinion that the Convention of 1924 was a very reckless promise by the State Department—which pins responsibility squarely on it."[35]

In a press release issued right after his arrival in the Dominican Republic (on July 31, 1922) Sumner Welles began with the denials of Root and Roosevelt, Bryan and Wilson. The United States coveted "not an inch" of Dominican Territory. And it had "no desire" and "no intention of assuming the right of intervention" because of the inalienable right of the Dominican people to control their own destiny.[36]

U.S. withdrawal was "conditioned" on the receipt of these assurances: other nations would be kept out of the Dominican Republic; peace and order would be maintained by (the marine trained) Guardia; and the island's government would recognize the validity of the tax and loan agreements promulgated by the military government.[37] "It is these guarantees alone which the government of the United States requires before it effects its withdrawal....Once my government has obtained these indispensible prerequisites to its withdrawal....we will leave."

If the occupation was a "dictated" government, how could Welles establish either political justice or economic stability by making the Dominicans accept tariffs that ruined their local producers? Why did they have to repay, for twenty years, loans made by American soldiers? How was it cooperation if the United States demanded a series of "indispensible guarantees" before it would begin the withdrawal scheduled for 1924?

In September of 1922, the Dominicans reluctantly accepted the terms offered by Sumner Welles. They saw no alternative to the tentative agreement and Horacio Vasquez (elected president of the Dominican Republic in March of 1924) saw no alternative to a final guarantee in the American's government's final agreement.

Before its troops would leave in September of 1924, the United States demanded that, in addition to the benefits of the 1920 tariff, the Dominican Republic grant it most favored nation treatment. While the United States kept its markets tightly closed to Dominican sugar and tobacco, the islanders had to give the United States any benefit it offered other trading partners. Dominicans angrily asked: Why would the English take our sugar and tobacco if the Americans got for nothing the trade preferences which came to the English only because they opened their markets to Dominican sugar and tobacco?[38]

Sumner Welles fought to open U.S. markets to Dominican sugar. He knew it was a small price to pay for the guarantees required for withdrawal. As President Coolidge stressed, the business of America was business.

The last marine left the Dominican Republic in September of 1924. Their influence, however, lingered. In the resentments of the Dominican people. And in the gratitude of the Guardia's officers. When a marine general visited the island in 1925, he was presented with a sword which was a replica of the weapon used by the marines. Gratified, the general listened as Colonel Rafael Trujillo told him, "We want you to know that we cherish the memory of the marines and that we have adopted your sword as our sword."[39]

Virgin Islands

One idea was to make it a penal colony, modeled after the French use of Devil's Island. Send to St. Thomas, St. John, and St. Croix the "desperate criminals who have been sentenced to life imprisonment." France had "rid herself of the scum of the earth, why should the United States not do the same thing?"[40]

This idea never received serious consideration, but what was going to happen to a possession the navy considered an "adopted child?" After a decade of military control, the islands were economically bankrupt, and, as the military governor told Congress (on December 20, 1926) "the trouble with the law under which we are working is that it is written in Danish and translated, and some parts of it are hard to understand."[41]

Even harder to understand was the nature of military rule. The navy had incorporated Danish law into American. A group of "colonial councils" acted as the will of the people. Since only property owners were allowed to vote—you needed $60 worth of assets in St. Croix, $75 in St. Thomas—less than five percent of the Virgin Islanders had any chance of particpating in the government. Since the laws were American and Danish, military and civil, translated and confusing, it required special training to administer the islands. As Attorney A.A. Berle told Congress, much of what the military did was modeled after the Foraker legislation that governed Puerto Rico. Islanders might not grasp the nature of their new laws but they were "well understood by our own colonial administrators and by the people who have to interpret the laws."[42]

In Washington and in the islands, the people who interpreted the laws were the soldiers and sailors who worked for the War Department's Bureau of Insular Affairs. General Frank McIntyre was the bureau's long-time chief and, as he listened to the testimony offered by Attorney Berle, the general agreed with this suggestion: "The bureau is equipped to do this sort of thing, and has done it well in the past, and it is our American colonial office for overseas possessions, and I think that is where the ultimate jurisdiction, or the departmental jurisdiction, should be."

Congress agreed when a prominient liberal attorney—Berle represented the Virgin Islands Congressional Council—discussed an American "colonial office for our overseas possessions." Representatives simply moved to the business at hand. What were we going to do with these islands?

Berle suggested that they pass laws giving islanders some basic rights (*e.g.*, U.S. citizenship), but remember to include section five, the special clause written in "when I [A.A. Berle] drew the act."

Congress had to remember "that the navy might want a last clear chance to absorb such territory as might be necessary....It may still be possible for the navy to take them over if it desires."[43]

How long should the navy have to make up its mind? Berle had said in ninety days, but General McIntyre said to give them more time. "If you provide that that must be done in ninety days and make it necessary for them to act hastily, the army or the navy will be apt to take everything. That is the only way they can protect their interests."

McIntyre reminded Congress of the situation in Puerto Rico. "We had an army and navy board there and they took everything and as a consequence San Juan has been crowded ever since, because the army and navy took so much."[44]

The political and economic consequences of a decade of American control impressed a U.S. Senator. Hiram Bingham of Connecticut had just visited the islands, and while he was surprised by the way many islanders "bowed, very cordially" when the governor rode through the streets, Bingham was also distressed by the "distinct, sullen hostility" of many Virgin Islanders. They blamed the United States for what had happened and the senator partially agreed with their reasoning.

Bingham pointed to four economic issues, all outside the islanders' control. First, the wireless destroyed the significance of St. Thomas' cable station. Second, the rapid transition from coal to oil put hundreds of people out of work. The usual way to load coal on ships was for three or four hundred islanders to carry baskets full of coal on their heads and walk them on board. For each trip a person received a token, and by the end of the day an individual had earned $1 or $1.50 for his or her many treks up the gangway. Bingham noted that St. Thomas possessed a mechanical coal loader, but, to keep people employed, it was rarely used.

Third, the Panama Canal's completion changed the "lanes of travel." Ships bound for the west coast of South America or the United States used to stop at St. Thomas for coaling. Now they didn't stop if they used oil and, even if they still used coal, it was much easier to use the facilities at the Panama Canal.

Technological change threatened an always tenuous economy. Congress struck the hardest blow of all—prohibition. Sea captains used to stop at St. Thomas because it was a free port. They could buy all the fine French wine or all the fine island rum they wanted. When Congress made the island a dry spot, captains went elsewhere, and the Virgin Islands received a fourth and final blow to their economy.[45]

Some Congressmen wanted to extend the coastwise shipping laws to St. Thomas, St. Croix, and St. John. Bingham managed to convince his colleagues that such a law would reduce the already reduced traffic to the islands, but even he said nothing about a series of taxes that mocked the ideals of the American revolution and democracy.

As a rider to the Naval Appropriations bill of 1921, Congress extended federal income tax laws to the Virgin Islands. Sugar growers in St. Croix paid an export tax on their produce, imposed by Congress as a temporary levy in 1918, which had no market at home because of the ban on rum, and no advantage abroad in a decade that saw the world oversupplied with sugar.[46]

154

The Virgin Islands had the distinction of arguably being the first people under American authority to be taxed without representation. In local newspapers like *The Emancipator*, columnists complained about taxes and about the Organic Act: "It upholds the very powers that Madison condemns. Section 1 gives to any Governor civil, military, and judicial powers." Governors, "endorsing the vicious practices of George III," appointed and discharged judges. This was the "prototype of Romanoff imperialism" to the editor of *The Emancipator*,[47] but to Congress, the islanders had to understand who had absolute power over their destiny.

Congress underlined its authority in a bizarre way when it did and did not grant citizenship to islanders in the bill drawn up by A.A. Berle. Passed in 1927, the law made many islanders aliens in their own country. If you were in the islands on January 17, 1917 (the day in which Denmark and the U.S. ratified the treaties) and in the islands, the U.S. or Puerto Rico on February 25, 1927 (the date of the new legislation), you were a citizen of the United States. If you were in the United States on January 17, 1917 and in the islands on February 25, 1927, you were also a U.S. citizen. Otherwise you were out of luck.[48]

The Virgin Islands were a colony owned by a democracy. Indeed, despite Robert Lansing's assurance that they would be a possession "exactly" like Puerto Rico and the Philippines, the Virgin Islands were always treated with a special brand of indifference. They still lacked a resident commissioner to plead their case in Congress; they remained under military rule until 1934; and, when Herbert Hoover visited the islands, he quickly summed up the first fourteen years of American rule: "The Virgin Islands may have some military value sometime...in any event, when we paid $25,000,000 for them we acquired an effective poorhouse comprising ninety percent of the population....Viewed from every point of view except remote naval contingency, it was unfortunate that we ever acquired them. Nevertheless, having assumed the responsibility we must do our best to assist the inhabitants."[49]

Puerto Rico

Next door was another poorhouse. Even though Puerto Rico was "desperately in need of economic rehabilitation," Theodore Roosevelt Jr. (appointed governor in 1929) hesitated to tell the president. He understood the faults of America's colonial administrators: "We think we are better than other people. Anyone who does things in different fashion from us is comic or stupid. We regard being a foreigner in the nature of a defective moral attribute."[50]

Despite his reservations, Roosevelt wrote the president a long letter in December of 1929. The governor was "ashamed" of its length (i.e., five pages) but the island's situation was desperate. What could Hoover do about the sugar legislation? Congressional proposals suggesting even more subsidies for the beet growers would strike "a most serious blow" at Puerto Rico; and the reluctance to allow the island to increase its tiny refining industry retarded any efforts at industrialization. Meanwhile, "we are throttled by exorbitant steamship rates. Porto Rico is under the coastwise shipping laws and there is no one to whom we can appeal for redress in any matter."[51]

Could Hoover help? In addition to the high costs of transportation, the island's small quantity of refined sugar paid an extra high tariff when it entered the United States. Ironically, Roosevelt's letter could have been written by the head of Puerto Rican Independence Party. In speeches and newspaper articles Pedro Albizu Campos made the same complaints as Roosevelt, with exactly the same results: nothing changed.

Roosevelt did suggest exporting the Puerto Rican people but "insofar as emigration is concerned, from the temper of our people here and on a general basis, I do not think that such a thing as forced emigration is possible. All we can hope for is facilitated emigration. Incidentally shipping rates largely block our attempts in this line."[52]

Despite letters addressed to "Porto Rico, Cuba" and "Ambassador Roosevelt, American Embassy, Porto Rico," the new governor worked hard. Theodore Roosevelt Jr. tried to learn Spanish, and empathized with the "weight of the problems" Hoover faced. He even considered this suggestion for providing jobs to Puerto Ricans: buy hundreds of canaries which would be given to the poor. Islanders would teach the (presumably American) canaries to sing the Star Spangled Banner, and, if the economy picked up, islanders could then sell the birds to American tourists.[53]

Dominican Republic

No one ever bought the canaries. The depression occupied the greatest part of the president's time, but, even before that catastrophe occurred, Herbert Hoover always thought of the Caribbean as a place to leave, never as a place to invest even more American time, money, and energy.

The president had some specific ideas. Assistant Secretary of State Francis White explained them to the U.S. ambassador in the Dominican Republic on February 26, 1930, "the president feels, I may say confidentially, that our interventions in the past have not been very successful and he does not want to land forces nor even to send a ship unless it is absolutely essential for the protection of American lives."[54]

Ambassador Charles Curtis received this message three days after General Rafael Trujillo used his marine-trained forces to overthrow the government of the Dominican Republic. Even though Washington knew that Trujillo murdered friend and foe alike, Curtis received this advice from his superiors: "We have not felt from your cables that Americans were menaced as such or ran any danger other than is incident to residence in a disturbed area from stray shots and therefore on account of the effect it will have on public opinion in this country and also in Latin America we have not wanted to send a ship at this time."[55]

In 1916, the possibility of a takeover moved President Wilson to initiate a military occupation. In 1930, a chief of state the American ambassador compared to Al Capone received no opposition from the United States. In 1965, stray shots in a Dominican hotel would be one of President Lyndon Johnson's pretexts for another American occupation of the Dominican Republic.

It was a century of change, but the most debateable policy of all was initiated by Herbert Hoover and

labeled by Franklin Roosevelt. The Good Neighbor
Policy had one principal aim—keeping the United
States out of the Caribbean and Latin America.
However, the United States never refrained from
using its soldiers because American policy makers
thought intervention was immoral, illegal, or perverse
in relation to its economic consequences. President
Hoover let men like Trujillo murder with impunity
because he thought interventions caused more problems than they resolved.

The intent of the Good Neighbor Policy was negative. White told Curtis they would not send a ship
because of the effect it would have on public opinion
in the United States and Latin America. The United
States did not want bad publicity so officials looked
the other way even when Caribbean governments
violated the very constitutions U.S. officials both
wrote and imposed.[56]

In 1926, the Dominicans had borrowed another
$13 million. This loan was not only approved by the
United States government, it came with guarantees
and problems not included in the 1922 loan.
Instead of assurances from a military government,
the 1926 money came with the firm support of
Calvin Coolidge. Investors who told clients not to
buy in 1922, told them to purchase the 1926 bonds
because "they were sold by the United States
Government and are signed by an officer of the
United States government, with the consent of the
United States and the State Department."[57]

The United States had let the loan go through
even though it disagreed with the terms demanded by
the Dominicans. They took the money because they
desperately needed it, and because they also wanted

to avoid *any* extension of the receivership, they agreed to terms which demanded a quick amortization of the debt. Assistant Secretary of State White asked the Dominicans to reconsider a loan which demanded stiff payments in only four years, but, for the purpose of expediency, he put the U.S. guarantee behind what he knew to be a bad deal for both countries.[58]

Another bad deal was the constitution demanded by Sumner Welles in 1924. All parties then agreed that the president elected under the Welles constitution would serve a four-year term. President Vasquez liked the job so much he discovered an "error." He had been elected under the 1908 document, instead of the 1924 constitution. That constitution gave him a six-year term, and it gave the State Department a problem. The U.S. ambassador agreed that in 1924 "all interested parties" not only knew the president served for four years, he had it in writing from the Dominican government itself. However, he counseled his superiors in Washington to avoid a "formal note of demand"; actions should be limited to no more than "friendly advice and counsel."[59]

Washington agreed. In April of 1927, Secretary of State Kellogg tried to have his cake, eat it, and still avoid responsibility for any crumbs that fell on the Dominican table. He told the U.S. ambassador to "express orally and informally" that serious consequences could arise if Vasquez tried to "arbitrarily prolong" his presidency or arbitrarily select a successor. However, "at the same time you should impress on him that responsibility for deciding which course he is to follow rests solely upon him."[60]

Horacio Vasquez did as he pleased. In February of 1928, he announced that he had, in fact, been elected for six years and, buoyed by the advice that he could chart his own course, Vasquez decided to pick a successor. He chose Horacio Vasquez, which was the dilemma Herbert Hoover confronted when he assumed the presidency in 1929.

Herbert Hoover sat in the audience as Rafael Trujillo plotted "the best announced revolution" in Caribbean history.[61] In February of 1929, a Dominican newspaper noted Trujillo's "veiled candidacy" for the presidency. He was "cultivating relations," he was a favorite of the Americans, and he was head of the army. Let something happen to Vasquez and "Good night Alfonseca!" The vice-president would be a forgotten name, Trujillo the military man of the hour.

Hoover understandably did nothing when, in September of 1929, a 20-year-old Dominican named Juan Bosch published an article with lines like this: "It is undeniable that a tyranny which will threaten the Dominican people is gestating in the presidential mansion."[62]

But when Horacio Vasquez continued his plans to succeed himself, Hoover also did nothing. He accepted this violation of the American demanded constitution with equanimity, and he waited along with the rest of the island when the 69-year-old Vasquez went to Baltimore for medical treatment.

Trujillo acted. His old marine commander, Colonel Richard Cutts, was in charge of the U.S. troops still stationed in Haiti. Trujillo sent his aides to inform Cutts of his plans to take over the government. Cutts listened, and on December 3, 1929, the

161

news was published in the *New York Times*. The story correctly noted a "secret conference" with American officials, but, instead of a Trujillo plot, it suggested a coup because of Haitian/Dominican border problems stemming from the absence of Horacio Vasquez.[63]

Rafael Trujillo took over the Dominican government on February 23, 1930. As a precaution, he kept $600,000 in cash in a small handbag. With a degree of conspiratorial skill that would have impressed Machiavelli, Trujillo loyally stood behind the now returned Vasquez, as he funneled useless weapons to units possibly loyal to the government, and simultaneously helped Rafael Estrella Urena and his forces to act as temporary custodians of Trujillo's prize.[64]

The American ambassador pleaded for help: "A naval vessel should be sent here without delay." Instead, the ambassador was told to sit tight. "Should fighting seem imminent, you might deem it wise to suggest the establishment of a new zone where Americans and other noncombatants would be safe." Otherwise "your aim should be, if possible, to handle this situation without show of force. If you can do it, it will materially strengthen our position in the Dominican Republic and in the rest of Latin America."[65]

Ambassador Curtis did his best. A temporary government was established on March 2, with Estrella Urena as acting president. Elections would be held in May, and Trujillo had agreed not to run, However, as Curtis told his superiors on March 1, "in spite of all the promises he made to my predecessors, Trujillo was disloyal to President Vasquez from the first moment after his return to the country (from the hospital in Baltimore) on January 6." Trujillo's word was meaningless; he and his "gangsters" ran the new government; and "unless we can eliminate Trujillo, a revolution by or against Trujillo is certain. This cannot be accomplished by the president. Will the Department make any statement on the subject or authorize the legation to do so?"[66]

The State Department told Curtis that "it expects to recognize Trujillo or any other person coming into office as a result of the coming elections and will maintain the most friendly relations with him and his government and will desire to cooperate with him in every way." However, the State Department did offer a suggestion. Colonel Cutts "exercised great personal influence" over Trujillo; the general "frequently consults him on important matters relating to Trujillo's conduct and attitude." Let Cutts come over from Haiti and see what he could do with Trujillo.[67]

Cutts, in a remarkable interview sent to Assistant Secretary of State White, noted that despite his many vices, "Trujillo was probably more Americanized than any other Dominican." Indeed, if only because he copied Americans with such evident pleasure, Trujillo had been "picked" out from obscurity as a soldier having the necessary qualifications to develop into the commander of the national police and to hold it intact and free from politics in order that the Dominican Republic might not fall into the old cycle of revolutions after the withdrawal of the American Military Government."[68]

That is exactly what happened. Cutts, however, seemed oblivious to a remarkable admission; the most Americanized of the Dominicans was a brute and a gangster! What did that say about the United States?

Cutts told his superiors that "Trujillo fully admitted that the whole revolution had been a frame-up, that there had never been a real revolution...and that Trujillo was not hostile to Minister Curtis." Trujillo was willing to forget the ambassador's criticisms which meant that "the Legation, in spite of its previous attitude would not have any loss of prestige or difficulty in working with the new government."

Cutts "frankly admitted that the Trujillo administration would be the dictator type of government." The general was unfortunately a "Jekyll and Hyde" personality, but he nonetheless, "through his control of the army," assured a government that would work with the United States.[69]

Ambassador Curtis read this memo and immediately pleaded, in letter after letter, for his superiors to tell Trujillo they would never recognize his government. On April 21, Curtis wrote that "the army has unquestionably been exceeding its legal powers in thousands of cases, its members have committed murders and other outrages at the orders of Trujillo, have committed others without his specific orders but with the intent to help him or please him, and yet others to accomplish personal spite or vengeance."[70]

Trujillo's response was to run for the presidency. In theory he had resigned from the army but Curtis explained the facts to his superiors. Trujillo never resigned. He was on a leave of absence, running a peculiar, yet effective presidential campaign: "He does not wear his uniform but he uses his official car with a plate describing it as that of the Commander-In-Chief of the army and he is accompanied in his car by officers armed with machine guns and automatic rifles, while another car filled with officers similarly armed goes ahead of his and yet another such follows."[71]

No one seemed to care. Curtis wrote the Trujillo-as-Al Capone letter on April 21, and three weeks later he received a long letter from Assistant Secretary of State Francis White.

Curtis was told not to worry about the prestige of the legation. It had not been "rendered ridiculous" by the lies of Trujillo and his mob. On the contrary, because the United States had not exercised any control over the Dominicans' internal affairs since 1924 (neither the receivership, the marine training, nor the new loan of 1926 were considered control of internal affairs), the United States "does not suffer if its advice is not accepted or if promises made with a view to bettering conditions are not lived up to." We could offer our help "because of our friendship for the Dominican people, our desire to see them prosperous and stable and to help them to avoid the recurrence of conditions such as led up to 1916 and our military occupation which, however distasteful to the Dominicans was far more so to this government."

White's attitude—"I do not see any other alternative than to recognize as president the successful candidate at the election of [May] the 16th instant."[72]—reflects the fundamental shift in policy which Hoover endorsed and Franklin Roosevelt called the Good Neighbor Policy.

Theodore Roosevelt's Corollary was a blend of

exceptionalism and inconsistency, imposed through the implied use of force. But its "good colonialism" assumptions were at least positive rather than negative, optimistic rather than cynical, principled rather than expedient.

Robert Lansing was always honest. His policies produced three occupations (including the Virgin Islands), but this secretary of state was openly selfish. The integrity of Caribbean nations was an "incident," not an end of American strategy.

Herbert Hoover (and Henry Stimson and Francis White) changed the nature of U.S. Caribbean policy. They supported an Al Capone in the name of neighborliness, and they washed their hands of murder as easily as Pontius Pilate washed his hands of Jesus Christ. However, Pontius Pilate only watched one man be crucified; Herbert Hoover saw it happen to a nation.

Rafael Leonidas Trujillo easily won the May presidential elections. As Curtis put it to the secretary of state, Trujillo was so popular that his total count—223,851 votes—"greatly exceeded the total number of voters in the country." Thus, "further comment on the fairness of the elections is hardly necessary." The gang of 42 (they were named for the 42nd marine company) had intimidated the citizenry long before the elections occurred, and with the opposition refusing to participate, there was no violence on election day.[73]

The United States sent a special representative to the general's August 16, 1930 inauguration. Trujillo remained in office until 1961, when he was assassinated with the help of the Kennedy administration.

The creature created by the United States was killed by the United States. Or, as one of the American "liquidation" planners put it in 1960, "if you [Assistant Secretary of State Thomas Mann] recall Dracula you will remember it was necessary to drive a stake through his heart to prevent a continuation of his crimes. I believe sudden death would be more humane than the solution of Nuncio, who once told me he thought he should pray that Trujillo would have a long and lingering illness."[74]

Trujillo died from gunshot wounds. CIA officials did not think the assassins had used weapons provided by the United States.

Haiti

If the Haitian occupation "was going to stand until 1950 or 1975," then the United States had an opportunity to effect real social change. Sydney La Rue (the U.S. financial advisor in Haiti) said he used 60 percent of Haiti's revenues to develop the country and, after 15 years of American control, he believed the occupation had created a Haitian middle-class. "You can today find little farms, now and then you will find a house with a tin roof; you will find fences. You will actually see a cow at some places....This is a very humble beginning but a real start toward improvement. We have just started to get at the development of the peasant."[75]

La Rue spoke to a commission established by Herbert Hoover. The president wanted to get the U.S. out of Haiti because, as in Cuba, Puerto Rico, and the Dominican Republic, American intervention was producing adverse publicity abroad and humiliating demonstrations in the Haitian capital.

When the commissioners arrived in Port-au-Prince in February of 1930, they found their hotel littered with "get out of Haiti" signs. A trip through the countryside found "throngs" of angry citizens on either side of the modern roads built with *corvée* labor. In a "dozen" different places commissioners were greeted with "the same paper flags, darkened with black paper bars to indicate a state of mourning for lost liberties." La Rue might want another 45 years to complete his work, but, as the commissioners told the president, "it is fair to assume that public sentiment in Haiti was more responsive to the opposition than to the government."[76]

That government was theoretically controlled by the Haitian people, but as Ambassador Dana Munro told his superiors, that was a "fiction" used to convince the gullible. The United States was in charge and could not be blamed for Haiti's unwillingness to change. The problem was that "the Haitians are totally unlike the Spanish-Americans. With the latter, one can usually appeal to their better qualities and count on a certain amount of real patriotism among the more enlightened leaders. The Haitian seems to think primarily in terms of jobs; even the president and the Cabinet take the position in conferring with me that it is a misfortune to have the Americans here drawing salaries when there are so many Haitians who need the money."[77]

The Haitians wanted to put their own people to work, and wanted the Americans to get out. Munro seemed genuinely amazed by their ingratitude. "There seems to be no readiness to recognize the fact that the work is more efficiently performed under American direction and that the Treaty Services are performing a real service to the Haitian people."[78]

Munro wrote this letter nine months *after* the president's commission left Haiti. It was an accurate reflection of the American mind—"force after all is the only thing these people have any respect for"— and a concise explanation of why the Haitian occupation produced such resentment. The *corvée* and the bayonet helped explain part of the Haitian's anger, but on this side of Hispaniola the arrogance of American culture joined hands with its legacy of racism. The result was comments like these: "It is my opinion, after long study of the negro race, that they will always require inspection by white men." This statement appeared in a public report issued by the American official in charge of public works; and, when Haitians complained, High Commissioner John Russell noted that "what has been said of the Public Works Department holds true of all the other Departments under the Treaty officials."[79] Russell had issued a 1930 annual report which argued that the "majority of the Haitian people have the mentality of a child of seven years."[80]

In a statement issued from Washington, Assistant Secretary of State Francis White explained why he refused to testify before Congress. Haitian attorney George Leger had leveled very serious charges, but, as White told Ambassador Munro: "I replied that I had no intention of doing so [*i.e.*, testifying]—that I had no idea of getting into an argument with a coon on the stand."[81]

The natives interfered with the efficient and honest Americans "who had to maintain the integrity of the treaty service so long as we were responsible for their work." Munro spent a good part of his day listening to the complaints of the Americans who had just listened to the complaints of the Haitians. The Americans wanted an apology, and the Haitians wanted power. After fifteen years, however, both desires were thwarted by a stalemate. The marines remained in Haiti as an insurance policy; Americans officered an army which contained no Haitians above the rank of captain; and, as late as 1928, no Haitian had ever participated in designing the budgets of the nation's various government agencies.[82]

Herbert Hoover wanted "to withdraw from Haiti bag and baggage immediately if possible." He knew an "ugly situation" when he saw one, and he had no intention of allowing Haiti's constitution to get in the way of a speedy retreat from Hispaniola. The 1918 constitution established by Smedley Butler's bayonets stipulated that an appointed council of state elected the president. For the last twelve years that council had selected Louis Borno for a series of two-year terms. Borno had refused to allow elections for a council of state. He could only call those elections in even years, he had never found the time to do so,;and High Commissioner Russell saw nothing contradictory in preparing a people for democracy by not allowing them to elect their own representatives. As the State Department noted in a long report, Russell always "acquiesced" when Borno came up with an excuse to again postpone elections.[83]

Russell thought that 1930 would be different. Borno, however, postponed elections at the last minute, and that put the State Department in a difficult spot. The plebiscite-approved constitution said elections could only be held in 1932. With a bit of verbal gymnastics it might be possible to argue that

an election in mid-1930 was a "delayed election."
The constitution specified the date for advising the
people of elections. That date had passed. The
hands of the Americans were tied by a constitution
allegedly written by the Democrat's probable presidential nominee, Franklin Delano Roosevelt.

History sometimes does repeat itself. With
Franklin Roosevelt waiting in the wings, Herbert
Hoover and his subordinates decided to follow the
precedent set in the Dominican Republic: let
Haitians interpret their constitution. Russell's only
tasks were to negotiate a compromise, produce early
elections, and absolve the United States of any
responsibility for what might happen. Russell should
tell the Haitians that, "while we do not object to it
[i.e., the illegal elections], we do not insist upon it."[84]

Some Haitians cooperated; others did not.
Russell thought that Borno had agreed to resign in
favor of a businessman, Eugene Roy, who would be
elected by the appointed council of state. Some
"radical" council members refused to abide by this
decision, Borno himself was rethinking his no candidacy promise, and Russell opted for another council of state. He told Borno to fire the lot, appoint a
group who would do as they were told, and thus
elect Eugene Roy temporary president of Haiti.[85]

Borno "absolutely refused" to follow orders.
That led the Hoover administration to point to
Colonel Richard Cutts and his marines. They would
"install" Roy if the Haitians refused to reconsider
their opposition to the American plan. The council
remained adamant, but Borno finally surrendered.
He agreed to appoint another council but asked for
time to find pliable members from Haiti's various

geographical divisions. Russell refused. His idea was to reinterpret the already reinterpreted Constitution. Since nothing specifically "precluded the replacing of councilors of state by men from Port-au-Prince," Borno should find enough cronies who would vote for Roy, the new president would oversee the elections, and the Americans could leave under a democratic cloud.[86]

Like so many of his Caribbean predecessors, Russell never grasped his own contradictions. On the one hand the Haitians were, in 1930, "little better fitted for self-government than they were in 1915." On the other hand, Russell issued orders cancelling the promised elections (in 1924, 1926, 1928, and 1930); he dismissed councils of state as if they were hired hands, and he settled for political puppets while he argued that "the main object of the Treaty of 1915 is for the United States government to so assist the Republic of Haiti that it will become capable of self-government."[87]

Hoover disregarded this contradiction. Even before the negotiations were concluded, the two sides almost came to blows. Stephen Vincent, elected president of Haiti in November of 1930, actually thought he had power; he and his "ardent nationalist" colleagues wanted to appoint members of their government while Ambassador Munro refused to concede such authority. He demanded that the Haitians give a Garde commission to an American, President Vincent said refused, and the secretary of state overruled his minister. As White told Munro, he was sorry to do it, "but the truth of the matter is that we just could not answer questions in Congress or in the press in this country to justify breaking off the Haitianization negotiations over the question of whether Aarons should be a first lieutenant or a captain."[88]

To Munro it was question of principle. In his April meetings with Secretary of State Stimson, he said that he "must 'kick them out' if the Haitians attempted any interference, and the department's telegram #36 confirmed my impression that I would not be permitted to make any concessions where the control and efficiency of the Garde was concerned."[89] In April, control of the Garde was paramount; in June, the end justified the means.

In April Stimson wanted to use the Garde to prevent "rioting and bloodshed in Haiti"; that "would have made an unfortunate impression in the United States."[90] In June Stimson still wanted to prevent riots, but, in order to leave Haiti, he was willing to consider conceding control of the military instrument that supposedly guaranteed peace and progress. Actually, there was no real worry about the Garde because Munro agreed that "the effort to keep the Garde free from political influence had encouraged a rather dangerous spirit of independence among Haitian officers, and the recent seizure of power across the border by General Rafael Trujillo at the head of an American trained military force had set them a bad example."[91]

The Haitianization agreement was signed on August 5, 1931. The United States agreed to transfer authority to the Haitians as quickly as possible, and they agreed to help the American financial advisor who would help Haiti's peasants pay off the country's debt for at least another decade.

The peasants paid for the occupation because

in 1915 and in 1932 coffee was the economy's principal export crop. The taxes on coffee and the taxes on imported food soaked the poorest Haitians. Those taxes allowed the American financial advisor to argue that the country was "in most excellent shape." Those taxes paid off the debt to American and French banks; they paid off the "wavy" railroad that the Americans exempted from the 1919 claims commission; and, finally they paid the salary of financial advisor Sydney La Rue and the other Americans. As La Rue noted, "the peasant is a very decent hard-working, primitive sort of fellow. He is not hard to handle—perfectly easy to govern. He is naturally peaceful."[92]

The peasant was in the countryside when the United States *helped* ignite "the indigeniste movement." During the occupation Americans favored light-skinned Haitians. This produced tensions, but, in Haiti, sixteen years of American racism also added different fuel to a fire that had its deepest origins in Haiti's own preferences for Western judgements. By 1930, one result of the two forms of prejudice was a movement that celebrated the peasantry. The "indigenistes" argued that the brutalities and failures of the light-skinned elite stemmed from their contempt for Haitian popular culture. They said celebrate the African roots of Haitian society and you would see that no culture was inherently superior to another; the most westernized Haitians were not necessarily the best Haitians.

The indigeniste movement was non-political, but, years later, politicians would use it to justify distributing political positions on the basis of skin color. The peasants were in the middle when François

Duvalier fought for power, and the occupation must assume some responsibility for the ideology he so brutally employed. Prejudice had always existed in Haiti; what the American occupiers did was substitute skin color for the other factors that traditionally allowed Haitians to discriminate against one another.[93]

One result of the occupation was the increased use of Haitian peasants in the sugar cane fields of the Dominican Republic. The first legal authorization of Haitian workers occurred in 1919 and, as the many American plantations increased in size, so too did the use of Haitian labor. Haitians always worked for less, but, as the price of sugar declined during the 1920's, Haitians became the preferred cane cutters. They could be exploited during the harvest and returned to the Haitian/Dominican frontier when they were no longer needed.[94]

The trouble was racial prejudice in the Dominican Republic, built on a foundation of bitter feelings against Haitians of any color. Dominicans, after all, dated their independence from the 1844 expulsion of Haiti from Dominican soil. Haitians were despised because they were the invaders, and because they were the wrong color. A long line of Dominican intellectuals sought to "whiten" the population and, building on these beliefs, in 1925 nationalists tried to prohibit the immigration of Haitians.

The Americans remained oblivious to the consequences of their ever increasing exploitation of Haitian labor. Through the 1920s plantation owners and diplomats lobbied to prevent restrictions against Haitian workers. President Vasquez responded with an effort to stimulate the colonization of the Haitian/Dominican frontier. He hoped to paint it white and so did Rafael Leonidas Trujillo. The general who wore makeup to hide his skin color, the general ashamed of his Haitian roots, was not a man to tolerate the blackening of his people. He too pushed for colonization, but, in 1932, he added a law that obligated sugar growers to hire Dominicans—as many as possible, and as soon as possible.[95]

In the middle of the Depression the law was disregarded. Trujillo gave in to the pressure exerted by American business and diplomatic personnel; he allowed Haitians to come to the Dominican Republic and he thus confronted a new American president with an old and terrible problem: the exploitation of Haitians by the sugar growers who came with the military occupation.

The occupiers brought the Haitians. Trujillo would get rid of them. No informed American of the time could argue that he or she did not see the potential for horror on the horizon.

Rum, Revolution, and Moral Embargoes

"An island or small group of islands acquired primarily for naval purposes does not differ greatly from a war vessel or fleet at anchor. It would be as improper to transfer the administration of such an island to another department as to turn over war vessels to any other than the Navy Department."
—General F. McIntyre, War Department, 1932

Frank Dillingham did his best. He bobbed, he weaved, he danced around the congressional ring, but, after the bout was over, senators had convincingly struck a few blows for the American taxpayer. Caribbean islanders would continue to suffer, but Congress had publicized the business beauty of Frank Dillingham's exploitation of three Caribbean islands.

In 1928, Dillingham's Central Romana owned roughly 75,000 acres of the Dominican Republic. It was "virgin soil," producing some of the best sugar in the world. Added to better quality was the lower cost of production. Dillingham hedged when asked about this but after Senator Smoot posed the question again and again, the businessman told the senator that "the difference is more or less two to two-and-a-half dollars a ton."[1]

The senator also still wanted to know how Dillingham got his produce into the United States. Dominican sugar was essentially closed out of the American market in 1920. What did Dillingham do with his cane?

He shipped it to Puerto Rico. He paid a dollar a ton tariff to do so but that still left him a dollar to a dollar-and-a-half of extra profit on every ton of the Dominican sugar. Senator Smoot began to multiply. Dillingham had sent 235,000 tons of Dominican sugar to Puerto Rico in 1928. Did that mean a profit of roughly $350,000 on this one transaction?

Dillingham said no. You had to factor in transportation costs of a dollar a ton from the Dominican Republic to Puerto Rico, so the actual, extra profit was only fifty cents a ton.

Senator Smoot produced the company's own records. Central Romana had earned $345,000 on the Dominican sugar and Dillingham had to admit the truth. That was the "absolute profit" he had earned, but Congress should continue to allow his Dominican sugar to pass through his Puerto Rican door.[2]

Dillingham defended his practices, and Congress never added up the information produced by its own hearings. Dillingham said that Puerto Rico sent 600,000 tons of sugar to the United States in 1928. His South Porto Rico sugar produced one-sixth of this total, but if you added the 235,000 tons that came in from the Dominican Republic, Dillingham's operations alone accounted for 40 percent of the sugar that came in from and through Puerto Rico.[3]

The (1928) net profit from this cross-Caribbean trading was a hefty $4.8 million. On sales alone

South Porto Rico earned a profit of 25 percent; on its capital investment the profit was nearly 50 percent. Over half of this profit returned to the United States in the form of stock dividends—in 1928 it was $5.20 a share on common stock, $85.57 for a share of preferred—and the remainder was deposited in the company's "surplus" account.[4]

Most of that yearly surplus also returned to the United States. Investors wanted to use their Caribbean profits on the mainland. Congress had made an exception here and there (e.g., 20 percent of Cuba's crop could be refined at home), but, on the many Caribbean islands wedded to sugar, where was an entrepreneur going to find opportunities for additional investment? Tobacco offered a possibility, but it was easier to invest in the businesses that monopolized the production and distribution of the Caribbean's imports. In 1928, fully 87 percent of Puerto Rico's imports came from the United States; the figure for the Dominican Republic was 75 percent.[5]

Economically these islands—and Cuba and Haiti and the Virgin Islands—were dependent upon sugar and the United States. Neither partner offered any hope of self-sustaining development when, added to a worldwide oversupply of sugar, came depression and disarray. Producers initially struggled to create a workable cartel; they each set production quotas, but instead of cooperation, the world witnessed a staggering *increase* in sugar production. Everyone tried to make the same amount of money by selling more cane so the result in 1930 was a doubling of the world's sugar surplus.[6]

In the United States the administration (and

179

Congress) tried to protect mainland producers by raising the tariff on Cuban sugar, but instead of the expected stabilization of supply, Americans responded with a 64 percent increase in production. In Puerto Rico, Frank Dillingham and his colleagues raised their output by 42 percent. Their sales (compared to 1928) dropped by almost a third. Profits, however, were still good; South Porto Rico Sugar earned $1.5 million in 1931.[7]

Dillingham was lucky. He increased production and used his Puerto Rican connection to fill in the supplies no longer arriving from "foreign" sources. Cuba was desperate; and, in a tragedy that would be repeated in the 1980s, the ripple effects of sugar's depression spread across the Caribbean.

Cuba's sugar industry had increased production from one million tons in 1902 to nearly three million in 1914. The war soon opened markets in Europe; and the postwar period fed the speculation that fed the spending that fed an even greater production of sugar. By 1928, Cuba produced nearly six million tons of cane for an industry now dominated by the United States. Fully 75 percent of the crop in the late twenties came from mills owned by American interests.[8]

White House officials accepted no responsibility for the development of Cuba's economy. Critics published a book (in 1928) called *Our Cuban Colony: A Study in Sugar*[9] but two "confidential" memos to President Hoover focused on politics and General Enoch Crowder's constitution. President Machado had violated the constitution when he sought another term, that produced opposition, and Machado had responded by "making clear his determination to remain in office until the expiration of his term and to put down by whatever means necessary any further attempts at his overthrow." Officials agreed that "the Cuban political situation has been characterized by a policy of terrorism on both sides," but instead of intervention, our policy was one of "strict impartiality." We would let them kill each other as they saw fit and admit no responsibility for the consequences of our thirty-year protectorate.[10]

The Cubans, locked out of Europe and priced out of the United States, lowered the price of sugar with each increase in the tariff. As an advisor explained the situation to the president, "Cuba must fix the price at which she sells sugar at a point which will enable her product to enter the American market. The result is that the price has gone down [it was 3.35 cents a pound from 1921–25, 1.70 cents a pound in 1929, and 0.70 cents a pound in 1933] to a point which is disastrous both for the American and for Cuban producers. It is evident that no increase of the American tariff can relieve the resulting situation in this country or in Cuba."[11]

The human dimensions of this price and production war created havoc throughout the Caribbean. The assistant secretary of the interior took to the radio, telling his listeners that, since 1900, "the extension of the sugar industry, while long yielding handsome returns to the stockholders of corporations which increasingly acquired lands on the island, benefited the Puerto Rican people little."[12]

Many islanders accepted this assessment, but Frank Dillingham and his colleagues maintained profitability by reducing the costs of production. They cut wages by a third, so the 60 cents a day earned by a *campesino* in 1933 equalled the wages of his father in 1900. Meanwhile, South Porto Rico Sugar earned $2 million in 1933, its common shareholders received dividends of $1.95 a share, and the *campesino* tried to use 1900 wages to pay for the imported rice and beans that now cost more than ever before. Between 1932 and 1933 prices for the staples of the Puerto Rican diet jumped 50 to 60 percent; and, when Washington later announced plans to help Puerto Rico, the maritime industry took immediate advantage of their shipping monopoly. They raised prices for essential items by 65 percent, knowing that the U.S. coastal shipping laws prevented Puerto Ricans from using the lower cost ships of foreign nations.[13]

In Cuba severe unemployment exacerbated the perpetual problem of six months of dead time. The small producers (*colonos*) who supplied the American mills went into bankruptcy; and, in October of 1933, Cubans took out their sugar problems on thousands of Haitians and Jamaicans. Since 1913, American and Cuban growers had "imported" close to 150,000 Haitians and Jamaicans to cut sugar cane. They worked for less, and they were politically docile because they were legal and, just as often, illegal aliens.[14]

By 1933, the Haitians and Jamaicans were accused of taking jobs that rightfully belonged to Cubans, and were deported. Soldiers did this dirty work by forcibly uprooting Haitians and Jamaicans who had lived in Cuba for a generation.

The Jamaicans returned to an island run by British colonists; the Haitians returned to a Hispaniola in turmoil, and entered an island devastated by the depression and dominated by a man who meant to whiten the Dominican Republic. In 1933–34, Rafael Trujillo was searching for ways to rid his society of Haitians at the same time as thousands of "immigrants" struggled to find work in a society that had none.[15]

Franklin Roosevelt inherited this problem of forced migration, unemployment, dead-time, and profits that always returned to the United States. In a better world, Congress, the president, and men like Frank Dillingham would have behaved unselfishly. In the real world, the Caribbean soon found its economies dominated by the Jones-Costigan law, a set of regulations that *indefinitely* dead-ended these already dead-time economies.

The president resorted to quotas. Since producers failed to limit production on their own, the president made himself legal head of a sugar cartel. The law estimated the consumption requirements of the entire nation, and it then allotted quotas to all members of the "stabilization agreement." Domestic producers (those in Louisiana, Florida, Puerto Rico and Hawaii) got 56 percent of the national total, and foreign suppliers (Cuba and the Philippines, which had been promised independence) 44 percent of the U.S. sugar needs.

The basis for the allotments was a system called "representative years." Even before the agriculture department decided what years were representative, the beet sugar interests had a quota 100,000 tons greater than the total sales of their best year. This reflected their political power in Congress. It was a sweet deal for the beet people and a message to Puerto Rico, Cuba, and the Dominican Republic that they were second class members of the new cartel.[16]

The president had designated sugar a "basic" agricultural commodity. He could use the taxes collected from processing sugar to compensate *American* growers in two different ways. They would be paid to keep land out of sugar production, and they would receive—using the processing taxes and other federal funds—such a "fair exchange" price for their product that it would remain "impregnable" to the fluctuations of world prices or changes in the tariff rates.[17]

Puerto Rican growers like Frank Dillingham received some of these processing taxes to keep land out of production. Because the island was in such wretched shape by 1935 that 42 percent of the population was on "relief," the law also permitted the taxes to be used for the "general benefit" of the island. In effect, with the revenues derived from processing sugar, Puerto Rico was to develop a comprehensive plan to rehabilitate the agricultural base that the Jones-Costigan Act had substantially deadended.

In Puerto Rico, the head of the Nationalist Party, Pedro Albizu Campos, saw the underlying futility of the rehabilitation plan. Not only did the quotas set limits on development, but, to Albizu, there was "nothing more illusory than to submit to the will of a foreign leader [*i.e.*, Franklin Roosevelt] nothing less than the rehabilitation of an entire nation." Didn't the beet sugar quotas indicate who had the real power? Was it sensible yet again to root Puerto Rico's development in perpetual dependence on the will of the United States Congress?

And, suppose the rehabilitation succeeded? Would Congress then close markets as swiftly as it lowered the island's sugar quotas?[18]

Rum, Revolution, and Moral Embargoes

While Puerto Ricans debated these questions, Cubans tried to deal with the consequences of their quota allotment. They secured a substantial share of the market offered to foreign producers, a significant reduction in the tariff, and a sharp increase in the per pound price paid for their cane. However, their quota was fifty percent below their 1929 sales to the United States, so as a sugar analyst asked in 1936, "Can Cuba rebuild her economic and political life on a sugar crop of 2.8 million tons with an annual value of $100,000,000?"[19]

The analyst expressed his doubts. Since the industry was 75 percent American owned, Cuba had no guarantees that profits would be reinvested on the island. Since the quotas indefinitely curtailed production, why invest in Cuba? Sugar had reached its peak, and, as in Puerto Rico, the openness of the American market was always limited by the roadblocks constructed by mainland cane and beet growers. Cubans could be grateful that they had "been taken under the protective wing of the United States"; but, in accepting that protection, Cuba "forever" linked its economy to the United States, and, because of the quotas, the terms left little room for negotiation. Along with the Philippines, Cuba already controlled virtually the entire foreign allotment. Where was the room for growth in the axis of the Cuban economy?[20]

The Dominican Republic was left out of this sugar debate. The island's quota was limited to a portion of the 2 percent left for "other" foreign growers. Peru, Nicaragua, El Salvador and Mexico also received part of this 2 percent, so the Dominican Republic now found itself "perpetually" confined to selling its sugar in the ten percent of the world market that was free of subsidies and other government support. The Dominican Republic had to achieve economic stability on the basis of its participation in one of the most volatile commodity markets in the world. Given the military occupation, the one-way trade agreement, and the continued control of the Dominican customs houses, U.S. treatment of Dominican sugar was arguably the most controversial result of the Jones-Costigan Act.

The act became law on May 9, 1934. In slightly altered versions it would continue in effect until 1974. The long-term impact of Jones-Costigan was to dam up the sugar-based economies of Cuba, Puerto Rico, and the Dominican Republic. It was one-sided legislation or, as Ernest Gruening (director of the Interior Department's Division of Territories and Island Possessions) told Congress in August of 1937, "it is the establishment of Old World Colonialism under the Stars and Stripes, something which should be repugnant and repulsive to our ideas of democracy."[21]

Ernest Gruening sounded like a Puerto Rican revolutionary. The Nationalists led by Pedro Albizu Campos also argued that American policies were "repugnant and repulsive." But, what was repugnant in Congress was "fanatical" in Puerto Rico. Directing a possession the president labeled "hopeless," Ernest Gruening refused to let his public statements reflect his public policies. Albizu Campos "hated" the United States and, as Gruening told the president, it was his job to enforce the sedition laws against a man "who began preaching hatred and finally used violence as a means of "free-

186

ing" the island of Puerto Rico from the United States."[22]

Revolution and Sedition

The newspaper *El Mundo* (the World) reported the story in July of 1927. The leader of the Nationalist Party was in the Dominican Republic, and, in response to the question, "Do you have a political platform?" Pedro Albizu Campos answered: "Yes sir. Our program, its general thesis, is to create in Puerto Rico the moral force which existed in 1868...when Puerto Rican heroes like Hostos and Betances preached the revolutionary creed. We seek to translate that spirit into any and all forms of resistance so we can use it against the foreign colonialists."[23]

In assessing Albizu's revolutionary posture, Franklin Roosevelt and Ernest Gruening focused on the color of his skin. He was dark, he had studied at Harvard, and, during WWI he served in a rigidly segregated American army; thus, to the president, Albizu preached revolution because "of his being assigned to a colored officer's training camp."[24]

The evidence which disproved this assessment was available, but American officials never read Albizu's first postwar speeches and articles. Those documents were full of compromise rather than hate, an extended hand rather than a clenched fist, membership in the dominant Unionist Party rather than the group that advocated only independence.[25] Albizu *became* a revolutionary. He changed for a variety of reasons, but presidents like Roosevelt never tried to grasp either his development or the reasons for it. They focused on his alleged personality problems and overlooked a crucial question: If

American laws represented a form of "Old World Colonialism," then wasn't Albizu's revolutionary resistance a legitimate response?

Albizu went to the Dominican Republic and all over Latin America because he respected the work done by the Dominicans during the United States' military occupation. They had ousted the United States by creating political and moral pressure. Albizu sought to do the same thing, so he traveled for three years (1927–29) trying to create the sense of moral outrage that would move others to help the Puerto Ricans in the same way they had helped the Dominicans.

With his Harvard law degree in hand, Albizu was celebrated for his brilliance but was kept at a distance because of his tactics. Albizu and his followers wore their guns on the outside.[26] They hoped to create the crisis that would move the Americans to leave Puerto Rico just as they had left the Dominican Republic.

However, Puerto Rico was a "permanent" possession of the United States. Despite reports from subordinates that "the active agitation has been for independence," Franklin Roosevelt sent FBI agents to follow Albizu. Added to that were a string of double agents who reported back to the military authorities in San Juan. There Colonel John Wright wrote "top secret" reports about the *public* pronouncements of Albizu and his followers.[27]

Albizu brought the crisis to a head. After police "murdered" members of his party, Albizu delivered a funeral oration in which he suggested that his followers kill Colonel E. Francis Riggs, the American head of Puerto Rico's police force. Riggs was assassinated on February 23, 1936, but before that A. Cecil Synder (the United States District Attorney in Puerto Rico) had decided to prosecute Albizu Campos. Legend had it that it was Riggs' murder that moved the Americans to act, but Synder told the president, "at my request two special agents had come to Puerto Rico on February 3, 1936 and had already completed their investigation and left Puerto Rico before Colonel Riggs was murdered."[28]

Riggs or no Riggs, Albizu was going to jail. Murder was the charge, but the assassination had occurred on the streets of San Juan. To try Albizu on that charge meant the Insular Courts and, as the president and Gruening both agreed, "it was probably impossible to convict a Nationalist in an Insular court."[29]

Albizu and his followers were the nation's soul. The islanders lived vicariously through his actions, and the leaders of the island's dominant political parties understood their supporters. After his arrest, the heads of the Republican (statehood) and Liberal (pro-independence one day, pro-something else the next) parties sent President Roosevelt a telegram: Stop the proceedings against Albizu and his followers. He was never a criminal; he was always a patriot.[30]

In Washington, officials decided to try Albizu on sedition; they used the federal courts because of the composition of the juries. The federal courts were "English Only" strongholds; you could not be on a federal jury unless you spoke English, and, since the vast majority of Puerto Ricans spoke only Spanish, American officials thought they had guaranteed a guilty verdict. The English-speaking Puerto

Ricans on such a jury would, after all, be the most Americanized of all.

In court, Albizu admitted he preached revolution. The five American jurors said "guilty," but the seven Puerto Ricans refused to convict. The case appeared to be at a standstill when District Attorney Synder managed, in a quickly convened second trial (on July 27th, 1936, eight days after the first trial) to create a jury with ten Americans and two Puerto Ricans.

This was such a kangaroo court (there were 5,000 Americans in a population of 2 million islanders) that one of the jury's North American members later wrote to President Roosevelt. Elmer Ellsworth explained that "my associates on the jury all seemed to be motivated by strong if not violent prejudice against the Nationalists and were prepared to convict them regardless of the evidence." Ellsworth told the president he was the only holdout. Eventually, however, he gave in. With a conviction in hand, A. Cecil Synder also wrote to the president: "I think I may say it [the trial] has been woven into the history of Puerto Rico. It is superfluous for me to add that in this case we did not infringe on civil liberties nor did we attempt to suppress the independence movement."[31]

Synder was satisfied. A kangaroo court violated no one's civil liberties, the ten-year sentences meted out to Albizu and his colleagues were richly deserved, and, instead of trying to suppress the independence movement, the president had initiated the Tydings Bill, a measure designed to give the Puerto Ricans independence if they desired it.

No one mentioned the independence bill to the

Puerto Rican people. It was submitted to Congress in April of 1936 without their knowledge or approval. Senator Tydings explained why: "The Puerto Ricans weren't consulted when Puerto Rico was annexed to the United States. It was not necessary to consult them about their independence. It was a matter for us primarily to decide."[32]

The decision was made at a cabinet meeting. Less than a month after the Riggs assassination, Roosevelt authorized Secretary of the Interior Ickes to prepare an independence bill because it would have a "quieting effect" on Puerto Rican public opinion. Administration officials would write the measure and deliver it to Senator Tydings; then, before Congress, the senator would take credit for the administration's work. Under no circumstances was the bill to be perceived as coming from the Department of the Interior or the Roosevelt administration.

Ernest Gruening took charge. He modeled his proposal after the independence bill submitted for the Philippines. But, instead of a serious offer of independence, Gruening wrote a measure that he felt was sure to be rejected by substantial portions of the Puerto Rican people.

Instead of the twenty-year economic transition offered to the Filippinos, the Puerto Ricans recieved four years. At the rate of 25 percent a year, tariffs on imports and exports would be introduced, the activities of all federal agencies would cease after independence and the island would also receive no further federal funds once the republic was established.

Gruening admitted that "the bill was not nearly as generous as it should have been," but that, of course, was the whole point of the Tydings Bill.[33] In the midst of an unprecedented depression, who would vote for independence if the already dead-ended sugar industry found itself in the position of the Dominican Republic, with no American market for its cane.

Puerto Ricans did as Gruening expected. The island's 1936 elections were correctly interpreted as a defeat for the Tydings Bill. The Roosevelt administration took credit for its adherence to democratic principles. Puerto Ricans were free to do as they pleased; it was not the administration's fault they chose to remain a colony.

Through 1936 and 1937 the Nationalist agitation for independence never ceased. Even with Albizu locked away in La Princessa, his followers first struggled and then died. In Ponce, on March 21, 1937, police first gave permission for a parade, then refused it, and, when the Nationalists began to march, someone opened fire. The result was nineteen Nationalists dead and over one hundred wounded. Puerto Rican history soon labeled this the "Ponce Massacre" but, as with his rigged jury prosecution of Albizu Campos, and his rigged advocacy of independence, Franklin Roosevelt pursued a policy that reaffirmed 38 years of American colonialism.[34]

In an April 8 letter written by Ernest Gruening, Roosevelt said he meant to continue a highly controversial means of Americanization; the use of English as the medium of instruction in the Puerto Rican school system. The president told islanders, "It is regrettable that today hundreds of thousands of Puerto Ricans have little and often virtually no knowledge of the English language." Thirty-eight years of instruction had clearly had no effect, but Roosevelt felt that the need for English was greater than ever.

"Puerto Rico was a densely populated island." Many of "its sons and daughters" would need to emigrate to the mainland ,and they "will be greatly handicapped if they have not mastered English."

Thus, because "of the unique historical circumstance which has brought to them the blessings of American citizenship," islanders had to become bilingual. English was their passport to economic success and an "indispensible part" of American policy. It was essential "that the coming generation of American citizens in Puerto Rico grow up with complete facility in the English tongue. It is the language of our nation."[35]

Our nation. The coming generation. It was a blueprint for the future built on a U.S. assessment of Puerto Rico and its people. A 1930s U.S. resident of the island noted, "everything American had to be accepted as being best and unassailable, lest the Puerto Rican who criticized it be regarded as un-American—and so, in some cases, even lose his job." Of course, "no matter how well qualified by education or skill, Puerto Ricans were not permitted to hold top level jobs in such [American business] enterprises...As colonial subjects, and with rare exceptions, they were not admitted to the clubs and social life of the resident Americans."[36] Puerto Ricans should learn English, to speak to the many Americans who would not talk to them, would not treat them as equals, and would not stop taking pride in this fact: "No Puerto Ricans had ever set foot in their homes, except as servants"[37]

Virgin Islands

In Puerto Rico, servants tended to the needs of those who owned the sugar and managed the colony. In the Virgin Islands, servants did the same, but to rehabilitate the nation's "effective poorhouse," the Roosevelt administration offered a unique proposal; they put servants at the center of the economic strategy.

Ernest Gruening explained the administration's predicament to Congress in March of 1936. The idea was to take the islanders, especially on St. Croix, "off the backs" of the American taxpayers. Since 1917 it had cost the United States close to $4 million in "operating expenses." The administration was doing its best to reduce those expenditures, but Congress had to remember the president's responsibilities. When Representative Francis Culkin of New York asked, "Do you think our responsibilities there are greater toward these good people in the Virgin Islands than they are toward the average resident of the United States?" Gruening responded, "I think they are as great. They are greater to this extent, that we took them over without consulting them; we just annexed them and they are our wards....We have the same responsibility for them that a parent would have who went out and adopted a child, which is presumably as great as that to a child born to him."[38]

Representative Culkin agreed. The United States was "in a position of loco parentis," and that moved him to support the dual strategy outlined by Gruening. St. Croix would once again make rum, but "for the islands of St. Thomas and St. John the program has to be different." These islands had no agricultural base so "one part of the administration's program is to try and develop the tourist business and, concomitantly with the tourist business, what might be called the winter resident or long-term resident business."[39]

In background meetings with staff members, Gruening had carefully analyzed the island's economic possibilities. St. Thomas and St. John were among the most beautiful islands in the Caribbean. They boasted a near perfect climate and a thoroughly inviting "Old World atmosphere." Unfortunately, the Virgin Islands were also "undiscovered." Only three tourist ships had visited St. Thomas in 1933, and the figure for 1934 was eighteen.[40] The Roosevelt administration proposed to make the islands a mecca for tourists and a haven for those in need of servants. Gruening told Congress, "We believe that St. Thomas might be developed as a place where continental Americans, people who are retired either in civil life, artists, writers, and so forth, or former Government officials who are able to spend a part of the year in warmer climates, may go."[41]

This vision was threatened by Congress. Gruening's testimony ocurred before the House Committee on Merchant Marine and Fisheries. The administration wanted a perpetual exemption from the coastwise shipping laws. When the president said the islands had sufficient ships arriving, then the U.S. laws would go into effect. Otherwise, the exemption would continue indefinitely, and Gruening would have the legal collateral required to attract the investors who would build hotels and the winter visitors who would build their part-time houses.

Chairman Schuyler Otis Bland (of Virginia) was skeptical. He explained the problems with the

Philippines. A presidential exemption had been granted to those islands, but every time the committee proved that the Philippines should be part of the American coastline, the president refused to rescind the exemption. The required U.S. ships existed, but the president never kept his word.

Would the same thing happen in the Virgin Islands? Bland said, "I have just wondered what is behind this thing, where the nigger is in the woodpile?" Bland suspected that "the nigger" was in Puerto Rico. Interests there were using the Virgin Islands as an opening wedge. When the Virgin Islands got their exemption, the Puerto Ricans would seek to ride their coattails. Congress would be stuck with the Philippines as an independent nation, and two Caribbean islands would be taken off the list of coastal protectorates.[42]

Gruening eventually allayed the committee's fears. The indefinite exemption was granted, and the administration thus secured the tourist and winter resident investments which had—by 1936—already been made.

A cornerstone of Gruening's plans was Bluebeard's Castle, a hotel. This was the once magnificent fort of an eighteenth century pirate; it overlooked the harbor, and Gruening had spent a considerable amount of time and money resurrecting it. Its newly constructed "adjacent accommodations" (for the winter residents) were a symbol of the "tourist mecca" to come.

To islanders like Knud Knud-Hansen, however, the hotel was a "temple for race prejudice." Five percent of islanders entered the hotel as servants while ninety-five percent were kept at "a safe distance" from the "white" monument. To Knud-Hansen, a Danish doctor who had lived and worked on the islands for more than twenty years (he was appointed Commissioner of Health by the Roosevelt administration), Bluebeard's Castle symbolized the reservations expressed by the Danish king in 1916. The king feared the Americans would bring their brand of racism to the islands. Knud-Hansen lived to see those fears realized. The Castle's lighthouse, once a symbol of love, was now a drawing card for tourists and long-term residents. They came "to criticize our shortcomings and do no more for us than try to buy a dollar's worth of stuff for fifty cents."[43]

Knud-Hansen was bitter. Franklin Roosevelt was optimistic. He took a very personal hand in all plans for the islands, but those for St. Croix moved the president to become an artist. He designed the label that would appear on the island's government produced rum, and he saw no problem with his suggested name: The label would say "Pure Colonial Rum." Under that heading would appear the designation "Virgin Islands, U.S.A."; and, in drawings that symbolized the old and new world, Roosevelt had a three masted sailing ship on the top of the label and a steamship, smoke bellowing from its stacks, on the bottom.[44]

In St. Croix, the heavy export duty imposed by Congress in 1917 had never been removed. It had been reduced in 1927, but in a world already overflowing with sugar, the small reduction (from $8 to $6 a ton) never saved the principal cane producers from economic ruin. The small growers received no relief from the stiff sugar tax. "A good squatter or homesteader" produced about 50 tons of cane a year. That was a possible income of $160, but even before he was paid for the cane, the small grower lost more than twelve percent of his income to the federal government. Few could survive, especially given the nature of land ownership on St. Croix.[45]

When Roosevelt assumed the presidency, twenty men owned 80 percent of St. Croix's land, and less than one percent of the families controlled more than ninety percent of all cultivated land. The island depended on sugar—83 percent of the employed were classified as farm laborers—but St. Croix's crop had no viable market and prohibition had long ago destroyed sugar's market in rum. The island appeared to be at a dead end when, thanks to the repeal of prohibition in December of 1933, President Roosevelt saw a market for colonial rum.[46]

Colonial rum was not the president's first choice. He had wanted "St. Croix Rum," but he changed his mind because the label had to make two points: this was "great-grandfather's rum come to life again," and it was "connected with the government." If the president ever caught the irony that the rum industry destroyed by Washington was now being resurrected by Washington, he never mentioned it in memos. His point was that those who pushed for the label "Government Rum" had no political sense; "there would be criticism in every part of the country if any liquor was put out as government rum. The fact is, of course, that while the government put up the necessary loan to get the company started, it is a corporation."[47]

The Colonial Rum label thus avoided a firestorm of protest. It suggested great-grandfather and the government, so President Roosevelt asked Secretary of the Interior Ickes to patent the colonial label for the U.S. government corporation. Ickes reported—in a memo underlined "restricted"—that "patent records show that colonial in combination with other words is used by six or more concerns as a trade name for rum." The president was out of luck. The secretary still voted for Peg Leg but, in order to stress the government connection, all the labelers compromised on "Government House" rum.[48]

Organizing the company was less difficult than choosing the rum label. The company received a one million dollar government loan; the finished rum would be the government's collateral; and the Virgin Islands Company would buy vacant sugar mills, oversee the growth of the cane, and then produce the liquor in the government's factory.[49] By 1936, the company was producing rum under the Government House label, and it gave 500 people desperately needed permanent employment. For all the joy on the islands, there was controversy in Washington.

The issue was taxes and who would get them. Roosevelt wanted to make certain that, as in Puerto Rico, the excise taxes returned to the island. He never raised the issue of taxation without representation—the president's idea was to help the islanders with much needed funding—but Congress refused to abide by the president's wishes. All taxes derived from the rum returned to Washington, and, for one of the first times in United States history, a group of people were taxed without representation. Roosevelt struggled to get the taxes back to the people. Congress refused to budge, and the president knew why. A fellow named McCarver "had been working overtime to prevent passage in the House [it had already passed in the Senate] of the bill to authorize the treasury to pay back to the Virgin Islanders the taxes it collects from them." McCarver wanted the company to fail. His idea was "to buy the rum business cheap," and the president's idea was to publicize McCarver's selfishness.[50]

The president lost, and so did McCarver. The rum business was quite successful, the islanders continued to work, and the taxes without representation were such a windfall for the federal government that, when President Truman received a report on the islands in 1947, his briefing papers included a Virgin Islands balance sheet. On the left side of the sheet was the $25 million paid for the islands, the ten million paid for naval and civil administration (1917-1946), and a variety of other costs. Total costs: $48,773,648. The right side of the sheet had only one heading: "Internal Revenue Collections on Rum Exports, 1934 thru June 1946." The total was $51,197,643. After thirty years in the Virgin Islands, the government showed a profit of more than $2.4 million.[51] It was good news for Washington but bad news for the islanders. In 1948, the government would once again seek to drive islanders out of the rum business it had first destroyed and then resurrected.

The Virgin Islanders lived under a military government for fourteen years. When Congress finally approved the Organic Act of the Virgin Islands in June of 1936, these "subjects" of the United States were once again denied many of the Constitution's most elemental and admired rights.

The governor was appointed by the president of

the United States. The governor's secretary, a very powerful position, was also appointed by the president of the United States. The former colonial councils became municipal councils (one for St. Croix, one for St. Thomas and St. John), and they had the right to overrule the governor but the ultimate authority rested with the president. He could veto any bill passed by the people's representatives, even if two-thirds of those representatives had passed it over the veto of the appointed governor.

Judges were also appointed by the president. The islands never received even non-voting representation in Congress. While they did get all the tax receipts (except the rum) returned to the island's treasury, they could not tax the main business of St. Croix. Since local taxes cannot be levied on the property of the United States, the Virgin Islands Corporation was never on St. Croix's tax rolls. Thus, it paid no taxes, except the ones that finally allowed the federal government to earn a profit on its Virgin Islands purchase.[52]

Universal suffrage was finally granted—out of 25,000 citizens only 1200 were eligible to vote in 1935—but not without a fight. Donald Boreham, an elected member of the St. Thomas Colonial Council, explained the people's predicament: "We are beggars, we have been bought by the United States and we are in the position right now of the dog that was bought and who is expected to go out into the butcher shop and get his own bone."[53]

The administration offered that bone, but Congressman Bert Lord of New York wondered if this was really the right time to feed the islanders. He understood Ernest Gruening's point: the vote actually meant nothing since "the president has a final veto and the governor has the power to exercise his persuasive powers with the local legislature, and it requires a two-thirds vote to overrule him." Giving islanders the vote was "not going too far."[54]

Lord still had his doubts. He wanted to put off universal suffrage for another five years. "You are bringing in a new element that has been kept out of the voting and they are going to be anxious to elect from their own class and I think we should hold more of a rule over them during that time and not have to bring all these things to the president...You are just making the president unnecessary trouble."[55]

Gruening won this battle. All islanders got the right to vote; but in the bill that finally became law, Virgin Islanders included a provision that might have appealed to Congressman Lord. Members of one American colony discriminated against members of another. For years the Puerto Rican migrants envisioned by President Roosevelt had traveled to the Virgin Islands for employment. Like the Haitians in Cuba, they had established a new life, a life that threatened "native" Virgin Islanders. So, the 1936 Organic Act said a person could vote if he or she was a U.S. citizen, twenty-one years of age, *and able to read and write the English language.*[56]

The Puerto Ricans were thus disenfranchised. It was a discrimination worthy of Washington and a fitting way of bringing democracy to America's second colony, the Virgin Island of the United States of America.

Cuba

What is a good neighbor? In the United States it's someone who minds their own business. They mow their lawn, they paint their house, and they talk over the fence when they see each other on the weekend or when they ask to borrow a needed tool or a cup of sugar. Few good neighbors ever become close friends; in fact, the essence of the everyday concept borders on indifference. You don't bother me, I won't bother you, and neither of us will do any-thing—e.g., sell our house to an undesireable fami-ly—that threatens property values.

In November of 1938, President Roosevelt wel-comed a visitor from Cuba. Just before Colonel Fulgencio Batista arrived, the president received a briefing memo from Sumner Welles, his Under Secretary of State.

As minister to Cuba in 1933, Welles told his superiors (on August 30, 1933) that the political tur-moil—murders, strikes, student demonstrations—enveloping the country was due to a simple fact: "the laboring classes have suffered under an absolute dictatorship for the last three years; and their lead-ers have been arrested and frequently assassinated." Welles suggested a "strictly limited intervention,"[57] but when President Roosevelt refused to follow his advice, Welles watched as Sergeant Batista took con-trol of the Cuban government. The under secretary understood Batista's character, so he now tried to explain it to the president.

Batista disliked Americans. His father had labored on a sugar plantation owned by the United Fruit Company and, "remembering the policy that the United Fruit Company pursued until recently in

203

its dealings with its employees in the smaller American republics, it is by no means unnatural that Batista should have reached adult age with a very strong prejudice against the United States in general and large American corporations in particular."[58]

The sugar companies the U.S. government sponsored exploited their employees, and the exploitation produced a "very strong prejudice" against the United States and its business interests. This was no basis for a friendship, but the president could win Batista over if he remembered these facts: the man was "inherently suspicious," "never surfeited with flattery," and "very quick to learn." Granted, "it is certain that he has profited from his position in a financial sense," but money always assumed a secondary position in Batista's hierarchy of goals. Power was this man's medium, "and at the present time he is determined to become, whether in the immediate future or a few years from now, President of the Republic."

Batista was already president. He lacked the title, but President Federico Laredo Bru had been installed by Batista and his soldiers. Bru was the third president "elected" by Batista since 1933, and there was really no doubt who ruled the Republic. The formal title would come in time, especially if President Roosevelt continued to practice the studied indifference of a good neighbor.

Welles made three suggestions, all followed by the president. First, stress national security. The United States needed Batista's help with Guantanamo, so get him to cooperate "in all that relates to the defense of the continent." Second, stress the need to preserve deomocratic institutions.

"Cuba had now drifted for five years without a constitution and without a constitutional government," but Welles nevertheless suggested that the president ask the dictator to hold early elections. "Any statement that you make to him with regard to the need to maintain democracy unimpaired throughout the continent will have a very powerful effect upon him and will tend to prevent him from resorting to dictatorial methods."[59]

Welles final suggestion concerned corruption. Because Batista was ignorant—he had a distinct "lack of knowledge"—and because "of the corrupt character of many of his closest advisors," Batista was "continually favoring projects" which, while said to benefit the people, "were in reality schemes to enrich the individuals who concoct these projects."

To a man with a good memory—and Welles had written a two volume history of the Dominican Republic—this sounded like Haiti's wavy railroad, McDonald's nonexistent bananas, or the Santo Domingo Improvement Company.

In 1938, the Good Neighbor Policy dictated this approach. Tell Batista "that you would be disposed to see that the advice of the best experts that we possess in the administration is gladly made available to him." The United States would do what it could because, even after forty years of failing, we still believed in the power of American expertise. But, we were not going to intervene because, in sharp contrast to a meddlesome neighbor, the only aim of a good one was to avoid "the creation of situations embarassing both to the Cuban people and to ourselves."[60]

The advice accepted by the president symbolized the Good Neighbor Policy. For example, when Welles assumed his Cuban post in early 1933, he agreed with his Hoover administration predecessor: President Machado was responsible for the "recent murder of students," his continued assumption of presidental power was unconstitutional, and his regime could be characterized as "a military repression."[61]

The United States had already given up on military interventions—except as an absolute last resort—by the time Batista installed his first president in January of 1934. Welles' ministry helped the president define the meaning of the Good Neighbor's nonintervention ideal. The United States would not use troops. When it did intervene, Washington would do its best to avoid being noticed. President Roosevelt stipulated that "it should of course be made clear that request for any assistance from Welles originates from the Cuban Government and people and is not suggested in first instance by Washington."[62]

Today it's called plausible deniability. In the 1930s it was the Good Neighbor Policy. But, whatever the label, the axis is expediency.

In 1933, the Caribbean was exploding. The chaos in Cuba was complimented by an armed revolution in Puerto Rico and destitution in the Virgin Islands. Al Capone's instructor was in charge of the Dominican Republic, the United States was still eager to get out of Haiti, and, now returning home to work for Frank Dillingham at Central Romana were the thousands of Haitians deported by the Cubans.

Given this level of failure, President Roosevelt

could have questioned the deepest assumptions of American policy. He could have tried to comprehend the extent to which the United States bore responsibility for a region ruled by dictators and dominated by sugar's dead-time.

What the Caribbean got was the Jones-Costigan Act, and, even before that, a presidential pledge of nonintervention: "The definite policy of the United States from now on [it was December 28, 1933] is one opposed to armed intervention."[63]

If this policy was based on a recognition of responsibility for Cuba (or Puerto Rico or the Dominican Republic), it might have produced change in the Caribbean. But what Roosevelt (and Hoover before him) wanted to avoid were situations embarrassing to ourselves and to the Cubans.

Thus, in May of 1934, the United States abrogated the Platt Amendment. The Cubans were free to do as they pleased, but, before they did so, the Roosevelt administration imitated the blackmail practiced in 1903. To get Guantanamo we held on to the Isle of Pines; to keep Guantanamo we erased the Platt Amendment, and the Cubans made no effort to question our military terms. Sumner Welles said that when he negotiated with the representatives of Sergeant Batista and President Mendieta in early 1934, "there was actually very little disagreement as to the provisions to be included therein." It was all worked out in Welles' office at the State Department, and, in exchange for abrogating the Platt Amendment, the Cubans gave the United States rights in perpetuity to Guantanamo. The United States would leave only if the two parties mutually agreed to terminate the lease, or, even more unlikely, the United States abandoned the base.[64]

Abrogating the Platt Amendment meant that the United States avoided responsibility for embarrassing political and economic situations; the navy and the president got the bases required for cruising the Atlantic as well as the Caribbean; and, all over Latin America, leaders praised the new president's now demonstrated commitment to nonintervention. Meanwhile, as his 1938 visit proved, Batista and his cronies milked the Cuban people; Congress bottle necked the Caribbean economies with its sugar quotas; and the president's brand of good neighborliness included sustained support, not only for a "mild" dictator like Batista, but for a man who, in October of 1937, would order the slaughter—using machetes and sharks—of 17,000 Haitians.

His name was Harvey Bundy. He worked for the State Department, and in 1931, he worked out the first of many financial compromises with General Rafael Trujillo. The general was broke. Given the amortization provisions of the 1926 and 1922 loans, there was no way he could meet the "solemn" obligations to the bondholders whose security was the will of the United States government to intervene in the Dominican Republic.

The State Department first tried to find bankers who would give Trujillo the funds needed to pay both his principal and interest obligations. As Bundy told his superiors, "the Dominican Government would not consent to the financial control which the bankers insisted upon writing into the proposed loan contract."[65]

The general made a bet that the Americans

would never intervene, and he was right. Bundy first found a way to divert funds from the payments due. He then indicated that, "even though treaty rights expressly permit interference," the United States refused to intervene. Such a policy would "benefit neither nation" and, even more important, such a policy might force Bundy and his colleagues to admit that they had built in General Trujillo's bribes to the diversion arrangements then being made. As the State Department put it in a memo which summed up the Republic's debts for the incoming Roosevelt administration, "President Trujillo also incurred campaign expenses of an unascertained amount of a nature usually assumed by the Government of a Latin American country in the case of a revolution."[66]

The general had bribed associates, and he had paid other associates to kill former associates. This was a costly way to do business. Trujillo could have paid these expenses out of the substantial earnings then being amassed by his wife. She was sharply discounting the paychecks of the many government employees who, desperate for funds, could not wait until the United States helped the Dominican government obtain the needed loans.[67]

No one asked the Trujillos to dip into their own resources. The State Department simply folded the bribes into the total sum owed; and the Trujillos cashed the discounted paychecks with portions of the funds they were permitted to divert. On October 23, 1931, Secretary of State Stimson sent a message to the general: He understood that the emergency loan arrangements made by the Dominican Government were "contrary to the provisions" of the treaty signed in 1924, and contrary to "the agreement with the bankers acting as fiscal agents of the loan." But, because "it is the firm intent of the Dominican Government to make as soon as possible the payments which are now being deferred," the general should please "accept, sir, the renewed assurances of my highest consideration."[68]

This was the first of the many diversions Trujillo would receive. By January of 1934, the general was refusing to make the payments which he had promised to make. Ambassador Arthur Schoenfeld reminded the Dominicans that the emergency law was itself "an admitted violation of solemn international obligations." To violate the violation was unthinkable, until his superiors explained to Schoenfeld that that was what the Roosevelt administration proposed to do. The American minister had assumed he was supposed to press the Dominicans to keep their word, but he was informed "that it had been more or less understood in Washington" that there would be another long postponement of amortization payments.[69]

By June of 1936, General Trujillo was threatening the president of the United States. He was still stalling on his financial obligations, but, when Schoenfeld asked about the money, he was reminded of the Good Neighbor Policy. The Dominicans "were at a loss to reconcile" the pressure to pay with the pledge to avoid intervention. The treaty certainly gave the United States those rights, "but the Dominican Government was confident that the American government entertained no aim in relation to the Dominican Republic which was out of harmony with the policy enunciated in recent years by the

Rum, Revolution, and Moral Embargoes

American government in relation to all the countries in this [the Caribbean] area."[70]

The general said "make me" and the president gave these instructions to his minister: "The existing obligations of the United States Government towards the holders of Dominican external bonds and other holders of valid claims against the Dominican Government remained *secondary* to the postulates of the Good Neighbor Policy."[71] [emphasis added]

In August of 1936, Sumner Welles told Ambassador Schoenfeld "that your government desires to concern itself in a minimum degree with the fiscal affairs of the Dominican Republic."[72] Schoenfeld soon wrote back that "I see no advantage nor even international honesty in keeping up the fiction that the two governments are governed by it" [the 1924 Treaty].[73] And in an assault on the principles which had moved the United States to control the Dominican customs houses for 31 years, the United States agreed to give "very careful consideration" to this request from the Dominican government.

The Dominicans wanted to be treated like the Haitians. The United States had formally evacuated Haiti in 1934, but, given its treaty obligations, the Roosevelt administration was trying to help the Haitians keep their fiscal house in order. *The deal given to the Haitians was permission to borrow from foreign bankers.* This was the same policy which had moved Bryan and Wilson to intervene in Haiti and the Dominican Republic. The State Department had told the Haitians that "the government of the United States would, of course, be delighted if Haiti could obtain at this time a refunding loan on reasonable terms from responsible bankers which would retire the 1922 bonds and thus automatically abrogate the Protocol of 1919." The loan could be obtained from "bankers either in this country or elsewhere," and, indifferent to the history in 1905 and 1911, the State department was even willing to allow the bankers to control Haiti's customs houses.[74]

The bankers selected were Schroder and Company. They were going to give the Haitians the money so that their banking group "could liberate all or part of blocked mark credits in Germany belonging to certain clients of Schroder and Company." The Haitians, however, would be forced to spend their borrowed funds in Germany. They would thus purchase from a nation controlled by Adolf Hitler "the construction equipment and materials to be used in Haiti's public works projects."[75]

It was this kind of deal that the Dominicans wanted. They never obtained it in 1937 because it was easier for the administration to concern itself to a minimum degree in Trujillo's financial affairs. Dominicans with a sense of history asked if the U.S. had planned to disregard the treaty for nearly a decade, why was it forced on the Dominican Republic in the first place? No one could argue that Roosevelt (or Hoover) had acted on democratic principles because, as he and Sumner Welles watched Trujillo use the new money to enrich himself, Dominican funds were still paying off the interest on the old debts contracted by the U.S. military occupation in 1922 and, going back even further, the Santo Domingo Improvement Company.[76]

Meanwhile, attracted by fascism, Trujillo had begun wearing "unusual tropical attire": a greatcoat and jackboots. He had also ordered members of his

Partido Dominicano to stop shaking hands. The new greeting was an imitation of Hitler's 'Seig Heil' salute, and it was offered in a city that had been renamed for the general. In 1935, he proudly changed the name of the oldest permanent European settlement in the New World. Santo Domingo became Ciudad Trujillo. The newspapers now referred to the general as "Generalissimo Doctor President Rafael Trujillo, Benefactor de la Patria."[77]

The general had a helper named Major Thomas Watson, on loan from the Marine Corps. His assigned task was to help train the Dominican army, but based on a marine brotherhood that dated back to the early 1920s, the major actually served as the president's "personal confidential advisor." Watson always had an envied access to the generalissimo. The American minister, for example, feared he would "wear out his welcome"; Watson saw the president every day. In the presence of the American minister, Watson told a mainland businessman that "all the Americans in this country were here for the purpose of exploiting it to the utmost."[78]

In his first tour of duty (which ended in 1932), Watson made social and political waves. He and his wife rarely associated with any Americans; she boasted that she preferred the company of Dominicans; and he not only believed "in the high character of Trujillo," he also argued that "peace and order can be maintained by military force alone." In Santo Domingo, ministry officials feared that Watson—and the United States—would be "blamed for continuing Trujillo in power by increasing the efficiency of the army."[79]

When Trujillo asked for an extension of Watson's

(and other marines) services, the Hoover administration refused. Undersecretary of State Francis White explained that "the marines feel that Trujillo pretty much belongs to them." White feared that Trujillo "would doubtless entrust many matters to them outside their military duties, just as he entrusted manifold duties to Watson in the past." Moreover, "men of their character and training are apt to feel in a foreign country that they are to some extent beholden to the president only and will endeavor to do what he wants; that is, they are apt to be inclined to put his personal fortunes ahead of the real interests of the country."[80]

President Roosevelt personally intervened when General Trujillo asked that Watson be returned to the Dominican Republic. Roosevelt signed a letter of approval on September 18, 1933, and he refused to consider the fears and criticisms expressed by the Foreign Policy Association. When it heard rumors that Watson had been reassigned, the association told the president that "Trujillo is regarded as a dictator and has been charged with various atrocities during his term in office....The assignment of the two United States marine officers would almost inevitably be used by President Trujillo to strengthen his position in the face of widespread opposition and to bolster up a tottering dictatorship. At a time when you are bending every effort to establish firmer relations of friendship with Latin American countries such a development in Santo Domingo might be extremely unfortunate."[81]

The association misread the president. Especially in the Dominican Republic, his interpretation of the Good Neighbor Policy was far more cynical than his Republican predecessor. Hoover refused to reassign him once Major Watson's problems arose. Roosevelt reassigned him even when the problems were part of a documented record, and Trujillo's atrocities were well known. So, to reassign Watson in 1933 was to give Trujillo the seal of approval he needed and the training he (and his army) desired. It was an act of friendship toward the generalissimo, and an act of enmity toward the Dominicans and Haitians who would be slaughtered by the deadly efficiency of the Dominican army.

Rafael Trujillo never killed 17,000 Haitians. He only ordered their deaths. Hundreds of Dominican soldiers killed 17,000 Haitians and, along with Trujillo and his murderers, those who trained the soldiers must bear some responsibility for the results of their military education.

Roosevelt wanted to avoid any and all political complications. Trujillo wanted to "whiten" Dominican society. What happened in October of 1937 was that a variety of other factors—large numbers of illegal Haitians near the border, deportations from Cuba, the failure of the Dominican government's deportation policy, Dominican soldiers refusing to stop profiting from the sale of Haitian labor— moved Trujillo to erase a population, but even he could never hide such unprecedented slaughter.[82]

The killings occurred over a number of days in October. In the remote areas near the border, soldiers simply herded the Haitians into large groups and then began to slaughter them with everything from guns to machetes.

Near the pier at Montecristi nearly a thousand men, women and children screamed as soldiers tied their hands behind their backs; when everyone was shackled, soldiers forced their captives to walk off the pier. With soldiers watching, sharks devoured the helpless victims. The next day the tide washed in scores of half-eaten men, women and children. The Haitian remains made the beaches a graveyard that contained heads but no headstones. Trujillo had finally whitened his society, but nothing could wash away the stories about his blood red massacre of 17,000 Haitians.[83]

The American embassy sent one of its first telegrams on October 7, 1937. Haitians were racing across the border because of an inflammatory speech given by Trujillo. The Dominican minister said he would check into the exaggerated reports, but he reminded the American minister that it was probably just another instance of Haitians refusing to pay the taxes owed to the Dominican government.[84]

By October 25 the American embassy knew the truth. In a "strictly confidential" telegram to the secretary of State, embassy officials indicated that the incident was "much more serious than we had originally thought." The horrors were "indescribable" because "in this barbaric massacre there was no respect for sex or age. Haitians were killed until the very last person. Even young children and babes in arms were grabbed by their ankles, their brains were blown out, or they were smashed against the closest rock or tree." The death toll was close to 5,000 people, but well-informed sources also indicated that from a population of 17,000 Haitians, "today practically none remain."[85]

Although President Roosevelt received detailed briefings from his ministers, in public he avoided

216

reporters' questions. Asked (at a November 9 news conference) if he was giving "personal attention" to the Dominican-Haitian trouble, he responded, "Yes and no. I am familiar with it as it goes on." He had just met with the American ambassador to Haiti, and, even though he told reporters that his meeting with the Haitian minister was a "tea visit," the president was actively trying to defuse an embarrassing political situation.[86]

The president offered to mediate. The Haitians agreed; Trujillo refused; and the president sent a letter to the Dominican Republic. He asked his "great and good friend" to follow the example of Haiti. Come to the bargaining table "in accord with the traditional desire for peace for our new world."[87]

Trujillo hedged. He wanted Dominicans to judge themselves, but on December 21, 1937, he accepted an arbitration procedure. President Roosevelt congratulated the general for his willingness to abide by the "peaceful procedures" of law.

As the president stressed, "Permit me to further express my gratification by reason of Your Excellency's statement that the Government of the Dominican Republic will not give the slightest ground for a disturbance of the peace of America, in which all the peoples of the New World have so great and legitimate an interest."[88]

Within hours of the president's message, Congressman Hamilton Fish made a courageous statement in Congress. What he wanted to talk about was something that "happened two-and-a-half months ago, about which everybody in the State Department knows....This is the most outrageous atrocity that has ever been perpetuated on the

American continent. It is true that there is a question as to the number of people slaughtered...but I do not think that anybody in this country or in Haiti denies the fact that the floodgates of hate, cruelty, terror, lust, and slaughter were let loose for three days there [in the Dominican Republic]."[89]

Fish was wrong. Not only had the president just congratulated Trujillo, in Congress, Fish's colleagues interrupted his speech. Congressman Rankin of Mississippi seemed amazed. "The gentleman is not leaving the impression that these were white people who killed these colored people is he? He is not attempting to leave that impression I hope."

Fish appeared to be caught off guard. Rankin noted "as a matter of fact, they are all colored people." Fish said "No, they were Spanish and mixed bloods." Rankin disagreed with that so the two men then discussed the "races" that peopled Hispaniola.

It was an ignoble performance by Fish's colleagues who, after criticizing his call for an expression of national indignation, listened to Congressman Rankin end the long debate with this comment: "I feel like an old woman in one of the Southern states did about her husband....He was always nosing into other people's affairs and accusing them of things of which they were not guilty, criticizing people when they ought not to be criticized....The old fellow finally passed away and his wife erected a monument to his memory and on it inscribed this epitaph: 'Rest in peace until we meet again.'"

That was Rankin's—and Congress'—message to Fish and the 17,000 Haitians. While their bodies lay in mass graves, he joked about funeral epitaphs on the House floor: "I hope Mr. Speaker that the gentleman from New York will now curb his indignation and rest in peace until we meet again." The Congressional Record indicates that there were two responses to Rankin's remark: "Applause and laughter."[90]

In February of 1938, the Haitians accepted a cash indemnity for their murdered population. It worked out to roughly $60 a body. "The agreement," said President Roosevelt, "was added proof, if such had been needed, that the peaceful solution of international controversies has become the established practice of this hemisphere."[91]

Elsewhere the president had a very different moral perspective. When the Japanese engaged in the strategic bombing of Nanking on December 10, 1937, an estimated 10,000 civilians were killed, and the president labeled this attack "immoral." Four months after Trujillo paid his blood money to the Haitians, President Roosevelt declared a "moral embargo" on the shipment of arms to Japan. He "strongly opposed" the sale of airplanes or aeronautical equipment that would aid or encourage the practice of civilian bombings."[92]

Trujillo's reaction to this display of American indignation was never recorded. Neither was the reaction of thousands of Haitians killed with American weapons (even the machetes were made in Connecticut). However, those victims knew the real meaning of the Good Neighbor Policy: it was all show and no substance.

The president, especially after 1938, always wanted to use the Caribbean as an island shield for the United States of America. Puerto Rico would be the center of that Caribbean shield, but, as Senator Lundeen told his colleagues on July 17, 1939, the president ought to also acquire every island from Trinidad to Greenland. "They are all American and should be under our defense control. Let us act now before it is too late."[93]

The president acted. His strategy revolved around the so-called "bases deal," and it represented the first systematic U.S. analysis of the entire Caribbean. It was a bold vision, guided by an underlying idea: As the president put it on January 11, 1941: "If we can get our Naval bases why, for example, should we buy them with two million headaches, consisting of that number of human beings who would be a definite economic drag on this country, and who would stir up questions of racial stocks by virtue of their new status as American citizens."[94]

The Island Shield

"There is a great moral question involved here and it is a question that will shape and color the history of the world after this war is over. To get right down to the question, what inherent right has France to territory which she has seized, sometimes by war, as recently as the 1880's, any more than has Japan to seize by force certain territories of China which she has now occupied? The only difference is in point of time."

—Sumner Welles, August 9, 1942[1]

The officers disobeyed orders. Even though Congress "strictly forbade" professors at the Air Corps Tactical School to advocate the terror bombing of civilian populations, "aviation enthusiasts" did as they pleased. From 1926 until the beginning of World War II, American fliers learned that an elemental aspect of the next war would be "to attack the people themselves, especially those concentrated in the cities."[2]

Terror, or obliteration, bombing was difficult for Americans to accept. Leaders like President Roosevelt labeled as odious and immoral, not only the Japanese bombing of Nanking, but the German Luftwaffe's devastation of Guernica during the Spanish civil war. As the *New York Times* noted on April 27, 1937, "the object of the bombardment was the demoralization of the civil population and the destruction of the cradle of the Basque race."[3]

221

Meanwhile, the U.S. Army Air Corps told Congress that anyone producing war-related supplies "is potentially a part of the warring forces and will be so regarded in future conflicts....The nerve centers of a nation will be destroyed so as to break the will of that nation to fight."[4]

Americans were confused about morality, and about the role of air power in the next war. What if the Germans managed to obtain a foothold in Brazil, and from there took control of Puerto Rico or Hispaniola? As Guernica showed, they would have no hesitation about using the Caribbean as a take-off point for the terror bombing of the North American mainland.

The president appointed a commission headed by Admiral A. J. Hepburn. His report to the president helped transform the significance of the Caribbean for the United States. In 1938 neither the navy nor the Army Air Corps had any meaningful installations in Puerto Rico. The forces at Guantanamo included 17 naval officers, 153 sailors, 5 marine officers, and 129 leathernecks.[5] Until the late thirties, Cuba and Puerto Rico, Trinidad and Jamaica were nothing more than potential bases of military operation. Nobody cared about these colonies and nations until, as the president noted, "the present war became imminent, [and] it was obvious that the chain of islands running in a great arc from Florida to the shoulder of South America, enclosing the Caribbean Sea, formed a vast natural shield for the Panama Canal, suited in distance and conformation to the uses of the military plane."[6]

Admiral Hepburn suggested a series of air bases all over the Caribbean. He argued, and the president agreed, that the need "for additional shore-based facilities for aircraft far overshadows that for destroyers, submarines, or mines." The problem was where to place the bases. The United States owned only small parts of the Caribbean. We had, said the admiral, a "dearth of U.S. possessions in the area." For the air bases he planned to establish, the admiral chose Guantanamo, San Juan, and St. Thomas.

In Cuba and the Virgin Islands, the admiral suggested small operations, but for Puerto Rico, the admiral had a grand vision. The island was in the center of the arc depicted by the president, so "a base this far eastward in the Caribbean will be of major strategic importance." The 340 acre site at Isla Grande, in the center of San Juan, was a "Category A" facility; it had the highest priority even if military planners had elected to build "on a quivering lake of mud 20 to 30 feet deep." The supervising engineer complained to Washington that he had already driven thousands of piles and poured tons of solid fill into the Isla Grande mud hole. It was frutiless to continue. His job was impossible. The response from Washington was blunt: "You were sent to San Juan to build an airfield, not to select a site."[7]

The building continued, but even before the site was finally completed, at a then-astonishing cost of $27 million, the president of the United States bombed it. From ships at sea, the president watched (on February 25,1939) as the navy held what has since become an annual Caribbean event: practice or "mimic war." Using 150 to 175 airplanes, fliers bombed San Juan for eighteen hours. Their stated military goal was "storage tanks for fuel oil" but, beyond the practice given to pilots was the political significance of the president's well-publicized participation: Puerto Rico was to become the Pearl Harbor of the Caribbean. It would be turned into a "keystone of our national defense." To illustrate this change, the president made Admiral William Leahy governor of Puerto Rico in May of 1939. His appointed task was to prepare the island for any military contingencies.[8]

Leahy focused on the Isla Grande Air Field, but as the threat of war escalated into the obliteration bombing of Warsaw (in September of 1939) and the fall of France (in May of 1940), American strategists perceived a naval opportunity. The British requested destroyers. If history calls fulfilling this request a courageous political act, it was also a hard-nosed deal to get exactly what Franklin Roosevelt wanted: "Complete control of the Caribbean."[9]

The president's military advisors said the Caribbean was a "highway literally filled with seaborne traffic essential to our economic life and welfare." Total control was "fundamental to our national defense" because the United States needed it to defend the canal, the "vital gulf area" and South America. So, when Winston Churchill's request for destroyers arrived in Washington, the president soon devised a way to help the British *and* get all the bases he wanted without any of the responsibilities, expenses, and criticism that came with managing colonial possessions.[10]

Prime Minister Churchill made his formal request in June of 1940. He told the president that, given the German submarine threat, "nothing is so important as for us to have 30 or 40 old destroyers you have already reconditioned. We can fit them very rapidly with our asdics and they will bridge the gap of six months before our wartime new construction comes into play. We will return them or their equivalents to you without fail at six months notice if at any time you need them. The next six months are vital....Not a day should be lost."[11]

President Roosevelt accepted the prime minister's evaluation; in an August 2, 1940 Cabinet meeting he and his associates agreed, "without any dissenting voice, that the survival of the British Isles under German attack might very possibly depend on their getting these destroyers." Despite this dire prediction, Roosevelt hesitated, primarily because he needed to find a way to bypass the certain congressional opposition. Wendel Wilkie said he would support the president, but he had no votes in Congress. Republican policy needed to be ascertained. Also, was it legal to send the destroyers?

Before these questions were answered, Roosevelt asked for two things from the British: an assurance that their fleet would never fall into German hands and rights to "landing grounds and naval facilities in British possessions off the East Coast." While Churchill accepted (on August 5) the request for landing fields and naval facilities, he stressed that the negotiations must remain a state secret. He still had "to make the arrangements with the various colonial governments concerned."[12]

The native inhabitants of Trinidad, Jamaica or St. Lucia never appeared in the dialogue between the two heads of state. One leader ruled colonies, the other wanted rights in those colonies. Even when Roosevelt began to talk about 99-year leases to large parcels of land on very small islands, nobody mentioned the people. The paramount issue was bases, linked to a British accusation that the Americans were driving a very "hard bargain" indeed.[13]

Roosevelt said he had a problem with the law and the American electorate. The former mandated that no weapons could change hands until and unless the chief of army or naval operations certified they were unnecessary for the nation's defense. Obtaining such permission would be easy but convincing the American people to effectively scrap their neutral stance was much harder.

The president explained his dilemma to Churchill in an August 13 message. He would deliver the destroyers, but, "such assistance, as I am sure you will understand, would only be furnished if the American people and the Congress frankly recognized that in return therefor the national defense and security of the United States would be enhanced."[14]

To get the boats, the British had to offer the United States the immediate right to buy or lease—for 99 years—bases on Newfoundland, Bermuda, the Bahamas, Jamaica, St. Lucia, Trinidad, and British Guiana. The president did indicate "that specific details need not be considered at this time and that such questions as the exact locations of the land which the United States might desire to purchase or lease could be readily determined upon subsequently through friendly negotiation between the two governments."[15]

Two days later Churchill agreed and stressed that his approval was contingent "on our being

226

assured that there will be no delay in letting us have the ships and flying boats." He agreed to the bases as long as they were leased since that was "much easier for us than the method of purchase."

Churchill never contemplated "anything in the nature of a contract, bargain, or sale between us." He told the president on August 22 that "our view is that we are two friends in danger helping each other as far as we can." Churchill thought a formal agreement spelled bad politics. "People will contrast on each side what is given and received. The money value of the armaments would be computed and set against the facilities and some would think one thing about it and some another."[16]

Churchill failed to grasp the president's intent. Americans never accepted the short end of the stick, even if their friends were in desperate shape. Sign the deal or forget the ships.

Churchill resisted. On August 25 he said he understood Roosevelt's problems. But, "your commitment is definite, ours unlimited." The United States would give the British fifty ships and the United States' part of the bargain would be concluded. The British would the United States as yet undetermined rights to lands which were so far undetermined. "Suppose we could not agree to all your experts asked for. Should we not be exposed to a charge of breaking our contract for which we have already received value."

Churchill said he required the proposed agreement to be more specific. England desperately needed the destroyers, but new construction was on the way "and we should not be justified in the circumstances if we gave a blank cheque on the whole of transatlantic possessions merely to bridge this gap through which anyhow we hope to make our way through with added risk and suffering."[17]

The president remained adamant. Lord Beaverbrook told Churchill that "if you are going to make a gift, well and good, if we are going to make a bargain, I don't want to make a bad one and this is definitely a bad one." Churchill finally agreed to the president's terms. The British would tell their people that legal and constitutional difficulties in the United States forced them to make an admittedly bad deal. Roosevelt would tell the American people that, for fifty decaying destroyers, he had "put a ring of steel around the United States that it would be impossible for Germany to penetrate and what could the president of the United States accomplish for his country greater than this?"[18]

Congress echoed this assessment of the agreement. In the House, members questioned the constitutionality of the deal, but even opponents found it hard to resist. As Cox of Georgia noted, "I cannot ignore the pragmatic results, and, though I do not accept the doctrine of justification, I would not withhold ratification. I think we exchanged a weaker for a stronger means of defense for our own security and safety....We transferred the destroyers for an insular ring that affords us a first line of defense. Self preservation is no less the first law of nations as it is for individuals."[19]

The president immediately sent Admiral John Greenslade and his colleagues to choose sites for the American bases. They were to make their decisions on military grounds, and, once they selected the sites, another Roosevelt envoy, Charles Taussig, would assess "social and economic conditions in the British West Indies." What kind of labor was available? What was the cost?

Answers to these questions were essential if anyone expected quick construction of the outer arc bases. But while the president impatiently waited for word about the British West Indies, he moved with dispatch in the American colonies.

The navy wisely decided to call the new Puerto Rican facility, Roosevelt Roads. It would become (in terms of land area) the largest *temporary* naval base in the world. To build the complex the navy planned to take over no less than 65 percent of the island of Vieques. Thousand of islanders would be forced to sell their lands and move to, among other places, the Virgin Islands. They agreed because of the pressure of the war, but, as Admiral Leahy later told President Truman, the unwritten understanding was that when the lands were no longer needed by the navy, "they would automatically revert to the People of Puerto Rico."[20]

The base promised to devastate Vieques. In the short term, islanders would make money in construction, but once the bases were completed, 65 percent of the island's best lands would have been removed from productive agricultural endeavors and would have been stricken from the tax rolls. As with rum in the Virgin Islands, the colony could not tax the federal government; with the navy on board the municipality would have no way to finance vital government services. Vieques reluctantly agreed to do its part, but the Americans had to leave once they won the war, or, if war was avoided, once they no longer needed the land.[21]

The navy also purchased 6,680 acres of land on the eastern side of the Puerto Rican mainland. This gave it control of both sides of the vital Vieques passage. The navy planned a base that would provide supporting services for 60 percent of the Atlantic Fleet. One plan envisioned 14 miles of breakwater to provide a "sheltered anchorage" for the entire fleet. All plans included a gigantic dry dock, fuel depot, hospital, and a major air station for both land and sea planes.[22]

Puerto Rico had been drafted into World War II. Some 25 separate facilities would be "requested" for military use as the island became the Gibraltar of the American Caribbean.

Elsewhere, however, the United States had Caribbean problems. Some of the British colonies threatened trouble because of the lands selected by Admiral Greenslade. In the Dominican Republic, Rafael Trujillo agreed to stop yelling 'Seig Heil' only if the United States would remove its customs receivership.

The Customs Receivership

Franklin Roosevelt agreed to eliminate the receivership even though his decision added up to a number of contradictions. If the proposed deal was approved by the Senate, the Dominican Republic would be thrown into default.[23] One major justification for the 1905 and 1916 interventions was to avoid default. The United States was now precipitating the condition it had sought to avoid. Why did the Dominicans have to endure two generations of lectures about fiscal responsibility if the United States could disregard what the Dominicans had been forced to accept?

When the United States intervened in 1905 it protected what President Theodore Roosevelt's advisor called a group of "merciless, blood-sucking money sharks." The investors who held the bonds in 1940 were scattered all over the United States; the "largest category" each held one bond of $1,000, and these Americans bought because of the government's ironclad guarantee. The United States intervened to save the sharks and disregarded the rights of a group of "average" Americans. In some cases the bonds were held by "churches, cemetery associations, and schools and universities."[24]

The United States knew that Trujillo was stealing the money earmarked to pay off the bonds. As early as 1936, the American receiver publicly reported that a series of new "consumption taxes" had surpassed in value the amounts formerly received in customs duties.[25] Trujillo had openly detoured large portions of the money required to pay off the debt; the United States had looked the other way for five years; and in 1940 Roosevelt proposed to do what he had intervened to avoid. In 1905, the idea was to have an honest, unbiased individual monitor the republic's finances. In 1940, the idea was to let a man the American minister compared to Al Capone supervise the funds that would be returned to the bondholders.

Why did Roosevelt make this "complete turnabout in attitude?"[26] What had happened to the solemn obligations Welles had forced the United States and the Dominicans to accept in 1924?[27]

Senators wanted answers to these questions. They agreed to hold hearings in executive session—

the two meetings were only declassified in 1980—but they nevertheless asked pointed questions of Green Hackworth, the State Department's legal advisor.

Hackworth said the receivership had been a "thorn in the side of the Dominican government for a long period of time." The Dominicans felt "somewhat humiliated at having in their ports foreign collectors of their revenues" so, "as a matter of national pride" the administration proposed to remove the receivership.[28] Senators Bennett Clark (of Missouri) and Arthur Vandenberg (of Michigan) were quite skeptical. Clark said that since the bondholders opposed the administration's request, "does that not confront the legal principle that security behind a debt cannot be changed without the consent of the creditor?"

Hackworth argued that having established the receivership, the United States was "fully competent" to dissolve it. Vandenberg presented a statement made (on November 28, 1933) by the American secretary of state to the Dominican minister in Washington. The statement said: "I beg to remind you that this department has no authority to vary or sanction the variation of the terms of the convention which provides for the service of the external debt of your government."

Hackworth said, "I do not try to get around that." Vandenberg had to recognize "that a government can always change its mind....That is one of the fundamentals of a government, that it cannot be bound forever and a day by what some official has said."

Senator Vandenberg: "Then we confront the naked proposition that the State Department's attitude in 1939 [when the agreement with Trujillo was first reached] was different from what it was in 1933 on this subject."

Mr. Hackworth: "There is no escape from that statement."[29]

Nor was there any escape when Senator Guy Gillette (of Iowa) said: "Your interest, I take it from your statement, is simply as a gesture or a concession in the interest of amity, and toward the pride of the Dominican Republic."

Mr. Hackworth: "Precisely so."

Senator Gillette: "And that is the only purpose?"

Mr. Hackworth: "That is the only purpose.[30]

Not really. At another point in his testimony he had underlined the effect of the dissolved receivership throughout Latin America. Senators called this to his attention and he agreed that, besides the Dominican Republic, the administration aimed to create "better feelings all around."

Vandenberg thought the administration had no "moral right" to change the treaty, and he agreed with the representatives of the bondholders when they cited the words of Franklin D. Roosevelt and (Secretary of State) Cordell Hull. On October 5, 1937, the president had said, "There must be a return to a belief in the pledged word, in the value of a signed treaty. There must be recognition of the fact that national morality is as vital as private morality." At the Inter-American Conference for the Maintenance of Peace, in Buenos Aires, Hull had stressed (on December 5, 1936) that "trust in each other's honor, and faith in its given word must be restored by the concerted resolve of all governments."[31]

Roosevelt's policy was rooted in expediency. As war approached, he wanted no problems in the Caribbean or in Latin America. His basic contention was that the end justified the means. To legitimize the government of a man who ordered the death of 17,000 Haitians was apparently an acceptable way to prepare the world for its struggle against fascism and communism. To enable a man who was mercilessly robbing his people to accumulate even more loot was an apparently acceptable way to create good neighbors.

The Senate did the president's bidding, and Trujillo had his way. No one asked questions such as, if Dominican pride was important in 1940, why was it not important in 1905 or 1916? And, if the U.S. had suddenly seen the error of its ways, was the nation not obligated to assume some significant responsibility for the last thirty-five years of Dominican history?

Throughout the hearings, and in the Congressional Record as well, senators stressed the rights of bondholders. But nobody talked about the Dominican people, the development of their economy under American auspices, or the nature of a regime that was created, sustained, and, in the 1940 policy reversal, thoroughly nourished by the United States of America.

The essential contention of this book is that we are not who we think we are. The United States has no right to a positive self-image in relation to the preservation of democracy or the creation of prosperity if the Caribbean is the issue. On the contrary, one administration after another acted only in its own interests. Even when an administration pursued a policy full of contradictions, it fled from the truth rather than facing up to it.

Consider a 1944 report to the secretary of state from the U.S. minister in the Dominican Republic. Trujillo's regime was "an enterprise operated primarily for the personal enrichment of himself, his relatives and his satellites. His greed results in the impoverishment of the Dominican people, economically and morally. The dictator's vanity, which not infrequently dictates his course of actions, is, colossal."[32]

The American minister also stressed that "Trujillo's dictatorship represents the negation of many of the principles to which the United States subscribes." However, Trujillo's overthrow was "not the responsibility of the American government nor would such action be consistent with our present commitments with respect to non-intervention. Trujillo is primarily a Dominican problem, for solution by the Dominican people."[33]

Our creation had become their problem. The United States would refuse to intervene until the Kennedy administration helped murder Trujillo in 1961. In the meantime, the Dominican Republic enjoyed the stability that allowed presidents to deal with the problems created by Admiral Greenslade's controversial selection of land in the British colony of Trinidad.

Trinidad

Admiral Greenslade had only one concern: how to get the best land for a major U.S. naval base. Trinidadians asked that he consider their economic and political prospects. The British planned to give the colonies some measure of self-rule in the near future, and no native "would ever consent to be sold for scrap" (*i.e.*, the destroyers). Political and economic power would have little meaning if the United States took—for 99 years—large chunks of the best land on the island.[34]

Greenslade's proposed base would hamper Trinidad's economic development and would also deprive poor Trinidadians of their only bathing beaches. Would he please consider a reclamation project of the Caroni Swamp? All concerned agreed that this would take much more time and money to build, but, given the 99-year American hold on the property, it seemed a reasonable compromise.

The admiral rejected this compromise after spending two weeks on Trinidad. As he told the Secretary of the navy in a report dated October 23, 1940, he agreed that the reclamation project was "extremely desireable" and technically feasible. But, "the engineering requirements for the proposed bases must give way to the military requirements, one of which is the earliest possible construction of the facilities."[35]

In an addendum to his report, Greenslade listed twelve other "military advantages" of the proposed Chaguaramas site. It was nearer to deep water, it had excellent locations for anti-aircraft defenses, it was "less susceptible to sabotage and dangers from internal disorders, it "provided a natural area for recreation for fleet personnel," and it was capable of being "immediately occupied."[36]

Immediacy was the operative word. His task was to prepare for war, and the Trinidadians sympathized with his military aims. But, in sharp contrast to the promises made to the Puerto Ricans on Vieques, the Trinidadians were being asked to relinquish their land for a century. They fought the admiral every step of the way, and they applauded the British governor when he went to Washington to plead the island's case for the Caroni Swamp.

Long before the governor left for the United States, Washington had asked London to pressure its colonial representatives. When the governor met with British and American officials at the British Embassy (on December 6, 1940), they let him talk and then told him what would happen. The governor reluctantly conceded defeat but, in a memo to President Roosevelt, the navy explained the public relations aspects of the governor's continued public resistance.

The British would "forward the governor's data to the State Department for such consideration as the United States might be able to give." The State Department would say that it had "carefully considered" the governor's arguments but, despite them, the navy would begin to build on Greenslade's preferred choice. Meanwhile, "the governor could read [the State Department's response] to his local legislature to show he had exhausted his efforts to have the United States undertake reclamation of the Caroni Swamp."[37]

With the Trinidadians on the president's team, Congress suddenly complained about "sordid" British behavior.[38] Senator Homer Bone (of Washington) wanted to know why "if Britain is in a death grapple with destiny, why cannot the British Government be as generous as this Government is being?" Bone had never read the summer 1940 correspondence in which the British complained that Roosevelt had driven a "hard bargain" indeed. Senator Bone had read a story about the Trinidadians complaints, and he then raised the issue foreseen by Winston Churchill: They had their destroyers so "it does not seem to me that on the part of Great Britain, there has been the ultimate of good faith, that ultimate of fair dealing with us, who have been very generous, which we had a right to expect."

Senator Wiley thought that his colleague "had made a real contribution to his country." He believed the United States had been "done good" in a number of international deals and, despite his pronounced British sympathies, the senator wished we took advantage of them the way they took advantage of us. "Taking into view that in the bloodstream of the British is the proverbial Scotch—and the Scotch know how to deal—we should have a few Scotchmen over here who would deal for America....We must have collateral. We must have good business brains on the job."[39]

The response in Congress was immediate; the Congressional Record notes there were even "manifestations of applause in the galleries." Senator Wiley had made a criticism with deep cultural roots; the United States expected full value for its destroyer dollars. However, neither Wiley, nor Bone, nor the Scotsman in the White House ever mentioned the long-range economic and political problems of Trinidad. No one discussed the possible indecency of 99-year lease rights for antiquated destroyers. Neither did anyone raise objections when Bone said that "some formula ought to be worked out whereby the United States government, or the local colonial

The Island Shield

government, as an agent of the United States..." would have the power to do as it pleased.

The United States would have colonial regimes act as agents. There was nothing wrong with this but there was something wrong with the British. "In a life-and-death grapple, it is not usually considered very decent, to say the least, to proceed on such a sordid basis as to retard an essential operation. That was my only reason for mentioning the matter. Any sordidness will, of necessity, not be on our part."[40]

Bone's complaints immediately produced a day of executive session hearings. Senator Ellender stressed "that anything that is said is not to be divulged on the outside," but the Senate Committee on Naval Affairs nevertheless wanted to know if the president had been hoodwinked.

Testifying for the navy was Admiral J. Moreell. In response to a question about ownership, he indicated that after 99 years the land did revert back to the British Government. The navy had considered buying the land, but since the U.S. government did not want to enter into questions of sovereignty— recall the president's January 11 decision to avoid the "two million headaches" who would be an "economic drag on this country"[41]—the navy settled for a century of control.

That satisfied most of the senators, who also were gratified that the navy would never pay any taxes to the colonies whose land they leased. Regarding the controversy, Moreell explained that the government of Trinidad had been "rather insistent"; they wanted us to take the swampland, but we said that that was "absolutely impossible," and they eventually gave in. So, said Senator Tunnell, "then there was no unfairness perpetrated on the American government, on the United States."

Admiral Moreell: "No. So far [it was February 25, 1941] we have gotten every site we wanted."[42]

Senators seemed satisfied by the admiral's assurances but Senator Lucas soon returned to the issue of swampland. "If you listen to some of these debates on the Floor of the Senate and some of these newspaper fellows you would think we are building them [the bases] all right out of the ocean."

Admiral Moreel: "As a matter of fact, it might interest the committee to know that down at Trinidad we are getting the very choice land, and it involves the acquisition of the swimming beaches used by the people from Port of Spain. I think that will be a considerable hardship on the local population."[43]

This statement satisfied the senators. They agreed that the bases deal "was the most important action in the reinforcement of our national defense that has been taken since the Louisiana purchase. Then as now, considerations of safety from overseas attack were fundamental."[44]

But, said Senator Gillette, what happened if a dispute arose before the final contracts were signed? "Say we do not accept the court award, say we cannot reach an agreement by negotiation, what is to be done? The destroyers are gone, the deal has been completed, and we have reached an impasse."

Senator Wiley: "We are in possession."

Senator Gillette: "In possession of what?"

Senator Wiley: "Of the land."

Senator Gillette got the point. Possession was ten/tenths of the law, and the courts meant nothing because, as the admiral assured his formerly skeptical audience, "essentially we have what we are after right now."[45] The British could do nothing in the midst of their life and death struggle; and the Trinidadians were powerless. It was a great deal for the United States, and, following the lead of Senator Bone, many Americans thought the bases deal underlined a cultural constant: the United States perpetually let its desire to help others overcome its need to obtain fair value for the nation's hard earned dollars.

Caribbean Commission

Charles Taussig had just returned from a two month tour of the Caribbean. His itinerary included virtually every island, but in his long report to President Roosevelt (submitted in early 1941), Taussig prefaced his analysis with this comment: He "did not attempt to make a detailed study of all the social and economic problems in the British West Indies." That was certainly necessary, but Taussig had a clear order: He was to "confine himself to a survey of the various factors in the life of these colonies which might affect directly or indirectly the government and people of the United States of America."[46]

Taussig wanted to know how the islanders felt about "our acquisition of bases in the area." What was the possibility of riots and revolts? Taussig was also told to analyze "the British experience in colonial government that might be useful to the United States in its Puerto Rican and Virgin Islands problems."[47]

In the late thirties a series of riots and strikes—

241

in Jamaica, Trinidad, St. Lucia and St. Vincent—
forced Great Britain to send a member of the nobili-
ty to study the Caribbean. The findings of the
Moyne Commission were so explosive that the
English published only a small portion of the entire
report. Lord Moyne stressed that "little can be said
for the social conditions which exist in the West
Indies today [in 1940]. The child, so often reared in
an ill-built and overcrowded home, passes from it to
what is, all too frequently, an overcrowded school."
Unfortunately, "it was also no exaggeration to say
that in the poorest parts of most towns and in many
of the country districts, a majority of the houses are
largely made of corrugated iron and unsound boarding...sanitation in any form and water supply are
unknown in such premises." Finally, turning to
labor—a big issue for the United States—Moyne
underlined terrible conditions and "abominably" low
wages. He blamed the colonial governments, and he
suggested that workmen not only be allowed to
picket, they should no longer be held potentially
responsible for the cost of a strike.[48]

Given these conditions, it was hard to understand what the Americans could learn from the
British. But the president, about to fight a war, did
not want to change or transform the Caribbean. He
only wanted to use and lease it, so he seemed willing to consider any advice that produced the desired
labor and social stability.

Racism permeated the British West Indies.
Winston Churchill told Taussig, "we will not let the
Hottentots by popular vote throw the white people
into the sea."[49] Those white people refused to educate the black people, but they did occasionally con-

descend to visit their homes. Thus, the United States should be careful to send white supervisors who kept their own racism in check. As Taussig told the president, "the supervisors will be in constant contact with colored or black officials. These officials will probably invite them to their homes. A refusal to accept the invitation may well cause unpleasant relations."[50]

Wages were also a big issue to many of the "reactionary" planters. Taussig noted that, long before the base construction began, "pressure was brought by local (Puerto Rican) planters and businessmen not to pay wages above those currently prevailing." The same problem existed throughout the British West Indies. Decent wages could raise expectations on the plantations that were the islands economic axis. Taussig suggested a joint conference "to determine a broad policy covering the labor problem." This broad policy was needed because of the possibilities of emigration; islanders would gravitate to the locations paying the highest wages; that would produce complaints when the better paid workers returned home, and those complaints would surely produce instability given the appalling conditions depicted by Lord Moyne.[51]

Taussig suggested that an emphasis be placed on economic development. As in Puerto Rico, Cuba, and the Dominican Republic, "the sugar islands, as the British West Indies were formerly called, have usually prospered or languished at the touch of international sugar politicians." Taussig suggested closer cooperation between the United States and Great Britain; he wanted to pursue progressive economic policies but, given the absence of sovereignty, linked to a British desire to keep the Hottentots at bay, and linked to an American focus on only military matters, long range planning took a decided back seat to wartime concerns. Traveling through Grenada in 1992, a visitor could still see a substantial number of corrugated iron homes, all lacking the most elemental of sanitary facilities.[52]

Taussig's report became one basis for what was later (in 1942) called the Anglo-American Caribbean Commission. American officials agreed (in late 1943) that a number of "sometimes shocking" reports had recently appeared; and, "as a result of some of these investigations, remedial or palliative measures had been taken." But, despite the commissions efforts, the Caribbean "remained a social and economic anachronism in a progressing Western Hemisphere"; and, added to that terrible foundation, was a war "that made it difficult to maintain even the normal sub-standards of living. The simple wartime formula 'tighten your belts' could not be applied to populations whose belts had already been drawn to the last notch."[53]

The Commission sought to maintain stability and it never hampered the interests of the United States, even when the navy was asked to take over another large chuck of Trinidad.

The original base site was twelve square miles. It included every advantage Admiral Greenslade predicted, but, because of his short stay on Trinidad, the admiral had missed an important military point. While the base was protected on three sides by the sea, and protected by mountains on the fourth side, between the mountains and the base lay another four square miles of open land. Invaders could use this land—it contained a plantation and a "whites only" hotel—to attack the base. By June of 1941, Captain A.W. Radford pressed the governor of Trinidad to help him purchase the land.[54]

One family owned the land. That "simplified the problem of acquisition" but nothing quieted the resistance of Trinidad's colonial governor. Radford said the governor had recently received a nasty communication from the British Embassy in Washington. They complained that he was an "obstructionist," but Radford said the governor was a "very fine man." He was neither "anti-American nor an obstructionist" because "his stand on various details in connection with the army and navy leases is understandable from a Trinidadian point of view."

Radford was an American who negotiated like a Scot. In a British colony, he was prepared "to be liberal with the British navy in regard to the determination of boundaries for their base" if the United States got the four square miles of additional land. Radford remained convinced that his facility could be turned into "one of the finest fleet bases in the world," but the acquisition of the new land was essential because Radford needed to wall himself off from two potential enemies: the Germans and the Trinidadians.[55]

In the original agreement signed with the British, "our people and theirs were to live together without even a fence, much less a frontier between them." But, as construction progressed and problems (e.g., strikes) multiplied, it seemed to Radford that "the army and navy will be much better off when they are for the most part located entirely in their own leased areas."[56]

By November of 1941,, Radford bought "notice
to the public" ads in the local press; he told the
angry Trinidadians that access to the base was now
restricted and he told the governor that he would
soon have to completely close the beaches—presumably for 99 years—to the general public. He had
waited as long as he could but security concerns
were paramount, and, even if the Trinidadians
posed no threats, Radford looked "to the development of the area involving the use for military and
naval purposes of the bathing beaches which had
hitherto been used by the general public." Radford
meant to build the fleet recreational facility advocated by Admiral Greenslade. He wanted to begin work
as soon as possible so islanders had to make way
for a complex the navy soon called its "honeymoon
base."[57]

When the navy bought the additional land containing the plantation, it discovered an easy way to
make money for the United States. It distributed
about 60 percent of its grapefruit and limes to the
Atlantic fleet; it sold a large portion of the surplus to
the United States army ("they called for the produce
at the plantation"); and, whatever was left over "was
sold to the local market at the request and with the
complete acquiescence of the colonial authorities."[58]

Even Senator Bone would have liked that deal.
The Trinidadians, however, continued to complain,
so the base was walled off from the general public.
Islanders resented this treatment but, as a navy
report later made clear, the United States had no
choice. "Past experiences have clearly demonstrated
that a goodly percentage of the type of people who
may be expected to use the recreational facilities in

246

the subject area have no scruples whatsoever about thievery or wanton destruction."[59]

Pearl Harbor of the Caribbean

In September of 1943, President Roosevelt summarized a significant portion of his Caribbean military policy. In a document entitled "Report on Progress of Puerto Rico," Roosevelt stressed that "during the 45 years of our sovereignty, the elements of world military and naval strategy have changed." When the United States "occupied" the island in 1898 neither the Panama Canal nor the airplane existed. Now that they were strategic realities Puerto Rico had become a permanent possession with a new, incalculable military significance. Indeed, Sumner Welles privately told the British (in April of 1943) that the United States had no intention of including Puerto Rico in any postwar plans for international control, while the president told the nation that the island's "possession or control by any foreign power—*or even the remote threat of such possession*—would be repugnant to the most elementary principles of national defense."[60]

Puerto Rico was a prisoner. Through no fault of its own, it had become the center of America's Caribbean shield. Thus the president said it was militarily repugnant to consider even the remote threat of foreign control but not morally repugnant to yet again (*i.e.,* the Dominican Republic) break the nation's pledged word. On Vieques the navy had constructed a quarry; they took the rock from this facility and began to build the breakwater that would theoretically extend for 14 miles. However, when they got to 7,000 feet of breakwater, the navy

247

stopped; Roosevelt Roads would not be the the Pearl Harbor of the Caribbean.[61]

Four months *before* the president's report, the navy issued a "cease operations" order on the Roosevelt Roads facility. To date, admirals had spent $56,000,000 to build the largest dry dock in the world, three 6,000-foot concrete runways, and, on Vieques, an ammunition depot of more than one hundred buildings. This monumental undertaking was formally commissioned an operations base in July of 1943, but, sixteen months later, the navy put the entire facility into "caretaker status." Like a Broadway play that had bombed, Roosevelt Roads closed right after it opened. The navy had no idea what it was going to do with the facility, but the people of Vieques immediately demanded: "Keep your word! Return the land!"[62]

Vieques had problems. Even before the cease operations order, a commission established by the government in San Juan noted that even though the navy had settled 350 of the 700 displaced families in the "slum community of Santa Maria," the other 350 still had no place to go—except to the thirteen thousand acres of land the navy never used but refused to share. The commission suggested (in March of 1943) that this land should be turned over to the displaced families and to the other 825 families who formerly made a living on sugar cane cultivation and milling.

In March of 1943, the navy refused, and in November of 1944, Acting Secretary of the Interior Abe Fortas echoed the navy when he "strongly recommended against" a House bill that would have returned a quarter of the confiscated land to its displaced and unemployed inhabitants.

Fortas agreed that "the navy has recently determined that a large portion of this acreage [the navy controlled 21,000 acres out of an island total of 32,000] is no longer needed." Moreover, "by acquiring so large a portion of the island and taking it out of civilian use and occupancy, the navy effectively destroyed the economy of the community." The navy, after all, not only took the land, it confiscated "the best of the sugar lands"; the result was that "the situation has now deteriorated to the point where almost the entire population of Vieques is dependent upon the insular government." Without work, and with "community facilities which have disintegrated almost to the point of nonexistence," the 8,000 American citizens of Puerto Rican birth who lived in Vieques lost the war a year before it formally ended. They lost when the Interior Department unconditionally surrendered their island to the United States navy.[63]

The idea was to return some of the navy's acreage to the municipal government. But Fortas noted that to restore the land required "careful administration and adequate funds." Unfortunately, "neither can be made available by the municipality of Vieques, which is as bankrupt as its people." Fortas suggested that the insular government do the work. They had the administrators and the cash. He would let islanders use roughly 5000 acres of their own land; this was only half of what the navy already considered surplus, but it was the best Fortas could do and at that it was a only temporary grant of the land the citizens of Vieques had temporarily loaned to the navy!

In late 1944, Roosevelt Roads was on hold, in

mothballs without ever seeing any action. But the navy might want it back. No one could foresee post-war contingencies. Thus, the insular government could lease the land "until it is again required by the navy." As Fortas emphasized in his instructions to the Puerto Ricans, "these transfers do not disturb the underlying title of the United States."[64]

The Federal Works Agency made this budgetary point to Representative Carl Vinson, Chair of the House Committee on Naval Affairs. After it confiscated the land, the navy did buy it. They used taxpayers money, and, "while the government, doubtlessly cannot hope to recover its investment in the property, this office is of the opinion that the property should not be disposed of without the payment of a money consideration." In essence, even though Fortas agreed that the navy "effectively destroyed the economy of the community," that now bankrupt community was to pay for the land that it had sold only after that land was first confiscated by the War Department.[65]

In a memorable novel about World War II, Joseph Heller later called this kind of thinking a "Catch-22." In 1944, it was called U.S. policy in the Caribbean.

Plebiscites and Self-Determination

Another policy concerned the status of Puerto Rico. At an independence day celebration in 1942 Governor Rexford Tugwell told islanders that even though the Declaration of Independence "did not end colonialism, it did remove that system to a moral category which made it indefensible."[66]

While critics argued that this strong message

was nothing more than 4th of July oratory, U.S. leaders said very much the same thing in private. Sumner Welles understood that French control of its Indochina colonies posed a "great moral question"; he never made the leap to Puerto Rico, but he seemed to believe that the French had no right to land "seized, sometimes by war, and as recently as the 1880's." President Roosevelt, discussing Morocco in 1944, said "I do not think that a population which is 90 percent Moors should be run permanently by France"; and, turning to Indochina, the president said, "France has had the country—30 million inhabitants—for nearly one hundred years, and the people are worse off than they were in the beginning."[67]

That was the case in Puerto Rico. Sugar brought profits to the United States and dead-time to the Puerto Ricans. The economic reconstruction promised by the New Deal in the 1930s died stillborn, and islanders "thrived" during the war only because Americans liked to drink. Unable to buy liquor abroad, mainlanders satisfied themselves with Puerto Rican (and Virgin Islands) rum. Liquor revenues of $1.7 million in 1939 increased to $13.9 million in 1942, and to an astonishing (to the Puerto Rican Treasury) $65.7 million in 1944.[68]

Figures like these gave a new meaning to the phrase "wartime economy.". Many islanders understood that peace promised a return to the depression. They wanted to make plans for a self-sustaining economy in an independent Puerto Rico.

Rexford Tugwell explained the situation in his diary. The head of the island's majority party, Luis Muñoz Marin, was "thoroughly scared."[69] When he formed the Popular Party in 1938, Muñoz made it clear that the economy was his top priority. Sometimes he also let voters think that independence was his ultimate goal, but in 1941 he told Congress that his party agreed to postpone the independence debate for two reasons: islanders needed to do something about the economy ("without the confusion of the political issue"), and they patriotically refused to "embarrass" the national government during the war.[70]

The war was now nearing an end, and, as Tugwell wrote in his diary, Muñoz had some real problems. About "90 percent" of his party's "politicos" desired independence as soon as possible. At the party's August 1944 convention Muñoz had managed to keep these representatives in line only with an "outright threat to resign." This gave him a bit of breathing room, but Muñoz feared that he would be ousted as party leader once the elections took place. To avoid political defeat, "his tactic to meet the threat" was to "advocate independence." However, he might not do that. Tugwell gave the impression that Muñoz, in a state of "near panic," changed his position every other hour.[71]

Tugwell tried to explain the realities of American politics to Muñoz. The Puerto Rican thought (on August 30,1944) that "independence was inevitable." He would swim with the tide but only if he got special treatment from Congress. Tugwell said that was out of the question. The states never got such a deal so why should Puerto Rico? The tack for Muñoz to take—"if he wanted time and scope for negotiation in a postwar world"—was to come out for statehood! That would give everybody a jolt, and it would also deprive the radical independentistas" of a major claim. Tugwell said that when they won the 1944 elections the politicos would argue that their victory was a mandate for independence.[72]

How could Muñoz, a man who had always opposed statehood, suddenly endorse it? In the 1940 elections Muñoz had often indicated his personal preference for independence. And in 1944, a pro-statehood position would have undermined his legitimacy among the party's pro-independence majority. Muñoz opted for a political compromise. In the 1944 elections, a vote for the Popular Party was not a vote for independence, but it was a vote for self-determination. Muñoz promised that, no later than the structuring of the peace, the Puerto Rican people would hold a plebiscite. Independent of any election, all islanders would be free to determine their future from the status alternatives placed on the ballot.[73]

Senator Millard Tydings introduced a bill to consider possible independence for Puerto Rico. Testifying in favor of independence, but not in favor of the bill, Muñoz Marin stressed that if the people got independence, "it should have no calendar dates on it." He wanted independence only when he thought the time was right, so he used this metaphor: "If a patient has a fever the doctor does not say, you take this pill and get up in three days. He says, You take this pill and whenever the fever goes down to 97 you get up. If it goes down in 3 days, it is all right for you to get up, or if it takes ten days, you get up in ten days."[74]

When would the Puerto Rican people get better? Muñoz never offered a date, but his colleagues did.

Their answer was "instantly," and they backed up their argument with the vote of Puerto Rico's elected representatives. Even after Muñoz applied very strong pressures, 57 percent of the Popular Party senators, representatives and mayors still favored independence. They expressed their sentiments to Tydings in March of 1945,[75] and they asked for the promised plebiscite.

Tydings answer was clear and direct: forget it. As he told President Truman's representative on October 3, 1945, he was "violently opposed" to a plebiscite. Didn't Tugwell (who at this point favored a vote) understand that Congress would never grant statehood? Had he not listened when Tydings told this to the Puerto Ricans in May of 1945: "Your proposition [for the plebiscite] is absolutely sound, but it would be unfair to the people of Puerto Rico if you were to take the initiative in this matter, for this very obvious reason: Suppose you asked for something—I do not say what it would be—and the Congress was not disposed to give it to you. In that situation you would be in the position of having assumed that whatever you asked for we would give you and we would be in the position of breaking faith if we did not give it to you."[76]

The Puerto Ricans thought that "governments derived their just powers from the Consent of the governed." They were wrong. Puerto Rico was ruled by Congress, and, since Tydings told the president that Congress would grant neither independence nor statehood (*e.g.*, "It would be improper to submit statehood as a possible alternative knowing full well we would not give it to them."[77]), there was no point in having a plebiscite that was sure to underline the hypocrisy of the United States.

In his January State of the Union message, the president said that the United States was "committed to the democratic principle that it is for dependent people themselves to decide what their status should be."[78] But, when the Puerto Rican legislature passed a plebiscite bill on February 20, 1946, the president told Tugwell to veto it. When the Puerto Rican legislature overrode the governor's veto on March 6, 1946, Truman acted on his famous saying. The buck stopped at his desk because he was the court of last resort. Only he could deny the expressed will of the Puerto Rican people, and, when he publicly did so, his message was a "Catch 22" every bit as damning as the federal government's reasoning on the land situation in Vieques.

The president said the plebiscite bill "might erroneously be construed by the people as a commitment that the United States would accept any plan that might be selected at the proposed plebiscite." The United States could never make such a commitment because, even though the president was committed to letting dependent peoples decide their own political status, that was not the case when the will of the dependent people conflicted with that of the American people. The president sustained Tugwell's veto because he wanted to protect Puerto Ricans from a plebiscite's "harmful" effects. Since islanders might be upset if they were permitted to vote for a status they could never have, the president avoided all "misunderstandings" by advocating self-determination but denying Puerto Ricans the democratic rights they most assuredly had.[79]

Containing Communism

One war recalls another. In 1917 and in 1945, the United States refused to legitimate the independence aspirations of the Puerto Rican people. The island had to remain a permanent possession of the United States. The decision to deny a plebiscite was a bridge into the second half of the twentieth century; it contained such a resourceful blending of old and new assumptions that it helped mark a turning point in U.S. Caribbean policy.

The Cold War changed the world; it produced such a unique form of combat that the Caribbean indefinitely lost its backwater status. After 1945 even the tiniest of islands (e.g., Grenada) could become a center of international concern; neutrality was suspicious, anti-communism a banner flown by Rafael Trujillo and François Duvalier.

The Caribbean nations were drafted to play a role in this world struggle because, as Truman knew when he vetoed the plebiscite, the Communists monitored his actions. Thus, as soon as World War II ended, the Caribbean found itself inextricably linked to a new American doctrine; this one was laid on still solid foundations of good colonialism, arrogance and racism, but instead of many aims, the Truman Doctrine only had one; the containment of Communism.

By 1947, the United States had decided its Roosevelt Roads facility would become a "permanent" training base in the battle against Communism. Although he despised the thought of being in the same room with Rafael Trujillo, President Truman agreed because of pending negotiations concerning the use of the Dominican Republic "in connection with a long range proving ground for the guided missiles program."[80]

The Truman Doctrine thus contained an important assumption. To contain Communism it was sometimes necessary to shake the hand of a man who ran (what the State Department called) a Caribbean "Gestapo."[81]

In January of 1945, there was a hint of change; when the American minister wrote that "the most representative gesture of a Dominican citizen is looking over his shoulder to see whether he is being overheard," his superiors responded by denying American firms the licenses required to sell Trujillo an arsenal of new weapons. The United States still refused to intervene; Trujillo was still a Dominican problem; but, in contrast to the receivership gift given to Trujillo in 1940, in 1945 Washington wanted to "scrupulously avoid even the appearance of lending him any support." As the secretary of state put it to President Truman, "President Trujillo is the most ruthless, unprincipled, and efficient dictator in this hemisphere. He holds the country in an iron grasp, rules by fear, and extracts an annual tribute estimated at $5 million from the economy of the country and the Dominican people."[82]

Trujillo never changed. The nature of American policy did. Once President Truman decided to apply "counterforce at a series of constantly shifting geographical and political points,"[83] the Caribbean assumed new significance. Bases like Roosevelt Roads played a part in grand military strategy, and the new doctrine changed Washington's assumptions about the meaning and legitimacy of intervention.

The Good Neighbor Policy was rooted in a sense

257

of failure. As President Hoover noted, the nation's interventions had not been very "successful."[84] Thus, for a mix of motives (e.g., opinion in Latin America and the costs and consequences of intervention), and with varying degrees of expediency (e.g., Hoover helping Trujillo to "refund" his obligations in 1930, or Roosevelt turning a blind eye to the slaughter of 17,000 Haitians), two presidents pursued a strategy designed to avoid the necessity of another Caribbean intervention.[85]

The Truman Doctrine transformed American policy. Postwar presidents would define "the adroit and vigilant use of counterforce" in different ways, but, in the service of containing Communism, national leaders now accepted the necessity of interventions. But by 1947, an intervention was no longer called an intervention.

Secretary of State Marshall expressed this view in a February 19, 1947 letter to the United States Dominican ambassador. Disgusted by what he called Trujillo's disregard for "human rights," Ambassador Butler had suggested possible "multilateral action." To the secretary, a recommendation for the use of force raised "the question of the nature of 'intervention' within the meaning of the non-intervention commitments assumed by this government in common with the other governments of the American Republics."[86]

How could you intervene if you had a commitment not to do so? Secretary Marshall explained that "action by the organized community of nations with respect to transgressions by one of their number, in accordance with established principles of the community, *does not constitute intervention*. On the contrary, the department believes that such multi-lateral action is the alternative to, and, in a sense, the *antithesis of intervention*. Such action by the community would be in substitution for arbitrary intervention by individual nations that have the power to practice it."[87]

There was one problem with the secretary's interpretation; a "majority" of the American republics "were not yet prepared" to accept the notion that intervention was not intervention. As Marshall explained, when the United States raised the issue of possible multilateral action, that proposal not only "aroused the suspicions" of many of the American republics, "it put them on guard against any proposal that would appear to limit their respective sovereignties, whether that limitation was imposed by individual powers or by the organized inter-American community."[88]

The secretary suggested a strategy of caution. Because it had "such preponderant power in the Hemisphere," any U.S. advocacy of multilateral action "was more likely to arouse resistance among the majority of the other American republics than to win their favor." This was inevitable because of what Marshall called "*the penalty of power*." America's military might made others so suspicious that it clouded their reasoning. In Mexico or Cuba leaders would think "that the United States might practice what was, in effect, unilateral intervention under the guise of community action."[89]

Those suspicions were the extra price America paid for its obvious political, economic and military hegemony. However, no matter how much caution and empathy the United States needed to employ, the secretary of state had nevertheless underlined a key assumption of America's foreign policy in general, and its Caribbean policy in particular.

In the postwar world, interventions were acceptable; labeling those interventions was a semantic problem, and gaining support for those interventions was a political problem. Despite these obstacles, the United States believed that the threat of Communism gave it rights and obligations as compelling as those which attached to ideals like the Monroe Doctrine and "good colonialism."

The former (as Secretary of State Lansing stressed) made "the integrity of other nations an incident, not an end" of American policy. And the latter imposed obligations that compelled the United States to assist people who were not yet ready for self-government. As the Interior Department's chief counsel told Congress in September of 1948, "I should point out that there is a period of tutelage, as we call it, from the time we acquired the Territory (i.e., Puerto Rico) which as a ward and guardian relationship we have to assist and help."[90]

The Truman Doctrine was added to these other national rights and obligations, but, in the postwar world, it often assumed a preeminent position. The fight against Communism took a back seat to nothing, and, if a unilateral action like the Bay of Pigs sometimes occurred, a more common practice was (e.g., in the Dominican Republic in 1965 or Grenada in 1983) "unilateral intervention under the guise of community action."

Either way, the Truman Doctrine supplanted the Good Neighbor Policy. After 1947, the United States was prepared to intervene at a series of constantly shifting geographical and political points. For a decade or more the nation's focus was on Europe (*e.g.*, Greece) and Asia (*e.g.*, Indochina and Korea). But a new assumption was in place. As the National Security Council (NSC) told President Eisenhower in a January 30, 1959 secret study of hemispheric policies, the United States should "continue to adhere to the policy of not intervening unilaterally in the internal affairs of the other American republics." However, in the only exception to the rule, "in the event of *threatened* or actual domination of any American state by Communism" the United States should use the OAS "to the extent necessary to remove the threat to the security of the hemisphere."[91]

Intervene, and obtain the support of other nations if possible. But expect to be criticized because, as the NSC warned the president, he would still encounter the suspicions of neighbors. Many of them believed that "the United States is, at best, disinterested in the development of democracy in the area, and, less charitably, that the United States favors authoritarian regimes as providing greater stability, greater resistance to Communist penetration, and a better climate for U.S. economic interests."[92]

It was a stalemate. U.S. leaders believed that intervention was not intervention, and the other American republics feared unilateral action. While the two sides debated words and deeds, Congress acted. Instead of fighting communism, the House of Representatives decided to wage war on "demon rum." In 1949, members rediscovered ancient history. The Virgin Islands produced Government subsidized liquor. This was intolerable so Congress turned over to private hands the most profitable part of the Virgin Islands economy. When the government's accounts soon showed major deficits, Congress unashamedly blamed the islanders.

Colonies, Contradictions, and Television Aggression

"I do not know of any better time than today, this week, and next week, for us to learn something about our colonial possessions and our subjects."

—Representative Fred Crawford,
Virgin Islands debate, May 5, 1949.[1]

"I would like to say at the outset that I think many Americans, if not most Americans, realized that there was room for some change, indeed perhaps for social and political revolution in Cuba."

—Assistant Secretary of State Roy Rubottom,
Executive Session Hearings, Senate,
February 18, 1960[2]

In 1949, Congressman Miller of Nebraska returned from a congressional junket to the Virgin Islands, and explained Caribbean realities to his colleagues. First, the United States bought the islands because we thought Germany wanted them. However, "since that time they have been sort of a burden on the American people....The United States taxpayers have been carrying this load. We pay for their deficits."

Miller said, "They will not work....You cannot go down in St. Thomas and find any Virgin Islanders working in the hotels. They are English people from Tortola [a nearby British colony] or from Puerto Rico." Now the Puerto Ricans knew how to work. They thrived in the islands, and "they wanted no help from the government." But the natives lagged far behind. "Remember that 90 percent of the population of the Virgin islands is colored, and since 1914 [Miller gave the wrong date] when we took them over they have expected this country to take care of them."[3]

The congressman went on, "I just do not believe that a people can long remain self-respecting when they are being supported by funds from another government." Adam Clayton Powell wanted to know if "the gentleman from Nebraska is in favor of the millions of dollars that the United States government is spending in Nebraska now to transmit power and light to the hitherto dark regions of Nebraska."[4]

Miller did not like the question. Nebraska had no "dark regions." But, said Powell, "until the United States government came into Nebraska and put up public power lines you had dark regions." Miller grudgingly admitted that that was true but the people "are paying back every dollar with interest."

Powell pointed out that the bill before the House to create a new Virgin Islands Corporation did the same thing. Miller said there were two differences: Nebraska was a state and putting up power lines was not socialistic.

Congressman Keefe (Wisconsin) tried to move

the debate in a different direction. He wanted to know how much power the municipal councils had? Could they "interfere in any way to change or to limit or to extend what you proposed to do in this bill for the benefit of the Virgin islands?"

Fred Crawford (Michigan) now took the floor. As a long-standing member of the House Committee on Insular Affairs, Crawford asked what power did the island's local councils have over the corporation its sponsors wanted to create?

"None," was Crawford's ready response. The Islanders had wanted power, but, when the governor asked that he be made president of the proposed corporation, "I protested against that and told them I would not support any such proposition."

Keefe had no worries about conflicts of interest; his concern was self-government. How were you training the people "if you set up a super-corporation on top of their local government than can obstruct or do away with anything that the local government might determine?"

Crawford responded about the nature of the United States insular possessions. "We can upset the local legislative acts of Puerto Rico, where they elect their own governor, and we can upset any council order they might put through in the Virgin Islands....They are dependent on us....They cannot interfere with the operation because we have power in Congress and the White House to stop those *interferences*. They cannot do anything about that."[5] [emphasis added]

Congress had all the power and exercised it in the best interests of the Virgin Islanders. As Fred Crawford later stressed, "we are working with the emotions, the lives, the desires, and the souls of the subjects of the Congress of the United States."

Subjects. Crawford used the word twice, Keefe once[6] and none of their colleagues expressed outrage or amazement. As if wearing a crown, congressmen lorded it over the islanders because, in the royal court at Washington, the only concerns that mattered were those of mainland Americans.

Congressman Rees (Florida) grasped the islands desperate economic position; he agreed this was a bad time to sell the rum plant and its machinery. But, what about pancakes? Rees stressed that if the corn used to make rum had instead been used to feed people, "the 39,295,948 bushels of corn would have produced 220,000,000,000 pancakes, enough to have given 25,000,000 a plateful of 5 pancakes for breakfast each morning for 1760 days, almost 5 years."[7]

This example hit home. The Congressional Record indicated no laughter from his colleagues. They breakfasted on pancakes, and they listened when Representative Rich (of Pennsylvania) explained the reasons Congress had decided to sell the rum distillery and its machinery.

Rich once had a bottle of the rum in his office. "And I had my picture taken; it was sent out all over the country. I do not want any more people telling me I have been in the rum business. Some of my people do not like it....I say it is a stench on the American people to force them into a business they do not want to be in."[8]

Engle of California tried to make sense. He explained that the introduction of prohibition in 1920 "dealt a severe blow to the economy." Congress had resurrected the industry in 1934 because it wanted "to provide employment through operation of the sugar properties and the distillery, as an alternative to the dole." Engle stressed that his colleagues who complained about burdensome deficits missed a fundamental clause of the original contract: "Under the terms of the agreement, the company is required to deposit any net profits in the federal treasury....Thus there have been, and can be, no profits which the company may devote to the economic rehabilitation of the islands."[9]

For fifteen years the distillery had been "consistently profitable." Congress complained about deficits, but Engle said his colleagues forgot that islanders were forbidden to follow sound business practices. A private enterprise would have kept portions of any profits in a surplus account. Because this was a public corporation, all profits always went into the federal treasury; and—in a point that did not come out in the debates—so did the over $51 million in rum export taxes. The islanders were taxed without representation. Just twelve years of revenues (1934-46) paid for the islands.[10]

Truman knew the truth, and he diligently pushed for the corporation's approval. But he apparently decided that the opposition was too strong. To get the corporation he had to give up the rum.

Despite Representative Engle's accurate account of past history, Congress disregarded the facts. Just before Congress voted, Representative Keefe once again took the floor. He had listened to the debate for two days; he was confused in the beginning, and he was confused at the end. Since the new Virgin Islands Corporation would only have the authority to run a hotel (which was losing money), run a distillery (which was about to be forbidden), and grow sugar (which everyone agreed was a losing proposition, "What are they going to operate? What are they going to do?" Keefe thought that because "they do not know what they intend to do" Congress had unintentionally made a terrible admission about its "subjects." "We are going to confess frankly here in this Congress that we can no longer have a government in the Virgin Islands that will permit those people any measure of self-government, and that we must adopt a socialistic or communistic set-up in order to carry on these activities in these islands."[11]

Although the "heart" of that socialist set-up was the rum distillery, the amendment prohibiting it became part of the new law. Congress had responsibilities—"the people are to a great extent wards of the state"—but Government House Rum had to be removed from the nation's shelves. It was a distasteful business which, thanks to this amendment, "removed this blot from our record of handling the Virgin Islands affairs."[12]

When, in 1978, the governor of the islands wanted to present its first constitution to President Jimmy Carter, he had to beg for a five minute photo session. And, even though the governor "is putting considerable pressure on us to schedule *five minutes* [emphasis in original] for him to deliver the Constitution," he never got it. Vice President Mondale accepted the document, and was told to "thank them for coming all the way to Washington to bring it to you, and promise that it will be carefully and thoughtfully reviewed before it is transmitted to Congress."[13]

Cuba

By 1948, Cuba's leaders acted so much like the heads of an independent nation that their behavior angered and confused American officials. In a blatant manifestation of "Cubanidad," the island's congress changed the name of its most important war. In 1947, the "Spanish American War" became the "Spanish-Cuban-American War."[14]

In public, President Truman applauded the Cubans desire for autonomy; on the fiftieth anniversary of Cuba's independence (April 18, 1948) he told a joint session of Congress that all members should laud the day that "the dream of José Marti became at last a glorious reality." With America's help, Cuba was "equally sovereign" and a fifty year friendship between "peoples of different races and cultures" had turned into a perfect model for the entire world: "The same harmonious relationship can prevail among all nations, provided they possess a genuine desire for peace and a firm resolve to respect the freedom and rights of others."[15]

In reality, the United States was so bothered by the island's assertion of its rights that President Truman received (on December 23, 1948) copy number one of a secret report on Cuba. The new Central Intelligence Agency had written a document which said that Cuba was important to the United States because of its ability to fill sugar requirements and because of "its tactical relationship to U.S. plans for defense of the Panama Canal and the U.S. itself."[16]

To achieve those goals the United States relied on a fact of Cuban life; their prosperity "depended almost entirely on the demand for sugar in the world market in general and the U.S. in particular." This produced such an "intimate" linkage of the economies that in 1947 the United States took 92 percent of Cuba's exports and supplied it with 84 percent of its imports.

The CIA focused the president's attention on one issue: "Cuba's international position, as a result of the close ties with the U.S. and as a result of the basic fact that Cuba is small and weak and the U.S. large and powerful, is subordinate by force of circumstances to that of the United States."

José Marti, a revolutionary, wrote (in 1891) "the peoples of America become freer and more prosperous in the same degree as they draw apart from the United States." On the other hand (in 1894), the United States was an "indispensible" friend who could be won over only if the Cubans "continuously demonstrated their capacity to create, to organize, to unite, to understand and defend liberty."[17]

Many Cubans tried to follow Marti's advice. In their encounters with North Americans they acted like the "virile and constructive" citizens Marti requested; but, instead of the respect forecast by Marti, they encountered the sense of frustration expressed in the CIA report. After assuring Harry Truman that president-elect Prio "would fully support the U.S. in its anti-Soviet policies," the CIA also predicted that "U.S.-Cuban relations will probably become embroiled in a series of vexatious disputes arising from president-elect Prio's and his associates desire to assert Cuba's sovereign rights rather than accept the more expedient course of deferring to the U.S."[18]

If the Cubans embraced expediency and subordination, no problems existed. But because they chose to assert themselves—"to promote their position as a sovereign and completely independent country within the family of nations"—the CIA criticized their "exaggerated sense of nationalism"; it also criticized Cuban support for Puerto Rican independence; and, finally, it tried to explain Cuba's bitter reaction to what one critic called "a new Platt Amendment."

In 1947, Cuba still retained its authorized (in 1934 and 1937) quota of much of the foreign sugar imported into the United States. This provided what the United States wanted—as the CIA told the president, "Cuba's principal contribution to the U.S. is cheap sugar"—and it gave Cubans a minimum degree of economic stability. Large profits still flowed north, but an increasing share of the sugar industry was in native hands, and an assured market provided the jobs that allowed islanders at least to survive.[19]

What bothered officials in Washington was Cuba's refusal either to change or enforce its laws. The United States wanted prompt payment of debts owed to American citizens; it demanded that Cubans do something about a constitutional prohibition (not always enforced) against joint ownership of sugar plantations and mills; and, it was also vexed by a labor law that required Americans to employ increasingly large numbers of Cubans.

The island wanted to protect its own. The United States included a controversial provision in the 1948 sugar law. It stipulated that if the secretary of state "found that any foreign country denies fair and equitable treatment to the nationals of the United States," the United States could retaliate by reducing that foreign country's share of the sugar quota.

This was the new Platt Amendment condemned

271

by Cubans of all political persuasions. In Washington, the island's ambassador charged "economic aggression," and his Caribbean and Latin American colleagues added a new article to the Charter of the Organization of American States. It read that "no state may use or encourage the use of enforcement measures of an economic or political character in order to force the sovereign will of another state and obtain from it advantages of any kind." State Department officials characterized these reactions as "hysterical threats." The Cubans were only screaming because Washington had used its power; that was our prerogative and their problem since, as Elisha Briggs, of the Office of American Republic Affairs noted, "it was high time that the Cubans grew up."[20]

The Cubans were trying to "circumscribe the U.S. in its use, for political ends, of the economic power it derives from its dominant position in the Cuban economy." The risk the president ran was of creating so much economic havoc that it upset "the delicate balance between nationalism and dependence on the United States." The CIA said the president could exacerbate anti-Americanism to the point that Cubans "opposed continuance of the naval base at Guantanomo or refused additional bases in case of an emergency."[21]

This 1948 document was a blueprint for the next decade. To get cheap sugar and strategic access, the United States helped produce something it didn't want, namely revolution. Since "ultranationalistis" threatened American interests, Cuba got its sugar quota, and most of the tonnage that was formerly imported from the now independent (in 1946)

Philippines. This assured that America's sugar needs would be fulfilled and it also increased profits for American (and Cuban) suppliers. However, it perpetuated the island's dead end, dead-time economy. Cubans still ran into a difficulty when they tried to export more refined sugar; even their refined tobacco (*i.e.*, Cuban cigars) faced stiff tariffs; and, in the face of extraordinary corruption in the Cuban government—the CIA said that "the national police now includes gangsters"—the United States openly trained an army that "was organized by its [American] founders for the purposes of maintaining domestic law and order and serving as a final arbiter in matters of major political importance."[22]

Fulgencio Batista used the army to once again take over Cuba in early 1952. As Sumner Welles told Roosevelt in 1938, Batista was corrupt and "he had a strong prejudice against the United States."[23] Thus, when the United States recognized the legitimacy of his coup d'etat, it once again sanctioned the use of power as the final arbiter of Cuban affairs. Batista was seen as America's man, and that perception greatly exacerbated the resentments which even the most corrupt Cubans (*i.e.* Batista) shared.

In a letter dated June 10, 1952, Assistant Secretary of State (for Inter-American Affairs) Miller told the U.S. ambassador in Havana "that the Cubans seem to be headed for a terrific mess both politically and economically." Miller—who had never read the CIA study—believed that the United States' "ability to limit these developments was almost nonexistent." He suggested that the Cubans "ought to turn some of their cane land into grazing land for cattle." They did well with steers and the United

States would gladly import all the meat they could produce.[24]

Miller, however, saw little hope that anyone would listen to his suggestions. He agreed with Luis Machado's pessimistic assessment of Cuba's future. Batista had taken over "at the worst possible time." The deposed president, Carlos Prio, "was sitting quietly in Miami enjoying life and almost relieved at being out from under in the nick of time." Meanwhile, "Batista was like the fellow who came in at the end of the party and was then handed the check."[25]

Fulgencio Batista paid the tab for a half century of subordination; and Americans clapped when Fidel Castro handed him the bill.

Colonialism

At the instigation of the United States, delegations from England, France and Belgium sat down to discuss colonial questions. The meeting opened the day after the United States celebrated its independence (i.e., July 5, 1950); the participants met for three days, and the agenda was quite clear. How could the countries reduce their problems at the United Nations? How could they "render less divergent our general attitudes on colonial questions despite the historical backgrounds?"[26]

The United States was conciliatory yet firm. It told the participants that it was hard enough to defend colonialism, but "we explained that we did not feel that a rigid and non-cooperative attitude in U.N. bodies on the part of administering authorities would have useful results but on the contrary would drive the majority of the members into taking more extreme positions, thus widening the gulf between colonial and non-colonial powers." For example, what was the point of suggesting to the United Nation's special committee on non-self-governing territories that England might refuse to participate?

The United States asked the British to change tactics. They initially refused, but after many hours of debate the UK delegation, led by Ambassador Franks, informed the United States that it would now take a "positive initiative" in all committee meetings. Indeed, "they have decided to follow our line of being more generally cooperative, generous in participation and discussion and less sensitive to unjustified criticism."[27]

"Positive participation" would delay social change by "*reducing the extremism of the non-colonial group* in the United Nations"; and it might even result "in developing a middle bloc of states who would initiate and support more reasonable and moderate resolutions than has hitherto been the case."[28] [emphasis added]

This was common sense, but not the kind preached by Tom Paine in January of 1776. Then, when some colonists said, "come, come, we shall be friends again for all this," Paine argued that if you "can still shake hands with murderers, then you are unworthy the name of husband, father, friend or lover, and whatever may be your rank or title in life, you have the heart of a coward, and the spirit of a sycophant."[29]

By 1950, Americans were doing onto others what had been done unto them; and the spirit of Tom Paine, celebrated on July 4, 1950, was forgotten as the United States conspired to "reduce the extremism of the non-colonial group."

In 1950, the extremists were causing military problems from one end of the Caribbean to the other. The Cubans complained about Puerto Rico, the Puerto Ricans complained about the 25 installations now controlled by the navy and army; and, in Trinidad, islanders wanted to lease from the United States the land the United States had leased from Great Britain.

The navy admitted it had no immediate need for the base. The facility's commander told the Chief of Naval Operations in Washington (in an exchange that began in September of 1949) "the continuance of the Naval Operating Base, Trinidad in its present status is not necessary to the peacetime operations of the U.S. Atlantic Fleet, and the activities at this base can be curtailed without adversely affecting the national security."[30]

This was good news for the Sisters of Mercy and for the native population of Trinidad. The former wanted to use the base hospital to care for the island's sick and needy, while the latter wanted to avoid being sucked into the sea. As the American council general told his superiors, since the U.S. Navy arrived in 1941, "the loss of bathing facilities has been rather keenly felt by the inhabitants of Port of Spain." Sailors had constructed a road which led to the new facilities at Maracas Bay, but they had forgotton the undertow. Any islander who swam at the bay was pulled underwater and, assuming he or she survived long enough to once again reach the surface, they then swam, not for enjoyment, but for their lives.[31]

The navy wanted to help. But, "it is felt that if all naval activities at Trinidad were completely inactivated there would be pressure from the local government for the return of the area and the termination of the lease." This was out of the question because the navy might want to use the base for "war emergency planning," for "training by self-supporting fleet units." Even on a standby basis, the base always served a number of diplomatic and political purposes (e.g., deterring Latin American Communists).[32]

It was hard to say no to the Sisters of Mercy. In early 1950, the navy considered leasing the facilities to the colonial government—the figure cited by the non-taxpaying navy was $75,000 a year just for the wharf facilities—if the lease agreement contained an "immediate recapture clause." This was what Abe Fortas had done with the land in Vieques (Puerto Rico) but, instead of the thirty days given to the Puerto Ricans, in Trinidad the nuns and locals would have sixty days to return the land to the navy. However, the navy stipulated that "the consideration of the lease should be the maintenance of the buildings and facilities in the area and of the roads leading thereto and proper police protection."[33]

The navy worried that islanders would "trespass" on U.S. property. They told the colonial government that "in order to clear the beaches by sunset" there must be two squads of police on duty every day. The British agreed, but the navy still hesitated because of the location of the beaches. To reach water, locals had to travel eight miles from the navy control gate to Scotland Bay. They would be using bicycles, cars and even buses. The navy envisioned a variety of problems; traffic jams would occur because the road was narrow and circuitous.

Since "the Trinidad public would have a free gang-way through the heart of the base," they might vandalize the vacant officers quarters or the enlisted housing project also located near the main road. Trinidadians could sabotage the base. When a native was injured, "it would mean an immediate call to the navy for aid, and failure to render such aid—no matter why—will react unfavorably to say the least."[34]

"The sole advantage accruing to the navy was the good will of the lower class of people." It would be nice if they liked the United States, but what about the "loss of the good will of the more substantial Trinidadian—those people who owned homes in the subject area prior to its acquisition by the U.S. Navy and who were now desirous of regaining their old homes." The navy asked Washington to "direct the discontinuance of negotiations for the leasing of the subject area."[35]

By the summer of 1950 the Secretary of State Dean Acheson informed the secretary of the navy that he should inform his subordinates not to inform the colonial authorities—who would, after all, inform the Trinidadians—that the Americans had withdrawn their offer. After a joint inspection of the base with local officials, the U.S. commander suggested a fence on either side of the road. The locals would pay for this fence, but they lacked the funds required for its construction. Since this "important stipulation" (i.e., the fence) had been omitted in the proposal first presented to the colonial government, the secretary of state suggested finding another way to "terminate the discussions." Trinidad was about to vote for a new government, and the British colonial secretary was "apprehensive lest political capital be made of it (the fence and the withdrawal of the American offer) during the forthcoming general elections"[36]

The navy never mentioned a "surplus account" which often contained more than enough money to build the fence. From the fruit plantation the navy managed, there was a neat profit. And, in contrast to the rum money made in the Virgin Islands, the navy kept the funds in its own accounts. In this case they planned to purchase "capital equipment" based on the profits earned by a plantation where, except for an ensign and a chief carpenter's mate, "work was done entirely by native workmen."[37]

In Puerto Rico the natives were American citizens; that made it harder for the navy to manage a plantation but much easier to obtain more land. By 1950 the navy "permanently" owned 70 percent of Vieques; and, while it also owned a "considerable area" on the four-by-seven mile (Puerto Rican) island of Culebra, it was still having problems with the island's roughly 1,000 residents. In fact, even though President Truman's special assistant (Admiral William Leahy) said, "I am unable to see any military necessity for the acquisition of additional land on Culebra," the navy wanted more room for its "impact bombing" and for the observers who kept score as ships bombarded and airplanes strafed the island and its people.

While tending cows a youngster risked being killed, not by an explosion, but by the rain of duds that missed the mark. So, if only "to keep out natives" and thus avoid, as on Trinidad, an embarrassing and costly incident, the navy wanted another 700 acres of the tiny island.[38]

President Truman called this a "real estate" deal. He asked the Puerto Rican leadership to agree, and they very reluctantly did so. Island patriots abhorred a situation in which the citizens of Culebra dodged bombs and watched, on the white concrete wall of the pharmacy, John Wayne war movies on a Saturday evening. The Puerto Ricans gave in because any serious complaints risked "the congressional blast which might have an adverse impact on other matters in which the Puerto Ricans wanted congressional help."[39] In essence, keep quiet about Vieques and Culebra or forget about the change of status then being proposed by Congress and the island's first elected governor, Luis Muñoz Marin.

In his victorious 1948 campaign, Muñoz had promised a plebiscite with only two options: statehood or independence. By 1950, he had agreed to what would later be called "commonwealth," and, instead of the promised plebiscite, Puerto Ricans voted (on June 4, 1951) in a referendum that approved the creation of a constitution that would still have to be approved by Congress.

In 1952, Congress returned an amended constitution to the Puerto Rican people. When islanders approved the alterations made in Washington, they certified what Congress had already emphasized; as the House Committee on Interior and Insular Affairs put it to the Puerto Rican people on March 3, 1952, "it is important that the nature and scope of S.3336 [the bill which allowed Islanders to write and approve a constitution] be made absolutely clear. The bill under consideration would not change Puerto Rico's fundamental political, social, and economic relationship to the United States."[40]

If Puerto Rico was a colony before the self-government law was passed, and the law changed nothing fundamental in the island's status, then Puerto Rico was still a colony after the adoption of Commonwealth status in July of 1952. As Representative Halleck told his colleagues on May 13, 1952: "What was the reason why the Congress of the United States said that the Puerto Rican Constitution should come back here for approval? Why, to my mind it is simply because Puerto Rico is yet to be governed under the basic law that existed before this thing ever started."[41]

The commonwealth law created serious international problems for the United States. For domestic political purposes. Muñoz had pushed the Eisenhower administration to have Puerto Rico removed from the United Nations list of non-self-governing territories. In Washington the new (and the old) administration had no problems with the governor's request, but, before they acted on it, Interior Deparment officials explained the real meaning of "commonwealth" status to Puerto Rico's governor.

Muñoz wanted to argue that Puerto Rico had ceased to be a territory of the United States and that its laws "could not be repealed or modified by external authority." The Interior Department reminded Muñoz that it "must stage-manage the presentation to the United Nations." The governor should not make statements "which may prove embarrassing or difficult to defend against hostile questioning in the United Nations." For example, "if Puerto Rico has not become an independent nation or a state of the union, and we are all agreed that it has not, then as a matter of domestic constitutional law, it must still be a territory of the United States."[42]

Article 4, Section 3 of the United States Constitution said that "the Congress shall have power to dispose of and make all needful rules and regulations respecting the territory or other property, belonging to the United States." In the commonwealth law passed by Congress, the first line said that Puerto Rico and its adjacent islands "belonged to the United States;"[43] and the general reading of Congress' power to make *all* rules for its possessions conspicuously undermined the theoretical power of the Puerto Rican people.[44]

Henry Cabot Lodge (U.S. ambassador to the United Nations) knew it and U.S. officials stage-managed a lie. Before the United Nations, Lodge and his staff let the Puerto Ricans claim that their laws could not be changed without the consent of the Puerto Rican people. They seconded the island's representatives when they argued that, as commonwealth grew and was modified, no changes could be made without the mutual consent of both parties.[45]

This was unconstitutional, and Krishna Menon said so. At the United Nations, the Indian representative abused the United States so frequently that Lodge brought him to the breakfast table. At a November 20, 1953 meeting at the White House Lodge complained about the United Nations reaction to Puerto Rico. Nobody seemed to have a suggestion until the president came up with an idea that Lodge said was a "ten strike." The ambassador would bowl over the Indian with an offer of independence to the Puerto Ricans. He would take an eggs and bacon brainstorm and potentially threaten the commonwealth status which the Puerto Rican people had just overwhelmingly endorsed.[46]

The secretary of state expressed concern. At 5:15 in the afternoon he called Lodge in New York. Dulles had had a talk with a congressional power-house, and he said "that a dramatic announcement about Puerto Rican independence would not sit well in Congress." Lodge reminded the secretary that he himself had introduced an independence bill in Congress, "and the only complaints were from the Puerto Ricans." The important issue was Krishna Menon, and the secretary should also remember that "I won't be offering them independence anyway, only Congress could do that, I will be just be saying how the president feels."[47]

Four days later Dulles sent Lodge a "for-your-eyes-only" telegram. He said the ambassador "knew better than he whether the president's authorization with reference to Puerto Rico was made after ade-quate consideration and weighing of relevant facts." Dulles worried about Congress; he thought the independence bill might be used by "extreme nationalists" in North Africa to "seriously embar-rass" the French; and, finally, the secretary of state expressed concern about the "loyal elements" in Puerto Rico. Lodge's announcement could "under-mine their position" and thus "seem to build up the disloyal minority."[48]

The disloyal minority were the advocates of independence, among them the revolutionary follow-ers of Pedro Albizu Campos and the 19 percent of the Puerto Rican people who had voted the indepen-dence ticket in the 1952 general elections. The Independence party was the island's second most powerful political entity at a time when any advocacy of independence bordered on the illegal.

In 1948, the Muñoz administration had passed "La Mordaza," the gag law; it banned a variety of illegal independence activities, but its practical effect was to frighten many Puerto Ricans. Muñoz had purged the many independence activists who worked for the island's government, so Lodge was potentially supporting the people whom the commonwealth leadership and Secretary of State Dulles regarded as seditious. Muñoz was arguing that commonwealth was a permanent arrangement, "a new alternative, equal in dignity although different in nature to independence or federated statehood."[49]

Lodge told the U.N. General Assembly about the president's breakfast idea on November 27, 1953, and the next day he wrote a "Dear General" letter to Eisenhower. The independence announcement had "received an unprecedented burst of applause from the delegates." Lodge thought the announcement would have a tremendous effect in Latin America; and, perhaps most important of all, Krishna Menon liked the statement. In a handwritten postscript to the president, Lodge said that "Krishna Menon has just praised the Puerto Rico statement! His first pro-U.S. statement since I have been here!"[50]

On November 27, 1953, Puerto Rico became the first colony to be removed from the United Nations list of non-self-governing territories. This was a U.N. coup for the Eisenhower administration, but, in private, the president received a worried letter from a former West Point classmate. Writing from San Juan on January 1, 1954, Major General Luis Raul Esteves told "Ike" that his statement "had been used by the minority who favors independence as propaganda to the effect that the United States does not want us and is ready to turn us loose." Ike should add something more to his U.N. pronouncement because, "as proved at the last general elections... we are preparing our people for permanent association with the United States and such propaganda, in my opinion, is doing considerable damage to our work of half a century."[51]

On January 12, 1954, the president himself dictated a personal and confidential response to "Steve." Eisenhower assured him that Lodge's statement "was simply to make clear that the United States did not, by force or compulsion, hold any possessive or other relationship with any other area or country in the world. I have made no proposals for United States initiative in changing the relationship between our two countries."[52]

The president neglected to mention a letter, dated January 8, 1954, which he had first read and then sent to the "secret files." The letter was from the State Department's Mason Sears, and it was addressed to Henry Cabot Lodge. The issue was Lodge's request "to give some thought as to how it might be possible to stimulate the Puerto Rican legislature to adopt a resolve requesting the United States to give full independence to Puerto Rico."[53]

Ambassador Lodge saw that by giving the Puerto Ricans independence he would win praise at the United Nations and simultaneously rid the United States of a possession with many dissatisfied citizens.

The problem was the Puerto Ricans. As Sears cautioned, it would not be easy to get Muñoz to "sell" the idea in Puerto Rico since the "principal reason for the existence of the Popular Party [which had won 60 percent of the vote since 1944] has been the belief that as an independent nation the Puerto Ricans could not enjoy the close integration with the United States economy, which is necessary if they are to stand on their own feet economically."[54]

Sears worried about increased immigration to the United States—they would come "while it can be done without any restrictions"—and he devised a strategy for Lodge to follow. Assure Muñoz that the economic benefits would continue after independence; find a way for him to make a "political about-face without risking a political loss of face"; remind him of "the almost certain honor" that would attach to being the first President of Puerto Rico; and, explain to him that independence for Puerto Rico "would have an international impact in view of the colonial issue which is so red hot in most parts of the world. It would be received with great satisfaction by the Asiatic-African nations and would enhance the influence of the two American continents in world affairs."[55]

Sears stressed that Muñoz's party was already based on an about-face (from a 1930s advocacy of independence to a 1940s advocacy of commonwealth) so another 180-degree turn would never sit well with the Puerto Rican electorate. All Mason Sears could suggest was an approach by a "very high level official, preferably yourself [Lodge] or the secretary of state." But, no matter what approach the ambassador took he should remember "that this whole matter is fraught with danger and any misstep could easily lead to violence and bloodshed in Puerto Rico."[56]

Two months after the president placed Sears' letter in the secret files, four members of the Nationalist Party visited the House of Representatives. They appeared on March 1, 1954—the House was debating the Mexican emigration law—and, posing as spectators, they suddenly unveiled a Puerto Rico flag, Lolita Lebrón shouted "freedom for my country," and she and her three companions open fired on the House floor. Five congressmen were wounded, Muñoz quickly apologized, and Secretary of State Dulles later told reporters that the four nationalists represented "a fanatical rejection of the democratic process." After all, "the people of Puerto Rico, by their own free choice have freely chosen their own status."[57]

The contradictions mounted. The Puerto Rican revolutionaries were "fanatics," but Henry Cabot Lodge, trying to find a way to "sell" independence to the Puerto Rican people, was an admirable member of an administration that was once again prepared to disregard the will of the people. The documents at the Eisenhower Library show that when the island's elected representatives wanted independence in 1946, the United States denied independence and a plebiscite. But, when the Puerto Rican people voted for commonwealth in 1952, the United States tried to sell them the independence that, as a result of the gag law, was being systematically repressed in every barrio in Puerto Rico.

The ambassador did not give up. In March of 1956, he wrote another letter to Sherman Adams, the president's chief of staff. Lodge pointed out that when the president offered independence at the United Nations, "there was no reaction from Puerto Rico to this move." He had another idea: "It is that Congress [unilaterally] adopt a resolution offering independence to Puerto Rico on precisely the same terms as the president offered it."[58]

Lodge said "if the offer were accepted many problems would be solved." But, "if the offer were rejected, our Congress would at the very least have taken a step which would be interpreted as 'anti-colonial' and do us great good throughout the world—notably in Afro-Asian countries." Lodge closed by indicating that the resolution "is an idea that has real merit and I do not see what we could possibly lose by it."[59]

Sherman Adams agreed. Two days later he started the process moving but stressed that there was no point in pressing the issue "unless the [congressional] leadership will 'wheel' it for us." Lodge went to see various members of Congress. Speaker of the House of Representatives Joe Martin and his colleagues would "gladly shed Puerto Rico" at any time. Martin would "talk to the boys" and see what he could do.[60]

As in 1954, the real stumbling block to independence existed in Puerto Rico. The islanders had settled on commonwealth, so, as Lodge and his colleagues tried to produce independence, FBI Director Hoover sent "personal and confidential" reports to the president which, as they ridiculed the commonwealth government, warned Eisenhower about the threat from the island's disloyal *independentistas*. In seeking commonwealth, Governor Muñoz Marin sought "to make the divorce final and increase the alimony." Speaker of the Puerto Rican House, Ramos Antonini, "wanted to bolt his cake and have it too." And, finally, "the Popular Democratic Party desired to have a banana republic with United States air conditioning."[61]

Hoover stressed that the president still needed to watch out for the independence activists, and he told the president that "Governor Muñoz Marin is alleged to have been responsible for having an order issued to the Puerto Rican National Guard [which was subsequently rescinded] that the Puerto Rican flag should not be dipped to the United States flag when both flags were exhibited."[62]

There is one final footnote to this flip-flop decade in U.S.-Puerto Rican relations. On June 9, 1959, Governor Muñoz Marin appeared before Senator Jackson's Committee on Interior and Insular Affairs. The only topic of discussion was the proposed Puerto Rico Federal Relations Act, a bill "to provide for amendments to the compact between the people of Puerto Rico and the United States." Muñoz wanted to increase his government's powers (*e.g.*, over tariffs), but Senator Jackson emphasized that this was impossible. Congress had plenary power, period.[63]

Muñoz listened to Senator Jackson, but, eight days after this lecture on power, the governor visited the White House. He presented a written complaint to President Eisenhower.

The president informed one of his aides that, "this is the memorandum handed to me by Governor Muñoz Marin when you accompanied him to my office. When you have examined the "commonwealth" question that seemed to bother him so much, please give me a report."[64]

The president never received a report. A note on the bottom of the memo said the matter had been concluded (which was not true) "to Muñoz' satisfaction." The most surprising thing about the president's short note is that after almost a decade of commonwealth status, Dwight David Eisenhower seemed to have no idea what the governor was talking about. The president did not grasp that what "bothered him so much" was the island's political status.

Muñoz knew what had happened. The president of the United States still needed an education about the island that Senator Lodge tried to make independent while J. Edgar Hoover helped repress the independence movement. All the while, the president's subordinates called Puerto Rico, America's "Showcase of the Caribbean."

The West Indies

If Puerto Rico was America's glossy showcase, the West Indies was Great Britain's decrepit warehouse. From Grenada to Jamaica, from Trinidad to the Cayman Islands, the West Indies epitomized the awful power of colonialism. This was a world on hold. However, if only because of their many problems at the United Nations, the British recognized the need for some political, economic, and social change. They started slowly—with the creation of a dead-on-arrival Caribbean federation in 1958—but, thanks to the demands of leaders like Eric Williams in Trinidad and Norman Manley in Jamaica, the U.S. president devised and debated a systematic approach to the British parts of America's lake.[65]

Eisenhower's policy was put together in the late 1950s and discussed at a March 17, 1960 meeting of the National Security Council. The West Indies were part of the "free world." The United States expected all the islands to "cooperate in world affairs" and pursue an economic strategy that was "conducive to the maintenance of political stability, pro-Western orientation, and free democratic institutions." Also required was "freedom from Communist influence," plus "U.S. access to such military rights and facilities as may be required by U.S. national security interests."[66]

These were the assumptions of the Truman containment doctrine. Even before Cuba became the only axis of America's Caribbean policy, the National Security Council saw the West Indies in narrow terms. Analysts emphasized that both before and after independence came to the islands, "the U.K. was to assume the basic responsibility of assuring that the needs of the West Indies for external capital are met." America would help because it wanted to "promote understanding of and friendship with the United States"; but the president said that the West Indies had to "appreciate" the role they could "play in over-all Western hemispheric defense by permitting U.S. retention of its military facilities in the area."[67]

The leases ran for 99 years, but of the 24 locations approved by the British, "it was extremely doubtful that, in international law, U.S. rights to these facilities will continue upon the achievement of independence." One idea was to negotiate with the British and with the West Indians *before* independence was achieved or conceded. Used as part of a package deal—e.g., the British had agreed to try and tie base rights to the demand for independence—the bases would be a tool which moved the West Indians to lease away a part of their island heritage even before they controlled it.[68]

Another suggestion came from the Joint Chiefs of Staff. At the National Security Council meeting they wanted to include a new sub-paragraph to the policy statement; the United States should "assist in the acquisition of a federal capital on land other than the leased base areas which the U.S. has declared that it requires."[69] Ten years after they refused the nuns and the people of Trinidad, the navy still had no desire to give up the base at Chaguaramas. It wanted the Caribbean Federation to find another place for its proposed capital, but the president refused. He didn't want to give up the base, but he refused to be "indifferent" to the West Indies. "Cuba should be a warning to us." Avoid "paternalism" but practice "benevolence." Or, as the president lectured his chiefs, "Eric Williams was try-ing to get us out of Trinidad. Perhaps our relin-quishment of our facilities in Trinidad would not be a bad thing except for the sums of money we have put into our base there."[70]

Eisenhower was a forceful participant in the National Security Council debates. The joint chiefs' new paragraph was rejected, and the president also tried to cut through what he labeled a "picayunish" difference between the meeting's participants. Both sides agreed that all economic aide would be used "as a means" to the same end—continued access to as many of the 24 facilities as the United States needed.[71] The only difference was whether the policy statement included larger objectives (e.g., economic viability for the islands), the elimination of trade barriers against the United States, and increased U.S. investment.

The president reminded all present that "the West Indies was at our backdoor and we should be careful we did not define our interests too narrowly in terms of our military bases in the area." For example, the United States was getting to be "a have-not nation" in relation to raw materials. We needed Jamaica's bauxite and, for a strong Organization of American States, the president "would be willing to trade several military bases."[72]

Like his predecessor from Hyde Park, New York, Dwight David Eisenhower was a yankee trader. He reemphasized that in approving the grander vision he never sought major obligations; the West Indies "two million headaches" would remain a British responsibility. The United States might need to offer other assistance. Thus, he introduced a change to the NSC document which indicated that if the British failed to provide the funds required for "internal security," the United States "would meet the Federation's minimum legitimate internal security requirements."[73]

This was normal U.S. policy. In 1940 and in 1960, each president put America first. In the United States citizens still thought of their country as the best, the biggest and the most giving of all the nations on earth. America was not like other great powers—unless you were a resident of the West Indies.

The president perceived that there was a major problem with U.S. policy in Latin America in general and the Caribbean in particular. Three months after the West Indies debate, the president began a

National Security Council meeting with a question that had been "troubling him" for some time. In the last months the world had witnessed a "rash of revolutions" in countries like Cuba and Turkey. Yet the United States had been working "since 1947, and very intensively since 1953, to achieve stability throughout the world." What bothered Eisenhower was that instead of stability, the United States confronted "unrest and unhappiness." He had heard from "some of our South American friends that all our aid merely perpetuates the ruling class of the many countries and intensifies the tremendous differences between the rich and the poor." He wondered "whether we were *stupidly* pushing ahead, carrying out programs without taking into account the effects these programs might be having."[74] [emphasis added]

The president had just summarized his West Indies policy. Giving money to underwrite the security forces that insured British control would certainly perpetuate the West Indies ruling class.[75] Given British (and American) racism, the president guaranteed that the United States would receive at least partial blame for one of the other problems underlined by the NSC policy paper. In a section labeled "anti-white sentiment," the NSC stressed that racial discrimination "creates difficulties for us in retaining the friendship of the new country and in retaining our installations there."[76]

President Eisenhower sat through the National Council debates and was intelligent, perceptive and informed. He asked probing questions and provided quick responses to the comments of his colleagues. As an explanation of the pursuit of self-defeating policy, the president said, "Perhaps the difficulty was this; perhaps we could only stand by and watch a wave of revolution sweeping the world."[77]

Nonsense. The president never passively watched revolutions occur; he tried to stop them. In supporting the British, Eisenhower was actively underwriting the imperialism that had produced more than four centuries of West Indian poverty and dependence. It was easier for the president to use his intelligence to rationalize—"we could only stand by and watch"—than to question the assumptions which shaped his interpretations of West Indian events.

The final section of the policy paper talked about "opportunistic leadership" in the West Indies. This was true in Trinidad where a man like Eric Williams "thrived on his efforts to make maximum political capital from the grievances against the United States."[78] Those grievances were real, but when Williams used them (and he did[79]), he was called an opportunist. However, when the United States traded destroyers for 99-year leases on Trinidad's best land, that was not deemed opportunistic. Nor was it considered opportunistic for President Eisenhower to express satisfaction about using independence as a lever to keep U.S. base rights.

But, of course, it was. The unrest and the unhappiness cited by the president were intimately linked to America's pursuit of its own self-interest. However, like his predecessors, the president behaved selfishly but interpreted his and others actions in light of inherited beliefs and actions. Eric Williams was an opportunist. The United States was benevolent. Communism had to be contained.

Islanders ignored "the mutuality of interest" between themselves and the United States.[80] And, even if the president shook hands with men like Rafael Trujillo and François Duvalier, that was only a distasteful means to an unquestioned end: support for the free world. More accurately, support for a world free of leaders like Fidel Castro.

Television Agression

The navy would use a "super-constellation aircraft." Flying over Key West, Florida pilots would—years before the Star Trek program was even an idea—"beam" the truth into Cuba by infiltrating its television network. Channel 8 was the proposed secret station but officials debating this idea (on April 14, 1960) worried about the reactions of others. George Allen (Director of the U.S. Information Agency) told the National Security Council that "if Mexico or Canada beamed programs to one of our cities from an airplane we would be furious." And what happened if Castro spied the plane? He might sense its mission, decide to retaliate, and "jam our programs" by turning his dial to the station used by the navy.

The most chilling prospect of all was making Castro a martyr. "Beaming television programs to Cuba from an aircraft would give Castro a platform from which to denounce the U.S. for television aggression." Thus, the NSC decided against television, but it did consider using baseball as a subversive influence in Cuban society. In this plan the Cubans would get to see free games, but, when they took their seventh inning stretch, the United States would include, along with the baseball scores, "other news" of interest to Cuban counterrevolutionaries.[81]

By January of 1960, the Eisenhower administration had decided to overthrow Fidel Castro. As Assistant Secretary of State Roy Rubottom explained it in a meeting of the NSC: "The honeymoon period of the Castro government" had ended in March of 1959. By June, "we had reached the decision that it was not possible to achieve our objectives with Castro in power"; and by July and August, the United States "had been busy drawing up a program to replace Castro."[82]

The president argued "that we could take whatever action we needed to take if we first made sure that the rest of Latin America was on our side."[83] That support, however, was very difficult to obtain. As early as 1947, the United States had changed its position on Caribbean interventions, but in Mexico and Brazil yesterday's actions still shaped today's perceptions. Thus, the administration's decision to intervene collided with the determined resistance of its inter-American neighbors. Before Eisenhower acted, Congress demanded some legally plausible justification for the intervention planned by his administration.

In secret sessions of the Senate Foreign Relations Committee, Senator Lausche had "just one question" for Assistant Secretary of State Thomas Mann. "Are you putting this solely on the basis of trying to help our own economy because you have no treaties upon which you can rely and because there is no principle in our international policy that warranted our people stepping in when a people have decided to choose a Communistic form of government? What international principle justifies us stepping in?"[84]

Instead of citing a principle which allowed the administration to intervene, Mann explained why the NSC's plans were legally and morally out of the question. "We have a commitment reaching to the very foundation of the good neighbor policy made by Cordell Hull in 1932 that we would not intervene in the internal affairs of another country." To Mann this was an insuperable roadblock because "in the inter-American system" intervention meant that one government could not use "military force or economic sanctions" against the sovereign will of another American nation. "This is what intervention means. You can't use force to force Cuba to do something, but what we are trying to do is avoid running headlong into that obstacle."[85]

The television or baseball schemes were among the first attempts to make an end run around the Good Neighbor Policy. They represented the administration's commitment to intervene. In the January 14, 1960 NSC meeting, the president hinted at what would later be the Bay of Pigs invasion when he told his colleagues that "the anti-Castro agents who should be left alone were being indicated,"[86] and "down in Latin America the danger is that if we don't conduct ourselves right we are going to arouse fears of such importance that we won't be able to carry out any kind of policy; so we are trying to select the grounds on which we fight."[87]

War had been declared. Dwight D. Eisenhower never doubted his right to intervene in Cuba. The administration found a way to convince others to participate in the multilateral interventions that were actually unilateral interventions and that were simultaneously the antithesis of intervention. The same administration plotted to assassinate Castro, but it refused to send in the marines because it did not want Caribbean and Latin American nations to think of us as we told them to think of the Soviet Union.

Senator Fulbright: "I don't want to be accused of being another Hungary."

Mr.Mann: "Exactly."

Senator Smathers: "If we don't stop Cuba quick we will really have another Hungary because they are going to move on Guantanamo and when they move on Panama then you have had it."

Mr.Mann. "When you were out of the room I said just what you are saying now. The objective is the same."

Senator Fulbright: "Thank you all very much for coming....I think it has been very informative to everybody."[88]

Hispaniola

After a long NSC discussion (in January of 1960) of the Caribbean, Vice President Nixon said that bad as the situation was in the Dominican Republic, he felt the situation in Haiti was even worse. To Nixon, Haiti resembled Africa, but to Secretary Of State Dulles "the situation in Africa was worse than in Haiti."[89] Neither man explained his reasoning; they simply compared evils and then moved on to an issue of real concern.

François Duvalier (he assumed office on October 22, 1957) never seriously threatened the containment of communism. On the contrary, as the Haitian president told Eisenhower on August 2,

1958, he immediately needed "military assistance for the defense of the national territory against the henchmen of international Communism."[90]

Duvalier created the brutal "Tonton-makutes" but had the audacity to call the Communists a bunch of henchmen. The White House gave Duvalier a quick $6 million to cover budgetary deficits, said it would consider his offer to use Haiti for military exercises, and sent in the marines to retrain the army that had recently used its (Wilson, Harding, Coolidge, Hoover, and Roosevelt) marine training to kill anyone who defied the government decree against khaki colored clothing.[91]

Eisenhower responded to Duvalier's brutality. When the Haitian president sent a letter (dated May 26, 1958) voicing his government's regrets about the treatment received by Richard Nixon in Venezuela, Eisenhower thanked Duvalier for his "gracious letter" and said, "I am encouraged by your remarks on the need for respecting and advancing the cause of freedom in this troubled world and I sincerely thank you for your assurances that you and the Haitian people are with us in this endeavor. This teamwork demonstrates the vitality of freedom loving peoples."[92]

In August of 1958, the teamwork collapsed. With help from American citizens, a group of Haitian exiles had organized a "revolutionary expedition" designed to overthrow the Duvalier regime. Using a small yacht, the exiles had left from Florida. Even though they were quickly defeated, the secretary of state suggested a presidential meeting with Haiti's foreign minister. "It is highly desirable that you receive the minister in order to dispel any impression that we countenance the organization of revolutionary expeditions in the United States against Dr. Duvalier's government."[93]

President Eisenhower, in a staged apology at the White House, conveyed his "sincere regrets" to the Haitian minister and did the same in a letter to Duvalier. Eisenhower "deplored" the involvement of American citizens and thanked the Haitian president for assisting in the struggle against communism.

The Haitian elite spoke French; the United States partially owed its existence to the patriots who left from French soil. Thus, in the American Revolution, Lafayette fought beside George Washington. In the counterrevolution led by Eisenhower (and Truman), the United States was reduced to fighting alongside the likes of "Papa Doc." Indeed, while he deplored the expeditions that would overthrow Duvalier, a year later the president sponsored the Florida mission that would turn into the Bay of Pigs.

The Eisenhower administration practiced expediency, not in the service of stability, but in the service of overthrowing "irresponsible" governments. In his support of dictators like Batista and Trujillo, Franklin Roosevelt did everything possible to avoid intervention. Stability was his goal and the president's definition of neighborliness was to turn a deaf ear to the screams of 17,000 Haitians.

Under President Eisenhower the U.S. Caribbean policy was no less expedient. In the service of anti-communism, the president of the United States advocated everything from intervention to murder. Dwight D. Eisenhower and Harry S. Truman removed the restraints imposed by Presidents Hoover and Roosevelt; and, in the process, he laid the groundwork for another U.S. intervention in the Dominican Republic.

In March of 1955, General Edwin Clark submitted a long report to President/General Eisenhower. Trujillo was misunderstood. The "benefactor of the Dominican Republic" was a man of great vision and dedication. His 25-year administration stood out as a "model of twentieth century government" and, added to that history of "democracy and statesmanship" was "the best and most continuous record of anti-communism of any democratic country today."[94]

Trujillo had commissioned this report. He often hired influential Americans to improve his image or, as in this case, obtain a greater share of the U.S. sugar market for the Dominican Republic. As the report noted, sugar still ruled the island's economy. It represented 68 percent of the invested industrial capital, it employed 74 percent of the total industrial employees, and its sales accounted for 43 percent of total sales. What Trujillo wanted was the same treatment accorded to Cuba. "With a stern assumption of all its responsibilities to its sister republics of the Americas," the Dominican Republic had been every bit as anti-communist as Cuba. Yet Batista received over 98 percent of the U.S. sugar quota and Trujillo, heir to the economy developed by the receivership, was supposed to remain content with less than 1 percent of the American market. The benefactor wanted justice.[95]

In Washington, the president read the report. While he never did anything meaningful to help Trujillo with sugar, he did order Nelson Rockefeller (then working at the White House) to send the document to a variety of government officials. They also read—in a report received from the president—about Trujillo's dedication to democracy. While the Generalissimo waited for word about sugar, he received a gift from the president. It was an autographed picture of Eisenhower—personally delivered by Richard Nixon—and it called for a response from Trujillo. The benefactor said that he and his wife were so grateful for the picture that "this fine portrait will occupy a preferential place in our home as a token of the high regard I have for one of the greatest statesmen of our difficult times whose efforts to preserve the Christian way of life to the West—to which I am firmly devoted—deserve the praise of all."[96]

The report, the picture, and Trujillo's response all point to the same thing; the Alice in Wonderland quality of the 1950s relationship between the United States and the Dominican Republic. In March of 1953, Eisenhower was asked to meet with then Dominican Ambassador-At-Large Rafael Trujillo. As the State Department's chief of protocol told the president, "receiving him might contribute towards strengthening Dominican cooperation in a number of sensitive areas." Never forget that "the Generalissimo is, of course, the sovereign power in the Dominican Republic notwithstanding the fact that his brother holds the office of the presidency."[97]

This report (dated May 5, 1954) verified the evidence accumulated in 1953: "The Generalissimo's megalomania is both dangerous and progressive.... His mental condition demands careful and constant study....His distorted sense of proportion countenances wild extravagances, including steps toward self-deification. Nevertheless he still performs brilliantly in many spheres and remains the indispensable and indisputable leader of the Dominican Republic." However, "Trujillo extended totalitarian controls to new areas of the economy and his greed for personal aggrandizement showed no signs of abating."[98]

American officials read reports about a maniac dictator's commitment to democracy, the island's sugar, trade and tax problems were never addressed (*e.g.*,the Clark Report stressed that the tax system was an antiquated outgrowth "of U.S. customs control from 1907 to 1940"), and Eisenhower said nothing about a budget that devoted the greatest share (39 percent according to General Clark) of its resources to defense. As in Cuba or Haiti, expediency was the order of the day—until the Generalissimo finally went too far.

In March of 1956, Trujillo ordered his subordinates to kidnap one of his enemies. Professor Jesus Galindez (who taught at Columbia University) disappeared when he tried to take a New York subway. To transport his enemy to the Dominican Republic the Generalissimo had used an American; this young man also disappeared into the Dominican night and his parents complained to their congressman. Representative Porter (of Oregon) complained to the nation, and that was the straw that broke the Dominican camel's back.[99]

Eisenhower sent a new ambassador to the island in 1957, and he told Joseph Farland that it was his job "to lead the Generalissimo gradually to an understanding that he should step down to avoid bloodshed."[100] The Generalissimo never listened, so, in March of 1960, General Eisenhower sent General Edwin Clark to the Dominican Republic to convince Trujillo to step down. Now.

In an April report to the president, Clark summarized his mission. "The climate for dictators has worsened in recent years." Trujillo knew that "his days were numbered." In fact, there was no doubt that "increasing opposition, both from within and without, might lead to a sudden collapse of the Trujillo regime...."[101] Clark suggested that Eisenhower take advantage of this opportunity "to utilize the present situation in the Dominican Republic to obtain for the United States a major psychological advantage by refuting critics who allege that our government coddles dictatorships and lacks initiative in Western Hemisphere affairs."[102]

He ended his report with the recommendation that envoys be immediately dispatched to the Dominican Republic. They should assist Trujillo in an "orderly transition to a free, democratic government." Given Trujillo's "known egoism and flair for dramatic actions," Clark suggested that our envoys arrange a retirement which would be announced before the Organization of American States. This dramatic transition to democracy would be an "unprecedented event that would establish Trujillo's unique place in history as a *wise dictator* who indeed was "El Benefactor" of his people."[103] [emphasis added]

And, what if the "wise dictator" refused to go? Washington would assure democracy by leaving "no misapprehensions as to the intentions of the United States....He should be given to understand that the

United States believes his "retirement" is only a matter of time and that it will probably happen soon, either voluntarily or involuntarily."[104]

President Eisenhower's hand-written notes indicate that he discussed this report with the secretary of state on April 25, 1960, and that "the secretary of state will follow up planning." Then Trujillo tried to assassinate the president of Venezuela. This was a second attempt because Trujillo had first tried to kill President Betancourt in 1951. That murder failed when the killer was unable to inject a lethal poison into Betancourt as he strolled down a crowded street. This time Trujillo chose explosives and was partially successful. He blew up the president's car and killed one of its occupants and a passerby; but, except for severe burns to his hands, President Betancourt escaped harm.[105]

The attack occurred on June 24th, 1960. By early July, the Organization of American States found Trujillo guilty, but, even before his public conviction, the State Department decided to "neutralize" him. In a meeting that occurred on June 28, 1960, Colonel J.C. King, Chief of the CIA's Western Hemisphere Division, met with Roy R. Rubottom, Assistant Secretary of State For Inter-American Affairs. The CIA needed to know "to what extent will the U.S. government participate in the overthrow of Trujillo." More specifically, would it allow the CIA to send in the "sterile weapons" that the opposition needed?

Rubottom said "yes." The CIA made plans to "rub out" Rafael Trujillo. His downfall appeared inevitable so, as the CIA said, "U.S. relations with the opposition should be as close as possible.

Providing arms as requested would contribute significantly toward this end."[106]

It would be another year before the assassins succeeded (the date was May 30, 1961). By then John Kennedy was in charge, and, with the father gone, Kennedy's problem was the son. General Ramfis Trujillo was a playboy who hated homosexuals. Indeed, as the new president read in a secret report, Ramfis once played a game. He put a homosexual in an airplane, and, since the local word for a gay person was "bird," Ramfis threw the fellow out of the plane and said, "You're a bird. Let's see if you can fly."[107]

Ramfis was a problem. The promised transition to democracy was on hold and President Kennedy needed a policy. Part of the advice he received from one of his most liberal Democratic advisors, John Bartlow Martin, was to "sash our hands of the Republic now, let matters drift, secretly encourage the opposition (to Ramfis), *get a massacre started*, try to see that it gets out of hand and American lives and property are endangered, then send the marines. There must be a better solution."[108] [emphasis added]

As officials searched for a different strategy, Martin offered the president this summary of the political situation:

"Our strengths: sanctions and the fleet.

"Ramfis' strength: the air force

"Opposition Strength: the people."[109]

The Eisenhower administration had helped murder Rafael Trujillo. Now John Kennedy and John Martin would try to dispose of the son. It was Camelot versus the people, the fleet of the New

Frontier against a century-long enemy: the Dominican masses.

Cemeteries and
Headless Bodies

*"And I said, what country is it? And he said, Haiti.
I said, my God, Haiti. I don't know anything about Haiti."*
—John Thurston, Ambassador to Haiti, 1962[1]

He had great writers. To read the speeches of John F. Kennedy is to enter a world of graceful prose, elegant thought, and high ideals. The words "Ask not what your country can do for you but what you can do for your country" has become a part of American culture. They still spark a sense of nostalgia. If only we had another John Kennedy...

He was a fine speaker. At a 1961 White House reception for the diplomatic corps of the Latin American Republics, the president announced an "Alliance For Progress." His writers, in a grandiose gesture, used dashes of Spanish in the address. The gesture, however, soon backfired. One translation of "Alianza para Progreso" is the "alliance that stops progress." Within months of the president's speech many Latinos used this translation to assess American efforts.

But on March 13, President Kennedy's writers referred to a host of North and Latin American heroes. Simón Bolívar, Benito Juarez, Tom Paine, José Marti and Thomas Jefferson all made an appearance because "our nations are the product of a common struggle, the revolt from colonial rule. And our people share a common heritage, the quest for dignity and the freedom of man."[21]

While this speech received high praise, in private the president's aides pointed to problems. One referred to an "ideological gap"; for all the talk about ideals "to many a Latin American eye the alliance was simply a money lending operation." Arthur Schlesinger warned that the focus on lending suggested that the alliance was reverting to the "failed" Eisenhower Latin American policy.[3] Schlesinger was right, about the alliance in particular and the Caribbean in general.

The head of the Alliance For Progress was a Puerto Rican. Teodoro Moscoso was given the job because he was said to have managed an "economic miracle" on the island, and the administration wanted a Latin American in charge. As John Bartlow Martin later noted, Moscoso's choice reflected the administration's ignorance of Latin America—"only afterwards did we realize that much of Latin America felt Puerto Ricans were nothing more than our colonial lackeys"[4]—but he was good for public relations. He would also help the president conclude a series of what the administration labeled "Puerto Rican real estate negotiations."[5]

The navy was tired of the Vieques residents who interfered with its military exercises and of the obstinacy of Puerto Rican officials. After months of negotiations, the islanders "were either unwilling or unable to accept our proposals or offer an alternative." They didn't want to move their citizens, and they also refused to dig up their cemeteries.

This was the Dracula plan. Puerto Ricans celebrate All Saints Day. Each year they visit the graves of their relatives. The navy had no objection to this religious ritual; the problem was the possible return of the banished citizens of Vieques. So, along with their belongings, the islanders had to take the bones and caskets of their departed ancestors. It was a terrible prospect but the navy was quite willing to provide the transportation.

The president agreed and then, in January of 1962, changed his mind. Governor Muñoz Marin convinced him that digging up cemeteries was bad politics. The governor said "that the political and human dismemberment which the project involves will be a fundamental shock. We know of no comparable action in American history. I believe that it is the kind of action which arouses instinctive disapproval."[6]

The governor got the president's attention. Kennedy told Muñoz that "his powerful letter" helped him understand the public relations impact of the Dracula plan. The islanders could stay, but that permission never signalled a change in U.S. beliefs and values. The everyday bombardment of Culebra continued—in the 1960s there were as many as 950 air sorties a month; and ship-to-shore gunfire, by as many as 22 different boats, took place every third day.[7] In an interview with Governor Muñoz, the president's special counsel asked this question about the plan to remove the people and cemeteries of Vieques: "Do you think that it was important enough to take the time of the president of the United States for the problems of seven thousand people?"[8]

No one had the time. John Kennedy's advisors

had a directive to stop communism and no hesitation about writing a memo which told the president of the United States that one of his options in the Dominican Republic was to "get a massacre started and try to see that it gets out of hand."[9] In this administration anything was possible, even using Oleg Cassini to do public relations work for Rafael Trujillo.

Juan Bosch

Three weeks before the CIA would help assassinate Trujillo, the president had sent Robert Murphy (a lawyer and vice-chairman of the Civil Aeronautics Board) and Oleg Cassini (he designed Jacqueline Kennedy's pillbox hats) to assess the situation in the troubled island. After the attempted murder of Romulo Betancourt, the United States had broken diplomatic relations with Trujillo. Murphy stressed that Washington had done so only to get "the pallid OAS resolution on Cuba." The rupture was not a matter of principle so, after meeting with Trujillo and President Joaquin Balaguer, Murphy concluded that "our hostility to the Dominican Republic is unwise....The groups at Ciudad Trujillo are willing and eager to be taken by the hand and to institute democratic reforms."[10]

McGeorge Bundy told the president to "fully disengage from any venture of this sort." It was a terrible idea because "the whole concept of the Alliance For Progress would be gravely shadowed in the eyes of Latin Americans if we were to move to anything like a policy of friendly guidance toward Trujillo."

And, what about Oleg Cassini? Bundy told the president that "if the public were to know that Oleg

Cassini is providing public relations help to Trujillo, your personal position as a liberal leader might be compromised."[11]

Bundy had no cause for concern. President Kennedy remains a beloved democrat and Rafael Trujillo a dead dictator as a result of plans which (as Robert Kennedy noted) "had been pending for some time."[12]

With Trujillo gone, the president focused on his options. Given the human and political disaster of his invasion of Cuba—the Bay of Pigs[13]—he needed a success. His problem was the Dominican Republic, and the shadow of Fidel Castro.

After the Bay of Pigs, it was impossible to make Caribbean policy without *first* considering Fidel Castro. He was the invisible presence that had to be considered. As John Bartlow Martin told the president, "Trujillo destroyed a *people*. There is little or nothing here on which to build a viable democracy. This should be viewed as a nation ravaged by a 30-years war, to be occupied and reconstituted."[14] [emphasis in original]

The CIA offered its assessment in July of 1961. "The real power in the Dominican Republic is still held by the Trujillo family through Ramfis' control of the armed forces and the police. The family also continues to dominate the economic life of the country." The CIA was nevertheless impressed by "the flexibility and skill" shown by Ramfis and Joaquin Balaguer. The opposition had "little or no chance" to win the elections planned for 1962, so Ramfis let them publicly voice their complaints. However, "on the separate issue of an orderly transition to a more representative political system, we believe that there

is no more than an even chance of a moderate program being carried out in view of the possibilities of
a return to a more forceful repression."[15]

By October, the president received a summary
of all the available analyses, written by Special
Assistant to the president Richard Goodwin, and it
started with a lament. Unless the president intended to invade, he could never avoid an uncomfortable
fact: "The Trujillo-[General] Sanchez group has the
guns and are prepared to use them to stay in
power." Thus, "I believe—sad as it makes me to say
this—that any solution which involves an actual
relinquishment of authority by Trujillo is not practical or possible or even desirable at this time."[16]

The United States had helped murder the
father. Now it was "forced" to support the son
because the Kennedy administration was more
Eisenhower than Eisenhower. At an NSC meeting in
January of 1960 Eisenhower officials said that the
"U.S. objective in the Dominican Republic was...to
neutralize the ability of Cuba to influence any post-
Trujillo regime."[17] In his recommendation to
President Kennedy, Goodwin said that "the primary
and overriding objective of the U.S. in the Dominican
Republic is the prevention of the establishment of a
pro-communist or neutralist state."[18]

Goodwin offered suggestions. Washington
would send a series of missions to the Dominican
Republic; "economic development, agriculture, organization of public administration, even a constitutional government mission"—we would send every
expert we could find and they would "help re-estab-
lish a viable society." Meanwhile, we would support
Balaguer; we would push for elections in late 1962

314

("no one can be ready for anything but a farcical election in May"); and, to keep the orgy-loving, "braid dripping" Ramfis in line, Goodwin suggested this: "It should be left reasonably clear in Ramfis' mind that if he begins to move to the left or towards neutralism we would find a pretext for coming in with the fleet."[19]

In the Eisenhower administration, the NSC considered a Dominican intervention if it could get an "invitation";[20] a "pretext" was sufficient for the Kennedy activists, a group that did send in aircraft carriers and high-ranking U.S. generals to keep Ramfis, his uncles, and the military at bay. They were told that the United States would assist no government that achieved power by force; and they were "persuaded," not only to hold elections, but to invite the OAS to supervise them.[21]

The elections were significant. As Martin noted, one of Washington's principal objectives "was to help get the winner in the palace alive"—the presidential mansion was originally the home of the American official charged with collecting the customs receipts—and they succeeded. In December of 1962, the leader of the Dominican Revolutionary party—Juan Bosch—was honestly elected president by an overwhelming majority. He promised major social change, the people expected it, and that meant the Kennedy administration had to resolve a crucial question: Which came first, support for democracy or the prevention of a government that threatened to make a left turn?[22]

In a nation where getting the president into the palace alive was a significant achievement, revolutionary social change was certain to produce instability. Bosch had condemned American support for Trujillo in 1930. Like so many Caribbean citizens, he shared the love/hate sentiments toward the United States of men as different as José Marti and Fulgencio Batista. Bosch might want to distance himself from the United States.

John Martin (American ambassador to the Dominican Republic) said that "we were not being much help." On April 28, 1963—Bosch took office in February—"the president had no cash now and would have none for several months. And to a considerable extent it was our fault. We were being far less generous and helpful to Bosch then we had been to the Consejo."[23]

Without money Bosch had no way to make good on his campaign promises. By April the lack of action had already produced disenchantment, but the surprising thing to Martin was the reaction of the Kennedy administration. Bosch asked for no loan; the United States owed the republic $22 million but it refused to pay up. This money had been withheld because the United States didn't want Rafael Trujillo to obtain a windfall as a result of filling portions of Cuba's former sugar quota. In 1960 and 1961, the U.S. imposed an extra tax "on political grounds." As Senator Hubert Humphrey told the president's advisors, the money was always supposed to be returned to the Dominican people. And, since Bosch had been elected by the people, the money was his.[24]

Washington refused. They advised Bosch to borrow—at commercial rates—against the money he was owed. While Martin called this "an outrageous request," he was powerless to produce change. Bosch was desperate, but, to Martin's dismay, "his public stance is clearly one of independence, especially independence of the U.S."

This bothered Martin. The receivership, the eight year occupation, Roosevelt's about-face on the treaty, Eisenhower's autographed pictures—Martin not only missed why Bosch wanted to be independent, he underlined the even more angry reactions of his Kennedy administration colleagues: "The more he shuns our help, the more we withhold it, and so the more he resents us. Both these situations tend to drive him even deeper into the arms of the left."[25]

Bosch lasted nine months. He was forced out by the military on September 25, 1963, and the next day the U.S. Senate held a set of executive session hearings (they were made public in December of 1986) which were a requiem for President Bosch.

Edwin Martin (Assistant Secretary of State For Inter-American Affairs) and Teodoro Moscoso (head of the Alliance For Progress) spoke for the Kennedy administration. They had heard about the coup two weeks before it occurred. Throughout this period U.S. civilian officials "vigorously" told the plotters "not to take unconstitutional action"[26]

What kind of president was Bosch? Martin said he "had worked 16 to 18 hours a day trying to make his government run. I think there are few examples of as much devotion to the job as he has put into it" He was honest in a corrupt society, and "there is no evidence that we can discover, and in view of the charges we have made an effort at this, that he is a Communist in any sense of the term." On the contrary, "he is a left of center liberal, a man of very high ideals and a very devoted desire to help his people, and very fixed ideas about how this should be done."

What were the man's problems? First was his idealism. Instead of using his party to deliver patronage, Bosch let it deteriorate. "He decided he was going to represent all the Dominican people and no party and that he didn't need the party." Second, Bosch abided by the Dominican constitution. Along with members of the exiled right, Bosch let Communists openly participate in the political process. This was "the central issue of the attacks on him," but Martin told the Senate that Bosch had a "defensible theory." He argued that "if I take vigorous steps against them I will merely drive them underground....What I want to do is let them come in, operate openly, where they can be watched and if they take any subversive action why then, of course, we can move in."[27]

In these executive session hearings, the left outdid the right. Teodoro Moscoso told the committee about the United States' responsibilities. What happened in Venezuela? The first thing Betancourt did was let "the Commies back in." And Bosch? What did he do? "The first thing he does is let all the Commies back into the Dominican Republic." To Moscoso, the United States had clear obligations: "We have a responsibility, it seems to me, to not get so deluded by this intriguing term "democracy" that we lose perspective in many of these countries; that you cannot operate these countries on a basis of democracy as we understand it and interpret it, that you still have got to have a strong central government."[28]

As for Juan Bosch, Moscoso noted that he had another fatal flaw: "I must say that he ran probably about the most conservative government, financially, fiscally responsible government, that I have seen." Bosch refused to run a deficit and that baffled the Kennedy people because, as Secretary of State Martin noted, "perhaps our difficulty on this particular point was that we really haven't had much experience trying to persuade left wing liberals to spend money."[29]

Over thirty-five years (1905-1940) the United States had forced the Dominican Republic to balance its budget. A reason for the receivership was the necessity to keep expenditures in line with receipts. Bosch personally approved every expenditure of more than $300, and, despite his campaign promises, he refused to run the deficits advocated by Moscoso and Martin.

In his State of the Union address President Kennedy underlined the crisis nature of the United States balance of payments deficit. He meant to do whatever had to be done to balance the nation's accounts, and one of those things was to refuse to send dollars abroad. Bosch never got his $22 million. A major cause of Bosch's problems—as Ambassador Martin noted in the spring, even a $10 million advance would have helped the Dominican's chances of survival—was our trying to balance our accounts at Bosch's and the Dominican people's expense.[30]

Bosch was gone. Edwin Martin said we had no intention of removing the ambassador, nor of stopping our feeding programs. The food helped the people at the "bottom fringe" and the ambassador would stay because "we feel that he and his staff have influence with the people who are operating there."[31]

There was talk of military pressure. It was rejected because of the difference between an elected and an imposed government. Martin explained that, last year when the provisional government was shaky, "we a couple of times brought in an aircraft carrier and took the president out with a lot of noise and publicity for lunch aboard it." We got away with that because this "was not an elected regime." However it was bad Caribbean politics to force a shipboard lunch on a freely elected executive. Martin said he had made the same offer to Bosch, but "he rejected the suggestion because he wanted to maintain a posture of independence from the United States."

Martin drew two lessons from this experience. It was easier to influence an imposed government. And, don't bluff: "If you are not prepared to back it up, you better not do it, because it won't work."[32]

Meanwhile the junta was persuaded of the danger of communism. Yet in January of 1964, the CIA told President Johnson that "his refusal to adopt a strong anti-Communist posture left Bosch vulnerable to rightist pressure for his removal," in reality, "for many of those working for his overthrow, the Communist issue was the excuse; their self-interest was the motive."[33]

In October of 1963, Kennedy severed diplomatic relations with the Dominican Republic and suspended aid. In November, he decided to recognize the military government, and, by the turn of the year, the Johnson administration formally completed Washington's about-face. As Assistant Secretary of State George Ball told the senators (in an October 11, 1963 executive session), "You have a people who are suffering from the very strange kind of psychological trauma as a result of their dreadful experiences under Trujillo, and it is a matter of nursing them back to some kind of political health. This isn't going to be easy."[34]

Virgin Islands

In 1953 President Eisenhower named Archie Alexander governor of the Virgin Islands. He was "friendly, had been a generous contributor to the Republican Party and is backed by the Iowa delegation." To date, Iowa had received little of the "limited patronage" available and this memo from the Republican National Committee reminded the president that he had to spread the jobs across the country. Even if he ultimately chose someone from another underrepresented state, "remember that there are some 20 important jobs in the Islands that the governor can fill. He must be our man."[35]

President Kennedy nominated Ralph Paiewonsky. They had spent a day together in 1958 when the Kennedys visited St. Thomas. Paiewonsky had also hosted Theodore Sorenson (the senator's assistant) when he later spent a week on the islands, and Paiewonsky led a 1960 convention delegation that strongly supported John Kennedy for the presidency. With these political qualifications, Paiewonsky's life-long residency in the islands, and his active participation in its political affairs, this governor was a potentially promising compromise; a patronage appointee who knew something about the Virgin Islands.[36]

The governor's nomination hearings were long, contentious, and a remarkable commentary on Congress. Paiewonsky was rich. He and his family owned everything from St. Thomas' movie theaters to its bakery and drugstore, from its real estate to the A.H. Riise rum distillery. There was nothing inherently wrong with money. What upset Senator Clinton P. Anderson (Chairman of the Senate Committee on Interior and Insular Affairs) was the Virgin Islands Corporation, its large losses, and its relationship to the distillery owned by Paiewonsky and his family.

The governor was a businessman. So, "as a businessman, with all these investments down there, can you explain the loss of $662,000 in sugar operations in one year, after several millions of capital had been poured into it by the United States over the years." Paiewonsky pleaded ignorance. He noted that he had nothing to do with the Virgin Islands Corporation, and, although he would try to make it profitable, sugar was a hard sell. He doubted that an operation "restricted into the narrow field of sugarcane cultivation" could ever earn large profits.[37]

The House debates in 1949 were not mentioned. The senators displayed a case of amnesia about the corporation's creation and a fit of anger when they questioned Paiewonsky about his distillery. Did he buy molasses from the Virgin Islands Corporation? Was it cheap? And was its low cost a function of the federal government's heavy subsidies? Was Washington underwriting the substantial profits earned by the Paiewonsky distillery?

The implication was that Paiewonsky had cheated the government. Days later he returned with a lawyer to refute the insinuations. He was a sharp businessman, and his very profitable rum business indirectly received government subsidies. But Paiewonsky had done nothing illegal, or even, by American standards, unethical. He bought the rum business when the government sold it. He said he didn't know why the government disposed of the property and neither did the head of the corporation. Kenneth Bartlett admitted that VICORP had lost $1.2 million dollars in the last eight years. When Senator Anderson demanded to know why the government sold the rum business, Barlett said "I have not any idea." And then Anderson responded with this question: "Did you not ever get curious?"[38]

As in 1926 and 1949, Congress argued that the islanders were a never-ending drain on the nation's resources. Generous Americans covered the corporation's losses and subsidized the profits of a private rum distillery. So, while Ralph Paiewonsky could be governor, he had a specific charge from Chairman Anderson: "Try to repair this loss to the federal treasury."[39]

Understandably, Paiewonsky failed. VICORP closed its doors in the late 1960s. But there were economic alternatives, especially for corporations using "Headnote 3"—a 1954 law which said that goods produced in the Virgin Islands could enter the United States duty free even if they contained as much as fifty percent "foreign content." The law was an attempt to do something for the possessions, and it worked—too well.

In 1959, islanders exported only 5000 watches; but, with Paiewonsky's assistance, the export total jumped to 4 million watches by 1966. This was a significant help to the local economy, but there were both foreign and domestic policy problems. On the foreign front, many of the watch parts came from the Soviet Union. Thus, Congress was subsidizing an American colony which was—however insignifi-cantly—helping to underwrite international commu-nism. Congress unsuccessfully pressured the islands to find another foreign supplier.[40]

Since few people knew about the Soviet parts, the real threat to the watch industry came from the United States. Too much success on the island threat-ened domestic producers who demanded that Congress impose quotas on Virgin Islands watches. This would forever limit one of the island's only "growth" industries, but Congress did as it was asked. In a formula that might have baffled Einstein, the Virgin Islands received seven-eighths of one-ninth's production of the last year's domestic consumption of watches. This immediately limited employment in the watch industry, and, equally important, it underlined the complete dependence of the islands on the will and whim of Congress.[41]

The Paiewonsky administration understood the dilemma. But the governor and his colleagues nev-ertheless sparked a transformation that increased dependence on Washington as it simultaneously made native islanders a minority in their own home-land. From a population of 34,000 people in 1961, the islands jumped to almost 70,000 inhabitants in 1969. Many of these new immigrants—labeled "aliens" on the islands—came from locations like Puerto Rico and Grenada. By the end of the decade the newcomers outnumbered the natives. As the Interior Department put it, "native Virgin Islanders had become a minority" in the colony.[42] This trans-formation was based on industries that made all residents "wards" of an undependable guardian: the United States Congress.

Governor Paiewonsky got a call from David Rockefeller. Chase Manhattan had a branch on the island, Paiewonsky was a founder of the bank (bought by Chase in 1959), and the governor jumped on the request made by Rockefeller. One of Chase's best customer—Leon Hess of Hess Oil—hoped to establish a petroleum refinery on St. Croix. Rockefeller "wanted Paiewonsky to show Hess some consideration" and the governor said, "tell him to come."[43]

Paiewonsky convinced reluctant land owners to sell to Hess. The governor thought it was a great opportunity and so did Hess. One beauty of a Virgin Islands refinery—it is today the largest in the world—was the ability to use foreign boats. As long as Congress allowed the exemption to continue, Hess could use much less expensive foreign bottoms, manned by much less expensive foreign crews. Hess received a sixteen-year exemption from all Virgin Islands taxes, a rebate on all import duties on raw materials and plant and equipment for sixteen years, and a 75 percent rebate on all income taxes paid to the Virgin Island government by Leon Hess or any of his resident stockholders.[44]

A final incentive was added in 1966. Congress reluctantly agreed to help the distressed economies of Puerto Rico and the Virgin Islands. Each received the right—which could be revoked whenever Congress succumbed to the strong pressures exerted by mainland producers—to export to the United States substantial quantities of refined foreign oil. In the Virgin Islands, Hess shrewdly agreed to share the wealth—the local treasury got $7500 a day for ten years—but its ripple effects were limited. Senator

J. Bennett Johnson (Louisiana) pointed to an irrefu-
table fact: "You know, these refineries employ a few
people but they are very capital intensive. They are
not that job intensive."[45]

Even into the mid-seventies the refinery only
employed 825 people and, despite promises to hire 90
percent legal residents, Hess never did so. He
brought in mainlanders, Puerto Ricans and immigrants from other Caribbean islands. They took the
jobs promised to native islanders—the unenforced 90
percent quota was for any "legal resident"—and, even
more damaging to the island's long range prospects,
many "aliens" stayed after the construction boom
ended. By 1970, the islands had the refinery, outsiders had the best jobs, pollution had increased substantially, and the local government used its oil tax
revenues to buy the new garbage trucks that were
used in a manner reminiscent of the loading of coal
in the early twentieth century. To keep people
employed, workers went into the rear of the trucks
and did manually what the vehicles could do
mechanically—dump out the garbage.[46]

Politically, a revised act of 1954 erased a clause
which formerly put "qualified natives" first in line for
government jobs, added a comptroller whose deepest roots went back to the Dominican customs
receivership, and, most important, again denied
islanders a non-voting resident commissioner.
Congress told islanders that "the business and
political activity of the Virgin Islands did not justify
the expenditure of $47,000 annually for 24,000 peo-
ple."[47] Thus, they would be governed by appointees
who lacked even nominal representation in the body
that "disposed of and made all needful rules and

regulations respecting the territory or other property belonging to the United States."

Under these circumstances, the governor and his supporters argued that Hess and the Soviet watches (and the Harvey Alumina plant) were the only way to achieve economic "growth." That they displaced natives and transformed the Virgin Islands was an incidental consequence of totally unplanned development. As Senator Long later lectured the governor in relation to Hess Oil, "that was a complete accident that various companies twisted arms in that bureaucracy down there to get first one tax allocation approved and then something else. I am happy to see that you have it, but if you can find a way to make your people feel safe and secure in those beautiful islands we can work with you and send you all the tourist trade that you can handle."[48]

Senator Long sounded—*exactly*—like Ernest Gruening in the 1930s. The Virgin Islands took the accidental crumbs that fell off Congress' table, and, if those crumbs produced garbage, they could always be picked up by the workers not using the latest in disposal equipment. Meanwhile, send those tourists. And make sure they see the exquisite national park the Rockefellers created out of their holdings on St. John.[49]

Governor Luis Muñoz Marin

The governor never got the point. Because Congress still had plenary power over Puerto Rico, enhancing commonwealth was a legal nightmare. What did the governor want President Kennedy to do with the proposal that Puerto Rico's constitution would supercede that of the United States? The "rights, privileges, and immunities of citizens" were to be guaranteed by the island's constitution and, when it came to defense, the "enhanced" compact proposed by the governor suggested that "Puerto Rico would be free to wage war independently, or together with the United States, or allied with the United States or against it."[50]

This was out of the question. Since Kennedy had opened a can of worms by willingly discussing change with the governor, he tried to close it by creating a commission. Distinguished citizens would examine the island's status, report back to the president, and by the time they issued their report Muñoz would have finally backed off.

Kennedy bet on the commission, but before it met, Congress had to approve its creation. That meant hearings (in May of 1963) and, for a proud Puerto Rican, a humiliating confrontation with an angry congressman. Muñoz said that "the basic thing that must be done is to clarify the noncolonial nature of a commonwealth status," to define "a feeling, a relationship of dignity, of political dignity between Puerto Rico and the United States beyond any shadow of a doubt."

Congressman John Saylor (Pennsylvania) didn't care about feelings.He made Muñoz listen to the (June 30, 1950) words of Congressman Fred Crawford—"we are not offering the people of Puerto Rico anything except the right to vote on a constitution to be submitted to the president of the United States who in turn is to submit it to the Congress of the United States for approval." He also said that enhanced commonwealth was nothing more than a figment of Governor Muñoz's imagination. The governor—not Congress—was responsible for the mis-conceptions which existed.[51]

Muñoz then made an admission. "If Fred Crawford was right then Puerto Rico is still a colony of the United States. If it is still a colony of the United States it should stop being a colony as soon as possible for the honor of the United States and for the sense of self-respect of the people of Puerto Rico."[52]

The audience had a biased response to this comment: Islanders applauded and North Americans "jeered." It was a terrible morning for the governor and an even worse afternoon. In its testimony the Kennedy administration reversed virtually every one of its resolutions. Premature talk of "permanent" commitments was likely to produce misunderstandings. The commission would decide the propriety of "juridical equality," and the plebiscite desired by Muñoz should be optional rather than mandatory.[53]

Once the commission was created, President Johnson received these assurances from James Rowe, his friend and the commission's chair. Rowe said that the president "would not have to devote more than 10 or 15 minutes of your own time to this, if it is politically desirable in terms of New York."[54] Puerto Ricans were registering as Democrats, so the president should take that into consideration when he allocated his time. Meanwhile, Lee White (the official who asked Muñoz if the 7000 citizens of Vieques were worth President Kennedy's time) had prepared a memo for the president.

White explained that the commission would foreclose the islanders options before they ever exercised their right to self-determination. "Statehood does not seem anywhere near feasible at this point; it cannot, however, be left out as a possibility, for political reasons."

Independence had a small following ("probably no more than 2–3 percent") but "this too has to be regarded as a possibility to offset charges of colonialism made by Castro and other Communist elements in the Caribbean and South America."

The "perfection of commonwealth...involved the most difficult and painstaking study and review in almost every aspect of government." This could not be avoided as an alternative because the island already enjoyed commonwealth status.[55]

What if, as in 1946, Puerto Ricans threatened to choose a status, *e.g.*, the still "nowhere near feasible" statehood that Congress refused to endorse? That would produce the United Nations' criticism endured by Henry Cabot Lodge in 1953–54, so White explained what he had done to avoid "an international loss of prestige." The commission "included congressional representation in order to provide the commission with some guide as to what would be acceptable to Congress and how to present it, and secondly to provide a natural body of support for it when its recommendations are made."

This was good politics. White then suggested to the president that in his 10 or 15 minute meeting with the commission he should stress "the firm dedication of the United States to the principle of self-determination for all peoples."[56]

This was a winning public posture as long as no one found out that, besides the president's commission, the FBI was simultaneously interfering with the self-determination of the Puerto Rican people. In a report that would later be submitted to President Carter, an aide who had examined some of the FBI's documents (he was sure that the FBI had withheld material from the president) explained "the vicissitudes of a steady campaign of disruption [of the independence movement] over the 1960-69 period." While the FBI plotted to use everything from stink bombs (which would stop the independence presses) to antagonizing letters to double agents, the president was told that "the U.S. has repeatedly and pridefully declared its policy on political status to be that of self-determination. Yet here is a record of a decade of hanky-panky....What is most damaging is the FBI swashbuckling at the time of the plebiscite (is that self-determination?) and even at the time of the 1968 election."[57]

This evidence did not appear until the end of the 1970s. A day *before* the plebiscite actually occurred, former Governor Muñoz Marin sent to now Supreme Court Justice Abe Fortas the celebration of commonwealth's victory that should be read by the president of the United States.

Lyndon Johnson was happy that the "wishes of the Puerto Rican people had been determined democratically in a [July 23, 1967] plebiscite." It was "especially gratifying" that commonwealth status had received such a "clear endorsement" (60 percent of the vote).[58]

As far as the United Nations (and any other international body) was concerned, the Puerto Rican people had freely chosen to continue their compact with the United States. Because nobody defined the meaning of commonwealth before the election occurred, Senator "Scoop" Jackson commented on the commission's work. Islanders had to grasp that the English language was Puerto Rico's mandated means of communication; and, they should also know that Congress "could act unilaterally"—in any political, economic, or cultural matter—whenever it chose to do so.[59]

Dominican Republic

Their formal name was Task Force 44.9, but to marines, sailors and civilians alike, these men were the "Caribbean Ready Group." Their task was to snuff out the Cold War's "brush fires" before they escalated into full scale conflagrations. They were ready for anything, even a call (on Saturday, April 24, 1965) to cruise from their Vieques, Puerto Rico base to the waters surrounding the Dominican Republic. Their orders were to hurry up and wait. They might be called into action; they might not.

Ambassador John Bartlow Martin later explained the president's role: "I do know this: The president was running the Dominican intervention like a desk officer in the State Department. I mean, I talked to him at least once a day [after Martin was sent back to the Dominican Republic] and sometimes I talked to him three times a day." In Martin's experience this was uncommon presidential behavior. "You know, the president ordinarily withholds himself a little bit. But this president did not. He was in that Dominican thing....I think that might account for his intemperate utterances on the television. He lost his perspective on the thing."[60]

The "thing" was a full scale military intervention of the Dominican Republic. It began on April 29, 1965, and Martin was right about the president's intense and personal involvement. A summary sheet in the Johnson Library indicates that in 17 days (between April 25 and May 11) the president held 42 separate meetings about the Dominican Republic. Eighteen of these were group strategy sessions and, when the president finished these, he turned to the phone. White House logs show that he made 225 Dominican calls in this period. First on the list was McGeorge Bundy (86 times) but second was an old friend of the president's and an old student of the Caribbean. Johnson called Justice Fortas 40 times in these 17 days.[61]

Fortas provided essential assistance. He helped educate Johnson about the Dominican Republic—in the early days the president did not realized that the Dominicans shared the island with the Haitians[62]— and on May 2 he made an important call to Puerto Rico. Juan Bosch lived there, and Fortas "unequivocally" instructed Governor Roberto Sanchez Vilella to keep Bosch in Puerto Rico. The president believed that his nine month government had been infiltrated by Communists, and Johnson "did not want another Cuba."

Bosch, informed of the order from Washington, said this: "El elefante le teme al raton." The elephant is afraid of the mouse.[63]

Bosch had a point, but the president's real fear came, not from the Dominican mice, but from the Cuban rats. In the president's mind, the Dominicans were almost irrelevant. As he told Martin, shooting up a capital city with American troops was not the last thing he wanted to avoid. That was another Cuba, "a Communist takeover in that country." So, no matter how remote the threat, the United States meant to squash every rat in the Republic.

CRUISING THE CARIBBEAN

As he debated military strategy, the president received a number of interesting suggestions. One came from Senator George Smathers. He thought "it was worth considering the use of the National Guard of Puerto Rico. These men are all Latins of the same general make-up as are the Dominicans who are now fighting each other." To Smathers "the Puerto Ricans (if they would fight) would obviously be better received than our own marines and para-troopers by the locals and throughout at least the Western Hemisphere."[64]

There is no evidence of a response to this suggestion. Phone logs show that the president called Luis Muñoz Marin, but, instead of using Puerto Ricans, Lyndon Johnson let the Eisenhower administration provide him with a plan of action.

On April 14, 1960 Treasury Secretary Douglas Dillon cautioned Vice President Richard Nixon that "in order to intervene [in the Dominican Republic] we would need an invitation." One never arrived, and the Eisenhower administration never requested a plea for troops. It waited for an invitation. Lyndon Johnson wrote his own. Indeed, even though the U.S. ambassador provided a perfect pretext for inter-vention—the day troops landed the ambassador said that "if Washington wishes they can be landed for purpose of protecting and evacuating American citi-zens"[65]—President Johnson not only insisted on an invitation, he specified its content.

The Dominicans based a request for troops on *their* need for military support. But Assistant Secretary of State Thomas Mann ordered a rewrite; he told the Dominicans to base the invitation on the threat to American lives. Conceivably, the massacre suggested by John Martin would occur before the marines landed but,, if not, the president would think of something. Meanwhile, the danger to Americans was so great that the first soldiers to land were ordered to go in unarmed; this "control element" evacuated the Americans "without a hitch....Of the Americans who arrived [at the harbor of] Haina none had been physically harmed."[66]

Officials hoped to generate support for the intervention. On May 2, 1965, the president received a long summary of "favorable reactions" from "politically moderate" statesmen and newspapers. The writers made Cuba—not the Dominican Republic—the center of their stories, and the *New York Herald Tribune* published this comment: "It may be too bad that the Castro betrayal has prejudiced revolution as a sovereign people's right for removing a wrong, but it is a fact....The charge of gunboat diplomacy is...as unjustified in this instance as the gunboats of old are obsolete....True American forces landed on a neighbor nation's shores....But what matters most is the purpose and the context."[67]

In January of 1915, Woodrow Wilson—also writing about the Dominican Republic—said "no more revolutions would be permitted." Our demand for stability took precedence over their rights to sovereignty or their solutions to political and social problems.[68]

In May of 1965, the United States still acted like a counterrevolutionary force. The underlying constant in the two interventions was the cultural beliefs of U.S. leaders; in 1915 and 1965 it was assumed that they had the right to determine when and if a revolution was acceptable.

In 1965, the purpose and context of the intervention pointed to the same fact; Castro, the revolutionary, had killed revolution. He set such a bad example that the United States was finally willing to pay what Secretary of State Marshall called "the penalty of power." The United States would intervene unilaterally and refuse to seek the assistance of a multilateral force. As the president's advisors later noted, the members of the Organization of American States were both "timid" and "paralyzed by legal inhibitions."[69]

Thomas Mann explained these inhibitions to the Senate in a long series (from April through July of 1965) of executive session hearings. They were made public in September of 1990 and illustrate the nature of the administration's reasoning.

Senator Fulbright (on May 3, 1965) read Articles 15, 17, and 18 of the OAS charter. They forbid any form of interference or intervention, so Fulbright said, "I don't see how we are going to escape the charge that, whether you like it or not, this is a return to gunboat diplomacy and intervention in spite of the charter."[70]

Mann began with what Fulbright later called a lie. The administration was neutral. It supported neither the rebels nor the junta. It did "not wish to oppose a revolution of the right kind."

This went on for quite a while until Mann offered a history lesson. The purpose of the nonintervention principles written into the OAS charter was "to check the power of the United States. They wanted to check our power because of our interventions during the days of Wilson and during the days of Theodore Roosevelt, the interventions."

The problem—"and I think this is quite serious for the Nation"—was that nobody in the mid-1940s foresaw that "the great problem of our decade is how you prevent Communist subversion in a collective, in a legal way. It is simply not written into the charter."

Mann thought that rewriting the charter was a good idea, but the Mexicans were sure to say no. On "superficial technical grounds" Mexico would adhere to a strict policy of nonintervention. Mann furnished this ideological basis for a military intervention: "The real intervention in the Dominican Republic took place when these 85 people [the Communists that Bosch had "coddled"] were trained to overthrow the government of the Dominican Republic." They were the culprits, and, instead of an intervention, "what we are doing in there now is taking a *counter-intervention* attitude."[71]

To Mann, the marines were the armed umpires who would transform chaos into free elections because "the best defense against communism in this hemisphere is a free election." But, echoing Teodoro Moscoso when he testified about the fall of Juan Bosch in 1963, Secretary Mann stressed that the senators must avoid naiveté. Democracy meant something different among the Latins; so, "we must not be so naive to think that just the mere holding of an election is a democracy...."[72]

Mann had just undermined the logic of his position. If the best defense was a free election, what did it achieve if the holding of an election was not democratic? Even if a fair election were held, we would still always find cause for criticism, interference or intervention because—as Mann lectured the senators—their systems were Latin, ours Anglo-Saxon, theirs centralized, ours federalized. It was a comparison of apples and oranges, but Mann had to turn one into the other because he had no palatable answer to a dilemma posed by Senator Church.

The senator pointed to a fact that would soon be made in a speech by Defense Secretary Robert McNamara: only a minority of the world's insurgencies involved Communists (38 percent according to McNamara).[73] And "our own national security was based on principles that we have since avowed, the right of revolution against tyranny as resting with the people."[74] The liberal church said the United States had to protect against "Communist infiltration"; but, it also had to be true to the principles upon which "we were born."

The trick was how to do both, especially after the United States had been repeatedly defeated in its attempts to change the OAS charter. Mann said that "this idea of nonintervention has such a tremendous and even irrational hold on the minds of many Latin Americans that they may not be willing to have any kind of collective action."[75]

The Latin Americans had been complaining about U.S. interventions for more than sixty years. The United States would do as it pleased because Mann finally reached to the deepest assumption of his and the president's thinking: *We could say this is justified on the grounds of self-defense....*[W]e hesitate to take that position publicly right now [May 3] because it would raise other questions of various kinds." But, a missile base in the Dominican Republic and Haiti would fall "in thirty minutes." And "if you cannot stop it there because of this and that and the other, then you cannot stop it somewhere else, which is more difficult, say, in Venezuela or Columbia, which is in great danger today, even

Panama is in great danger." [emphasis added]

These were Caribbean dominoes. They would fall without U.S. intervention which was, in truth, based on a new variation of the Monroe Doctrine. The United States had the right to unilaterally protect itself against the threat of a Communist takeover. In a CIA report received by the president on May 7, 1965, the agency said that the Communists were "a harmless and isolated minority" under the Bosch government. They had gained some strength under the junta and they were "intent on winning influence in the rebellion." But, as of May 7, the rebels "presented to the world the picture of a moderate leftist regime dedicated to the fulfillment of a popular revolution."[76]

The rebels had received help from the Communists, and what would the Communists do if the rebels emerged victorious? The United States resorted to tortured reasoning. Before the committee the intervention was a counterintervention. Before the world a "White Paper" tried to make it legally palatable while, in private, Justice Abe Fortas assessed the paper: "Its soundness as a matter of legal analysis is subject to effective challenge; and it will confuse and obscure the United States *best* position which is moral and pragmatic."[77]

Fortas was honest. The president tried to make the illegal, legal for two reasons: his beliefs contradicted those of the OAS, and he never had the courage to make the argument offered by Secretary of State Lansing in 1915. "While, therefore, the Monroe Doctrine and Pan-Americanism may come into conflict, the Monroe Doctrine will in case of conflict prevail so long as the United States maintains the Doctrine and is the dominant power among the American nations."[78]

Ambassador John Martin said, "the reason for the [General Antonio] Imbert government was that I felt we needed a third force....It was the United States military versus the rebels. I wanted a third force in between that would fight the rebels. I didn't want us to fight the rebels. I wanted some Dominican to fight the rebels. And Imbert was the guy; he was the only one with any guts, the only one with any troops.[79]

Secretary Mann made the same point in executive session. "The great difficulty [it was now July 14, 1965] was to get any Dominican of any stature and reputation to step forward and assume responsibility." Balaguer wanted to be elected, no one else wanted the president's job, so the United States faced two choices: "Impose a government by force or alternatively permit the armed forces, if they have the capability, to impose a government by force."[80]

The president chose the general. And that meant using an Assistant Secretary of State For Economic Affairs, Anthony Solomon, as a "bag man." Solomon brought "a hell of a bundle of money down to meet the payroll of the Imbert government. I [Ambassador Martin] remember going into the back room of the embassy one night, and there were a lot of girls counting stacks of hundred dollar bills."[81]

Secretary Mann told the Senate that "the history since Trujillo" was that the military resisted anyone who tried to change the rules of the game. Soldiers were accustomed to buying things—*e.g.*, cars, televisions—in the United States and then selling them on the island's active black market. This was an institutionalized part of Dominican military life, and if an honest man like Bosch "tries to tangle with them, they throw him out."[82]

They also threw out anyone who interfered with their phantom payrolls. Senator Carlson asked Mann if it was true that "the chief of police collects checks for about 300 deputies, of which he has no deputies, and he pockets the money himself." Mann said that "we all understood that there would be some leakage." Since nobody had the time or the authority to revise the payrolls presented by loyalist soldiers, the United States simply forked over the hundred dollar bills. Thus, even though Mann could not confirm this particular bit of corruption, "I have no doubt that when this is all over...that we will find instances of this kind."[83]

The United States was now operating under street rules. Johnson and his subordinates saw no alternative to secretly subsidizing corruption; for the foreseeable future the phantom employees would receive their checks while, in public, the president sought to justify the intervention. At a June 17 news conference he told the country that "some 1500 innocent people were murdered and shot and their heads cut off." This was pure fabrication but the need to accuse the rebels of savagery underlined the weakness of the administration's position. The consequences of this lie symbolize the absurdities to which a blind anti-communism had driven the United States and its officials.

In the executive session hearings, Senator Fulbright said that the president's statements were "very inflammatory." They "affect the attitude of the public and can influence policy." So, in a question to Under Secretary of State Jack Vaughn, Fulbright asked if it was true. Had these people been beheaded? Vaughn said the president never said that. Fulbright cited his source; it was a State Department press release. Now Vaughn, backed by Thomas Mann, said, "I really see no purpose in printing newspaper rumors about what the president of the United States said."

Fulbright agreed but then asked "Why does the Department of State do it if it is not verified?" Mann now argued that he, too, doubted the president said what he said. In the name of democracy, and in the service of anti-communism, the United States of America was perpetuating institutionalized corruption and underwriting the men trained by Rafael Trujillo.[84]

Meanwhile, the president resented the press ridicule to which he was subjected. Somebody had to find the headless bodies. A search was conducted, and the president received this summary on August 12, 1965. Ambassador Bennett wrote that "we have put a great deal of time and effort into trying to confirm the numerous stories of this type that have circulated. Now I believe we have finally found some definite proof."

Bennett first mentioned an OAS report which discussed one body without its head. However, "we have also now come into possession of a picture of the remains of a human body on which no head can be seen. Ellsworth Bunker [the president's Dominican trouble shooter] and other members of the staff and I have examined it very carefully." It definitely lacked a head. However, Bennett had no way of knowing if the headless person was killed by a rebel, a loyalist, or a personal enemy. As luck would have it, "there was no reason to believe that the two bodies mentioned in the previous paragraphs are the same." Thus, even though the president was still 1498 heads short, he had two possibilities in his corner. A third fell through when Bennett sent aides to the Red Cross; they supposedly had a headless body but "the story was inaccurate."[85] McGeorge Bundy summarized this report for the president: "I am afraid it doesn't make the matter as clear as we might like, but it is the best he [Ambassador Bennett] can do."

While young women counted stacks of hundred dollar bills in the back rooms of Bennett's embassy, he and Ellsworth Bunker sat in the front office looking for pictures of headless bodies. It was a low point in the Dominican intervention, but the Senate added a much needed dose of humor and nostalgia.

Senator Hickenlooper asked (on July 14, 1965) about feeding both sides. Deputy Secretary of Defense Cyrus Vance said that was true and then Hickenlooper made this point: "We cannot have a good war without both sides being fairly fed, and are we sort of feeding them so they can fight tomorrow?"

Secretary Vance: "We have been trying to be impartial, Senator...."

Senator Hickenlooper: "That is impartial."

A final exchange (also on July 14) occurred between Senator Aiken and Secretary Mann. Mann explained that Bosch was not a Communist; he was a "do-gooder" and a "crusader." This was a problem because "while the preponderance of rebel strength is on the side of the non-Communists," it was questionable if a "do-gooder" could restrain such a ruthless opponent."

Senator Aiken: "Bosch apparently demonstrated

that he was not a competent administrator...for a government, not nearly as competent as his predecessor Trujillo had been."[86]

When the United States finally had a provisional government in place (in September of 1965), officials called for elections. Joaquin Balaguer headed the ticket of the Reformist Party and Juan Bosch (allowed to return on September 25) headed the ticket of the Dominican Revolutionary Party.

Five weeks before the June 2 election, the CIA sent the president a report entitled "Prospects For Stability in the Dominican Republic." Nobody could predict the results of the election—it was too close to call—but "even if the elections are relatively fair and free...we believe the political prospects are for further tension, instability and disorder." Moreover, given the society's "intractable" social, political and economic problems, whoever won would have a hard time making significant progress for the next year or two. Thus, the chances for stability were always poor—"and without foreign aid impossible."[87]

The United States was not leaving the Dominican Republic, and Juan Bosch was not leaving his house. As the CIA told the president, there was "no doubt" that during the campaign "elements of the extreme right have conducted terrorist operations against members of Bosch's Dominican Revolutionary Party and against former "constitutionalist" military figures." Bosch had a hard time campaigning without leaving his house, but the ambassador saw a silver lining in this: "We do not rule out the possibility of a successful assassination attempt on Bosch but consider it unlikely on the assumption he would remain in his house until inauguration by which time the immediate danger would hopefully have been brought under control."[88]

Balaguer did travel about the country in a fashion that, as the ambassador noted, reminded his critics of Rafael Trujillo in 1931 or 1961. Balaguer used "a large and sometimes unsavory" group of bodyguards on several of his campaign junkets. They assured his safety, but the unsavory bodyguards also reminded the people that Balaguer was Trujillo's chancellor when the 17,000 Haitians were slaughtered in 1937.

Balaguer won 56 percent of the votes cast on June 2, 1966, and Bosch 41 percent. However, the CIA cautioned the administration not to misinterpret the results. "Balaguer's election demonstrated the desire of most Dominicans for a return to peace and order." They feared that a Bosch victory would produce another junta, and it also was hard for Bosch to run a campaign while locked inside his own home. Moreover, "anti-US sentiment is intense among a considerable number of Dominicans" because they blamed us for the thirty years of Trujillo, for the 1965 intervention, and for Joaquin Balaguer, a man "many such people regard as a US puppet."[89]

The CIA was pessimistic. In Washington, W.W. Rostow asked the president if he wanted to "gloat." Aides had prepared a list of positive stories from the Latin American press so Rostow asked the president to check off one of three choices: "Leak to the press; leak for Congressional Record; no gloating: clam up."[90]

The president chose to gloat. As his press aides tried to "inspire" stories for *Life, Look,* and *Harper's,* Johnson received this memo: "Our people should answer the question of why we went through this long and troublesome intervention to 'keep Bosch' out of office. If we were genuinely willing to let Bosch win the election a year later, what did we gain by the intervention?"[91]

Haiti

The new U.S. ambassador, Raymond Thurston, admitted that he knew nothing about Haiti (he had wanted to go to Rumania), and neither did the man interviewing him for the job. Presidential Assistant Ralph Dungan recognized that he "didn't know a damned thing about foreign affairs," but he nevertheless "netted" all of Kennedy's diplomatic appointments. He took a special interest in the Caribbean because of "Goddamned [Richard] Goodwin and [Arthur] Schlesinger, crazy nuts on Latin America." They had talked the president into the Bay of Pigs disaster. Dungan decided that, despite his ignorance, he could not do a worse job than the "crazy nuts."[92]

Thurston did undergo a "policy review" process but, "I found, frankly, that I had very little guidance." He went through the files and tried to discover for himself some indication of Kennedy's real desires but all Thurston got from his superiors was vagueness.[93]

He was in the Caribbean when he encountered a political hot potato—the cut-off of aid to Haiti. Theoretically this was a matter of principle; Duvalier received no more money because he systematically murdered his people and because he and the Dominicans had a "slave deal" for plantation labor. In reality, the aide was lost because Duvalier refused to pay Senator Everett Dirksen's brother-in-law $300,000. That was the amount owed to the American contractor, and, when Duvalier refused to pay, Dirksen tacked on a rider to the foreign aide bill; no funds to any country in default to American companies or individuals.

Thurston worked to "get around the Dirksen amendment" because he wanted to influence Duvalier. He hoped to provide aid to the Haitian masses when Secretary of State Rusk used the Haitian aid to obtain a vote against the Cuban government. The United States wanted to keep Castro out of the OAS and Haiti had the vote required for a two-thirds majority. As Rusk told Thurston, "they tell me that I bribed the Haitians. That was just diplomacy."[94]

Rusk knew what to do. Duvalier did not. In May of 1962, he made a major diplomatic mistake. Against the orders of Thurston, the Haitian president used U.S. aid trucks and jeeps to provide mass transportation for a political celebration. This was bad public relations for the United States, so most of Duvalier's aid was cut off in the summer of 1962. However, the United States maintained a "foot in the door" by continuing to help with the new jet airport. It also allowed Duvalier to keep a military mission that was "certainly a waste of the taxpayer's money if ever I saw one." Duvalier used his "tame marines" for two purposes: to underline his support from Uncle Sam and to train his internal police. Thurston said this was ridiculous—"we were sending a million dollars a year in ammunition, small arms, etc."—but he nevertheless allowed the soldiers to stay because the United States had let the opposition know it was desireable to assassinate the president. Washington wanted the marines in place when Duvalier died, but "that was, of course, never put in writing or anything like that."[95]

The low point for the Kennedy administration came in October of 1962. In Thurston's words, "the impact of the Cuban missile crisis was, in effect, for me to go to Duvalier and the word 'beg' is not the right word, but in the atmosphere of cold war...." Washington needed to use Haiti. Duvalier loved this encounter; "he was as unpleasant, and yet chuckling to himself that here I was, you know, coming." At the meeting (in October of 1962) Duvalier hedged; the next morning he announced that "in the great struggle against Communism they were going to, you know, be part of it and that this would bring about a new relationship with the United States."[96]

A full-scale policy review was conducted by the Johnson administration. It sent Benson Timmons to Haiti and in February of 1964, he provided a summary of his first meeting with François Duvalier.

The president was not wearing a gun, nor was there (as rumor had it) a holster attached to his chair. However, "a large number of armed soldiers stood outside the palace, at the main entrance, at the bottom and top of the staircase, and within the corridor leading to the yellow room and to the president's office." Timmons saw "an impressive pile of heavy caliber machine guns and other weapons on the floor just inside the door to Duvalier's office."[97]

Timmons listened as Duvalier praised President Eisenhower. That man loved Haiti, and he liked Duvalier so much that he still sent the Haitian president a Christmas card every year. Duvalier hoped for that kind of relationship with Lyndon Johnson, and, after touching on every issue from the Tonton Macutes, to aid, to tourism, Timmons was told that all the problems boiled down to "the man." To the extent Timmons wished it, collaboration would be good because the Haitian president wished to nourish the "integral humanism" that forever bound our great republics.[98]

Timmons, after his departure, helped to write a plan that characterized American policy for the next decade. Timmons and his colleagues agreed that for the foreseeable future Duvalier would remain in power. Moreover, "for nearly fifty years, the United States had played a *preponderant* role on the Haitian scene." Many islanders resented us, but, given our half a century of technical and economic assistance—$47 million since 1957 alone—islanders also believed that we "could not afford to turn our backs on Haiti."[99]

The strategy paper stressed that Duvalier's foreign and domestic policy were two sides of the same coin: His "primary domestic objective" was to retain power, and a primary means was success with his "foremost international policy objective...stringless aid from the United States."[100]

President Johnson decided to cooperate because there was no apparent alternative to Duvalier and because "the overriding objective for the United States was to deny Haiti to the Communists, preventing either a takeover or gradual infiltration of Communists and their stooges into a position of de facto control."

The United States had other aims: Haitian assistance at the OAS; protection of American citizens and their property rights in Haiti; and the long range development of democracy and respect for human rights.[101] But, as in the Dominican Republic, Fidel Castro made American policy in Haiti. All other priorities were a distant second to stopping Castro and his "stooges." That was the thrust of this detailed May 1964 policy review; it was the conclusion of a "secret, special report" in December of 1965, and of a solid CIA analysis in October of 1966.[102]

The United States decided that, even though "corruption, apathy, favoritism, irresponsibility, and brutality continue (in December of 1965) to permeate the regime," this was better than the possible infiltration of Communists into a possible position of "de facto control."[103]

The CIA did discuss a possible "military occupation" if and when Duvalier fell—or was pushed— from power; but the CIA also said that caution should be America's watchword. "The problems in Haiti are such that it might prove more difficult to get a force out than to put it in, as was the case in 1915."[104]

The United States had played a preponderant role in Hispaniola for the last fifty years; and, as the Johnson administration came to an end, the loyal supporters of Rafael Trujillo controlled one side of the island and the machine gun toting thugs of François Duvalier the other.

In the name of "democracy," the leader of the free world supported dictators. Meanwhile, in Miami and New York, Caribbean political exiles tried to understand why the perpetuation of Haitian slavery—in the sugar fields managed by Joaquin Balaguer—was endorsed by the free world.[105]

Designs for
Development

"The Virgin Islands are ghettos in the sun. Only worse. They don't even have the grey areas and buffer zones of U.S. central cities. They are black (largely poor) and white (largely tourists—spending, spending, spending). So the situation is explosively bad and getting worse."
—Nixon White House, January 5, 1973[1]

Describing his strategy of decolonization, the Puerto Rican revolutionary Pedro Albizu Campos wrote in 1937 that "Puerto Rico has to create a grave crisis for the colonial administration in order for it to be able to attend to the island's demands."

Testifying before the House of Representatives in 1973, Professor Robert Crassweller described the results of his detailed presentation to State Department staff. House members expressed interest and they even agreed about the urgent need for a comprehensive solution. But, "nobody on Capitol Hill would buy these arguments [meaningful change in U.S sugar quotas and policy] and beyond that no one else in the executive. People are not going to focus on the [Caribbean] problem unless a national security threat comes up, if there is a possibility of a second Cuba and so on."[2]

Campos and Crassweller were both right. Americans disregarded the Caribbean until a crisis arose. But, instead of the empathy desired by Albizu, or the scholarship urged by the professor, even a crisis produced no significant reevaluation of U.S. beliefs and practices.

The murders occurred on September 6, 1972. Sixteen people filled the clubhouse of Fountain Valley, one of the Virgin Island's most exclusive golf courses. Five men—carrying guns and wearing army fatigues—turned a round of golf into political slaughter. After taking everyone's money, the assailants turned to a white couple, shouted "I hate those white motherfuckers!" and the men opened fire. Eight people died (seven of them were white), and the Virgin Islands had to confront a terrible reaction to Governor Paiewonsky's development schemes. The murders were allegedly a revolutionary act designed to help eliminate "the alien, white ruling class."[3]

In the Nixon White House Leonard Garment (one of the president's former law partners) called the Virgin Islands "ghettoes in the sun." He wanted to "award the Pollyanna Prize of 1972" to the Justice Department official who said he could make the Virgin Islands "the economic and social leader of the Caribbean." Garment also wanted to protect his boss. He said to "keep the White House at arms-length from any conspicuous involvement in the area's emerging mess," and he offered two suggestions for action. Send someone to the islands to "non-bureautically" assess the situation; and "concentrate on enlisting and/or training tough police cadres (principally black) who will go down and take maximum action against the Mau Maus in the hills."[4]

Aides forecast trouble as early as March of 1969. A memo to the president said that it would be "unwise to discount the potential of the Virgin Islands' status as an issue to be exploited by black militants. The conditions in the islands described below [indentured servants, "substantially rising crime," and, as in 1930, 1949 and 1960, an insufficient island contribution to the federal treasury] suggest that the fodder for radical speeches does exist."[5]

In response to this memo, President Nixon appointed the first black governor in the islands' history. Dr. Melvin Evans got the nod because he worked hard for the Republican Party; and *despite* a White House memo which said that, while serving as a Commissioner of Health, "he made a shambles of the department as he showed no talent whatsoever as an administrator." In fact, "he shows indications again of a poor administrator by making many promises recently to many unqualified individuals for positions if he is appointed."[6]

Once Richard Nixon congratulated Doctor Evans, White House aides sought to digest a report they had commissioned. Trying (in March of 1970) to understand "why did we let the situation get so bad? Why have we not acted earlier?" the president's aides prepared a first-class analysis. They stressed the terrible results of the tourist buildup, they suggested that people who worked on the government's thoroughly padded payroll were the "aphids of the system," and they offered an evaluation. "To put people in this kind of a responsibility without broad supportive help would be *revolting* in any other circumstance but somehow it is excused

353

when it comes to the Virgin Islands."[7] [emphasis added]

This was normal for the Caribbean in general and the Virgin Islands in particular. Evans, after all, followed Ralph Paiewonsky who followed Archibald Alexander. Until a crisis occurred, nobody noticed; and when they did, officials made this suggestion: "Just why should the president become involved? If immediate, decisive action cannot be accomplished, then we should let [Interior] Secretary Hickel wrestle with the problem and take the heat that results."[8]

By 1975 in Puerto Rico, 60 percent of the people were on food stamps (they were introduced in 1974) and, as the head of the island's Development Bank told a Ford administration official, "we couldn't even attempt a Khmer Rouge. There are no cane fields to drive our people back to."[9]

Nobody listened—in 1950 or in 1975—because no administration wanted to accept responsibility for the existence or consequences of American colonialism; because U.S. strategies were always rooted in emergency and expediency; and because large numbers of American (*and Puerto Rican*) businessmen made such huge profits from the island's economic development.

Operation Bootstrap

In 1921, Americans doing business in the Philippines complained to Congress. They were double-taxed (by Washington and Manila), their British competitors were not, and Congress should eliminate federal taxation as a means to fairer competition for America's Far Eastern entrepreneurs.

Designs for Development

China and the Philippines were the sole focus of these fascinating debates.[10] But, like the Philippines in 1921, Puerto Rico was an American possession. So, Congress extended the exemption to Puerto Rico. It was a question of equity. You could not help one possession and exempt another.

This 1921 exemption was the federal axis of what islanders called (in 1948) "Operation Bootstrap." Industrialists would flock to Puerto Rico because they paid no taxes and, theoretically, islanders would enjoy long term benefits because of the industrialization of their society.

Self-sustaining success was contingent on manufacturers who meant to stay on the island, and, equally important, on manufacturers who reinvested their significant profits in Puerto Rico. This would not happen because the American head of the Puerto Rican tax program counseled investors (in 1950) to do this; "The corporate activities of the [Puerto Rican] subsidiary should be carefully conducted with a view to *liquidation* rather than continuation of operations."[11] The 1921 law contained a loophole. If an American business returned profits in any one year they did pay federal taxes; but, if they kept their profits in a foreign account, and, upon liquidation, brought the money home, *all* the years of profits were exempt from all federal taxation.

In Puerto Rico, companies took their profits and sent them to Guam (another American possession); from Guam the money was invested in Europe; and, when the corporations liquidated, bankers passed the money from Guam to Puerto Rico to the United States. As Puerto Rico's resident commissioner told

Congress in 1976, for nearly thirty years the law has "forced a U.S. subsidiary to place this investment abroad until such time as the company is liquidated...these investments are not available in the United States or Puerto Rico while they are outside of both countries."[12]

Money banked in Guam was never used in the Caribbean and, even more important, a report complied in 1964 showed that 35 percent of the enterprises opened since 1953 had already closed. Some failed, others liquidated, and still others—the triple whammy—liquidated and immediately reopened as a new entity. Islanders legalized this fiction because they saw no alternative; they were running fast just to stay in place. Meanwhile, Puerto Rico received no benefits from the exempted federal taxes.[13]

To attract corporations island, planners used a "fishing net approach to industrialization." They advertised their Caribbean tax haven and they exempted anyone who came to the island *if the new manufacturer did not take away jobs from the mainland.*

Washington said the island could take only what the mainland discarded or never wanted. Before Congress islanders stressed that "there is a careful scrutiny, a careful examination and investigation of each case to make sure that it is not a runaway plant. The States know that we do not accept runaway plants...they will raise a turmoil if one of their plants moves to Puerto Rico and creates unemployment in their location."[14]

So, instead of an industrial strategy, islanders used fishing nets; and, because the States came first, if Puerto Ricans somehow caught too big or too valuable a fish, they had to send it back to the mainland. The result was industrialization rooted in firms that "at best represented entrepreneurial mediocrity; and, at worst, a motley group of entre-preneurial migrants, some of whom were frankly attracted by low-cost labor and a tax holiday."[15]

One Harvard professor spoke of a "gold rush psy-chology." Profits only two times the mainland average were insufficient to attract investment; four to five times the norm was the magnet that drew investors who came to make a killing. No one asked how "entrepreneurial migrants" looking for gold would contribute to self-sustaining, long-term development. Instead, island planners focused on tax exemptions to lure new investments (which only filled in the holes left by the liquidators) because it was the "unani-mous opinion" of the officials involved that tax exemption was always an investor's "main motiva-tion."[16]

Puerto Rico could have demanded quid pro quos; as in Singapore, it could have demanded that substantial sums were reinvested on the island; or that after five years a firm had to sink or swim, and, if it swam, it also had to pay taxes.

Options like these were never exercised. The island's planners lacked vision; they (and Congress) were in a hurry; the East Coast absorbed significant numbers of the unemployed; and, most important of all, the island was politically and economically dependent on Congress and the president.[17]

From federal tax exemptions, to the permission of the United States, to the coastal shipping laws, to the minimum wage, the island rooted its economic development in the will of Congress and the president. Mainlanders made the rules, and, even when no one mentioned quid pro quos, they changed the rules whenever Puerto Rico proved to be too much of a threat. Over a period of years Congress continually extended minimum wage to the island.

Every time islanders asked for the concessions that promised self-sustaining growth, they were rebuffed. They responded to changes like minimum wage by disregarding their own rules and regulations. Initially officials examined the applications of those companies seeking tax exemptions; by the mid 1960s the hearings were staged. Petitioners received the answers to the questions they would be asked; the need for new business was so great that no one cared if the end result was greater dependence on Washington.[18]

Interior Secretary Stewart Udall—and a group of oil companies—offered to help. They understood the island's terrible dilemma (*official* unemployment in 1948 was 11.2 percent; in 1965, it was still 11.2 percent and this with a program of industrialization, a significant drop in the rate of labor force participation, and a net migration of nearly half a million people![19]), and they offered to build a world class petrochemical industry if Congress agreed to exempt the island from import quotas on foreign oil. After a fight, the companies got the exemptions, and Puerto Rico got the facilities. The companies wanted to pan for black gold in the Caribbean and the Interior Department wanted to avoid economic disaster. As Udall noted in a letter to the president's budget director, "the island will soon be in serious difficulties unless new approaches are taken to assure sustained economic growth."[20]

Designs for Development

The oil industry depended on exemptions granted by Congress, the liquidation law was still in
effect, and, in a nation overflowing with labor, capi-
tal-intensive industries promised few jobs. But,
despite a federal ruling that destroyed a similar oil
scheme in 1959, Puerto Rico turned the other
cheek. Its planners saw no alternative to oil and
Senator Long saw no alternative to new legislation.
In 1967 he and a number of other senators put quotas on the quotas; they restricted the number of
import exemptions Secretary Udall could grant, and,
as with sugar in the 1930s, Puerto Rico suddenly
had another dead end industry.

Puerto Ricans' political status limited their economic options. So, in 1974, islanders again asked
Congress to enhance commonwealth. Give them some
of the economic tools requested for more than twenty
years (e.g., the right to impose tariffs) and they could
achieve a measure of economic self-sufficiency.

In making this request, Puerto Ricans neglected
powerful senators like Henry Jackson. He told
islanders in April of 1974, that they "became a part
of the United States by an act of conquest." Moreover, "even if the people were to vote for independence Puerto Rico can't become so…neither independence, developed commonwealth, or statehood
can be had. *Puerto Rico must remain a colony.*"[21]
[emphasis added]

Islanders responded with a request to censure
Jackson. But all the senator did was tell the truth,
albeit bluntly. Congress made *all* the important rules
in Puerto Rico, in the Virgin Islands, and, if President
Ford had his way, in the independent nation of
Jamaica.

Dollar Diplomacy

Bauxite is mined in stages. First you scoop up the bauxite using huge mechanical shovels. Then, for every two and a half tons of bauxite dug, a manufacturer extracts one ton of alumina by crushing it, dissolving it in caustic soda, and drying the result into a fine powder. Finally, by using enormous quantities of electric energy, the alumina is smelted into the aluminum that wraps leftovers and frames storm doors and windows.

In Jamaica the bauxite industry developed in the same manner as sugar in Cuba, Puerto Rico, or the Dominican Republic. Islanders were "permitted" to extract the raw material but most of the second stage processing (in 1972 Jamaica processed only one-sixth of the bauxite it mined) and all of the third stage transformations occurred abroad. In this manner developed nations monopolized the refining of a raw material and, in the process, they denied Jamaica an opportunity to expand the number and quality of its manufacturing jobs. As in Batista's Cuba, outsiders reaped the greatest rewards from the Caribbean's minerals and produce.

Michael Manley not only demanded change, he agreed with the U.S. Government Accounting Office. Something had to be done about a situation in which an industry that accounted for 72 percent of Jamaica's export earnings provided only 1 percent of the nation's jobs.[22] He wanted more processing to be done at home, and, to tax differently the bauxite exported to the United States and Canada. As he noted in *Jamaica: Struggle In the Periphery*, the nation's goal was to keep the surplus that permitted investments that fueled a dynamic, self-sustaining economy.

Michael Manley wanted money. There was no doubt of a struggle with companies like Reynolds and Kaiser. The transnational corporations inventively managed their accounting ledgers. This was commonplace all over the world but especially destructive in Jamaica because it taxed bauxite at the price paid by the parent company. Thus, if Reynolds' Jamaica Mines underestimated the costs of production, Reynolds in Louisiana saved the tax dollars that Jamaica lost. It was a struggle without end until Michael Manley challenged the developed nations rules of the game. Because he had no way to control a company's books, Manley decided to establish a bauxite levy that was indexed to the price of aluminum in the United States. In 1974 this 7.5 percent levy increased Jamaica's bauxite revenues by 60 percent. The companies immediately reacted violently and in 1975 this formerly peripheral struggle reached the White House's Oval Office.[23]

In a memo to General Brent Scowcroft (then President Ford's Assistant For National Security Affairs), subordinates said (on November 21, 1975) that Michael Manley wanted to see the president. The Jamaican prime minister had been asking for such a meeting "for the past several years but neither State nor we [*i.e.*, the National Security Council] have wanted to recommend such a visit because of the uncertain status of the negotiations between Jamaica and the American aluminum companies." The memo argued that Manley had "arbitrarily increased the tax on bauxite sevenfold in 1974" and, equally ominous, that tax increase "breached the contracts with the American companies." Thus, following the advice given by Henry Kissinger, the president had refused

361

to see Manley until the negotiations were satisfactorily completed.[24]

This was "dollar diplomacy" 65 years after the term was invented. Three separate memos show no appreciation of Jamaica's tax or employment dilemmas; the focus was on the United States—the island provided 54 percent of the bauxite and 25 percent of the alumina used by the U.S. aluminum industry in 1974—and the final recommendation was to allow Manley a visit with the vice president of the United States. President Ford would be out of the country when Manley arrived so Nelson Rockefeller served as a stand-in, because "we do not want to overdo the connection between our political relations and the bauxite negotiations."[25]

The vice president's job was to "improve our bilateral relationship" with an "emerging Third World spokesman"; to convince Manley that even though he and his neighbors felt "neglected," the United States cared about the Caribbean; to express the president's regrets that Washington was unable to provide the "large program of concessional assistance" Manley had requested; and, finally, the vice president should hold out the carrot of an Oval Office meeting "when the bauxite negotiations were satisfactorily completed."[26]

This exercise reflected a century-long cultural constant. In 1910 and in 1975, the United States seemed unable to empathize with the dilemmas faced by Caribbean nations. In 1973, the four major aluminum companies boasted net earnings of $249.1 million; in 1974, after the levy, their earnings skyrocketed to $581.7 million.[27] Yet neither they nor their government was willing to share the wealth. The companies cut back on production and moved their operations to other nations. Meanwhile, the United States helped destabilize Michael Manley because he often supported Fidel Castro; and, in a significant assertion of U.S. corporate interests, the federal government provided an insurance package that was even better than the Haitian and Dominican customs receiverships.

Developmental Insurance

Created in 1969, OPIC (the Overseas Private Investment Corporation) is a federal agency with a unique mission. It encourages U.S. investment in developing nations by providing insurance against a variety of adverse *political* actions. Expropriation, war, revolution, insurrection, currency changes: OPIC insures a corporation against all these eventualities and it does so because "without the imagination and resources of [multinational] corporations and their willingness to assume some of the unusual risks involved in overseas investment, the tremendous developmental advances of the last two decades could not have taken place."[28]

This sounds like the Santo Domingo Improvement Company in 1892. The rationale for that company's high interest rates was the company's high exposure to risk but its control of the customs houses—underwritten by Washington—eliminated the risk that theoretically justified the huge profits.

The beauty of OPIC was that it avoided the everyday humiliation of a customs receivership. In the event of political turmoil, Washington would simply reimburse a corporation for its investment risks. Thus, in 1974 Jamaica led all nations in the federal government's exposure to expropriation, war, revolution or insurrection. At the White House General Scowcroft learned that the companies had investments of $660 million; meanwhile OPIC insured them—the average policy lasted 20 years—for more than $500 million on all political risks.[29]

Who received the insurance? And what were the criteria OPIC employed to accept or reject a particular client?

The first concern was any adverse impact on U.S. employment. As in Puerto Rico's Operation Bootstrap, OPIC told Congress that in the last three years it had rejected 34 separate projects because they would take jobs away from Americans. However, where the Puerto Ricans asked only if it was a runaway plant, OPIC first asked that question and it then asked whether "it will have a negative effect on U.S. employment." A "yes" to either question and the company received no government net for its proposed operations.[30]

A second concern was the ripple effect on the American economy. OPIC boasted that the operations it insured bought their goods and services in the United States. It estimated that the companies it assisted provided nearly 27,000 man years of employment in only the last five years. OPIC officials assured the Senate that their clients provided jobs that were "derived from the U.S. exports that are initially involved in the capitalization of these projects, the follow-on spares and supplies to these projects from the United States and financial flows."

A final concern was "adequate developmental benefits." OPIC said it had rejected 31 projects because they offered little help to nations like

Designs for Development

Jamaica and the Dominican Republic. However, it was unclear what standards OPIC used to determine adequate development. After a four-month scrutiny of its many clients, analysts argued that the Washington insurance company was primarily a service to U.S. multinational corporations, who are the principal beneficiaries of its programs. *"Any positive developmental impact OPIC may have on needy people seems to be almost incidental."*[31]

Senator Frank Church (Idaho) not only agreed with this assessment, he cited the case of Puerto Rico. "There is no doubt that companies came to Puerto Rico as they came to no other place. But what has happened there, Mr. Chairman?" Church said (in July and August of 1977) that agriculture was a "disaster," 60 percent of the population was on food stamps, the import of food had continued to rise, and all this despite the migration of 40 percent of the people to the mainland. To Church there was good reason to question the premises of OPIC; indeed, "anyone who can accept the proposition that the investment of the big multinational companies is a boon to the host countries, who does not thoroughly look at the example of Puerto Rico, is not serious."[32]

Henry Kissinger was serious. The Secretary of State testified in full support of OPIC. He did agree with Church's comment that OPIC rarely insured enterprises in the poorest countries, the ones who most needed the development OPIC sought to foster. But, besides Jamaica, the federal government underwrote investments in the Dominican Republic and Trinidad. It actually spread its insurance nets widely but, even if it focused its assistance on a few countries, the senator had to remember that OPIC only insured the business judgments of others because, "basically it is true that OPIC will have to follow the decisions of the private investor, and, basically, OPIC, by itself, cannot substitute for the necessity of creating an investment climate for private capital."

Kissinger stressed the "fundamental dilemma of the present development situation." Governments lacked the money needed to underwrite their developmental needs so the federal government underwrote the private wealth that was the world's "largest source of untapped capital." To Kissinger there was "no alternative" to corporate power, but Senator Church once again cited the case of Puerto Rico.

The Senator said that he and Kissinger were grappling with "a very basic argument that will continue for a long time to come." Puerto Rico contained "the largest concentration of corporate investment that we can point to anywhere in the world"; yet if Kissinger meant to use it as a "showcase of how private capital contributes to the wholesome development of the host country," Church thought it was time to reevaluate theories with such obvious deficiencies.

Kissinger disagreed. Puerto Rico had special problems; the senator had to remember the impact of the oil crisis on the island's budding petroleum industry. Kissinger also wanted "to put Puerto Rico aside." He simply saw no alternative to private capital, even though he echoed Church when he concluded with this statement: "I am not saying that private investment, left to its own decisions, simply by the operation of the free market, is going to bring about the economic development of the least developed countries." On the contrary, "its incentive is going to be to go into the *most developed* situations in the less developed countries, and it may pursue policies that are not in every respect compatible with the long-term interests of the countries involved."[33] [emphasis added]

The companies made the decisions in the interests of profit. After all, in the U.S. brand of capitalism, satisfying stockholders was the top priority.[34] With a twenty year guarantee from OPIC, the companies made decisions based on *their* developmental interests. OPIC insured the expansion of Citibank and Chase Manhattan branches in the Dominican Republic; it also insured the manufacture of electronic inductors in Barbados, the assembly of electronic connectors in Haiti, and the cutting of diamonds in the Dominican Republic.[35]

Nobody in OPIC had a plan of what would most benefit the United States, much less the Caribbean. Instead of listening to the warnings of Senator Church, Caribbean nations followed Puerto Rico in using a fishing net approach to industrial development. They took what they could get, and what they could get usually came with an OPIC guarantee.

OPIC is a symbol, a stark reminder of the way in which the United States publicly underwrites the private development of its third border. However, despite it significance, OPIC "only" provides risk insurance; it kicks in when disaster strikes but investors hope that that eventuality never arises. They want to make money and to do that the principal lure used in the 1970s was the creation of "free zones." These were modeled after the Puerto Rican experience, and, like OPIC, they called to mind the fundamental dilemma addressed by Secretary of State Kissinger. Could a nation using free zones as a magnet for investment create self-sustaining development? Or, as with OPIC, would the free zones only underwrite what was in the best interests of the corporations and their limited number of island beneficiaries?

Free zones varied but the normal incentives included lures which suggested the U.S. military occupation of the Dominican Republic in 1920. The free zones offered duty and tax free importation of all machinery, equipment, spare parts, construction materials, and other items. This kept people working in the United States as did the duty free entry of imported materials and other goods destined for re-export.

Besides these duty free import incentives, the free zones offered cheap labor, free factories, free infrastructure, long term exemptions from all local taxes and fiscal charges, freedom from foreign currency and exchange restrictions, and no financial reporting requirements.[36]

Using free zones, countries like Haiti and the Dominican Republic became the U.S. showcases of the seventies. Under "Baby Doc," the assembly industries in Haiti became the most dynamic sector of the island's economy. From 6.5 percent percent of exports in 1970, the assembly industries climbed to 15.2 percent in 1977. This dramatic growth was based on the manufacture of items like clothing and baseballs. Using cork from Portugal, rubber from Vietnam, and centers made in Mississippi, the New York Yankees hit baseballs that were sewn in Haiti.

Women—often very young women—did the work and in some instances the women who made garments, toys, and baseballs had money deducted from their pay when they used toilet paper or took a drink of water.[37]

These were supposedly extreme examples but, putting labor conditions aside, the norm in any of the free zones was an enormously increased dependence on the will of Congress and the president. The balls, toys, and electrical inductors were exported to the United States, and, as with oil in Puerto Rico or watches in the Virgin Islands, the Caribbean took a backseat to the mainland. For example, in Haiti the production of garments was too successful, so in 1975 Congress imposed the quotas that reminded an observer of sugar in 1930s.

Nothing changed, least of all the flow of profits. From Puerto Rico, they went to Guam. From Haiti they took a number of banking detours but, however circuitous a route, one study showed that for every dollar earned in Haitian manufacturing, 85 cents went to the United States, and in the late seventies that added up to $50 million a year returning to its point of origin.[38]

The free zones never offered self-sustaining development. Their success depended on two factors outside the control of Caribbean nations: the willingness of the United States to accept what the companies wanted to export; and the willingness of the companies to continue doing business. If a company found a freer free zone, it could threaten to leave and thus blackmail host countries in the same way liquidators blackmailed the Puerto Ricans.

A memo in the President Ford Library notes

that in 1974, American textile manufacturers made it difficult for Washington to negotiate a new multi-fiber textile agreement with the Haitians. "The negotiations were probably one of the most difficult we have had; aside from normal resistance on the part of the Haitian government, there was enormous pressure from a number of U.S. manufacturers. These U.S. citizens put pressure on Haitian officials including attempts at threats and bribes. They went so far as to create layoffs of employees and informed the Haitian government that it was the result of their negotiations. They even called the minister of commerce and demanded that he break the negotiations."[39]

Since self-interest was the political and economic posture of the United States, the free zones were at the mercy of forces outside their control, while the people of Haiti and the Dominican Republic were at the mercy of leaders like "Baby Doc" Duvalier and Joaquin Balaguer. The former murdered with only slightly less impunity than his father and the latter used a group called "La Banda" to assassinate his enemies and destroy their personal property.[40]

In Washington legislators decided to make the next ten years easier for American investors. Congress relaxed the tax laws for its possession's corporations and, in the process, created profits for the pharmaceutical companies that soon made them the legal drug lords of the Caribbean. For example, in 1992, a GAO study commissioned by Senator David Pryor (Arkansas) found that Pfizer employed 500 Puerto Ricans, its average annual tax savings equalled $69 million a year, and its tax savings as a percentage of its compensation to workers was a whopping 636 percent. In the case of Upjohn, it had 775 island employees, tax savings of $68 million a year and a 238 percent rate of tax savings to workers' pay.[41]

The 936 Laws

In Puerto Rico, the treasury department knew little about the many companies earning tax free profits. Baxter Travenol Laboratories accounted for 40 percent of world profits in Puerto Rico but the island's government had no knowledge of the number of Baxter's island subsidiaries, or knowledge of the firm's foreign currency transactions. The treasury department lacked even a list of the corporations doing business on the American colony.[42]

Island planners believed that tax exemptions were the principal enticement of their industrial program. As Resident Commissioner Jaime Benitez told the Senate Finance Committee in March of 1976, "unemployment stands officially at 21 percent; unofficially it is much higher...we are caught in the double vise of federal minimum wages and coastwise shipping laws." So, "we come here because the approval of this section [the new tax law] constitutes one of the few rays of hope for a potential amelioration of the extremely critical problem of employment and income presently choking industrial development in Puerto Rico."[43]

The House Ways and Means Committee finally focused on Puerto Rico because of its economic problems and because the tax laws had produced controversies that were increasingly hard to neglect. Statehooders eager to undermine the commonwealth called attention to the flow of U.S. tax dollars to Europe and that called attention to the amount of stockpiled profits—the estimate was $5 *billion.* Island subsidiaries of mainland parents took their Puerto Ricans profits abroad and used the island's profits to establish new foreign subsidiaries of the mainland corporation. The tax laws were providing resources which enabled multinationals to use Caribbean capital to finance European development.[44]

Puerto Rico cited the Ways and Means study which proved that the tax exemptions made no significant contribution to the island's economy. Instead of reevaluating the island's approach to industrial development, the only thing needed was a quick fix of the tax laws. Keep the companies free of federal taxation. But, in justice to Puerto Rico, and in justice to the United States, the goal was "to harness income that is presently outside of the United States and outside of Puerto Rico and refund, rechannel it into the economy of *both* countries."[45]

What was good for Puerto Rico was good for the United States. That was the red, white and blue flag waved by islanders and Congress saluted it for at least five reasons:

(1) Few senators and congressmen knew or cared about the details listed above. This was the Caribbean, not something important.

(2) America had balance of payments problems; bringing home $5 billion was at least a small step in the right direction.

(3) The lobbying was intense. The old tax laws had built up a mainland constituency that wanted the exemptions to continue; and the lure of new leg-

islation brought additional lobbyists to Washington. They would help Puerto Rico as they helped themselves.

(4) For almost thirty years Congress had received no tax revenue from Puerto Rico. Thus, "because no loss of U.S. tax revenues was involved when amendments were made to the U.S. tax laws, Congress was willing to change the tax rules to conform with whatever Puerto Rico wanted."[46]

(5) After thirty years of failure, no one knew what to do about Puerto Rico. Developing countries throughout the world competed with the island for new factories. And, in the last decade Congress had quadrupled federal transfer payments to the island. Washington simply got in deeper and deeper. *Anything* that promised to help was better than a serious reevaluation of the results of (what then amounted to) 75 years of colonialism.[47]

The few congressmen with knowledge knew *exactly* what they were doing. There was the public commentary of Senator Frank Church and, by 1978, a detailed and very critical report submitted to President Carter.[48] However, faced with a crisis, Congress voted for expediency, the president kept quiet, the corporations said thank you, and accountants scrambled to locate loopholes in the new, 936 laws.

The corporations made their usual threats, so under 936 they were allowed to bring home all profits—free of federal taxes—whenever they pleased. In 1977 the island tried to impose a modest tollgate tax of 10 percent but even that stopped the corporations from returning money to the mainland so, within a year, the tollgate tax was reduced. The corporations refused to share their incredible profits. The pharmaceutical companies totaled only 10 percent of the island's corporations but they earned 45 percent of the net income. In 1978 that equalled a net profit of $1.1 billion, a much envied 30 percent return on sales alone.[49]

The companies also received a tax exemption on their financial investments in Puerto Rican banks. Say you put $50 million of drug money in an account and received 8 percent interest. Everything was tax free and also theoretically available for use in Puerto Rico. However, the corporations quickly escaped this trap by investing over sixty percent of their funds in short term (60 and 90 day) certificates of deposit. Thus, the banks had use of the money—and in Hato Rey there are now a number of imposing American and Puerto Rican financial skyscrapers—but there was no way they could use short term funds for long term investments. Over time both the American and Puerto Rican banks simply began to once again reinvest the money in Europe.[50]

A lovely loophole—"closed" in the early eighties—was the tax treatment of intangibles. What the companies did was transfer the patent rights to a drug or invention to their Puerto Rican subsidiary. All profits then flowed South; they made a pit stop in the Hato Rey banks; and they then flowed North after having been cleaned in the Caribbean's new laundromat. Meanwhile, the corporations deducted the research and development costs attributable to intangibles from the taxable income of their mainland operations.[51]

This was a farce. The Carter administration knew that in 1978, and the Reagan administration knew it in 1986. But, as the next chapter shows, Congress only agreed to save the program when its supporters pledged to use the 936 billions as an engine of development, not only in Puerto Rico, but in the entire Caribbean.

Carter and the Caribbean

"I view the United States as a Caribbean nation." This assertion appeared in an (April 9, 1980) speech by President Carter. He argued that geographically, Texas and Louisiana, Puerto Rico and the Virgin Islands "either face the Caribbean or swim in it." There were ties of kinship and culture because "there are perhaps more Dominicans, Jamaicans, and Barbadians in New York than anywhere other than their native countries." The economic links were also strong, and strategically, "all the people of the region will remain concerned as long as Castro permits his nation to be the outpost and staging areas for Soviet imperialism."[52]

The president cited the empty promises of Castro and he underlined the limits of even the best foreign policy. "The foundation of foreign policy is a nation's values and people. Governments don't have relationships; people do."[53]

Well said. It was a speech full of laudable statements which, in the Caribbean, bore little relationship to the actions of the Carter administration. They lacked a Caribbean policy and openly admitted this before Congress in a set of late 1979 public hearings.

The speaker was John Bushnell, a high ranking official in the State Department's Bureau of Inter-American Affairs. He summarized conditions throughout the Caribbean and discussed the recent coup (on March 13, 1979) in the tiny island of Grenada. "The repressive, corrupt and frequently erratic regime of Eric Gairy (Gairy made UN speeches about UFO's) was ousted in a nearly bloodless coup by a group of young radicals calling themselves the New Jewel Movement." Not only was there no evidence of weapons coming from Cuba, the guns and rifles employed "were apparently smuggled into Grenada from the United States."[54]

Bushnell stressed that despite democratic progress throughout the Caribbean, "we would have to recognize that the degree of freedom, human rights, and so forth which had existed under the previous government in Grenada was probably the weakest in the Caribbean area." It was in some respects a deviation from the norm but, "the Soviets themselves have not played any significant direct role that we can identify in the Caribbean." The Carter people had of course looked but "the Soviet direct influence is certainly negligible in the Caribbean and is the normal sort of diplomatic establishment in places like Jamaica."[55]

Bushnell echoed the comments of his predecessors. For example, when (in late 1974) Grenadian Prime Minister Eric Gairy personally asked President Ford for money at a luncheon, Secretary Kissinger said to tell him no. As in 1979, the island was then in crisis and Kissinger knew why: "A general strike, called to protest the violence of Gairy's personal police force, resulted in substantial economic losses for the country and demonstrated Gairy's unwillingness to compromise. This, combined with the Gairy government's mismanagement of the economy and financial over-extension, has resulted in the current crisis."[56]

Representative Benjamin Gillman asked about policy. Did we have one? Bushnell hedged. Policy was made "on various levels."

Gillman pressed. "What you are telling me then is, we really don't have a Caribbean policy-making group; is that right?"

Bushnell: "We do not have something that is a Caribbean policy-making group separate from a policy-making group for other parts of Latin America."[57]

Gillman: "It is folded into the Latin American considerations?"

Bushnell: "That is correct."

As Bushnell reluctantly admitted, the Caribbean was an addendum, nothing more than a footnote, despite the rhetoric of the administration.

Representative Gus Yatron (Pennsylvania) had listened to a witness explain the economic problems confronted by Caribbean nations. He did not disagree with the assessment of "the economic underpinnings of the political trends in the Caribbean." He sensed that poverty produced a desire for change. However, "the radicalism which concerns me and which I believe clearly threatens the interests of the United States is the type which can only breed the kind of instability which has plagued most of the South American and Central American independence."

Arguably Yatron had been reading the 1915 correspondence between Secretary of State Bryan and President Woodrow Wilson. Whatever the case, he indicated that "the movement toward the left in the region will generate a backlash. This kind of instability, this seesawing from the left and to the right is what concerns me. No one stands to gain from this sort of instability."

Now Yatron sounded like Secretary Thomas Mann and his colleagues discussing the Dominican Republic in 1963 or 1965. U.S. officials worried only about instability and Fidel Castro. That upset Willard Johnson (representing an African-American organization called Transafrica) and he said so.

Johnson did not "share the view that instability was the enemy and that no one had anything to gain by it." On the contrary, Johnson pointed to an issue which cuts across the century when he said that "instability offers very little in and of itself but it is rare that there can be changes in power and economic distributions without instability. And so if you see instability as the principal threat, then you commit yourself to the status quo which I think many people would find unsatisfactory in the Caribbean today."[58]

Johnson had asked a crucial question: Whose side are you on? The Caribbean was a sea of profound political and economic problems but, instead of a policy which focused on the Caribbean in a comprehensive fashion, what islanders heard was a call to stay calm and, as President Carter noted, help us stop Castro from perpetuating the "Soviet imperialism" which, according to Secretary Bushnell, was a "negligible" factor throughout the Caribbean.

Jimmy Carter generally supported the status quo. More importantly, his reaction to three separate issues—Joaquin Balaguer, sugar, and the Mariel "entrants"—provided a "don't rock the boat" blueprint for the eighties and the nineties.

President Carter met with Joaquin Balaguer on September 8, 1977. He noted that the United States had "an extremely good relationship" with the Dominican Republic and he then said that "President Balaguer had set an example for all leaders in this nation in changing his own country and his own people away from a former totalitarian government to one of increasingly pure democracy." The Dominican leader deserved great praise because "the commitment he has shown in preserving human rights and leading the other nations in this effort have been an inspiration to me...."[59]

In the 1974 elections—Balaguer won with 84.6 percent of the vote—the president's forces "unleashed a violent reign of terror" against his opponents. In parades soldiers shouted that they would permit only Balaguer to govern and they taunted potential voters with this campaign slogan: "Ustedes tienen los votos y nosotros las botas." ["You have the votes; we have the boots."][60]

It was vintage Trujillo. Representative Donald Fraser (Minnesota) wrote a letter complaining about the president's comments—"our statements have shown an unreserved partiality towards the government of President Balaguer"—and he cited a number of instances in which Balaguer and his followers were already violating the electoral rules of the game. Fraser therefore asked that "your administration take some meaningful concrete action to correct the strong impression, however unintended, that we favor President Balaguer. Otherwise we can be fairly criticized as intervening in and influencing the elections."[61]

In the correspondence which ensued the reaction of the Carter administration was fascinating. When Fraser suggested that they meet with Balaguer's opposition, the president's staff said no; that would be "unnecessarily provocative"; they wanted "more distance from the election" despite the tributes accorded to Balaguer. When Fraser asked for a check on campaign irregularities, the staff secretary of the National Security Council handwrote, "I don't want any major effort on this request, please." And, finally, when Fraser's complaints were brought to the attention of Zbigniew Brzezinski, Robert Pastor told him that "Fraser and his staff appear obsessed with the Dominican elections. This is his third letter in less than two months."[62]

Congressman Fraser was apparently too concerned with the need for fair elections. Whatever the case, the Carter administration kept its distance, the elections were held, Balaguer lost, he and forces tried to overturn their defeat, and President Carter issued a very forceful statement about the need to abide by the will of the electorate. Faced with the prospect of serious political and economic repercussions, Balaguer and his soldiers backed down; and, however belatedly, the United States had supported the forces of instability.

In the Dominican Republic the president hesitated. When it came to U.S. sugar policy, he and his advisors believed that significant change was required but they nevertheless surrendered to the small group of growers whose self-interest did nothing to help the many Caribbean nations (the

Dominican Republic, Haiti, Jamaica, the Eastern Caribbean) who still depended on sugar for portions of their export earnings.

The memos and analysis of the Carter administration make one thing instantly clear: These men and women believed that sugar policy was a boondoggle. In 1979, the world price was 7.5 cents a pound, the price maintained in the United States was 15 cents, the growers and their congressional backers (*e.g.* Senators Long and Church) wanted 17 cents and some even spoke of reimposing quotas.

The quotas had been eliminated in 1974 when the price of sugar was so high that even the American growers found it impossible to make a case for further protecting their already record profits. Whether from price supports or quotas, the Carter analysts said that "this wide margin of protection has nothing to do with national security. Its *only possible justification* is to protect about 13,000 farmers, that is, less than one-half of one percent of the total farm population, many of them corporations, and most of them with other good uses they would devote their land to, and *would but for their protection from the market.*"[63] [emphasis added]

U.S. support prices were based on the costs of production in the highest cost states. In Idaho (with its sugar beets) and Louisiana (with its cane) it cost more to grow sugar than in any other farm situation, so these states became the model for everyone. This made no sense if the goal was a measure of justice for the nation's consumers. It was also hard to explain in terms of free market capitalism. His advisors told the president, watch out for Senator Long (of Louisiana): "Your conversations with him on finance committee matters have been very much like ours; they inevitably turn to sugar, and he talks about it with a passion not seen on any other legislation."[64]

Long favored sugar because his state contained hundreds of farms. The senator depended on sugar's vote but the Carter people were bothered by the consequences of Long's effective lobbying; the benefits of the sugar support program were highly concentrated. As analysts told the president, in 1977 "the 25 largest sugar cane farms in Florida and Hawaii accounted for *61 percent* of total sugarcane production. In contrast the *1000* smallest sugarcane farms (mostly in Hawaii and Louisiana) accounted for less than *3 percent* of production. Five Hawaiian firms received nearly $56 million under the payment program we operated last year."[65] [emphasis in original]

The Carter administration worked hard to obtain an International Sugar Agreement which was meant to provide a floor price for Caribbean and other world producers. At the national level the president pushed for means to shift producers out of sugar; he believed that "the best long-term solution for Louisiana and Hawaii is to identify other economic activities and provide means by which human and capital resources now employed in sugar production can make an adjustment."[66]

Carter tried for a small victory when he suggested direct payments to farmers instead of price supports. This would have permitted prices to be set by market forces but the large producers refused. They feared that Congress would impose payment ceilings so it was safer (and much more profitable) to keep prices at double the world average. When the president balked at a price of 17 cents a pound—the administration proposed a ceiling of 13.5 cents— Senator Church told the president (in April of 1978, and then again in February of 1979) that the Senate would never approve the International Sugar Agreement achieved by the administration's negotiators unless Idaho and its farmers received the support they desired.[67]

The administration pondered its options. "The gut issue that underlay all the talk about different levels of price support" was simple: how much of the American industry was the Carter administration "going to protect from foreign competition." His answer was the same as that of Presidents Kennedy, Johnson, Nixon, and Ford. Carter set the yearly import level at 5.3 million tons, the average for 1960-1978. In addition the administration accepted an import fee (on top of the sugar tariff) and also settled on a price of 15 cents a pound. Even that failed to satisfy the sugar interests, so when the House rejected a 17 cents a pound bill, the Senate did in fact reject the International Sugar Agreement achieved by the president and his staff.[68]

Sugar won and the American consumer lost. Meanwhile, the Jamaicans who found no work at home came to Florida and Louisiana where their American jobs were protected by the sugar legislation that was a prime cause of their migration.[69]

Migration became a problem right after the president's April 9, 1980, address about the Caribbean. The president "welcomed all of you here to celebrate the establishment of Caribbean/Central America Action." This was a quasi-governmental group (sponsored by officials like Congressman Dante Fascell) that represented two concerns; the "vital importance" of the entire Caribbean to the U.S,. and the "deep importance we as Americans attach to people-to-people relationships as the foundation for building genuine friendships among nations."[70]

These admirable sentiments were about to be tested because a number of Caribbean people suddenly wanted to enter the United States. It started in Cuba. For at least a year small groups of Cubans had sought political asylum in the Peruvian and Venezuelan embassies. On April 4, 1980 a group of Cubans tried to crash into the Peruvian compound. They killed a Cuban guard in the process. The Castro government removed the forces stationed outside the embassy, and announced that anyone who wanted to leave via the Peruvian route was free to do so.

Within days 10,000 Cubans camped in and around the Peruvian embassy. This was far more than the Peruvians could resettle so on April 14 President Carter not only agreed to admit 3,500 of the Cubans, he offered to fund their transportation and other costs through a $4.25 million "drawdown" from an emergency refugee and migration assistance fund.[71]

Castro responded to the flight of so many Cubans with an offer—on April 20—to let any who wished to emigrate to the United States ship out from the port of Mariel, a city twenty miles from Havana. By late May over 69,000 Cubans were in Florida and the Carter administration faced a dilemma that, within a month, generated more negative reaction than any other issue decided by the president.[72]

Congress offered the president little or no help. A mid-May summary of congressional reaction told Carter that the "biggest concern" in the Senate was "where the money will come from." In the House, representatives "had basically not focused on the issue." The immigration status of the Cubans concerned some members, and the president could expect a bit of cooperation from the speaker, but beyond that many in Congress happily let the president assume full responsibility.

The tens of thousands fleeing the "repression" of President Castro's communist regime would be welcomed in an "orderly flow", and, while the president certainly wanted to slow down the flotilla of desperately eager migrants, an action memorandum (May 13) stated that the goal was to have a "*modest* enforcement of our entry laws (fines and citations but few seizures and no attempt to block boats seeking to go to Cuba)."[73] [emphasis in original]

The Cubans continued to come, and so did roughly 15,000 Haitians. They had begun arriving even before the mass exodus from Cuba but their simultaneous appearance in Florida gave the president a definitional dilemma of the first order. Since 1970 only 250 Haitians had received asylum in the United States. The Carter administration agreed that "the regime in Haiti was, without question, as repressive as that in Cuba." Since both countries were then experiencing serious economic problems, "there was no reason to *presume* that persons leaving Cuba do so for political reasons and those leaving Haiti do so for economic reasons."[74] However, despite these arguments the Haitians had always been treated differently. They were aliens to be returned, the Cubans victims who would be saved from Communist oppression.

In mid-1980, the two groups of migrants appeared at the same time, their numbers posed staggering short and long term problems, and, perhaps most important, Congress had just passed the Refugee Act of 1980.

The new law partially eliminated the old discrimination. Instead of making an exception for those fleeing communism, it adopted a United Nations standard rooted in universally acceptable terms.

Race, religion, nationality, political affiliation; any of these was now a basis to be granted asylum or to be a refugee if the individual was "unable or unwilling to return" to his or her native land "because of persecution or a well founded fear of persecution."

No one expected this law to apply to more than one hundred thousand people at the same time. The asylum provisions were intended for individuals like ballet dancers and it was expected that the refugee decision would be made while the person(s) was in *another* country. The Haitians and Cubans threw a hot potato in Jimmy Carter's lap. His decision could open America's doors to so many Haitians that a fleet of oceans liners would never provide sufficient room for that country's eager departing citizens.

Even before he and his advisors considered specific options, this administration laid out a variety of policy objectives. Owing to "its international position vis-à-vis Castro," only criminals and other threats to national security would be returned to Cuba; all others could stay. The overall Carter policy—by law—had to treat the Haitians and Cubans in an "even-handed" manner. This done, somebody had to find the money to underwrite the resettlement effort; and, because all concerned wanted "to minimize incentives for persons with economic motivation to migrate to this country," the administration's ultimate solution must be "an exceptional measure that can be contained as precedent."[75]

Precedent was the axis around which all thinking revolved. Instead of answering questions that went to the roots of America's treatment of Caribbean refugees—for example, if Haiti was, "without doubt," as repressive as Castro, why did we help one but economically blockade the other; and, why never question keeping the vast majority of the Cubans but always question keeping the Haitians?—the Carter administration searched for a one time solution, a way to resolve the immediate crisis in a manner that never dealt with the increasing stream of migrants from all over the Caribbean.

The law focused on the motivation of the migrants; but another issue was the motivation of the officials labeling the new arrivals. Thus, when the Carter administration tentatively decided to call everyone "entrants," it focused on a word which artfully underlined the ambiguity desired by the president and his advisors.[76] It was one thing for Americans to bathe in the Caribbean's warm sun, another to give Haitians or Dominicans the idea that they would somehow receive a sunny welcome in Florida.

If only as an emergency measure, President Carter struggled to help the people now massed on America's shores. The president dutifully asked for congressional input. On the right Senator Thurmond said that "the only refugees to be allowed in should be those who qualify under the present law. Those who are here for economic reasons should be returned. The people of South Carolina feel very strongly about this."[77]

On the left, Senator Frank Church presumably spoke for the people of Idaho. He suggested that except for the few who qualify under the present law, "we put the Cubans on a destroyer and send them back, forcing the gates of Guantanomo if necessary." As aides told the president, "Senator Church did not want to discuss the options or relative merits of various strategies. He stated that he could care less about them."

In the middle was Senator Chiles. He told the president "that there are 80 Strom Thurmonds in the Senate on this issue. This had been illustrated by the reactions exhibited during talk shows all over the country."[78]

The president received a "final" memo on June 14, 1980. It came from, among others, Zbigniew Brzezinski and it put "avoiding undesirable precedents" as the administration's number one objective. Jimmy Carter had two options; he could let the migrants in via a "broad interpretation of the refugee definition," or he could continue to keep them on parole and "seek special legislation for the long-term solution." The president chose parole for the "entrants" because to use the brand new law (to define the Cubans and Haitians) was to "significantly weaken the refugee standard for these and future groups." The president's advisors unanimously opposed such a move: "All favor [of the parole option] including Brzezinski."[79]

On June 20, 1980, President Carter announced his decision. He named 129,000 people (114,000 Cubans, 15,000 Haitians) entrants and asked Congress for "special, one time only" legislation. Any of the entrants who arrived after April 20, but before June 20, would be covered by the new legislation; anyone coming after the president's announcement would be treated very differently. Indeed, although he never suggested using a destroyer to push them through the gates of Guantanomo, President Carter stressed that new arrivals would be processed on a rigorous, case by case basis. The peoples of the Caribbean had to understand that on June 20, 1980, the United States of America had indefinitely removed the welcome mat so reluctantly offered to the people of Cuba and Haiti.[80]

The president's compromise was a very controversial—even a very courageous—decision. He helped over 100,000 people but, like Congress, he did nothing to resolve the long term problem posed by the Caribbean's "economic" migrants. The Haitians would not only never disappear, they (and the Dominicans who sailed to Puerto Rico in hopes of "passing" through to New York) were a major consequence of a century of America's preponderant influence throughout the Caribbean. The United States chose to do what was best for Idaho or Louisiana and then had the audacity to turn away the migrants who were a direct consequence of America's political and economic hegemony in the Caribbean.

Critics of the "entrant" decision stressed that the president's compromise allowed the special status of Cuba to remain intact. Because of Castro and Communism, Cubans who had lived in the United States for more than a year could be granted permanent status. Meanwhile, the president never justified his relations with the governments of men like Duvalier and Balaguer.

The problem was the result of never facing up to the economic consequences of a century of exploitation, indifference, and intervention.

The Haitians were not about to disappear. Not for Jimmy Carter, Ronald Reagan, George Bush, or Bill Clinton.

Cultural Constants

"For the 13 sugar producing countries of the CBI...lost sugar earnings have cost them half a billion dollars since 1983, and more than offset any CBI benefits...your bill forcefully expresses the intent of this committee to address the appalling effect of current U.S. policy on these countries we are supposed to be helping."

—David Rockefeller, Congress, 1988[1]

It was one of the closing acts of his administration. On October 25, 1980, President Carter transmitted a constitution to Congress. This was the fourth draft of the document and even though the president never found five minutes to formally receive the constitution from the governor of the Virgin Islands (in August of 1980), he had no compunctions about offering a number of significant corrections, deletions, and suggestions. It was paradoxical that a U.S. official for whom no islander had the right to vote could nevertheless edit and alter the document that assured both self-government and the rights of a free people.[2]

One of the president's former aides offered an explanation for the president's behavior: The administration was "somewhat schizophrenic" when it came to the territories. The White House said one thing, the bureaucracy did another, and, meanwhile, the fellow writing the letter—Jeffrey Farrow—called himself "State Chairman" of the Democratic

Party of the Virgin Islands. He apologized for his complaints; Farrow wanted no one to assume that a "politically insignificant population" was dissatisfied with Washington's policies, but, could the president please consider these injustices.[3]

In a bill submitted to Congress (in April of 1978), the Department of the Interior wanted such a "great increase" in the power of federal comptrollers that it "would appear to reestablish colonial control." So far no sponsor had been found for the bill, but, "while Interior had been dreaming up back-to-colonialism legislation," it not only offered no assistance with the island's fiscal and social problems, it sought to maintain a policy of taxation without representation.[4]

Every year Washington officials withheld millions of dollars of excise taxes on the gasoline refined at the Hess' St. Croix plant. To islanders this was both contradictory and undemocratic because while Hess paid no federal taxes, they were taxed even though their resident commissioner still had no right to vote in Congress.

Farrow thought it was one thing to send Vice President Mondale to accept the constitution but why did no one at the White House grasp "the necessity for the president to personally receive a document about which the White House may have some reservations." This was bad politics and a potentially damaging manifestation of the White House attitude.[5] The president should read the document and make the necessary adjustments.

Jimmy Carter did as he was asked. Aides read the constitution and, as in the debate about Puerto Rico in 1950–52, they focused on the preamble to the Virgin Islands model for self-government.

Former drafts had "explicitly recognized the sovereignty of the United States"; this document only did so by implication so Carter aides wondered if it was "necessary for the president to point out that the current draft recognized the supremacy of U.S. law and that the official analysis [the body of the constitution] recognizes U.S. sovereignty?"[6]

The answer was yes. In his message to Congress the president underlined the sovereignty of the United States. He also revealed the schizophrenia suggested by his former White House aide. After four pages of proposals, corrections, and deletions, the president stopped. He said the courts might be the ultimate arbiter of many of the document's problems, so, to avoid extensive litigation, the people of the Virgin Islands should engage in "serious discussion." Make the changes before the constitution went to the courts because, as President Carter told Congress, "this document should truly be one of their own making."[7]

The president had just rewritten a constitution. He simultaneously reaffirmed the islanders right to self-determination when he said their constitution should be made by the people. At the same time, he never addressed the contradiction embedded in the final paragraph of his message; mainland senators and representatives made all "needful rules and regulations" for the Virgin Islands.

As in the United States, "largest non-state, offshore entity" (i.e., Puerto Rico)[8], Congress wore the crown. Its prerogatives not only had nothing to do with self-determination, they represented a reassertion of the mentality manifest in 1949, namely that the Virgin Islands were a colonial possession and islanders mere subjects of the United States.

That was the reality under President Truman. And it was the reality when President Carter handed the reins of power over to a man who extolled the virtues of free markets and private enterprise.

Caribbean Basin Initiative

President Reagan drew a wide arc. While even the most expansive definitions of the Caribbean never included countries like El Salvador and Nicaragua, these nations were the military axis of what the president called his Caribbean Basin Initiative. It was a cold war, free enterprise approach to development because three Central American nations (El Salvador, Costa Rica, and Honduras) received 67 percent of all the proposed funding (the figure for the entire Eastern Caribbean was 3 percent) and neither Nicaragua nor Cuba received any form of assistance. Before Congress the president's representatives said they "must work closely" with other interested countries but, despite pleas from the Mexicans to include Cuba, the United States refused. As Assistant Secretary of State Enders put it, "clearly, we do not contemplate giving any assistance to Cuba and we have simply agreed to disagree (with the Mexicans) on this."[9]

By excluding Cuba, Nicaragua, and Grenada, the president had sanitized the Caribbean Basin. He made it free for free enterprise, a phrase which symbolized the administration's "innovative" approach to Caribbean development. Countries throughout the Basin faced "a plague of economic disasters," which a Reagan official summarized as "high rates of unemployment, low growth or negative growth, high inflation, and massive debts and capital flight.

In other words, conditions which undermine the confidence of the people in these countries that they can survive, much less prosper."[10]

It was a desperate situation which could be transformed by a proper stimulation of the private sector. The Reagan officials had a plan and they asked Congress to fund it as a Caribbean *means* to U.S. ends. Under-Secretary Lawrence Eagleberger cited six reasons for the president's initiative: "Greater security and new economic opportunities for the U.S."; protection of an important sea lane and its many passageways; protection from the "possibility of hostile powers in the region"; protection from the political disruption that could threaten access to raw materials like bauxite; and, perhaps most important of all, protection from "massive migration."[11]

In his speeches the president supported supply side economics; in the Caribbean Basin the "centerpiece" of his program was an effort to stimulate demand. He wanted to have an immediate economic impact so he focused on an "offer of one way trade." The Caribbean economies—traditionally bottled up by a combination of U.S. export quotas, tariffs, and taxes—would suddenly find a welcome American outlet for their goods and services. They could sell what they made, and, given a gigantic market for the output of small to tiny nations, the demand package would send ripples of wealth across the Caribbean Basin.[12]

There were a variety of immediate problems with this approach to development. Since its centerpiece was even greater dependence on the U.S. marketplace (*e.g.*, in 1982 the United States bought close to 60 percent of the Basin's exports and an even greater percentage of its tourists came from the United

States) the demand stimulus offered no sure help of a self-sustaining economy. On the contrary, the Basin package had a twelve year limit and if a Caribbean nation proved to be too successful, Congress had the power to suspend the privileges just granted. Thus, an economy on the move could be halted by a stop sign from Congress; paradoxically the Caribbean initiative would fail if it produced successes that seriously threatened any American job or business.

Thomas Enders (Assistant Secretary of State for Interamerican Affairs) perceived this problem and another as well. Since 86 percent of the Caribbean's goods already entered U.S. markets on a duty free basis, where was the room for growth? Did the Reagan administration plan to open up the U.S. marketplace to the 14 percent of the goods (*e.g.*, sugar and textiles) that accounted for the major part of the Caribbean's export earnings?

Enders told Congress that he and his colleagues recognized that "the remaining 14 percent of our imports from the area that are dutiable are nearly all sensitive areas"; so, in order to quell the fears of the sugar producers in Idaho and Louisiana, Enders stressed (as early as July of 1981) that "we hope to work closely with industry, labor and Congress to make sure those interests are appropriately listened to *and secured*."[13] [Emphasis added.]

Size was the key to the Caribbean's development. Since the economies were so small, "new access" need not "upset the balance of the market in the United States." It was a simple matter of "appropriately designing" the program of demand stimulus so that it produced development which simultaneously furnished adequate safeguards for U.S. producers.[14]

In Congress, no one broached the administration's ideological contradiction: A centralized government program was the means to success in a world where economies succeeded only if the government practiced a hands-off approach to prosperity. The appropriate design would come from federal officials and they would produce economic growth by opening up the theoretically free markets which were, in reality, tightly controlled by the federal government.

To stimulate the supply side of the equation, Reagan officials promised a package of investment incentives. They planned to ask for tax breaks for new businesses, they suggested bilateral treaties with a number of Basin countries, and, to insure the well-being of the attracted entrepreneurs, the Reagan administration planned to overuse the Overseas Private Investment Corporation. As a result of its huge program in countries like Jamaica, OPIC was already (in 1982) at or near its country limits in many Basin nations. To push free enterprise, the Reagan officials planned to increase the federal government's insurance exposure in areas like nationalization, expropriation, and revolution.[15]

When it came to the administration's designs for demand Congress posed some disturbing questions. Representative William Thomas (California) asked about the "3 cent break under duties" being given to sugar importers. Was it true that "a substantial portion of the excised duty was actually being used to move their sugar?" Were the producers making a windfall profit from the "benefits" of the Caribbean Initiative? And, most important of all, "how, if they are using a portion of those duties to move the sugar, the diversification—does that not mean that they would continue emphasis on sugar if they have an ability to undersell other countries on the sugar?"[16]

In the hotseat was the Department of Agriculture's Richard Smith. He agreed that diversification was a must and he saw no problem with the duty break because in the Caribbean the major producers confronted an "absolute quota." The United States refused their sugar as soon as it threatened American interests so what was the point of producing more sugar if it had no market?

Smith thought he had satisfied the congressman but Thomas introduced a series of provocative issues. To the extent that the sugar fields were owned by the government (this was the case for many in the Dominican Republic) was a free enterprise society underwriting socialism in the Caribbean? Was there a quid pro quo in terms of windfall profits? What assurance did the Reagan administration have that the reduction in duties would be used to diversify agriculture and/or create viable, export industries?

And, "does anyone have any figures" on what percent the private sector is involved in the production of sugar? Smith said "there was a mix" and the congressman then retorted; "So the duty reduction would benefit private companies. Are these nonnative? Are they Dominican companies or American companies?" Smith was familiar with Gulf and Western. They owned Central Romana so Thomas asked if someone would "explain to me how removing duties on sugar produced and sold by Gulf and Western, an American company, will benefit the Dominican Republic in terms of diversification of agriculture and the movement [toward democracy and a more viable economic system] you indicated?"

This was a good question. What never came out at the hearings was the extent of the benefits received by Gulf and Western. When (in 1971) the Nixon administration considered a change in sugar policy, the president received a memo which stated that "32 percent of the sugar entitlements within the Dominican Republic are controlled by Gulf and Western." Fully one-third of the Caribbean nation's entitlement had always benefitted an American corporation whose headquarters were in the middle of Manhattan. This was great for Gulf and Western in 1971 and to Congressman Thomas it looked like an even better deal in 1982.[17]

In answer to the question about benefits to the Dominican Republic, the Reagan officials again cited the quotas which limited the likelihood of increased production. "There certainly are very clear limits to which any expansion could take place. The program is such that one would not expect an expansion of the industry and of the exports to the United States."

Congressman Thomas: "So they simply take the profits and bring them home?"

Mr. Calingaert (Deputy Assistant Secretary of State): "obviously one does not know what happens to the profits. *The free system works in different ways.*"[18]

What free system? There were absolute quotas on sugar production; the 14 percent of the American market that mattered to the Caribbean was still closed by a mix of tariffs and other quotas; the federal government was insuring free enterprise against the perils of government-engineered investment; and the entire initiative lasted only as long as Congress agreed to permit the entry of additional Caribbean products. By 1988, members of the International

Garment Workers Union pleaded for limits on apparel exports from the Caribbean, while, in Florida, growers complained about too many tomatoes. CBI imports had increased nine-fold in four years and Congress had to stop importing tomatoes before constituents started to throw the tomatoes at them.[19]

Reagan officials celebrated free enterprise as they used a public program to stimulate both demand and private investment. As with Gulf and Western in the Dominican Republic, the public program often helped private enterprises who neither helped the Caribbean nor protected the United States. The administration admitted it had no idea where the profits went and, equally important, sugar symbolized the deeper schizophrenia of the whole CBI activity. If new or additional sugar quotas were imposed, one federal program (i.e., sugar policy) would conceivably wipe out all the benefits of another (i.e., the Caribbean Basin Initiative). Meanwhile, the Reagan administration would continue to extoll free markets while the new sugar quotas—which could generate the political turmoil that forced the government to pay off its OPIC insurance policies—protected the well established group of privately owned farms whose only interest (according to the Carter administration) was self-interest.

CBI helped start a war. In the name of competition and capitalism, one government program battled with another, and, since the Caribbean nations lacked electoral clout in Congress, they sat in the wings as a group of federal officials decided who would win and who would lose the public war over private profits.

Islanders lost, although they did get a chance to

tell Congress about their problems. On March 30, 1982, Felipe Vicini explained the significance of sugar to the Dominican Republic. One in ten islanders (Vicini did not include the paid and slave labor of the Haitians) worked in cane; sugar provided close to 35 percent of all the nation's foreign exchange receipts and with that money Dominicans not only bought a variety of items manufactured in the United States, they purchased virtually "100 percent of our energy requirements at OPEC prices." Without sugar the lights went out in the Dominican Republic.[20]

Vicini thanked Congress for thinking about the Caribbean. Even though U.S. duties added 45 percent to the price of Dominican sugar, a controlled market was much better than a free one. As Vicini stressed, "it is important to understand that about 80 percent of global sugar production is sold under protected or preferential marketing arrangements." The free market was the exception rather than the rule but the Dominican Republic (except for outfits like Gulf and Western's Central Romana) nevertheless sold most of its sugar on the volatile free market. The European Economic Community heavily subsidized its continental production but, whenever an oversupply developed, it violated international trading rules by throwing millions of tons of subsidized sugar on the free market. That sent prices tumbling; the lower prices had recently moved President Reagan to increase the variable tax on imports, and, as the higher prices reduced the demand for free market sugar, the Dominican Republic was stuck with a product it could trash but never sell.[21]

Vicini asked for empathy; grasp the position of the Dominican Republic and understand that even without quotas the future of sugar looked dim. World consumption was down, world production up.[22] To even consider the agricultural diversification that everyone wanted, Congress had to—at a minimum—provide the export stability (730,000 tons annually) of recent years.

While one congressional committee listened, another acted. Two months after Vicini's plea Congress reimposed the sugar quotas that, in five short years, reduced the Dominican Republic's U.S. sugar exports by 75 percent.[23]

Votes and deals partially explain the president's capitulation (Reagan agreed to support sugar quotas if he got the votes required for his budget and tax packages) but even more significant was a government sponsored loan program that put Ronald Reagan in the same position as Felipe Vicini.

Under President Carter Washington sponsored a program which gave farmers low interest loans to grow their sugar and, as collateral, the government took the produce that the farmers had not yet produced. Instead of the 15 cents which Carter agreed was too high, the Reagan administration set the "market stabilization price" for this sugar at 20 cents a pound. This was generous but, as long as the domestic price remained *above* the price guaranteed by the president, farmers had no incentive to forfeit their crops.[24]

As the EEC and other producers threw their surpluses on world markets, the free market price of sugar plummeted. Instead of selling their crops, farmers simply offered Reagan the collateral for their loans. The president was stuck with millions of tons of subsidized sugar and a *billion* dollar bill for the produce that, by law, he had to purchase and store.

On May 5, 1982, Ronald Reagan reimposed country quotas on sugar. He could have let the free market work but he chose instead to support sugar at prices 60 percent greater than the world price. The Commerce Department estimated that the policy cost American consumers an extra $3 billion a year but the beauty of quotas was the money they saved Ronald Reagan. He only agreed to let the loan program continue if it operated at *no* cost to the government. The farmers could have use of the government's money, but Ronald Reagan did not want their sugar. Because even the maximum duties and fees failed to bring imported sugar up to American levels, the only way to maintain the 60 percent greater price at no cost to the government was for a supply side president to sharply reduce the supply of imported sugar.[25]

The consequences of the president's contradiction were significant and immediate. In the Caribbean sugar imports dropped by fifty percent in the first year of the new import program while, in the United States the high prices moved farmers to increase production. As if a slap to the Caribbean's other cheek, the president unintentionally nourished a new and powerful vested interest when he imposed the quotas. For years high fructose sweeteners had competed with sugar; the higher prices moved consumers to use the sweeteners and they also moved the industry to support the sugar growers. The fructose companies set their price below sugar so, the higher the sugar price, the higher the price for sugar substitutes. It was a terribly vicious circle, which soon had negative ripple effects throughout the Caribbean.

In the Dominican Republic, the country had borrowed far too much money in the 1970s. They had to repay their loans but with a significant drop in export earnings they now had less and less money to cover a balance of payments deficit that was large even before the imposition of the sugar quotas. Mills closed, unemployment increased, Haitians built boats, Dominicans complained about "abogados del diablo" (the devil's lawyers sent by the International Monetary Fund),[26] and, meanwhile, President Reagan did something which was both unique and typical. For the first time in history, the United States militarily intervened in the English speaking Caribbean. When U.S. soldiers stormed the shores of Grenada they did so on the basis of (intervention) invitations that were even more questionable than the ones received by Teddy Roosevelt in 1905 and Lyndon Johnson in 1965.[27]

Grenada

Grenada is small, even for the Caribbean. It's a roughly 10 by 13 mile strip of land which, before the American invasion, was best known for nutmeg, exploitation, and a brutally peculiar prime minister. The nutmeg is everywhere; merchants hawk it on street corners and a tour of the island's warehouses produces a sight of a literal mountain of bulging bags all waiting for a buyer in Europe or the United States. Throughout the island nutmeg shells provide a lovely covering for footpaths; you crunch as you walk. Before those shells hit the ground, someone cracked them. Traditionally a woman working all day at home received $7.10 for cracking 150 pounds of nuts. When those nuts finally found a marke,t the finished product sold for one dollar an ounce. That was 300 times the women's daily wage, a figure rivaled only by Puerto Rico's pharmaceutical companies.[28]

The peculiar prime minister was Eric Gairy. Addressing the United Nations on October 7, 1976, he opened with this statement: "Man is the greatest thing that God has created on this earth plane and man is everything that he himself has invented. But, as I said before on another occasion, man is afraid to unlock the door to himself."[29]

Not Gairy. Spiritually he lived on one plane but, on earth, he unlocked the door to the island's treasury and to its armory. His Mongoose Gang cracked heads in the same way workers cracked nuts; Congressman Jonathan Bingham (New York) even suggested that Gairy was "sort of a Trujillo" so, after more than twenty years of repression and thievery, few sympathized when Gairy was overthrown in March of 1979. A group of revolutionaries called the New Jewel Movement assaulted the island's only encampment of soldiers, secured the cooperation of Sir Paul Scoon, the governor-general appointed by the Queen of England, and they quickly formed a government that immediately received a lecture from the United States.[30]

The Carter administration did agree to work with the new government. It had no choice since, among others, Barbadian Prime Minister Tom Adams said Gairy was "indefensible." Within days of the takeover the Carter administration turned the conflict into a battle to contain communism. Officials testified (two months *after* the coup) that "the Soviets have not played any significant direct role that we can identify in the Caribbean."[31] Despite this knowledge, Grenada's leaders were quickly told "that the United States would view with displeasure any tendency on the part of Grenada to develop closer ties with Cuba."[32]

In assessing this message a Carter official later wrote that it was a question of delivery. U.S. Ambassador Benjamin Ortiz had lectured the Grenadians. He walked into offices without knocking; he threatened the government's leadership; he warned the head of security at the Grenadian airport; and he was "condescending with blacks." As Prime Minister Maurice Bishop noted, "Ortiz did everything possible to arouse a black man."[33]

Personality is undoubtedly a part of this equation. But, Ortiz did have instructions from the president—"he was to tell Bishop of the U.S. concern about his establishing a military relationship with Cuba"—and those instructions manifested a Great Power thrust that was typical rather than unique, shared rather than special. Reading General Smedley Butler's testimony about the 1916 occupation of Haiti a reader also encounters a strong personality acting on the basis of cultural instructions: "We were all imbued with the idea that we were trustees of a huge estate that belonged to minors."[34]

Grenada never belonged to minors, but it was the United States to control and whether Ortiz acted politely or abrasively he carried out orders that could have been issued at any point in the century. As in 1916 the Caribbean was still an American lake; but, in 1979 the lake contained a few Communists. The president sent a message: Maurice Bishop could drown if he decided to swim with Fidel Castro.

Bishop reacted to President Carter's threat with an angry denunciation of the United States. On April 13, 1979, he tried to distance himself from the

United States: "No country has the right to tell us what to do or how to run our country or who to be friendly with; we are not in anybody's backyard and we are definitely not for sale...."[35]

President Carter set the tone that helped produce the invasion of Grenada. Unquestionably the members of the New Jewel Movement were Communists. If they significantly improved everything from medical care to the literacy rate, they also demonstrated a pronounced disregard for political and human rights. The New Jewel government closed newspapers, it threatened religious rights, it cut off opponents' telephones, and it held a variety of Gairy and New Jewel supporters without trial and under brutal conditions.[36]

This happened after President Carter issued his threat, and no matter how repressive the regime became it was never a match for Claude Duvalier in Haiti. As the president's advisors indicated when they discussed the Mariel flotilla, the regime in Haiti was, "without question," as repressive as the one in Cuba.

For Jimmy Carter the dictators could stay but the Communists had to go—peacefully if possible, forcefully if necessary. Thus, President Reagan inherited a climate alien to Grenada. There was a freeze in the Caribbean on January 20, 1981, and that freeze remained in effect throughout the first years of the Reagan administration. As Representative Michael Barnes noted in 1982, "if the United States had a policy toward Grenada, it appears to consist of not answering mail and avoid being seen in the same room with officials from Grenada."[37]

Maurice Bishop was assassinated on October 19, 1983. His New Jewel colleagues proclaimed a new government while, in Washington, officials issued new orders to the fleet. Go to Lebanon by way of the Caribbean. Stay close just in case the United States decides to act in a forceful way.

At the White House CIA Director William Casey was eloquent: "Fuck it, let's dump the bastards."[38] His colleagues at first hesitated, but by October 21 they decided to imitate the behavior of Lyndon Johnson in 1965. When Ambassador Bennett received a verbal request for aid from the Dominican military, Johnson said to get a written request specifying danger to American citizens. On Friday, October 21, the Reagan administration sent word to the Organization of Eastern Caribbean States (OECS), meeting in Barbados, that an invasion was much more likely if the administration received a written request from the concerned nations. Just to make sure that the request contained the appropriate wording, on Saturday Reagan sent an emissary "with a list of essential points to be included in any formal OECS written request for assistance."[39]

The man who wrote that laundry list was Michael Kozak. His formal title was Deputy Legal Advisor for the State Department and, if his language lacked the flair of William Casey, it nevertheless betrayed the same arrogance and indifference to the Caribbean and its peoples. As Kozak noted in a November 3, 1988 interview, "you do what you have to do and then you look for a legal justification."[40]

Kozak looked for a legal justification, which was very hard to find from the OECS. Two articles (Numbers 6 and 8) of the organization's charter did offer some help but they also stipulated that any decision had to be unanimous and any prospect of collective action was contingent on the danger or reality of external aggression. The assassination of a head of state never fit into the charter's provisions but, despite that, Reagan officials would use the OECS as a justification for the invasion.[41] As Secretary of State Marshall noted in 1947, the United States suffered from the "penalty of power"; despite the decided weakness of the OECS as a legal justification, the organization performed a vital public relations service. It turned unilateral intervention into collective action.

Another justification was at least a century old: Americans were in danger. The students who attended the medical school on Grenada could be killed at any moment. This was a fine excuse except that, among others, the president of the medical college "felt they were never in any kind of danger." He said that on TV and it was embarrassing to the administration so, as Langhorne Motley (Assistant Secretary of State, Bureau of Interamerican Affairs) later told Congress, after the invasion "we chatted with him... and he *finally* changed his mind."[42]

The biggest contradiction revolved around the alleged role of Sir Paul Scoon. He owed allegiance to the Queen yet Scoon was also bound to act in accordance with the advice offered by Grenadian officials. After the assassination of Bishop Buckingham Palace said Scoon expressed no reservations about his new colleagues. On Saturday, October 22, he not only never mentioned any need for assistance, he offered officials in London his best guesses about the composition of the new government.[43]

Washington heard about the invitation on Sunday, October 23 at 2 in the morning when word came that Tom Adams (Prime Minister of Barbados) said that David Montgomery (British deputy high commissioner) said that Sir Paul Scoon said he wanted the Americans to invade. It sounded like the children's game of telephone (you sit in a circle and pass a message from one ear to another) so, at the White House, officials were skeptical. They had already made a tentative decision to invade and they also had the requested OECS invitation in hand. Was another invitation needed? Was it true? And what authority did Scoon have? Legal researchers immediately went to work as Assistant Secretary Motley summarized their thinking: Scoon's invitation could provide a "nice legal justification" for American action.[44]

It took almost two weeks to finally play the Scoon card. Meanwhile, officials told a story that would thoroughly contradict their definitive account. Testifying before Congress on October 27 Deputy Secretary of State Kenneth Dam tried to dispel any doubts about the legitimacy of the OECS decision. "On the question of unanimity, first of all, there had been a communication from the governor general to the OECS countries *as to his assent or approval*, with the action of the OECS." Dam made no mention of any request or appeal and he also indicated that Scoon "was expected to speak to the people today [October 27th]." That sounded good to Congress. Asked what had happened to the governor general during the invasion, Dam left no doubts: "*We secured his safety.*"[45]

In fact Scoon had been removed from Government House on the 26th. According to Foreign Service Officer Larry Rossin, "on the morning of October 26th I, together with [Barbadian General]

410

Rudyard Lewis, received a written request from Sir Paul Scoon for intervention."[46]

Dam had the request and a "secured" Scoon in hand when he testified before Congress on the 27th. However, when he presented (on November 4, 1983) the definitive legal explanation for the Grenada invasion, Sir Paul's assent or approval had become an appeal, and Dam also said that "we were unable to make this request public until the governor general's safety had been assured, but it was an important element—legally as well as politically—in our respective decisions to help Grenada."[47]

It was a contradictory argument in 1983, and it is a contradictory argument now. However, the most important question is why do intelligent officials waste time with rationales that they themselves publicly contradict?

John Bartlow Martin provided an answer to this question in October of 1965. Writing to President Johnson about the White Paper which provided the legal rationales for the Dominican invasion, Martin said that "its sweeping unsupported conclusions will be attacked as lacking evidence." He "did not believe any department paper can successfully meet the attacks, particularly on lack of candor...." The president should scrap the legal argument "but he had no apology to make for the result, which was to preserve freedom of choice for the Dominican people. It is results that count."[48]

In the Caribbean, U.S. officials have repeatedly done as they pleased, but they have also refused to concede a disturbing fact: the "results" argument is the brutal rationale of a Great Power. It is the CIA explanation offered to President Truman in 1948:

411

"Cuba is small and weak, the U.S., large and powerful."[49]

As officials championed democratic ideals they simultaneously used guns to illegally overthrow any undesirable Caribbean government. In the Dominican Republic in 1965 the White Paper was issued and in Grenada in 1983 officials hastily constructed a series of rationales which, however contradictory, offered explanations in harmony with the ideals professed by the United States and the United Nations. Meanwhile, in private, they talked like William Casey; indeed, after the invasion in 1983, "Grenada grew as a positive symbol in administration lore. It was routinely invoked as a sign of a new toughness, reaffirming the Monroe Doctrine, big stick and gunboat diplomacy...."[50]

In Grenada islanders heard about democracy but settled for a large dose of arrogance, irony, and indifference. When a group of U.S. Quakers visited Grenada in 1984, they discovered that the made-in-Washington blueprint for the island's economic development had never been shown to Grenadian officials; the advisory council installed by invasion authorities ruled as a figurehead while Americans made the economic and political decisions for the Grenadian people.

An airport that was supposedly built for military purposes—it would be used by Soviet and Cuban forces—was finished by an American government whose rationales seconded those of Maurice Bishop and the New Jewel Movement. As Secretary of State George Schultz said in February of 1984, "I must say, having landed here and looked around a little, it certainly is needed here and in one way or another, it will be completed."[51]

That airport now prominently displays a sign thanking the United States for its construction. There is no mention of the support given by Cuba, Canada, or the European Economic Community. It is a case of amnesia in Grenada and indifference in the United States.

These lines were written almost a decade after the invasion, and Grenada is now what it was before—a tiny, forgotten part of the Caribbean. The United States efficiently completed its work. So, as in the Dominican Republic in 1965, Haiti in 1934, or the Dominican Republic in 1924, U.S. officials and U.S. culture refuse to look backwards.

Forward is the only direction for the American people, because the past is a challenge to the conventional wisdom; and, on a deeper level, the past is a challenge to the positive assessment of the officials and practices that have shaped a century of U.S. Caribbean policy.

The 936 Laws Again

The Governor was unequivocal: "Section 936 works." Rafael Hernandez Colon told Congress (on October 3, 1985) that without the federal tax exemption for "possession corporations" Puerto Rico had no meaningful way to stimulate employment and "sustain our economic development." Money from the 936 corporations provided at least 30 percent of Puerto Rico's existing jobs and those corporations generated 40 percent of all funds on deposit in the Puerto Rico banking system. Without 936, Congress would have to provide even more money to "reduce the welfare burden" and, on the positive side, Congress needed to remember that "compared to our neighbors in the

Caribbean, we have achieved through 936 an *economic miracle....*"[52] [emphasis added]

Antonio Colorado, head of the island's Economic Development administration, questioned the governor's assessment. In May of 1986 Colorado told Congress that unemployment remained the island's greatest social problem. In a nation with an official unemployment rate of 21 percent, "unemployment among youth aged 16 to 19 years was 53 percent, and the rate was 40 percent among those 20 to 24 years old. Fifty-one percent of our unemployed persons had 13 or more years of school."[53]

Colorado said the disaster had many explanations. The imposition of minimum wage made Puerto Rico far less attractive than many other developing economies. Since 1960, Congress had substantially reduced tariffs on 60 percent of the products entering the United States. What was good for Taiwan and Hong Kong was not good for Puerto Rico. The oil crisis had "destroyed" the promising petrochemical industry and, while the extension of food stamps "reduced the pressure for persons to migrate to the mainland," whether in Puerto Rico, Chicago or New York, the bottom line was always the same; nobody had a job.

To Colorado, all these factors created an economic scenario in which only Section 936 prevented a major recession in Puerto Rico. Critics asked how, with 60 percent of the people on food stamps, and official unemployment at 21 percent, the island was not already experiencing a major recession. In his view, 936 was the axis of an economy that achieved progress by celebrating laissez faire. Colorado said that "as far as the government is concerned our policy within Puerto Rico and outside of Puerto Rico is that private industry is the one that decides what project they go into. We do not push one company one place or the other."[54]

In a world where both giant and small competitors (Japan and Singapore) used sophisticated industrial strategies, Colorado's faith in the beneficial effects of the free market was an anachronism. He felt that Puerto Rico enjoyed substantial advantages as a result of the free hand given to 936 companies. Colorado said the island now boasted a number of high level jobs, all sending positive ripple effects across the nation.[55]

One way to test Colorado's assertions was to use the figures provided by Puerto Rico's Labor Department. From 1977 to 1985 the island's economy had generated 227 new jobs in manufacturing. That was abysmal at best but (again from 1977-1985) there had been 8909 new jobs in pharmaceuticals. However, since 1982 that industry had only generated 668 new jobs and, in areas like computer equipment and electronic and electrical equipment, the economy has also seemed to stall. Computers showed a net decline of more than 2500 jobs (since 1983) and the highly profitable electronics sector had only generated 1200 new jobs in the last five years.[56]

Despite these figures, Colorado said to keep 936. President Reagan disagreed. He challenged the status quo because "despite the fact that inflation-adjusted tax-exempt income of corporations which have elected the benefits of section 936 has more than doubled since 1972, employment levels (both overall and in the manufacturing sector) have been flat. *The credit rewards generating income in the possessions; it provides no direct incentive to generating employment.*"[57]

Companies like Westinghouse, General Electric and Baxter, "that are big employers in Puerto Rico, and have the major operations down there...repatriate 100 percent of their funds. They do not have any funds in Puerto Rico."[58] And, of the $10 to $15 billion of corporation money in the island's banks, "approximately 75 percent of them (the deposits) would be CD's issued for tenures of 90 days or less...."[59]

Twelve years after President Carter received a report about 936, and four years after a second president also lambasted the tax exemption program, the companies still did as they pleased and Puerto Rico still enjoyed depression levels of unemployment.

How did the president lose? In 1986, Ronald Reagan met the 100 to 200 (out of 600) companies who earned the lion's share of the *$2 billion a year* in tax savings. Companies like Upjohn, Squibb, and Johnson and Johnson had no intention of losing a program that generated (for the pharmaceuticals) $265 in tax benefits for every $100 in wages. In league with the government of Puerto Rico they convinced Congress to support a continuation of 936 if Puerto Rico and the companies agreed to use 936 as a model for development in the entire Caribbean Basin. As Congressman Charles Rangel (New York) angrily told a possessions corporation spokesman, "You know and I know and the Chair knows that this Caribbean thing was just thrown in to save the program."[60]

This Caribbean thing was a promise to use $100 million a year in 936 funds to underwrite the president's faltering Caribbean Basin Initiative. This was only 5 percent of the companies yearly profits and .007 percent of the money deposited in Puerto Rico. It was nevertheless enough for Congress and President

Reagan to support the 936 program. They surrendered to a combination of carrots and sticks (no 90 day CD's if the tax exemptions were repealed) and, putting a happy face on bad policy, Congress and the president agreed to make Puerto Rico the investment hub of the Caribbean.

Puerto Rico was always second in line for economic development. Now, with the $100 million 936 proposal, the rest of the region would be second to Puerto Rico. An island with 21 percent official unemployment planned to use the promised funds only if they did not have a negative effect on Puerto Rico. It would be suicidal to do for others what the United States refused to do for Puerto Rico. So Congress, eager to avoid the crucial issues raised by Reagan, continued a program that continued to repatriate 75 percent of the profits earned in Puerto Rico.[61]

Meanwhile, the Caribbean would try to stimulate private investment by using one federal program (the 936 tax laws) to overcome the effects of another federal program (the sugar quotas) that had overcome the effects of another federal program (the Caribbean Basin Initiative).

David Rockefeller pleaded for a little sanity. Before Congress (in March of 1988), he stressed the appalling effects of the sugar quotas—a loss of 400,000 jobs compared to the 136,000 created by the CBI initiative—and he indicated that not only had sugar policy "more than offset all the benefits" of CBI, "it is hard for me to see how without at least restoring the quotas to where they were at the beginning (in 1982), there could be any other satisfactory solution."[62]

Rockefeller said Congress should immediately implement the sugar re-export program passed in

December of 1987. It would allow the Caribbean nations to import 290,000 short tons of sugar and, even though "we all know this was purely a stop-gap measure," Rockefeller pleaded with Congress to obey the law. "It was inexcusable that the administration had refused to implement this (re-import) program, which is the law of the land...."[63]

The president used a technicality to ignore the law for a variety of political and economic reasons. Like the National Rifle Association, the sugar lobby wanted *no* exceptions to the rule; even a stop-gap measure provided the precedent for abolishing the quota system. Moreover, the president knew the six year results of the new legislation. Domestic production had actually increased by more than 20 percent since 1982 so the last thing the sugar lobby wanted was free market competition from abroad.[64]

Once again speaking for the free market was Felipe Vicini, a man whose testimony alerted Congress to a possible breakdown of authority. The CBI stipulated that the Dominican Republic could export more than 875,000 tons of duty free sugar to the United States. Projected shipments for 1988 were no more than a 177,000 tons, so, instead of earning $344 million a year on sugar exports to the United States, the Dominican Republic netted a mere $70 million in sugar earnings. Since 1984 the island had lost over $1.1 billion dollars in promised sales to the United States, with the result that thousands of Haitians (many of whom worked in the Dominican Republic) were fleeing to the United States on boats destined for Florida, thousands of Dominicans were fleeing to Puerto Rico in hopes of entering the United States as citizens, and, "because of the massive cuts

418

in the U.S. sugar quota, the economy of the Dominican Republic is in critical condition. Foreign debt service is draining a large portion of the limited foreign exchange earnings, and the country must again reschedule its bilateral commercial debt or run the risk of a default."[65]

Vicini was being kind. He wanted to sell his sugar. But the realitites were even worse that the dismal picture painted by the Dominican. While exports from the Caribbean decreased, exports from the United States had substantially increased. A commission (its task was to explain unauthorized migration) established by the president noted that since 1983 U.S. exports to the Caribbean had jumped 37 percent; "interestingly the Caribbean Basin is one of the few regions of the world in which we have a trade surplus."[66]

The surplus existed because the principal aim of CBI was to stimulate U.S. exports. Japan was an equal or a superior; the Caribbean was so weak and dependent it offered one of the few spots in the world where the U.S. had a decided edge. The United States took advantage of a sure thing. Without the sugar quotas the trade results would have shown a better balance; with them the situation was so bad the Dominican Republic approached the predicaments first confronted in 1905.

Bankers were at the Republic's door. They had made high risk, *variable interest* loans all over the Caribbean but, instead of paying the price, they expected the government to act like Teddy Roosevelt; step in and collect for the banks the money their debtors would never otherwise repay.

As *bankers* told the president's commission on Unauthorized Migration, "A rolling loan gathers no loss." Even though a country like the Dominican Republic (or Haiti) paid nothing on the principal of its debt, the banks loaned the countries new money to pay off the interest on the old debt. Analysts confused debt payments and the effect of those payments on the bank's books. "They are *not* reciprocals of each other. The terms 'debt relief' and 'debt reduction' describe the effect on the creditor's books after a transaction is executed. They do not reflect the before and after actual cash burden of the debtor."[67] [emphasis in original]

The Dominican Republic used new money to pay off the *interest* on ten to twenty year old loans. The island still owed all the original principal but the banks lent the new interest money because they were involved in a "death dance" with countries like the Dominican Republic and Haiti. The banks never discounted the value of the loans. In the so-called secondary market the Dominican debt might fetch 20 or even 45 cents to the dollar. The banks nevertheless valued the debt at 100 cents to the dollar. The moment they accounted for the debt in a truthful fashion, regulators would require the banks to reclassify the loans as duds, or, in banker's language, as non-performing assets. The net worth of the bank would immediately tumble, its stock prices would fall, and banks which deserved to fail might actually do so.[68]

The banks had a solution—call in the government. The banks, after all, had no time to worry about the long term welfare of the Caribbean. Their goals were short term; they needed to protect their balance sheets and income statements. Instead of giving the countries the options offered in bankruptcy court (lower interest rates and significant reduction of debt), the banks required that countries like the Dominican Republic pay their interest on a timely basis and at the highest market rates. Ironically, a debtor like Mexico got better rates because its huge debt threatened the world banking system; the smaller Caribbean nations had to pay top dollar for their new money, and, all the while, the payment plans were orchestrated by officials like U.S. Secretary of the Treasury James Brady, and, behind him, the International Monetary Fund.[69]

In 1905 and in 1990, the free market was protected by the federal government. While the conventional wisdom argues that the rich nations transfer resources to the poor, "as a result of the build-up of massive debts, high interest rates, and the drying up of new credit, the direction of the resource flow has reversed. In a perversion of economics and ethics, the Third World is now transferring resources to the industrial nations."[70]

Dominican Republic: Its total external debt in 1982 was $2.5 billion. In 1990 the figure was over $4 billion and debt as a percentage of gross domestic product had jumped from 30 percent to 60 percent.

Jamaica: Its total external debt in 1982 was $2.8 billion; in 1990 the figure was $4.1 billion. Debt as a percentage of GDP had risen from 80 percent to a frightening 120 percent of GDP.

Haiti: Its total external debt in 1982 was $500 million; in 1990 it was $800 million. Its debt as a percentage of GDP had increased from 25 to 30 percent.

Barbados: Its total external debt in 1982 was $425 million; in 1990 the figure was over $1 billion.

Its debt as a percentage of GDP had moved from 30 to 60 percent.[71]

In each country, national policy accounts for part of the problem. The Dominican Republic or Haiti could design tax policies which at last drew substantial funds from their richest citizens.[72] But, in the Caribbean the United States is the dominant economic force. Thus it must assume responsibility for the consequences of the government protection afforded to its banks, its sugar growers, its unions, and its export industries.

Those consequences always add up to much more than a negative bottom line. Women, men and children were so affected by the negative numbers that thousands of Haitians were—and are—willing to crowd themselves into homemade boats. They sailed for the United States, they were sequestered on Guantanamo, and, all the while, Congress closed its eyes to the results of the 936 program.

In April of 199,0 Congress held oversight hearings. Had Puerto Rico and its corporations kept their word? Did they invest a hundred million a year of 936 funds in the Caribbean? And how many jobs had they produced?

Testifying for the Bush administration was Assistant Secretary of the Treasury Kenneth Gideon. He was the flak catcher for a program that had made few investments, and, of the investments actually made, the money went to companies like AT&T and for products like airplanes in Jamaica. As Congressman Anthony (Arkansas) complained, Puerto Rico had used tax exempt funds to purchase from Brazil planes manufactured in Europe. The program appeared to be out of control so Congress wanted an explanation.

Cultural Constants

Gideon admitted that no jobs had been created by the airplane sale nor by the funding of AT&T to install a fiber-optic lightguide submarine cable system. It didn't look good for 936 when Gideon said he "hoped" that the 936 projects created jobs but "we don't specifically look at the issue of job creation beyond the general requirement that this be a new development project in the country." Congress had to remember the regulations; they specified no numbers, no strategy, and no long or short term perspective. It was assumed that a new business created new jobs and the reason the money went to corporations like AT&T was that the 936 funds were funneled through institutions like Citibank. They made loans to only the most creditworthy customers. Double or triple A banks and corporations got to use the drug money; other customers went to Miami where the normal interest rate was 20 percent, and 40 percent was a figure sometimes required for the native investors of Jamaica or the Dominican Republic.[73]

But what about the "big papacito?"[74] That was what Congressman J.J. Pickle (Texas) called Puerto Rico and in April of 1990 he and his colleagues grilled the head of the island's Economic Development administration. Charles Rangel (New York) was incensed: "We have actually said that a bunch of Puerto Rican bankers should determine what investments are going to be made in these countries...." The purchase of European planes with American tax dollars upset Rangel so much that he decided to switch punching bags. "Our Treasury Department could not tell me who is in charge of the overall economic development of Puerto Rico. And I assumed if he could not do it for *one of our possessions* he darn

423

sure could not do it for a foreign country [Jamaica or Haiti]. So, let me start from the beginning. Is there a U.S. National Economic Development Program for the government of Puerto Rico?"[75] [Emphasis added.]

This question was 42 years too late, but Rangel pushed, so Antonio Colorado had to provide an answer. He said, "not that I know of." Rangel then asked about other programs. Did the federal government have, besides 936, additional ways to provide jobs for islanders? Mr. Colorado responded "no" and both men now agreed that while Puerto Rico lacked a plan, it nevertheless had $15 billion in 936 funds. So, for the record, what had happened to Puerto Rico's 1986 promises?

Colorado and his colleagues argued that the solemn pledges of 1986 had turned into a "so-called commitment" of $100 million a year. Puerto Rico was $230 million off target—Colorado and his colleagues guessed that roughly $70 million had been invested—and a report submitted by the Grenadians explained why.

George Brizan (the island's Minister of Finance) told Congress that "Grenada has not benefited from the 936 loan program. None of the projects sent to Fomento for consideration has received funding...." Brizan thought the Puerto Ricans were helpful but the funds were always short term "and this makes them somewhat unattractive for international lending to developing countries which generally need funds for infrastructural development." In addition, 936 was a closed shop. Outsiders got no money until they proved they posed no risk; and, for the 936 companies themselves, there was "little incentive to use their own funds in CBI countries." In

Puerto Rico their "passive" banking deposits produced earnings that were tax free; in Grenada the 936 companies might have to pay taxes to the federal government. Why give back to Uncle Sam what he had given to you?

At the conclusion of these hearings Congressman Rangel said, "Let me make it abundantly clear to you; whenever this committee believes that jobs are not being created for our Puerto Rican citizens, you are not going to have a 936 program...So we are going to make certain not only that it works but the members know it is working."[77]

But the members knew it wasn't working. That was proven in the report to President Carter in 1978, in the courageous efforts of President Reagan in 1986, in the Treasury Department's six reports on possession corporations, and in the testimony just presented to Rangel in 1990.

Rangel reiterated his refusal (when he finally received proof that no jobs were being created), the pharmaceutical representative solemnly said the companies would do better in the coming years, and Chairman Pickle responded to his colleague's possible rejection of 936 with this comment; "well, I am not serious about that position of course."[78]

The 936 laws were an institution. The facts made no difference in 1978 and even less in 1990. Indeed, the companies soon began to offer a new rationale for the tax exemptions. Instead of helping Puerto Rico, the billions saved helped citizens in Texas and Iowa, New York and Oregon. The companies were patriotically using the money to fund the research and development that kept them in front of the Japanese. So, forget about Grenada or the

Dominican Republic. Instead of the $100 million promised in 1986, the companies—seconded by Puerto Ricans of all political persuasions—would invest $200 million a year to make certain that one federal program overcame the effects of another federal program that overcame, etc....

A Plebiscite in Puerto Rico

At times U.S. Caribbean policy seems like a ride on a ferris wheel. You go round and round, you stop in different places, you get queasy if you have a weak stomach, and, ultimately you come back to where you began. This was true for the 936 laws, for their predecessors (the 931 regulations), and it was also true for the endless debate about the political status of what is now the oldest colony on earth, Puerto Rico.

The island is full of experts. Everybody knows what the Puerto Rican people want. In February of 1991, for example, now Resident Commissioner Carlos Romero Barcelo assured Congress that the advocates of independence spoke for only 5 percent of the population. "That is what independence has gotten in the votes." However, "the majority of the people want the permanent union and want to have U.S. citizenship."[79]

Romero forgot his own book. He was before Congress to ask for a referendum and in his book *Statehood Is For the Poor* Romero stressed that a referendum had to be held separately from a regular general election. "The reason for this is that the results of the general elections held every four years hinge on a great many issues, most of which have little or no bearing on the ultimate resolution of

Puerto Rico's political status question."[80]

Romero knew the truth: Nobody, absolutely nobody, knows what the Puerto Rican people want. After almost a century of U.S. colonialism an intelligent choice is impossible unless islanders *first* receive answers to a variety of crucial questions. What happens to the military bases which now occupy roughly 14 percent of Puerto Rico? What about the 936 corporations and the banking system which depends on their funds? What about the coastwise shipping laws? What about the private universities who have 71 percent of their students paying for tuition with federal Pell grants'?

Citizenship? The Spanish language? The English language? Social security? Food stamps? The questions are endless and answers are required if islanders are to make a choice that is both meaningful and—just as important—satisfactory *once the referendum is over.*

Islanders tried to explain their predicament to the Senate. They had read history. They remembered the Truman-refused plebiscite in 1946. They recalled the lost battle for specifics with Presidents Kennedy and Johnson. Congress had the power or, as Assistant Attorney General Stuart Gerson noted on February 1, 1991, senators did not want to create "the false impression that there is residual power in Puerto Rico. There is not. I mean the Tenth Amendment describes that which the States retain. Puerto Rico does not retain that power, because the Congress can trump it whenever it chooses under the territory clause."[81]

Gerson was right. In a rare manifestation of unanimity, Independence representative Reuben

427

Berrios Martinez said, "it is Congress' obligation to speak clearly because we are tired of waiting. The three of us [Berrios, Carlos Romero Barcelo, and Governor Rafael Hernandez Colon] are tired of waiting. Now is no time to say go back and you arrange things between yourselves and come out. We have done that hundreds of times, dozens of times. We do not want to do that any more. We want you to fulfill your obligation now."[82]

This was a surprising outburst from the normally diplomatic Berrios. But, for the last two years the House of Representatives had refused to provide specifics. As Morris Udall said on May 9, 1990: "It must be made very clear that the exact details of status implementing legislation cannot be determined in advance, and that while we can assure through this legislation that a winning status will be *considered* by both houses of Congress, we cannot assure enactment or that the bill will be precisely what the winning political party will prefer."[83]

It was paternalism from the mouth of a liberal Democrat. So, Berrios and his colleagues wanted the Senate to provide the non-revocable specifics never offered by the House of Representatives.

Senators did as they were asked. But the answers given to the Puerto Rico people symbolize, not only this one island's predicament, but the dilemma of every other nation and colony (the Virgin Islands) in the Caribbean. The U.S.A. refuses to accept responsibility for the consequences of its actions. And, on a deeper level, it refuses to discard the cultural exceptionalism which shaped Caribbean policy in 1900, and still shapes today.

Consider the Senate's approach to a new U.S.

state. The banner flown by the Puerto Rican statehooders is this: Statehood Is For the Poor. To critics
this is "bellyism, in other words betraying one's
birthright for a full stomach." But to men like Carlos
Romero Barcelo it's a question of pluses and minus-
es. "Puerto Rico's per capita contribution to the federal treasury, were we a state, would come to less
than that of any other state in the Union. At the
same time the per capita benefits we'd reap from
federal aid programs would be greater than those of
any other state in the Union."[84]

Finally, Puerto Rico would also have seven or
eight islanders "working up in Washington at all
times to help draft and pass new and improved
social welfare legislation."[85]

Romero sounded like former Governor Luis
Muñoz Marin. The latter wanted a permanent status
called commonwealth because that was the only
way for Puerto Ricans to economically survive. The
former wants statehood because that is the only
way for islanders to economically survive. Both
men—one first writing in 1938, the other in 1978—
understood that the economy was a disaster. They
asked Washington for a state of perpetual dependence. Save us from poverty or, as one of Barcelo's
followers threatened in 1987, Puerto Rico "may
become a colony in a state of civil insurrection."[86]

Guns in hand, the Statehooders would apparently appear at the federal treasury today to confront Lloyd Bentsen, the senator who (as chair of
the Senate's Finance Committee) made poverty the
touchstone for the list of specifics finally provided to
the Puerto Rican officials.

The Senate was worried. "It did not want to

enact statehood if it costs a huge amount of money. As a practical, political consideration, it would be very difficult to enact statehood and have it cost billions of dollars to the treasury."[87] So, the Puerto Ricans got their specifics but ones that were quite different from those anticipated. As Senator Bill Bradley (New Jersey) noted, "what you are saying is that the poverty level in the United States, those who are in poverty would receive more than those who are in poverty in Puerto Rico, is that correct?"[88]

It was. The Senate proposed a "permanent" second class statehood. Programs like Medicaid, Aid to Families With Dependent Children, and Food Stamps would all have budgetary caps. But, there was "another cap" on top of the separate caps. If the total for *all* the poverty programs was, for example, $10 billion then if Food Stamps went up, Medicaid or some other program went down. The cap on the cap set definite limits because the Senate said islanders could have statehood only if it was "revenue neutral."[89] That was a euphemism for 'Puerto Ricans are too poor to be equal' and Senator J. Bennett Johnston (Louisiana) wondered if that was constitutional. Could you really treat 50 states in one fashion and Puerto Rico in another?

Assistant Attorney General Gerson assured the senators that it could be "permanently done." And critics should stop using the word discrimination. "The issue that you [the Senate] face in terms of constitutional analysis is whether there is a rational basis for the distinctions. As I say, discrimination is an unfortunate term. It carries an opprobrium with it. There is a rational basis for the distinctions that the Congress would make.[90]

That basis? Money. It was rational to permanently cap the state of Puerto Rico and thus offer it another peculiar distinction. It was the nation's first colony, its first unincorporated territory, and now its first second class state.

In this projected move from permanent possession to permanent poverty, no senator questioned the negative impact of the 936 laws. None offered the economic strategy sought by Congressman Rangel. None mentioned almost a century of Puerto Rican requests for real economic power. And none discussed paternalism's most incredible achievement; a statehood movement that proudly sought indefinite dependence on the federal government.

The House saved the Senate. It refused to commit to any specifics and that left Puerto Ricans with the familiar refrain; we are tired of waiting. The Senate, however, was tired of the Puerto Ricans. Staffers indicated that Congress would do nothing more until islanders once again clamored for action; meanwhile, the Puerto Rican economy produced more poverty, the 936 corporations more profits, and Congress rested on a series of discriminatory proposals.

As Senator Pete Domenici (New Mexico) summed up the hearings, "It is fun for this committee to have this kind of issue. We do not get this kind of issue very often. And I think it is always somewhere else that such matters of individual freedom, rights, choices by people; those are never discussed by us. I think we go in, not necessarily without strong feet, but we go at it a little slower perhaps because we do not do this very often."[91]

Domenici did indicate that the novelty of the issue might move the Committee to do a better job but he prefaced that comment with this one: "I also want to conclude by saying I am remiss by not going there thus far. I always find something else and say I am too busy...I do not know where I am going to find the time to be an adequate participant in this...but I think we ought to make at least a public commitment to your people, Puerto Ricans, that we will try to come there and get to know you better. I urge that more of us do."[92]

The senator would squeeze Puerto Rico in when and if he ever had the time. Or, as Senator Malcolm Wallop (Wyoming) noted, "I would caution patience for all parties, and that is not to say that I regard 92 years of waiting as impatience. But we are in a moment in time in which real decisions can be framed...and I think we ought not to back off from that simply because timetables get jiggered off track."[93]

The senator never got the point. The Puerto Ricans, Haitians, Virgin Islanders, Dominicans, Cubans, Grenadians, and Jamaicans are tired of waiting. As of early 1994 they continue to sit in relative silence. But for how long—and how peacefully— is anybody's guess.

Our third border is about to be overrun, by the poverty that drives people to swim with sharks, and by the injustice that moves them to violence.

The United States can recognize that it is the predominant part of the problem. Or, as in Puerto Rico, it can try to put a permanent cap on the consequences of a century of colonial policy.

The choice is ours. But the situation is so desperate—in Haiti, Cuba, Puerto Rico, and the Dominican Republic—that only a complete reevaluation of the past offers real hope for the future.

Epilogue:

Wilson, Roosevelt, Carter, Clinton

The *New York Times* reports (April 28, 1994) that President Clinton has "repeatedly" complained that Haiti's military leaders "are chopping people's faces off." However, despite the President's accurate analysis, and despite speeches which laud "America's moral authority in defending the rights of refugees around the world," President Clinton has continued to send fleeing Haitians back to a Caribbean nightmare. In some instances, U.S. soldiers have even provided Haitian authorities with neat lists containing the names and addresses of the boat people captured on the high seas.

The president's contradictions are rooted in a policy of expediency. Like Jimmy Carter in 1980, he wants to prevent a flood of refugees into southern Florida. Thus, on the campaign trail, he complains about the Bush administration's "callous response to a terrible human tragedy," but once in office, behaves even more callously than his predecessor.

There is an alternative: Recognize that Caribbean economic and political refugees are a twentieth century constant and that the United States bears a significant responsibility for the displacement of Caribbean peoples. The terrible consequences of the

433

sugar quotas imposed in 1982, the long standing support for Duvalier, the continued training of Haitian officers by U.S. soldiers on U.S. soil in such areas as Fort Benning, Georgia—all these practices have helped lead directly to the present horror in Haiti.

The president might consider this summary: the United States has been training Haitian and Dominican soldiers since 1915 and the results are still the same. Whether it's 2,000 Haitians slaughtered in 1919, 17,000 chopped to pieces in 1937, or an estimated 4,000 since 1991, innocent people continue to die and presidents from Wilson to Clinton provide the guns.

The United States has no moral authority in the Caribbean. We own Puerto Rico, the oldest colony on earth. We have trained three generations of Haitian murderers. We invaded Grenada and then forgot about its existence. We bought the Virgin Islands and we have consistently taxed them without representation. We knew Rafael Trujillo was a gangster and we installed him in power and kept him there.

The United States can help produce meaningful change only if our leaders root policy in the actual results of a century of U.S. influence and intervention.

We can either face the truth about ourselves and our behavior or, with President Clinton, watch sluggers hit the baseballs sewn in Haiti, as our ambassador (in April of 1994) plays tennis on courts lit up by the fuel purchased in violation of the president's supposedly strict embargo.

Notes

Supreme Hypocrisy

1. Congressional Record, 56th Congress, 2nd session, March 1, 1901, p. 3370-3371.
2. Congressional Record, 55th Congress, 2nd session, April 14, 1898, p. 3841-2.
3. Ibid., p. 3842
4. For the message itself see Congressional Record, 55th Congress, 2nd session, April 11, 1898, p. 3704-3707.
5. Congressional Record, 54th Congress, 1st session, February 28, 1896, p. 2244, 2247-2248.
6. Ibid, p. 2249; see too the comments of Senator Allen, p. 2251 and Senator Lindsay, p. 2242.
7. Congressional Record, 55th Congress, op. cit., p. 3840.
8. Ibid., p. 3838 and 3840.
9. Ibid., p. 3846
10. See Paul S. Holbo, Presidential Leadership in Foreign Affairs: William McKinley and the Turpie-Foraker Amendment, *The American Historical Review*, Volume 72, April, 1967, p. 1328. See, too, Louis Perez Jr., *Cuba Under the Platt Amendment* (Pittsburgh: University of Pittsburgh Press, 1986).
11. United States Caribbean Policy Part I, Hearings Before the Subcommittee on Inter-American Affairs, Committee on Foreign Affairs, House of Representatives, 93rd Congress, 2nd session, 1973, p. 43. The statement was made by Robert Crassweller.
12. Congressional Record, Senate, 55th Congress, 2nd session, April 18, 1898, p. 4033; on McKinley's threat see Margaret Leach, *In the Days of McKinley* (New York: Harper and Row, 1959), p. 188.

13. Ibid., p. 4033.

14. Ibid., p. 4034.

15. Ibid., p. 4038.

16., Congressional Record, House, 56th Congress, 2nd session, March 1, 1901, p. 3343; on McKinley's satisfaction, Holbo, op. cit., p. 1333.

17. Congressional Record, Senate 55th Congress, 2nd session, April 20, 1898, p. 4095, 4097.

18. Ibid., p. 4097; for the McKinley quote see Stanley Karnow, *In Our Image* (New York: Random House, 1989), p. 108.

19. This definition belongs to William Elliot, a member of the National Security Council Staff in the administration of Dwight D. Eisenhower. See, Dwight D. Eisenhower Library, White House Office Files, Office of the Special Assistant For National Security Affairs, OCB Series, Box 5.

20. For the autocracy comparison see William F. Willoughby, *The Government of Modern States* (New York: Appleton-Century, 1932), p. 105-107; for the British model see William F. Willoughby, The Executive Council of Puerto Rico, *American Political Science Review*, Volume 1, August, 1907, p. 561-582; finally, see, Willoughby, *Territories and Dependencies of the United States* (New York: The Century Company, 1905), p. 86. Willoughby was Secretary of Puerto Rico's government and President of the Executive Council from 1901 to 1908.

21. Eisenhower Library, op. cit., William Elliot.

22. On Puerto Rico's status see Ronald Fernandez, *The Disenchanted Island: Puerto Rico and the United States in the Twentieth Century* (New York: Praeger, 1992); for the Supreme Court decision see Downes vs. Bidwell, reprinted in *Documents on the Constitutional History of Puerto Rico* (Washington: Office of the Commonwealth of Puerto Rico, 1964), p. 130.

23. Leonard Wood, William Taft, Charles Allen, Perfecto Lacoste, and M.E. Beale, *Opportunities in the Colonies and Cuba* (New York: Scribner and Company, 1902).

24. Eisenhower Library, William Elliot's unpaginated manuscript.

25. Congressional Record, Senate, 56th Congress, first session, April 2, 1900, p. 3638.

Notes

26. Congressional Record, House of Representatives, 56th Congress, 2nd session, March 1, 1901, p. 3371-3372.

27. For example, Ralph Eldin Minger, William H. Taft and the United States Intervention in Cuba in 1906, *Hispanic American Historical Review*, Volume 41, February, 1961, p. 75-89. N.B. p. 86-87.

28. Franklin Knight and Colin Palmer, eds., *The Modern Caribbean* (Chapel Hill: University of North Carolina Press, 1989), p. 7.

29. Congressional Record, House, 56th Congress, 2nd session, March 1, 1901, p. 3344; Congressional Record, Senate, 56th Congress, 1st session, April 2, 1900, p. 3635; Michael Hunt, *Ideology and U.S. Foreign Policy* (New Haven: Yale, 1987) has a superb discussion of this issue on p. 46-91.

30. Congressional Record, House, 61st Congress, 1st session, June 7, 1909, p. 2921.

31. Robert Nisbet, *The Present Age* (New York: Harper and Row, 1988), p. 29; see too Albert Weinberg, *Manifest Destiny* (Baltimore: Johns Hopkins, 1935); also Merle Curti, *The Roots of American Loyalty* (New York: Columbia University Press, 1946); finally, Hunt, op. cit., Chapter Two.

32. Sumner Welles, *Naboth's Vineyard: The Dominican Republic* (New York: Payson and Clarke Limited, 1928), Volume II, p. 918, 920.

33. Weinberg, op. cit., p. 29, 30, 31; emphasis added in the Jefferson quote.

34. J. Reuben Clark, Memorandum on the Monroe Doctrine, Senate, 71st Congress, 2nd session, Document 114, Washington, Government Printing Office, 1930, XIX.

35. Congressional Record, House, 55th Congress, 1st session, February 4, 1899, p. 1448.

36. Congressional Record, House, 55th Congress, 1st session, February 4, 1899, p. 1448.

37. Arthur S. Link Editor, *The Papers of Woodrow Wilson* (Princeton: Princeton University Press), p. 246.

38. Franklin Roosevelt Library, Papers of Charles Taussig, Box 35, see the paper entitled "Some Aspects of the Caribbean Problem, July 1, 1941, p. 1.

39. For these characteristics see Michael Manley, *The Politics of Change* (Washington: Howard University, 1990, 2nd edi-

tion); see too James Ferguson, *Far From Paradise* (London: Latin American Bureau, 1990), p. 4.

40. Alex Dupuy, *Haiti in the World Economy* (Boulder: Westview Press, 1988), p. 34.

41. On Puerto Rico see, for example, Pedro San Miguel, *El Mundo Que Créo El Azucar* (San Juan: Huracan, 1989); and, on Barbados, Cyril Hamshere, *The British In the Caribbean* (Cambridge: Harvard University Press, 1972), p. 112.

42. See Claypole and Robottom, op. cit., p. 15; On Jamaica see Sandra W. Meditz and Dennis M Hanratty, editors, *Islands of the Commonwealth Caribbean* (Washington: Federal Research Division, Library of Congress, 1987).

43. Irvin Bettman, The Beet-Sugar Industry: A Study in Tariff Protection, *Harvard Business Review*, Volume 11, Number 3, April, 1933, p. 369-375; see too John E. Dalton, *Sugar: A Case Study of Government Control* (New York: The Macmillan Company, 1937).

44. Bettmann, Ibid., p. 370.

45. Willoughby, op. cit., especially Chapter Four of *Territories and Dependencies of the United States*; also Fernandez, op. cit. Chapters One and Two.

46. On Hollander's role see Hearings Before the Subcommittee on Expenditures in the State Department, House of Representatives, House resolution 103, Number 2, May, 1911, p. 36-37.

47. Elihu Root, *The Military and Colonial Policy of the United States* (Cambridge: Harvard University Press, 1916), p. 170.

48. James L. Deitz, *Economic History of Puerto Rico* (Princeton: Princeton University Press, 1986) especially Chapter Two.

49. Rexford Tugwell, Report on the Five Hundred Acre Law, in *Puerto Rican Public Papers* (San Juan, 1942), p. 291-347.

50. Oscar Pino-Santos, *El Asalto A Cuba Por La Oligarquia Financiera Yanqui* (Havana: Casa de Las Americas, 1973).

51. Paolo E. Coletta, Editor, *United States Navy and Marine Corps Bases, Overseas* (Westport: Greenwood Publishing, 1988), p. 147.

52. Ibid., p. 147.

53. Perez, op. cit., p. 47; see, too, the superb book by Jules Robert Benjamin, *The United States and Cuba* (Pittsburg: University of Pittsburg Press, 1986).

Notes

54. Ibid., p. 47.

55. For the use of the word 'ultimatum' see Morgan in The Congressional Record, Senate, 56th Congress, 2nd session, February 27th, 1901, p. 3147; in the House see Congressman Grosvenor on March 1, 1901, 56th Congress, 2nd session, p. 3340.

56. Ibid., Senate, p. 3146.

57. Adjustment to the Isle of Pines, Senate Committee on Foreign Relations, 59th Congress, 1st session, Senate Document 205, p. 11.

58. Morgan, op. cit., February 27, 1901, p. 3147.

59. Ibid., p. 3149.

60. Congressional Record, House of Representatives, 56th Congress, 2nd session, March 1, 1901, p. 3340.

61. Congressional Record, op. cit., March 1, 1901, p. 3370.

62. Scudder, op. cit. Congressional Record, March 1, 1901, p. 3371.

63. See, for example, Perez, op. cit., p. 40-41.

64. See Coletta, op. cit., p. 147; George Mowry, *The Era of Theodore Roosevelt* (New York: Harper, 1958), p. 129; Richard Challener, *Admirals, Generals and American Foreign Policy, 1898-1914* (Princeton: Princeton University Press, 1973), p. 95-98.

65. See Congressional Record, Senate, 68th Congress, 2nd session, January 17th, 1925, p. 2015.

66. Russell H. Fitzgibbon, *Cuba and the United States, 1900-1935* (Menasha: George Banta Publishing Company, 1935), p. 98.

67. Challener, op. cit., p. 95-96.

68. Ibid., p. 96.

69. Senate Document 205, op. cit., p. 130-131.

70. Ibid., p. 10.

71. Ibid., Harrington's letter appears on p. 48 of Senate Document 205; McDowell's letter is on p. 43.

72. Ibid., see the correspondence p. 34-188.

73. See Coletta, op. cit., p. 148.

74. Ibid., p. 10.

75. See President Dwight D. Eisenhower Library, Abilene, Kansas, Ann Whitman Files, National Security Council

Series, Box 12.

76. For example, Robert Heilbroner, *The Nature and Logic of Capitalism* (New York: Norton, 1988).

77. For example, George W. Stocking and Myron W. Watkins, *Cartels In Action: Case Studies In International Business Diplomacy* (New York: Twentieth Century Fund, 1946), Chapter Eight.

78. See Benjamin, op. cit., p. 11-12; also, Commission On Cuban affairs, *Problems of the New Cuba* (New York: Foreign Policy Association, 1935), especially Chapter Ten.

79. On the Spanish and other foreign investors see, especially, Perez, op. cit., p. 56-87.

80. Charles Callan Tansill, *The Purchase of the Danish West Indies* (Baltimore: Johns Hopkins University Press, 1932), p. 225; Chapter Four discusses the Christmas dealings in some detail.

81. Ibid., p. 270.

Merciless, Blood-Sucking Money Sharks

1. William H. Wynne, *State Insolvency and Foreign Bondholders,* Volume 2, (New Haven: Yale University Press, 1951), p. 199–203.

2. Ibid., p. 203; see too Sumner Welles, *Naboth's Vineyard,* Volume I (New York: Payson and Clarke Limited, 1928), Chapter Five.

3. Jacob Hollander, *Debt of Santo Domingo* (Washington, 1905), p. 5.

4. Ibid., p. 7; see, too, Antonio de La Rosa, *Las Finanzas de Santo Domingo and El Control Americano* (Santo Domingo: Editora Nacional, 1974).

5. Doctoral Dissertation of Joseph Glenn Kist, The Role of Thomas C. Dawson In United States-Latin American Diplomatic Relations: 1897–1912, Loyala University of Chicago, 1971, p. 64–66; also Wynne, op. cit., p. 225–226.

6. Hearings Before the Subcommittee on Expenditures, House, House Resolution 103, No. 2, May, 1911, p. 50; Wynne, op. cit., p. 221–224.

7. Summary by the U.S. Dominican Minister, Thomas Dawson, in Foreign Relations of the United States, 1905, p. 380; See,

Notes

too, J. Fred Rippey, The Initiation of the Customs Receivership in the Dominican Republic, *Hispanic American Historical Review*, Volumes 17, 1937, p. 419–457 (especially p. 427–428).

8. Ibid, p. 347.

9. Dawson, Ibid., p. 380.

10. Hollander, op. cit., p. 41;

11. Ibid., p. 110–112; see too Foreign Relations, op. cit., p. 347; also Wynne, op. cit., p. 231.

12. Wynne, op. cit., p. 232.

13. Foreign Affairs, Ibid., p. 348.

14. Dana G. Munro, *Intervention and Dollar Diplomacy, 1900–1921* (Princeton: Princeton University Press, 1964), p. 87; see, too, *The United States and the Caribbean Area* (Boston: World Peace Foundation, 1934).

15. Healy, op. cit., p. 100–104; also Munro, Ibid., p. 66–75.

16. For example, Healy, Ibid., p. 102–105

17. Kist, op. cit., especially p. 69–73; a similar account appears in Munro, p. 89–91.

18. Kist, op. cit., p. 74; also Healy, op. cit., p. 117.

19. Ibid., Kist, p. 74; on Loomis idea for the customs house takeover see Rippey, op. cit., p. 441.

20. On the malcontent remark and circumventing the constitution see Foreign Relations, p. 350–352; also Kist, Ibid., p. 140; see also Rippey, op. cit. p. 448.

21. Foreign Relations, p. 308; also Munro, op. cit., p. 100.

22. Foreign Relations, p. 319.

23. House Hearings, op. cit., 1911, p. 33.

24. Foreign Relations, p. 329.

25. Foreign Relations, p. 334.

26. Foreign Relations, p. 336.

27. Congressional Record, op. cit., January 24, 1906, p. 1474.

28. Foreign Relations, p. 340–341.

29. Foreign Relations, p. 342; Rippey, op. cit. has a fine summary of the president's multiple aims, see p. 419.

30. Foreign Relations, p. 358.

31. House Hearings, op. cit., p. 36.

32. Hollander, op. cit., p. 41, 44; the comment about moral

barbarism appears on p. 59.

33. Congressional Record, Senate, op. cit., p. 797.

34. Congressional Record, Ibid., p. 797–798.

35. Congressional Record, Ibid., p. 799–800.

36. Congressional Record, January 23, Ibid., p. 1424, 1428.

37. Congressional Record, January 24, 1906, p. 1472–1473.

38. Munro, *Intervention and Dollar Diplomacy*, op. cit., p. 119.

39. House Hearings, 1911, op. cit., p. 56.

40. House Hearings, Ibid., p. 52.

41. House Hearings, Ibid., p. 50–51; also Wynne, op. cit., p. 254.

42. House Hearings, Ibid., p. 51.

43. House Hearings, Ibid., p. 71.

44. For the letter see President Harry S. Truman Library, Independence, Missouri, White House Central Files, Box 38; a fine biography of General Trujillo is by Robert Crassweller, *Trujillo* (New York: Macmillan, 1966).

45. Congressional Record, January 24, 1906, p. 1473.

46. Melvin Knight, *The Americans in Santo Domingo* (New York: Arno Press, 1970, the original appeared in 1928), p. 44; for a fine Dominican account see, Roberto Cassa, *Capitalismo y Dictadura* (Santo Domingo: Editora de la Universidad Autonoma de Santo Domingo, 1982), especially Chapter 5.

47. For example, Frank Moya Pons, *Manual De Historia Dominicana* (Santo Domingo: Universidad Catolica Madre y Maestra Santiago, 1980), especially p. 447–456.

48. The Caribbean Basin Initiative, Committee on Foreign Relations, Interamerican Affairs, House of Representatives, 97th Congress, 2nd session, 1982, p. 153.

49. Healy, op. cit., p. 125.

50. For example, David McCullough, *The Path Between the Seas* (New York: Simon and Schuster, 1977).

51. Ibid., p. 475.

52. Michael Conniff, *Black Labor On A White Canal* (Pittsburg: University of Pittsburg Press, 1985), p. 33.

53. Ibid., p. 38; on the financing of the schools see p. 39–40.

54. For example, Barry Levine, editor, *The Caribbean Exodus* (New York: Praeger, 1987).

55. Herbert Hoover Library, West Branch, Iowa, Francis White Papers, Box 14, from a confidential report labeled "Report Covering Haiti Prepared in the Division of Latin American Affairs," p. 172–173.

56. Ibid., p. 173.

57. Anthony Maginot, Haiti: Problems of Transition to Democracy in an Authoritarian Soft State, *Journal of Interamerican Studies and World Affairs*, Volume 28, number 4, Winter 1986–87, p. 75–102; see too Michel–Rolph Trouillot, *Haiti: State Against Nation* (New York: Monthly Review Press, 1990).

58. Franklin Roosevelt Library, Hyde Park, New York, Papers of A.A. Berle, Box 2, manuscript is labeled "Occupation of Haiti and Santo Domingo", p. 1–2.

59. Huntington Wilson, The Relation of Government to Foreign Investment, Annals of the American Academy of Political and Social Science, Volume 68, number 157, November, 1916, p. 300–301; also David Healy, *Drive To Hegemony* (Madison: University of Wisconsin Press, 1988), p. 145–146; finally Scott Nearing and Joseph Freeman, *Dollar Diplomacy* (New York: B.W. Huebsch and the Viking Press, 1928).

60. Ibid., p. 301–302.

61. Ibid., p. 304.

62. Brenda Gayle Plummer, *Haiti and the Great Powers, 1902–1915* (Baton Rouge: Louisiana State University Press, 1987), p. 153.

63. Ibid., p. 152–155.

64. Wilson, op. cit. p. 300.

65. Plummer, op. cit. p. 164.

66. Ibid., p. 165.

67. Moya Pons, op. cit., p. 446–473; for the Down With McDonald remark see Danna Munro, *Intervention and Dollar Diplomacy* (Princeton: Princeton University Press, 1964), p. 257.

68. Herbert Hoover Library, West Branch, Iowa, Records of the president's Commission For Study and Review of Conditions in Haiti, Box 1069, memo by Farnham labeled "Financial Operations Under the Haitian Regime" dated February 20, 1926.

69. Plummer, op. cit., p. 171; also Hans Schmidt, *The United*

States Occupation of Haiti (New Brunswick: Rutgers University Press, 1971), especially p. 48–51.

70. Plummer, op. cit., p. 182; also Hoover Library, op. cit., papers of Francis White, p. 174–175.

71. For example, Munro, op. cit., p. 258–259.

72. Inquiry Into Occupation and Administration of Haiti and Santo Domingo, Hearings Before a Select Committee of the Senate, 67th Congress, 1st and 2nd sessions, Washington, 1922, Volume 1, p. 108.

73. Foreign Relations of the United States, 1912, (Washington: Government Printing Office, 1919), Cuba, p. 302.

74. Congressional Record, 68th Congress, 2nd session, January 15, 1925, p. 1866.

75. Foreign Relations, op. cit., 1912, p. 303.

76. Ibid., p. 247.

77. Louis Perez Jr., Politics, Peasants, and People of Color: The 1912 "Race War" in Cuba Reconsidered, *Hispanic American Historical Review*, Volume 66, number 3, 1986, p. 509–539; my quote is from p. 529; see too, Perez's *Cuba Under the Platt Amendment* (Pittsburg: University of Pittsburg Press, 1986), especially p. 148–152.

78. Ibid., Perez, Race War, p. 519.

79. Ibid., p. 534–535.

80. Foreign Relations, op. cit., 1912, p. 254.

81. Fernandez, op. cit., especially Chapter Three.

82. Message From the president of the United States, United States Senate, 61st Congress, 1st session, Senate Document #40, p. 3, 6.

83. Congressional Record, House of Representatives, 61st Congress, 1st session, June 7, 1909, p. 2924.

84. Ibid., p. 2924.

85. Congressional Record, House of Representatives, June 8, 1910, especially p. 7606–7608.

86. Delma Arrigoitia, José de Diego: A Legislator in Times of Political Transition (1903–1918), A Doctoral Dissertation done at Fordham University in 1985.

87. Woodrow Wilson *The New Freedom* (Englewood Cliffs: Prentice Hall, 1961), p. 125.

Notes

Popes, Plebiscites, and Possessions

1. Hearings Before a Select Committee on Haiti and Santo Domingo, Senate, 67th Congress, 1st and 2nd sessions, 1921, Vol. 1, p. 516.

2. Hearings Before the Committee on Insular Affairs, House, 63rd Congress, 2nd session, Washington, 1914, p. 31, 51.

3. Ibid., p. 32; p. 31 for quote in preceding paragraph.

4. Ibid., see, for example, p. 13, 56, and 58; see p. 34–35 for Garrison.

5. Congressional Record, House, 63rd Congress, 2nd session, April 15, 1914, p. 6718–20; document dated March 27, 1914.

6. Congressional Record, Congress, June 19, 1922, p. 8962; the benevolent dictatorship phrase comes from The United States Military Government in the Dominican Republic, 1916–1922, case history prepared by 2nd Section, Group V, U.S. School For Military Government and Administration, Folder F1938.45/ U58, Hoover Institution Archives.

7. For a solid approach to Wilson's character see David Barber, *The Presidential Character* (Englewood Cliffs: Prentice Hall, 1972).

8. Arthur S. Link, editor, *The Papers of Woodrow Wilson* (New York: Harper, 1955), Volume XXVIII.

9. Herbert Hoover Library, West Branch, Iowa, Papers of Francis White, Box 14, document is entitled Report Covering Haiti Prepared in the Division of Latin American Affairs, January 1, 1930, p. 174.

10. Brenda Gayle Plummer, *Haiti and the Great Powers, 1902–1915* (Baton Rouge: Louisiana State University Press, 1988), p. 209–210.

11. Ibid., p. 210.

12. Arthur S. Link, editor, *The Papers of Woodrow Wilson* (Princeton: Princeton University Press, 1982), Volume 42, January 7, 1915, p. 27.

13. Ibid., p. 28; for a fine overview of many of these issues see Selig Adler, Bryan and Wilson Caribbean Penetration, *Hispanic American Historical Review*, Volume 20, 1940, p. 198–226.

14. Papers of Woodrow Wilson, July 27, 1914, p. 307–308.

15. Frank Moya Pons, *Manual De Historica Dominicana* (Santo Domingo: Universidad Catolica, 1980), p. 463–465; see, too, Melvin Knight, *The Americans in Santo Domingo* (New York: Arno Press, 1928).

16. Papers of Woodrow Wilson, op. cit., July 27, 1914, p. 307.

17. Papers of President Woodrow Wilson, January 15, 1915, p. 76.

18. Papers of Woodrow Wilson, February 25, 1915, p. 288–289.

19. Ibid., p. 472–73.

20. Ibid., p. 473.

21. David Healy, Gunboat Diplomacy in the Wilson Era: The U.S. Navy in Haiti, 1915–1916 (Madison: University of Wisconsin Press, 1976), p. 45.

22. Hearings, Senate, op. cit., 1921, V.1, p. 334.

23. Ibid., p. 302–303.

24. Healy, op. cit., p. 54–55.

25. Healy, op. cit., p. 57–58.

26. Caperton, Hearings, op. cit., p. 307.

27. Ibid., p. 307–308.

28. E. David Cronon, Interpreting the Good Neighbor Policy: The Cuban Crisis of 1933, *Hispanic American Historical Review*, 39, 1959, p. 538–567, especially p. 542; on the no guidance see Dana A. Munro, The American Withdrawal From Haiti, *Hispanic American Historical Review*, 49, 1969, p. 1–26, especially p. 3; a fine overview by Hans Schmidt, *The United States Occupation of Haiti* (New Brunswick: Rutgers, 1974).

29. Healy, op. cit., p. 84.

30. Ibid., p. 90–96.

31. National Archives, Record Group 45, SF 1911–1927, Box 1000, p. 140–143 of a manuscript written by Captain Edward Beach.

32. The Lansing Papers, Foreign Relations of the United States (Washington: Government Printing Office, 1940), Volume 2, p. 501–502.

33. Papers of Woodrow Wilson, November 24, 1915, p. 246.

34. Ibid., p. 249–250.

35. Arthur Link, *Woodrow Wilson and the Progressive Era* (New York: Harper and Row, 1954), p. 33.

Notes

36. Wilson Papers, op. cit., p. 252.

37. Hearings, Inquiry into Occupation...., op. cit., Volume 2, p. 1094; also Bruce Calder, *The Impact of Intervention* (Austin: University of Texas Press, 1984), p. 6–7.

38. Hearings, Inquiry into the Occupation...., op. cit., Volume 2, p. 1094–1095; also Calder, , op. cit., p. 8–12.

39. Army School For Military Gov. (footnote 6), p. 17.

40. This last line is from a November 4, 1930 memo written by Assistant Secretary of State Francis White to Secretary of State Henry Stimson. In this memo White confirms the "selfish" thrust of the Lansing interpretation of the Monroe Doctrine. See President Hoover Library, West Branch, Iowa, Papers of Francis White, Box 11.

41. Papers of Woodrow Wilson, op. cit., p. 249.

42. Maurice Egan, *Recollections of a Happy Life* (New York: George H. Doran, 1924), p. 240.

43. Maurice Francis Egan, *Ten Years Near the German Frontier* (New York: George Doran, 1918), p. 250.

44. Foreign Relations of the United States, Washington, Government Printing Office, 1926, p. 594.

45. Ibid., p. 665 and 692.

46. Cession of the Danish West Indies, Hearings Before the Committee on Foreign Affairs, House of Representatives, 64th Congress, 2nd session, February, 1917, p. 4.

47. Downes vs. Bidwell, reprinted in *Documents on the Constitutional History of Puerto Rico* (Washington: Office of the Commonwealth of Puerto Rico, 1964), p. 130.

48. The Virgin Islands, Hearing Before the Committee on Insular Affairs, House of Representatives, 69th Congress, 2nd session, December 26, 1926, p. 14.

49. Hearings, 1917, op. cit., p. 9, 14, 15.

50. Ibid., p. 15; also p. 10 and 7.

51. Gordon Lewis, *The Virgin Islands* (Evanston: Northwestern University Press, 1972), p. 51; also Ralph Paiewonsky, *Memoirs of a Governor* (New York: NYU, 1990), p. 59.

52. Congressional Record, 64th Congress, 1st session, May 5, 1916, p. 7473, 7488–9.

53. Ibid., p. 7474, 7486.

54. Papers of Woodrow Wilson, Volume 40, p. 516.

55. Hearings, Occupation of Haiti, Volume I, p. 517, 537.

56. Frank Freidel, *Franklin D. Roosevelt: The Apprenticeship* (Boston: Little, Brown, 1964), Chapter 16. Freidel says that Roosevelt never actually wrote the Constitution.

57. Hoover Library, op. cit., Report Covering Haiti, p. 27.

58. Hearings, Occupation, 1920, Volume 1, p. 566.

59. Ibid., p. 56.

60. Ibid., p. 567.

61. Franklin D. Roosevelt Library, Hyde Park, New York, Papers of A.A. Berle, Box 2, book is labeled "Occupation of Haiti and Santo Domingo"; also Paul Douglas, The American Occupation of Haiti, *Political Science Quarterly*, Volume 42, 1927, p. 228–258, especially p. 251.

62. Hoover Library, op. cit., p. 41–42.

63. Hans Schmidt, op. cit., p. 109.

64. Hearings, Occupation, op. cit., p. 530; and p. 589.

65. For the military slavery comment see Roosevelt Library. Papers of A.A. Berle, op. cit., no pagination in this section of his Haiti manuscript; for Butler's comment, Hearings, Occupation, op. cit., p. 530.

66. Hearings, v. 1, p. 553, 600; see too, James H. McCrocklin, *Garde D'Haiti* (Annapolis, 1974), especially Chapter 3.

67. Ibid., p. 560; also Berle, Roosevelt Library, op. cit.

68. Herbert Hoover Library, West Branch, Iowa, Francis White Papers, Box 14, strictly confidential letter from Dana Munro to Assistant Secretary of State Francis White, dated January 27, 1932, p. 2; for the expenditures see the testimony of John McIlhenny, Hearings, Occupation, op. cit., Volume 2, p. 1347.

69. Berle, Roosevelt Library, op. cit.; also Hearings, Volume I, p. 551.

70. Hearings, Occupation, op. cit., Volume 1, p. 435–436; also Berle, Roosevelt Library, op. cit.; for a soldier's memoirs see Lowell Thomas, *Old Gimlet Eye* (New York: Farrar and Rinehart, 1934).

71. Michel-Rolph Trouillot, *Haiti: State Against Nation* (New York: Monthly Review Press, 1990), p. 61.

72. Hearings, Occupation, op. cit., Volume 2, Testimony of John A. McIlhenny, Financial Advisor, p. 1345, 1401.

Notes

73. Ibid., p. 1437; also p. 1351.

74. Ibid., p. 1439.

75. Ibid., p. 1429.

76. Ibid., p. 1410; on the racism see, for example, Trouillot, op. cit., p. 128–130.

77. Samuel Guy Inman, *Santo Domingo and Haiti: A Cruise With the Marines* (New York, 1919), p. 9; also Mary White Ovington, The United States in Porto Rico, *The New Republic*, July 15, 1916, p. 271.

78. Ibid., p. 9; also Wilfredo Lozano, *Proletarizacion y Campesinado En El Capitalismo Agroexportador* (Santo Domingo: Instituto Tecnologico de Santo Domingo, 1985), p. 81.

79. School For Military Government, op. cit., p. 30. The full citation appears in endnote 10.

80. Ibid., p. 30; also Inman, op. cit., p. 9.

81. Stephen Fuller and Graham Cosmas, *Marines in the Dominican Republic, 1916–1924* (Washington: U.S. Marine Corps, 1974), p. 48; Lieutenant Edward Fellowes, Training Native Troops In Santo Domingo, *Marine Corps Gazette*, V. 8, No. 4, Dec., 1923, p. 216.

82. Ibid., p. 228–229, 231.

83. Fuller and Cosmas, op. cit., p. 48.

84. Fellowes, op. cit., p. 220.

85. Fuller and Cosmas, op. cit., p. 48; on the makeup see Mark Kurlansky, *A Continent of Islands: Searching For the Caribbean Destiny* (Reading: Addison Wesley, 1992), p. 49.

86. Ibid., p. 43.

87. Army Military School, op. cit., p. 51, 65.

88. Calder, op. cit., p. 76–77; also Frank Moya Pons, Import Substitution Industrialization Policies in the Dominican Republic, *Hispanic American Historical Review*, 70, No. 4, p. 539–577.

89. On the commissions see Army Military School, op. cit., p. 59.

90. Lozano, op. cit., p. 81; Knight, op. cit., Chapter 12.

91. Calder, op. cit., p. 92; the figure on 1907 monies still owed is from the U.S. Army Military School Study, op. cit., p. 65.

92. Ibid., Calder, p. 76; also the U.S. Army Military School

Study, p. 63–64; also Knight, op. cit., p. 142.

93. Military School Study, p. 61; see the very important insights of Roberto Cassa, *Capitalismo y Dictadura* (Santo Domingo: Editora De La Universidad Autonoma de Santo Domingo, 1982), p. 354–55.

94. Sale of Foreign Bonds or Securities in the United States, Hearings Before the Committee on Finance, United States Senate, 72nd Congress, 1st session, Washington, 1932, p. 716–717.

95. Joseph Juarez, United States Withdrawal From the Dominican Republic, *Hispanic American Historical Review*, V. 42, May, 1962, p. 152–190; Congressional Record, Senate, June 19, 1922, p. 8942.

96. Ibid., p. 8962.

Gangsters and Good Neighbors

1. For the Roosevelt comment see Franklin D. Roosevelt, Our Foreign Policy: A Democratic View, *Foreign Affairs*, Volume 6, number 4, July 1928, p. 573–586; the quote appears on p. 583; for the comment of Ambassador Curtis see President Herbert Hoover Library, West Branch, Iowa, Papers of Francis White, Box 3, comment is on p. 4 of letter dated April 21, 1930 to Assistant Secretary of State For Latin American Affairs, Francis White.

2. Warren Harding, Presidential Papers, Manuscripts and Archives Section, The New York Public Library.

3. Congressional Record, Senate, June 19, 1922, p. 8956.

4. Ibid., p. 8958.

5. Hearings, op. cit., p. 8956–8957.

6. Dana Munro, *The United States and the Caribbean Republics, 1921–1933* (Princeton: Princeton University Press, 1964), p. 5.

7. Joseph Robert Juarez, United States Withdrawal From Santo Domingo, *Hispanic American Historical Review*, Volume 42, May, 1962, p. 152–190, see p. 168.

8. Congressional Record, op. cit., p. 8955.

9. Harding Papers, Ibid. p. 6–7 speech.

10. Harding Papers, op. cit., letter dated November 11, 1922.

11. Pedro Albizu Campos, *Obras Escojidas*, Tomo I (San Juan:

Notes

Editorial Jelofe, 1975) p. 42, 44.

12. Harding Papers, op. cit., p. 4 of letter dated September 17, 1921.

13. Hearings Before the Committee on Territories and Insular Possessions, United States Senate, 68th Congress, 1st session, Washington, 1924, p. 6.

14. On the insistence see Munro, op. cit., p. 17; on the foregone conclusion see David Lockmiller, *Enoch H. Crowder: Soldier, Lawyer, Statesman* (Columbia: University of Missouri Studies, 1955), p. 22.

15. Munro, op. cit., p. 17.

16. Lockmiller, op. cit., p. 230; Munro, op. cit., p. 18; also Louis Perez Jr., *Cuba Under the Platt Amendment, 1902–1934* (Pittsburgh: University of Pittsburgh Press, 1986), p. 190.

17. Perez, Ibid., p. 188.

18. Oscar Pino–Santos, *El Asalto A Cuba Por La Oligarqia Financiers Yanqui* (Havana: Casa De Las Americas, 1973), p. 93.

19. Perez, op. cit., p. 212.

20. Perez, Ibid., p. 200; also Lockmiller, op. cit., Chapter 16.

21. Pino–Santos, op. cit., p. 162–164.

22. Jules Benjamin, *The United States and the Origins of the Cuban Revolution* (Princeton: Princeton University Press, 1988), p. 110–111.

23. Lockmiller, op. cit., p. 240.

24. Ibid., p. 244

25. Perez, op. cit., p. 259–260; also Lockmiller, Ibid., p. 244–246; Munro, op. cit. p. 40–42.

26. On the plan itself see Bruce Calder, *The Impact of Intervention* (Austin: University of Texas Press, 1984), p. 204–206.

27. Sumner Welles, *Naboth's Vineyard* (New York: Payson and Clarke, 1928) Volume 2, p. 916.

28. Ibid., p. 920–921.

29. Ibid., p. 925–926.

30. See, for example, the testimony of Thomas Mann, The Situation in the Dominican Republic, Executive Sessions of the Senate Foreign Relations Committee, 89th Congress, 1st session, July of 1965, Washington, 1990. See p.

451

514–516.

31. Welles, op. cit. p. 926; also Sumner Welles, Is America Imperialistic?, *Atlantic Monthly*, V. 134, Sept., 1924, p. 412–423.

32. William Roger Lewis, *Imperialism At Bay: The United States and the Decolonization of the British Empire* (New York: Oxford University Press, 1978), p. 238.

33. Mann's Oral History Interview, The Harry S. Truman Library, Independence, Missouri, July, 1979, p. 29.

34. Welles, op. cit., p. 929.

35. National Archives, State Department, 839.51/3284, memo to Assistant Secretary of State Francis White, dated October 17, 1930. The quotes are from p. 1, 5, 6.

36. National Archives, Department of State, Series A., No. 128, Dominican Republic, No.3, Washington, 1923, p. 5.

37. Ibid., p. 5.

38. Bernardo Vega, *Trujillo y el Control Financiero Norteamericano* (Santo Domingo: Fundacion Cultural Dominicana, 1990), p. 5–6.

39. Stephen Fuller and Graham Cosmas, *Marines in the Dominican Republic* (Washington: History and Museums Division, 1974), p. 52.

40. Hoover Library, West Branch, Iowa, Presidential Papers, Cabinet Officers, Box 21, This was a suggestion made to President Hoover by attorney John Barrell.

41. Hearings Before the Committee on Insular Affairs, House, 69th Congress, 2nd session, Washington, December, 1926, p. 24; for the adopted child comment see the Hearings held in February and March of 1926, 69th Congress, 1st session, p. 88.

42. Ibid., Hearings in February and March of 1926, p. 68; for who could and could not vote see Hearing Before the Committee On Insular Affairs, House of Representatives, 74th Congress, 2nd session, Washington, April, 1936, p. 10–11.

43. Ibid., p. 69; preceding quote is from p. 70.

44. Ibid., p. 69.

45. Hearings, December, 1926, op. cit., p. 2–3.

46. Herbert Hoover Library, West Branch, Iowa, Presidential

Notes

Papers —Cabinet Officers, Box 40.

47. Roosevelt Library, Hyde Park, New York, F.D.R. Papers: Official File, Division of Territories and Insular Possessions, Box 40.

48. Luther Harris Evans, *The Virgin Islands* (Ann Arbor: J.W. Edwards, 1945), p. 63.

49. Hoover Library, op. cit., Presidential Papers—Cabinet Officers, Box 21.

50. Theodore Roosevelt Jr., *Colonial Policies of the United States* (Garden City: Doubleday and Doran, 1937), p. 83.

51. Hoover Library, States and Territories File, Box 975, p. 3 of letter.

52. Ibid., p. 4.

53. Roosevelt, op. cit., p. 110.

54. Hoover Library, Papers of Francis White, Box 3, p. 1 of a letter to Ambassador Curtis dated February 26th, 1930.

55. Ibid., p. 3.

56. Henry L. Stimson, Bases of American Foreign Policy During the Past Four Years, Foreign Affairs, V. 11, April 1933, p. 394–395; also Munro, op. cit., Chapter Eleven titled "The Transition from Intervention to the Good Neighbor Policy"; for a solid critique see Eric Paul Roorda, *The Era of the Good Neighbor Policy in the Dominican Republic, 1930–1940*, an unpublished doctoral dissertation done at Johns Hopkins University, 1990.

57. (Confidential) Dominican Republic—Convention Relating to Customs Revenues, Hearings, Committee on Foreign Relations, Senate, 66th Congress, 3rd session, Washington, 1940, p. 46.

58. Ibid., p. 24.

59. Foreign Relations of the United States, 1927, Volume 3, Washington, 1942, p. 546.

60. Ibid., p. 548.

61. Bernardo Vega, *El 23 De Febrero o La Mas Anunciada Revolucion de America* (Santo Domingo: Fundacion Cultural Dominicana, 1989).

62. Ibid., p. 16–17, 25.

63. Ibid., p. 30.

64. Robert Crassweller, *Trujillo: The Life and Times of a*

Caribbean Dictator (New York: Macmillan, 1966), p. 64–68.

65. Foreign Affairs, op. cit., p. 701.
66. Ibid., see especially p. 711 and 718.
67. Ibid., p. 718–719.
68. National Archives, Department of State, Division of Latin American Affairs, File 839.00/3398; three page memo dated May 7, 1930. The visit to Trujillo occurred in late March.
69. Ibid., p. 1 and 3 of the memo.
70. Hoover Library, Papers of Francis White, Box 3.
71. Ibid., letter dated May 6, 1930, p. 2.
72. Ibid., see p. 2, 3, 4 of the letter.
73. Foreign Affairs, op. cit., p. 723; also Howard Wiarda, *Dictatorship and Development: The Methods of Control in Trujillo's Dominican Republic* (Gainesville: University of Florida Press, 1969), p. 30–31.
74. Alleged Assassination Plots Involving Foreign Leaders, an Interim Report of the Select Committee to Study Governmental Operations, Senate, 94th Congress, 1st session, 1975, p. 195.
75. Hoover Library, The Haiti Commission, Box 1069, from an interview with de La Rue for the president's Commission, p. 5–7.
76. Foreign Relations of the United States, 1930, Volume 3, p. 221.
77. Hoover Library, Francis White Papers, Box 8, from a letter to White from Dana Munro. dated January 31, 1931; the fiction comment appears on p. 5 of the letter. For the other quote see p. 2–3.
78. Ibid., p. 3.
79. Hoover Library, Haiti Commission, Box 1069, memo March 13, 1930, p. 3.
80. Ibid., p. 4.
81. Hoover Library, Papers of Francis White, Box 8, p. 3 of letter dated February 24, 1932.
82. Clarence Streit, Haiti: Intervention in Operation, *Foreign Affairs*, Volume 6, number 4, July 1928, p. 623; for Munro remark see Hoover Library, Papers of Francis White, Box 8, p. 8 of a letter dated January 9, 1931.
83. For example, Munro, op. cit., p. 311.

84. Foreign Relations of the United States, 1930, op. cit., p. 206.

85. Foreign Relations, 1930, op. cit., p. 244–245.

86. Ibid., p. 246–247.

87. Hoover Library, Haiti Commission, Box 1073, see p. 2 of the memo dated March 13, 1930.

88. Hoover Library, White Papers, Box 8, letter dated July 3, 1931.

89. Ibid., p. 2 of Munro's June 27th letter.

90. Munro, op. cit., p. 323.

91. Dana A. Munro, The American Withdrawal From Haiti, 1929–1934, *Hispanic American Historical Review*, V. 49, No. 1, p. 21.

92. Hoover Library, Haiti Commission, Box 1069, interview with La Rue, see p. 3.

93. Michel-Rolph Trouillot, *Haiti: State Against Nation* (New York: Monthly Review Press, 1990), p. 128–136; also Alex Dupuy, *Haiti in the World Economy* (Boulder: Westview, 1988), Chapter 6.

94. Bernardo Vega, *Haiti y Trujillo* (Santo Domingo: Fundacion Cultural Dominicana, 1988), Volume 1, p. 19–22.

95. Ibid., p. 390–391.

Rum, Revolution, and Moral Embargoes

1. Tariff Readjustment, 1929, Hearings Before the Committee on Ways and Means, 70th Congress, 2nd session, Washington, 1929, p. 283.

2. Ibid., p. 281-282.

3. Ibid., p. 287.

4. Moody's Manual of Investments, 1931, p. 368.

5. On Puerto Rico see James L. Dietz, *Economic History of Puerto Rico* (Princeton: Princeton University Press, 1986), p. 120; also Extension of the Sugar Act of 1948, Hearings, Committee on Agriculture, House, 82nd Congress, first session, 1951, p. 173.

6. Report of the Commission on Cuban Affairs, *Problems of the New Cuba* (New York: Foreign Policy Association, 1935), p. 250.

7. Moody's, op. cit., 1937, p. 3008.

8. Hearings, 1948, op. cit., p. 34-35.

9. Leland Jenks, *Our Cuban Colony: A Study in Sugar* (New York: Vanguard Press, 1928).

10. Herbert Hoover Library, West Branch, Iowa, President's papers—Cabinet Officials, Box 49; see the summaries marked "Review of Questions of Major Interest in the Relations of the United States with the Latin American Countries, 1929-1933."

11. Hearings, 1948, op. cit., p. 37.

12. Vital Speeches of the Day, Volume 1, Affairs of U.S. Territories, Oscar Chapman, Assistant Secretary of the Interior, October 10, 1934, p. 85.

13. Deitz, op. cit., p. 139; Ronald Fernandez, *The Disenchanted Island: Puerto Rico and the United States in the Twentieth Century* (New York: Praeger, 1992), p. 121.

14. *Problems of the New Cuba*, op. cit., p. 214-215.

15. Ibid., p. 216.

16. John Dalton, *Sugar: A Case Study of Government Control* (New York: Macmillan, 1937), p. 103-105.

17. Ibid, p. 99; see, too, Department of Commerce, *United States Sugar Policy: An Analysis*, Washington, 1988, especially Chapter One.

18. Pedro Albizu Campos, *Obras Escogidas*, Tomo II, p. 47.

19. Dalton, op. cit., p. 256.

20. Dalton, Chapter 14.

21. Sugar, Hearings Before the Committee on Finance, United States Senate, 75th Congress, 1st session, Washington, 1937, p. 132-133.

22. For the hopeless comment see Ernest Gruening, *Many Battles* (New York: Liveright, 1974), p. 181; the comment to the president is from a letter dated August 29, 1936; see Franklin Roosevelt Library, President's Personal Files, Puerto Rico-400. This letter was written by Ernest Gruening for President Roosevelt in response to a letter from Henry Epstein, then Solicitor General of the State of New York. The president said that Gruening's letter was "extraordinarily good."

23. Pedro Albizu Campos, *Obras Escogidas*, Tomo 1 (San Juan:

Notes

Editorial Jelofe, 1975), p. 50.

24. Roosevelt Library, op. cit., p. 1 of the letter.

25. Ibid., for example, p. 12-31.

26. José Luis Gonzalez, *Nueva Visita Al Cuarto Piso* (San Juan: Libros del Falmboyan, 1986), p. 178-181.

27. On the permanent possession see Ernest Gruening's comment in Truman Clark, *Puerto Rico and the United States, 1917-1933* (Pittsburgh: University of Pittsburgh, 1975), p. 146 ; on the active agitation for independence see Frank Otto Gatell, Independence Rejected: Puerto Rico and the Tydings Bill of 1936, *Hispanic American Historical Review*, V. 38, (February, 1958), p. 38.

28. Roosevelt Library, Hyde Park, New York, President's Official File, 400, Box 24, memo dated December 8, 1937, see p. 2.

29. Roosevelt Library, op. cit. see p. 3 of the letter dated August 29, 1936.

30. Fernandez, op. cit., p. 127-128.

31. The Ellsworth letter to President Roosevelt is dated October 17, 1938; it can be found in the archives of the American Civil Liberties Union, at the Princeton University Library, see Volume 2053; Roosevelt Library, Synder, op. cit., p. 3.

32. Gatell, op. cit., p. 33.

33. Gruening, op. cit., p. 198-199.

34. Fernandez, op. cit., p. 131.

35. National Archives, Division of Territories and Insular Possessions, 9-8-65, letter dated April 8, 1937.

36. Earl Parker Hanson, *Transformation: The Story of Modern Puerto Rico* (New York: Simon and Schuster, 1955), p. 42-43.

37. Ibid., p. 39.

38. Exempting Virgin Islands From Coastwise Shipping Laws, Hearings Before the Committee on Merchant Marine and Fisheries, House of Representatives, 74th Congress, 2nd session, Washington, March, 1936, p. 1-2, 16.

39. Ibid., p. 2.

40. Gruening, op. cit., p. 185.

41. Hearings, 1936, op. cit., p. 2.

42. Ibid., p. 3.

43. Knud Knud-Hansen, *From Denmark to the Virgin Islands*

(Philadelphia: Dorrance and Company, 1947), p. 124; on Knud Hansen's position in the island's administration see Gordon Lewis, *The Virgin Islands: A Caribbean Lilliput* (Evanston: Northwestern University Press, 1972), p. 70.

44. Franklin Roosevelt Library, Hyde Park, New York, F.D.R. Papers: Official File, 3434.

45. For the sugar duty figures see To Provide A Civil Government For the Virgin Islands of the United States, Hearing before the Committee on Insular Affairs, 74th Congress, 2nd session, Washington, 1936, p. 62-63.

46. William Boyer, *Virgin Islands: A History of Human Rights and Wrongs* (Durham: Carolina Academic Press, 1983), p. 157.

47. Roosevelt Library, F.D.R. Official Files, 3424, memo for the Secretary of the Interior dated November 16, 1936.

48. Ibid., Ickes memo dated November 30, 1936.

49. Roosevelt Library, Papers of Charles Taussig, Box 40, memo to Governor Pearson dated January 10, 1934.

50. Roosevelt Library, Official Files, 3424, from a message to the president dated December 2, 1940.

51. Harry Truman Library, Independence, Missouri, Papers of Charles G. Ross; the balance sheet is part of a package dated February 26, 1947.

52. Luther Harris Evans, *The Virgin Islands: From Naval Base to New Deal* (Ann Arbor: J.W. Edwards, 1945), p. 304.

53. Hearings. op. cit., Civil Government For the Virgin Islands, p. 51; for the suffrage figures see Boyer, op. cit., p. 180.

54. Ibid., p. 49.

55. Ibid., p. 49.

56. Boyer, op. cit., p. 182.

57. Foreign Relations of the United States, Diplomatic Papers, Volume Five, The American Republics (Washington: GPO, 1952), p. 376, 397.

58. Franklin Roosevelt Library, President's Special Files: Welles, memo dated November 7, 1938.

59. Ibid., p. 2, 4.

60. Ibid., p. 4-5.

61. Foreign Relations, op. cit., p. 327 and 280.

62. Ibid., p. 310-311; also 323; for two superb summaries of

Notes

the Welles mediation see Jules Robert Benjamin, *The United States and Cuba* (Pittsburgh: University of Pittsburgh Press, 1984), especially Chapters 6 and 7; also Louis Perez Jr., *Cuba Under the Platt Amendment* (Pittsburgh: University of Pittsburgh Press, 1986), especially Chapter 11; finally E. David Cronon, Interpreting the Good Neighbor Policy: The Cuban Crisis of 1933, *Hispanic American Historical Review*, Volume 39, November, 1959, p. 537-567.

63. Ibid., Cronon, p. 561.

64. Foreign Relations of the United States, Diplomatic Papers, 1934, Volume 5, The American Republics (Washington: GPO, 1952), p. 185.

65. Herbert Hoover Library, West Branch, Iowa, Cabinet Officers, Box 49, from a long memo dated February 21, 1933, see p. 13.

66. Ibid., p. 18.

67. Eric Paul Roorda, The Era of the Good Neighbor in the Dominican Republic, 1930-1940, unpublished Doctoral Dissertation, Johns Hopkins, 1990, p. 137.

68. Hoover Library, op. cit., see p. 3 and 4 of an annex to the February 21, 1933 memo; for a good overview of this whole process see Dana Munro, *The United States and the Caribbean Republics, 1921-1933* (Princeton: Princeton UP, 1974), p. 306-308.

69. Foreign Relations of the United States, Diplomatic Papers, 1934, Volume V, Washington, 1952, p. 191.

70. Foreign Relations of the United States, Diplomatic Papers, 1936, Volume V, The American Republics (Washington: GPO, 1954), p. 446-447.

71. Ibid., p. 448.

72. Ibid., p. 455.

73. Foreign Relations of the United States, Diplomatic Papers, 1937, Volume V, The American Republics, Washington: GPO, 1956, p. 452.

74. Ibid., 1937, p. 527, 548, 552.

75. Ibid., 1937, p. 529.

76. By far the best examination of this period is Bernardo Vega, *Trujillo y el Control Financiero Norteamericano* (Santo Domingo: Fundacion Cultural Dominicana, 1990).

77. Roorda, op. cit., p. 346.
78. Herbert Hoover Library, West Branch Iowa, Francis White Papers, Box 10, by Minister Curtis, September 15, 1930.
79. Ibid., p. 2 of a letter from Ambassador Curtis dated February 16, 1931.
80. Ibid., letter from White to Minister Schoenfeld June 3, 1932, see p. 1, 4.
81. Roosevelt Library, Personal Papers, 138, the letter is dated October 26, 1933; the president met to consider Trujillo's request on September 13, 1933.
82. Bernardo Vega, *Trujillo y Haiti* (Santo Domingo: Fundacion Cultural Dominicana, 1988), Chapter Ten summary of the "causes of the massacre".
83. Roorda, op. cit., p. 335-336.
84. Vega, op. cit., p. 331-332.
85. Ibid., p. 343-344.
86. Roorda, op.cit, p. 346-347.
87. Foreign Relations, 1937, op. cit., p. 136.
88. Ibid., p. 141.
89. Congressional Record, December 21, 1937, 75th Congress, 2nd session, p. 2040.
90. Ibid., pp 2040 and 2043.
91. Roorda, op. cit., p. 357-358.
92. Ronald Fernandez, *Excess profits: The Rise of United Technologies* (Reading: Addison Wesley, 1983), p. 114.
93. Congressional Record, July 17, 1939, 76th Congress, 1st session, p. 9248.
94. Foreign Relations of the United States, Diplomatic Papers, Volume III, The Britsh Commonwealth, Washington, 1959, p. 3.

The Island Shield

1. William Roger Lewis, *Imperialism At Bay* (New York: Oxford University Press, 1978), p. 165.
2. General Haywood S. Hansell, Jr., *The Strategic Air War Against Germany and Japan* (Washington: USAF, 1974), p. 11-12.
3. Philip Knightley, *The First Casualty* (New York: Harcourt,

Notes

Brace Jovanovich, 1975), p. 205.

4. Air Defense Bases, Hearings Before the Committee on Military Affairs, House of Representatives, 74th Congress, 1st session, Washington 1936, p. 106.

5. Paolo E. Coletta, Editor, *United States Navy and Marine Corps Bases, Overseas* (Westport: Greenwood Press, 1988), p. 150.

6. Report on the Progress of Puerto Rico, Message of the president, 78th Congress, 1st session, House Doc. 304, Sept. 28, 1943, p. 2.

7. Coletta, op. cit., p. 302; also Report on Need of Additional Naval Bases To Defend the Coasts of the United States, Its Territories, and Possessions, House of Representatives, 76th Congress, 1st session, Document 65, p. 8, 16, 35.

8. *The New York Times*, February 26, 1939; for the Pearl Harbor of the Caribbean remark see *The New York Times*, May 13th, 1939.

9. Navy Yard, Washington D.C., Operational Archives Division, Report of Admiral Greenslade, January 6, 1941, p. 15.

10. Ibid., p. 15.

11. Foreign Relations of the United States, Diplomatic Papers, 1940, Volume III, Washington, 1958, p. 52.

12. Ibid., p. 58 and 62.

13. Ibid., p. 68.

14. Foreign Relations, 1940, op. cit., p. 65.

15. Ibid., p. 63-64.

16. Ibid., p. 67 and 69.

17. Ibid., p. 70.

18. Ibid., p. 73; see too James McGregor Burns, *Roosevelt: The Soldier of Freedom* (New York: Harcourt, 1970), p. 10-12.

19. Congressional Record, House, 76th Congress, 3rd session, September 24, 1940, p. 12571.

20. Admiral Leahy's memo written in April of 1948. See Naval Historical Center, Operational Archives Division, Washington, files marked Roosevelt Roads, Memo for the president, p. 2.

21. Ibid., March, 1943, Report of the Committee For the Investigation of Conditions in the Island of Vieques.

22. Building the Navy's Bases In World War II, History of the

Bureau of Yards and Docks and the Civil Engineer Corps, 1940-1946, Volume 2 (Washington: GPO, 1947), p. 8.

23. (Confidential) Dominican Republic-Convention Relating to Customs Revenues, Hearings Before the Committee on Foreign Relations, United States Senate, 66th Congress, 3rd session, Washington, November 27 and December 4, 1940, p. 44.

24. Ibid., p. 20.

25. Ibid., p. 53.

26. Congressional Record, 77th Congress, 1st session, Washington, 1941, February 14th, p. 1028.

27. Negotiations and Initial Preparations For American Evacuation of the Dominican Republic, Department of State, Series A., No. 128, p. 5. the National Archives.

28. Hearings, 1940, op. cit., p. 2.

29. Ibid., p. 10.

30. Ibid., p. 10.

31. Ibid., p. 42.

32. Foreign Relations of the United States, Diplomatic Papers, Volume VII, The American Republics (Washington: GPO, 1967), p. 1015.

33. Ibid., p. 1016.

34. On the sold for scrap see Eric Williams, *Inward Hunger: The Education of A Prime Minister* (London: Andre Deutsch, 1969).

35. Naval Historical Center, U.S. Naval administration in World War II, The U.S. Naval Operating Base Trinidad, B.W.I., Guide 166, p. 212.

36. Ibid., p. 213.

37. Franklin Roosevelt Library, Hyde Park, New York, Papers of Charles Taussig, Box 35, four page memo dated Dec. 28, 1940.

38. Congressional Record, 77th Congress, 1st session, Washington, February 20, 1040, p. 1218.

39. Ibid., p. 1219.

40. Ibid., p. 1221.

41. Foreign Relations of the United States, Diplomatic Papers, 1941, Volume III, The British Commonwealth (Washington: GPO, 1959), p. 3.

Notes

42. Executive Session, The United States Senate, 77th Congress, 2nd session, Committee on Naval Affairs, H.R. 3325, Washington, February 25, 1941, p. 4, 8, 10.

43. Ibid., p. 15.

44. Ibid., p. 21.

45. Ibid., p. 25-26.

46. Roosevelt Library, *Report of the United States Commission to Study Social and Economic Conditions in the British West Indies, Appointed by the president of the United States on November 13, 1940,* Charles Taussig Papers, Box 35, p. 2.

47. Ibid., p. 3.

48. William Claypole and John Robottom, *Caribbean Story,* Book Two, The Inheritors, (London: Longman, 1989), p. 118-123; Clive Y. Thomas, *The Poor and the Powerless: Economic Policy and Change in the Caribbean* (New York: Monthly Review Press, 1988).

49. Roosevelt Library, Taussig, Box 35, Report of his luncheon with Winston Churchill, December 17, 1942, p. 1 of the memo.

50. Roosevelt Library, Taussig Commission Report, p. 86.

51. Ibid., p. 150-151.

52. The Caribbean Islands and the War: A Record of Progress in Facing Stern Realities (Department of State, United States Government Printing Office. 1943).

53. Ibid., p. III.

54. Naval Historical Library, U.S. Naval Base in Trinidad, op. cit., p. 227.

55. Ibid., p. 226.

56. Ibid., p. 227.

57. On the Honeymoon Base see Williams, op. cit., p. 216; on the plans for the Trinidad base see Ibid., p. 235-236.

58. Naval Historical Library, Operational Archives, Washington, page of an office memo dated October 20, 1950; in the Trinidad files of the Atlantic Command.

59. Ibid., p. 4 of a Trinidad naval memo dated March 23, 1950.

60. Report on the Progress of Puerto Rico, op. cit., p. 2, emphasis added; William Roger Lewis, *Imperialism At Bay* (New York: Oxford University Press, 1978), p. 237.

61. Coletta, op. cit., p. 272.

62. Building the Navy's Bases, op. cit., p. 8-9; Ibid., p. 272.
63. To Provide For the Donation of Certain Property of the United States in Vieques, P.R. to the Municipal Government of P.R. (H.R. 4863), Interior Department, document dated November 13, 1944, p. 1, government document designation Y4 N/22/1a: 943-44/264.
64. Ibid., p. 2 of Fortas' memo.
65. This is from a November 17, 1944 letter from Major General Philip B, Fleming. Its government document classification number Y4.N22/1a: 943-44/267.
66. Rexford Tugwell, *Puerto Rican Public Papers* (San Juan, 1946), p. 95.
67. Louis, op. cit., p. 165 and 355-356.
68. Ronald Fernandez, *The Disenchanted Island* (New York: Praeger, 1992), p. 145.
69. Roosevelt Library, Papers of Rexford Tugwell, Box 47, p. 67 of the diary, August 30, 1944.
70. Nomination of Rexford Tugwell, Hearings Before the Committee on Territories and Insular Affairs, United States Senate, 77th Congress, first session, August, 1951, p. 49-50.
71. Tugwell Diary, op. cit., p. 67.
72. Ibid., p. 67.
73. Luis Nieves Falcon, *Diagnostico de Puerto Rico* (San Juan: Edil, 1970), p. 242-243.
74. Independence For Puerto Rico, Hearings, Committee on Territories and Insular Affairs, Senate, 79th Congress, 1st session, p. 383.
75. Carlos Ramon Zapata-Oliveras, United States-Puerto Rico Relations in the Early Cold War Years (1945-1953), Doctoral Dissertation, University of Pennsylvania, 1986, p. 131.
76. Independence Hearings, op, cit., 1945, p. 376.
77. Truman Library, Rosenman Papers, Box 3, op. cit., memo to the president dated October 3, 1945.
78. Zapata Oliveras, op. cit., p. 173.
79. Truman Library, Rosenman Papers, Box 3.
80. Truman Library, Independence Missouri, PHST, Records of the National Security Council, memo labeled Conversation

with Ambassador Thomen concerning a long range proving ground....

81. Foreign Relations of the United States, Volume VIII, 1947, The American Republics, Washington, 1972, p. 659.

82. On the looking over his shoulder comment see Foreign Relations of the United States, Diplomatic Papers, 1945, Volume IX, The American Republic, Washington, 1969, p. 982; for the secretary's comments see Truman Library, PHST, Box 585, memo from Secretary of State James Byrnes to the president, undated.

83. George Kennan, The Sources of Soviet Conduct, *Foreign Affairs*, XXV (July, 1947), p. 566-582.

84. Hoover Library, Francis White Papers, Box 3, letter to Minister Curtis dated February 26, 1930.

85. The policy was defined in Cuba in 1933; see the superb summary by E. David Cronon, Interpreting the Good Neighbor Policy: The Cuban Crisis of 1933, *Hispanic American Historical Review*, Volume 39, 1959, p. 538-567.

86. Foreign Relations of the United States, Volume VIII, The American Republics, Washington, 1972, p. 629.

87. Ibid., p. 629-630.

88. Ibid., p. 630; for a longer summary see the Oral History Interview of Assistant Secretary of State Thomas Mann, Truman Library, p. 25-80.

89. Ibid., p. 630.

90. Hearings Before a Subcommittee on Interstate and Foreign Commerce, United States Senate, 80th Congress, 2nd session, September, 1948, p. 784.

91. Dwight D. Eisenhower Library, Abilene, Kansas, NSC Policy Papers, Box 26, See p. 8 of the NSC study entitled "U.S. Policy Toward Latin America."

92. Ibid., p. 64.

Colonies, Contradictions, and Television Aggression

1. Congressional Record, 81st Congress, 1st session May 5, 1949, p. 5709.

2. Executive Sessions of the Senate Foreign Relations

Committee (Historical Series), Volume XII, 86th Congress, 2nd session, 1960, (Washington: GPO, 1982), p. 110.

3. Op. cit., p. 5611.

4. Ibid., p. 5612.

5. Ibid., p. 5615.

6. Ibid., Crawford's use appears on p. 5709; Keefe's on p. 5708.

7. Ibid., p. 5713.

8. Ibid., p. 5695-6.

9. Ibid., p. 5704.

10. Harry S. Truman Library, Independence, Missouri, Papers of Charles G. Ross, Box, from a balance sheet presented to the president in February, 1947.

11. Ibid., p. 5708.

12. Ibid., p. 5713.

13. President James Carter Library, Atlanta, Georgia, ST51-3; also Domestic Policy Staff-Special Projects, Stern, Box 90. Memos are dated May 15, 1978, June 1, 1978, and July 19, 1978.

14. Javier Figueroa, La Vinculacion Militar Entre Cuba y Los Estados Unidos Al Finalizar La Segunda Guerra Mundial, 1944-1952, *Historia y Sociedad*, Ano II, 1989, p. 90-118; also Jules R. Benjamin, *The United States and the Origins of the Cuban Revolution* (Princeton: Princeton University Press, 1988), p. 99.

15. Harry S. Truman Library, Papers of Clark Clifford, Box 33, p. 1-2.

16. Harry S. Truman Library, Independence, Missouri, President's Secretary's Files, Central Intelligence Agency, *Cuba*, p. i.

17. Emilio Roig De Leuchsenring, *Marti Anti-Imperialist* (Havana: Book Institute, 1967), p. 18, 21.

18. CIA, op. cit., p. ii.

19. Thomas J. Heston, Cuba, The United States and the Sugar Act of 1948: The Failure of Economic Coercion, *Diplomatic History*, Volume 6, Number 1, Winter 1982, p. 1-21.

20. Ibid., p. 14.

21. CIA, op. cit., p. 27-28.

22. Ibid., p. 29, 31.

Notes

23. Franklin Roosevelt Library, President's Special Files, Sumner Welles' memo dated November 7, 1938.

24. Foreign Relations of the United States, 1952-54, Volume IV, The American Republics, Washington, 1983, p. 875; for a fine overview of this period see Louis A. Perez Jr., *Cuba: Between Reform and Revolution* (New York: Oxford University Press, 1988).

25. Ibid., p. 876.

26. Truman Library, White House Central Files—Confidential Files, "Weekly Review", Policy Information Committee, Department of State, review for the week of July 5, 1950, p. 15-16.

27. Ibid, p. 15-16.

28. Ibid., p. 16.

29. Howard Fast, Editor, *The Selected Work of Tom Paine* (New York: Modern Library, 1945), p. 23.

30. Naval Historical Library, Operational Archives Division, Washington, D.C., from a letter dated September 23, 1949, included in the files of the Trinidad Base, The Atlantic Command and United States Atlantic Fleet, Headquarters of the Commander-In-Chief, p. 1.

31. Ibid., the Consul General's report dated May 16, 1950, stamped confidential, p. 2.

32. Letter of September 23, 1949, op. cit., p. 1.

33. Ibid., p. 2; $75 figure from a letter dated February 6, 1950 titled "Rental Payments For Inactivated Leased Military Areas".

34. Ibid., confidential memo dated March 23, 1950, p. 2-4.

35. Ibid., p. 4.

36. Ibid., from a confidential memo from the secretary of state, dated June 5, 1950, p. 2.

37. Ibid., memo labeled Macqueripe Plantation; it is dated October 20, 1950, p. 2.

38. Admiral Leahy's report can be found at the Naval Historical Center, Operational Archives Branch, box marked Roosevelt Roads, file marked Admiral Leahy's Report; the material on Culebra, p. 14-15.

39. National Archives, Record Group 126, see 9-8-93. quote from letter dated January 20, 1948, to Governor Jesus

Pinero from James P. Davies, Director of the Department of the Interior's Division of Territories and Island Possessions.

40. House of representatives, Committee on Interior and Insular Affairs, 82nd Congress, 2nd session, Report 1832, p. 3; for the Senate Committee on Interior and Insular Affairs, see Senate, 81st Congress, 2nd session, Report 1779; p. 3 stresses that "the measure would not change Puerto Rico's fundamental political, social, and economic relationship to the United States."

41. Congressional Record, House of Representatives, 82nd Congress, 2nd session, May 13, 1952, p. 5119.

42. National Archives, Office of Territories, Record Group 126, 9-8-68, letter from James Davies to Governor Muñoz.dated September 25, 1952, p. 1,3.

43. Documents on the Constitutional History of Puerto Rico, Office of the Commonwealth of Puerto Rico, Washington, D.C., 2nd edition, 1964, p. 155.

44. For example, Hearing Before the Committee on Interior and Insular Affairs, United States Senate, 86th Congress, 1st session, June 9, 1959, especially Senator's Jackson's comments on p. 35-55.

45. Carlos Ramon Zapata Oliveras, United States Puerto Rico Relations in the Early Cold War (1945-1953), unpublished Doctoral Dissertation, University of Pennsylvania, 1986, especially Chapter Six, p. 378-382.

46. Dwight D. Eisenhower Library, Abilene, Kansas, Ann Whitman-Administrative Series, Box 2. Lodge describes the breakfast meeting in a letter to the president, dated November 28, 1953.

47. Eisenhower Library, Secretary of State Dulles—Telephone Series, Box 2, memo dated Friday, November 20, 1953.

48. Eisenhower Library, Dulles-Chronological Series, Box 5, telegram dated November 24, 1953.

49. On the gag law see the superb book by Ivonne Acosta, *La Mordaza* (San Juan: Edil, 1987); for a good general overview see Roberta Johnson, *Puerto Rico: Commonwealth Or Colony?* (New York: Praeger, 1979).

50. Eisenhower, Ann Whitman-Administrative Series, Box 23, the letter dated November 28, 1953.

51. Eisenhower Library, Ann Whitman-International Series,

Notes

Box 41, letter to the president dated January 1, 1954.

52. Ibid., Eisenhower's response is dated January 12, 1954.

53. Eisenhower Library, Ann Whitman Papers—International Series, Box 41, p. 1 of the letter.

54. Ibid., p. 1 of the letter.

55. Ibid., p. 1-2 of the January 8, 1954 letter.

56. Ibid., p. 2.

57. *New York Times*, March 2, 1954, p. 16; for a detailed account of this attack see Antonio Gil de Lamadrid Navarro, *Los Indomitos* (Rio Piedras: Edil, 1981).

58. Eisenhower Library, White House Central Files, 147-F, letter from Lodge dated March 27, 1956; it has a number of relevant attachments stapled to the main document.

59. Ibid., p. 1 of the letter.

60. Ibid., these comments appear on the four attachments to Lodge's letter.

61. Eisenhower Library, Office of Special Assistant For National Security Affairs—FBI Series, Box 4, long memo from FBI Director Hoover dated November 14, 1956 and the comments quoted appear on p. 5 of the memo.

62. Ibid., p. 6 of Hoover's memo.

63. Senate Hearings, June 1959, op. cit., p. 49.

64. Eisenhower Library, White House Office Files, 147-F, note dated June 17, 1959.

65. For Example, Eric Williams, *History of the People of Trinidad and Tobago* (London: Andre Deutsch, 1968); Franklin Knight and Colin A. Palmer, Editors, *The Modern Caribbean* (Chapel Hill: University of North Carolina Press, 1989); Clive Thomas, *The Poor and the Powerless* (New York: Monthly Review Press, 1988).

66. Eisenhower Library, White House Office Files—Office of the Special Assistant For National Security, Policy Papers Subseries, Box 28, p. 1.

67. Ibid., p. 2-3.

68. Ibid., p. 6, 14-15.

69. Eisenhower Library, Ann Whitman Papers—National Security Council Series, Box 8, meeting occurred on March 17, 1960, see p. 9.

70. NSC meeting, March 17, 1960, op. cit., p. 7.

71. NSC study, op. cit., p. 4.
72. NSC meeting of March 17, 1960, op. cit., p. 9.
73. Ibid., p. 9-10.
74. Eisenhower Library, Ann Whitman Papers-National Security Council Series, Box 8, meeting on June 30, 1960, p. 9.
75. For one example of development under Great Britain see Robert Thompson, *Green Gold: Bananas and Dependency in the Eastern Caribbean* (London: Latin America Bureau, 1987).
76. NSC study, op. cit., p. 20.
77. NSC meeting of June 30, 1960, op. cit., p. 9.
78. NSC study of the West Indies, op. cit., p. 24.
79. Eric Williams, *Inward Hunger: The Education of a Prime Minister* (London: Andre Deutsch, 1969), especially Chapter 22.
80. NSC policy paper, op. cit., p. 19, 22.
81. Eisenhower Library, Ann Whitman Papers-National Security Council Series, Box 8, meeting of April 14, 1960, p. 6-7.
82. Ibid., meeting of January 14, 1960, p. 8-9.
83. NSC meeting of January 14, 1960, p. 10.
84. Executive Sessions of the Senate Foreign Relations Committee, op. cit.; this is footnote #2. This quote is from p. 159.
85. Ibid., p. 159-160.
86. NSC Meeting of January 14, 1960, op. cit., p. 12.
87. Executive Session Hearings, op. cit., p. 160.
88. Ibid., p. 160.
89. NSC meeting of January 14, 1960, op. cit., p. 13.
90. Eisenhower Library, Ann Whitman Files—International, Box 25, from letter dated August 2, 1958.
91. Michel-Rolph Trouillot, *Haiti: State Against Nation* (New York: Monthly Review Press, 1990), p. 152.
92. Eisenhower Library, op. cit., Box 25, from a reply signed by President Eisenhower, undated.
93. Eisenhower Library, Box 25, op. cit., see the memo to the president dated August 7, 1958.
94. Eisenhower Library, Clark Papers, Box 6, p. 1 of the report, also letter to the president dated February 16, 1955.

95. Ibid., p. 24, 43.

96. Ibid., Rockefeller memo dated March 4, 1955; for the portrait correspondence see White House Central Files, Box 859, letter dated March 22, 1955, roughly three weeks after the president received the Clark report.

97. Ibid., Box 859, memo dated February 27, 1953.

98. Foreign Relations of the United States, 1952-54, Volume IV, The American Republics, Washington, 1983, p. 960-961.

99. For a good summary of this incident see the Congressional Record, 85th Congress, 1st session, February 28, 1957, p. 2815-2827.

100. Eisenhower Library, White House Office Files, Office of the Staff Secretary—International Series, Box 4, memo for the president dated May 12.

101. Eisenhower Library, Clark Papers, Box 6, report dated April 14, 1960; includes note from President Eisenhower to discuss this with the secretary of state.

102. Ibid., p. 1 of the memo.

103. Ibid., p. 5.

104. Ibid., p. 5 of General Clark's report.

105. For a fine summary see Robert D. Crassweller, *Trujillo: The Life and Times of a Caribbean Dictator* (New York: Macmillan, 1966), p. 412-420.

106. Alleged Assassination Plots Involving Foreign Leaders, Senate, 94th Congress, 1st session, Report 94-465, p. 193.

107. John F. Kennedy Library, Boston Massachusetts, President's Office File, Box 115A, undated report labeled "Dominican Republic—Martin Report." See p. 2 for Ramfis example.

108. Ibid., p. 104.

109. Ibid., p. 102.

Cemeteries and Headless Bodies

1. John F. Kennedy Library, Boston Massachusetts, see the oral interview with John Thurston, p. 13.

2. The president's speech is reprinted in Jerome Levinson and Juan de Onis, *The Alliance that Lost Its Way* (Chicago: Quadrangle Books, 1970), p. 333-339, quote used appears

on p. 334.

3. Kennedy Library, first memo from Arturo Morales Carrion, see National Security Files, Box 290, memo dated May 3, 1963; the Schlesinger comment can be found in the Schlesinger Papers, Box 2, memo labeled "Alliance For Progress", dated October 15, 1962.

4. John Bartlow Martin, *U.S. Policy in the Caribbean* (Boulder: Westview, 1978), p. 70.

5. Kennedy Library, National Security Files, memo for the naval aide to the president, dated December 14, 1961.

6. Kennedy Library, White House Central Files, four page letter from Muñoz to the president, dated December 28, 1961.

7. Carmelo Delgado Cintron, *Culebra y La Marina De Estados Unidos* (Rio Piedras: Edil, 1989), p. 207.

8. Kennedy Library, oral interview with Governor Muñoz Marin, June 11, 1965, p. 5.

9. Kennedy Library, President's Office Files—Countries, Box 115A, p. 104.

10. Kennedy Library, memo to the president, dated May 2, 1961.

11. Ibid., p. 1.

12. Alleged Assassination Plots Involving Foreign Leaders, Senate, 94th Congress, 1st session, Report 94-465, p. 215.

13. For example, the fine study by Peter Weyden, *Bay of Pigs: The Untold Story* (New York: Simon and Schuster, 1979).

14. Kennedy Library, President's Office Files—Countries, Box 1115A, op. cit., p. 89.

15. Lyndon Johnson Library, Austin, Texas, National Security Files—National Intelligence Estimates, Box 8-9, CIA assessment dated July 25, 1961, p. 1, 3.

16. Kennedy Library, National Security Files—Country Files, Box 66-7, 3 page memo dated October 3, 1961.

17. President Eisenhower Library, Abilene, Kansas, Ann Whitman Papers-NSC Series, Box 12, meeting of January 14, 1960, p. 12.

18. Kennedy Library, Goodwin's October 1961 memo, op. cit., p. 2.

19. Ibid., p. 2-3; remarks about orgies and dripping braid from Martin's report, op. cit., p. 2-3.

Notes

20. Eisenhower Library, op.cit, NSC meeting of April 14, 1960, p. 4.

21. Martin, op. cit., p. 76.

22. Bernardo Vega, *Trujillo y el Control Financiero Norteamericano* (Santo Domingo: Fundacion Cultural Dominicana, 1990), p. 25.

23. John Bartlow Martin, *Overtaken By Events: The Dominican Crisis From the Fall of Trujillo to the Civil War* (Garden City: Doubleday, 1966), p. 352-353.

24. Kennedy Library, Central Subject Files—Tariffs, Box 950, memo to the president's special counsel dated April 30, 1962.

25. Kennedy Library, Papers of Arthur Schlesinger, Box 7, 34 page memo from Ambassador Martin dated April 28, 1963. The quote appears on p. 29. The outrageous comment is from Martin, *Overtaken By Events*, op. cit., p. 352.

26. Executive Sessions of the Senate Foreign Relations Committee (Historical Series), Volume XV, 88th Congress, 1st session, 1963 (Washington: GPO, 1987), p. 596-597; for attitudes of American soldiers see p. 629.

27. Ibid., p. 601, 603.

28. Ibid., p. 611; preceding quote p. 613.

29. Ibid., p. 609.

30. Ibid., p. 610; Martin, *Overtaken By Events*, op. cit., p. 414; Theodore Sorensen, *Kennedy* (New York: Harper and Row, 1965), p. 406-408; for Bosch's interpretation see Juan Bosch, *The Unfinished Experiment* (New York: Frederick Praeger, 1966), p. 150-151.

31. Hearings, op. cit., p. 604, 686.

32. Ibid., p. 684-685.

33. Johnson Library, NSF, Box 8-9, op. cit., report dated January 17, 1964; quoted lines appear on p. 2. This document was declassified on October 5, 1990.

34. Hearings, op. cit., p. 846-47.

35. Eisenhower Library, Central Files—Official Files, 147H, Box 757, memo to Sherman Adams dated November 19, 1953.

36. Ralph Paiewonsky, *Memoirs of a Governor: A Man For the People* (New York: New York University Press, 1990), p. 156-160.

37. Hearings Before the Committee on Interior and Insular Affairs, Senate, 87th Congress, 1st session, March 1961 (p. 17 for the senator's quote).

38. Ibid., p. 156.

39. Ibid., p. 18.

40. Jimmy Carter Library, Atlanta, Georgia, Domestic Policy Staff—Special Projects—Farrow, Box 27, Interior Department Report labeled "The Economy of the Virgin Islands," p. 25-26 for the watches, p. 21 for Headnote Three.

41. Ibid., p. 26-27; see also, Paiewonsky, op. cit., p. 232-238.

42. Ibid., p. 5, 51.

43. Paiewonsky, op. cit., p. 228-229.

44. Carter Library, Interior Department Study, p. 29.

45. Amend the Merchant Marine Act of 1920, Hearings Before the Subcommittee on Merchant Marine, Committee on Commerce, Senate, 94th Congress, 2nd session, 1976, p. 7; for the original debates about oil see Hearings Before the Subcommittee on Mines and Mining, Committee on Interior and Insular Affairs, House, 90th Congress, 2nd session, 1968.

46. On the number of workers see Carter Library, Interior Department, op. cit., p. 30; also Gordon Lewis, *The Virgin Islands* (Evanston: Northwestern University Press, 1972), especially p. 124-125.

47. Paiewonsky, op. cit., p. 150.

48. Hearings, Merchant Marine, 1976, op. cit., p. 19.

49. On the park see Edward A. O'Neil, *Rape of the Virgin Islands* (New York: Praeger Publishers, 1972), Chapter Seven.

50. Kennedy Library, White House Central Files, Box 18, memo to Arthur Schlesinger (dated Dec. 29, 1962) from the Justice department's Harold Reis, quotes from p. 8, 14 of memo.

51. Ibid., p. 50.

52. Ibid., p. 50.

53. For example, Ronald Fernandez, *The Disenchanted Island* (New York: Praeger, 1992).

54. Lyndon Johnson Library, Executive File Group 759, Box

408, this 2-page. memo to the president dated May 6, 1964.

55. Johnson Library, Executive File Group 759, Box 408, 3 page memo to the president dated June 8, 1964.

56. Ibid., p. 2.

57. Jimmy Carter Library, President's Personal Files, Box 80, memo dated May 5, 1978, p. 1, 3.

58. Johnson Library, Papers of Harry McPherson, Box 27.

59. Ibid., p. 2 of a memo from James Rowe to the president, dated July 28, 1996.

60. Johnson Library, Martin's oral interview, op. cit., p. 21.

61. Johnson Library, National Security Files—Dominican Crisis, Box 8.

62. Martin Interview, op. cit., p. 24.

63. Juan Manuel Garcia Passalacqua, *Vengador del Silencio* (Rio Piedras: Editorial Cultural, 1991), p. 69.

64. Johnson Library, National Security—Defense, Box 201, letter dated April 30, 1965.

65. Johnson Library, National Security Files, Boxes 48, 49, 50, Ambassador Bennett's Critic Number Four, dated April 28, 1965.

66. For example, Yates, op. cit., p. 50; also p. 39-43.

67. Johnson Library, National Security Files—Latin America, Box 39, survey from Carl Rowan, Director of the United States Information Agency.

68. Arthur S. Link, Editor, *The Papers of Woodrow Wilson* (Princeton: Princeton University Press), p. 76.

69. Johnson Library, NSF—Dominican Crisis, Box 8, undated summary labeled "Dominican Crisis: Presidential Decisions", p. 5.

70. Executive Sessions of the Senate Foreign Relations Committee, Historical Series, V. XVII, 89th Congress, 1st session, 1965, p. 486-87.

71. Ibid., p. 514-515.

72. Ibid., p. 515.

73. Robert McNamara, *The Essence of Security* (New York: Harper and Row, 1968), p. 148.

74. Hearings, 1965, op. cit., p. 516.

75. Ibid., p. 517.

76. Johnson Library, NSF—Country File, Dominican Republic, Boxes 48, 49, 50, 28 page report entitled "The Communist Role in the Dominican Revolt"; p. 2, 7, 12.

77. Johnson Library, NSF—Dominican Crisis, 65, Box 7, memo dated May 6th, 1965, p. 1.

78. Arthur Link, Editor, November 24, 1915, p. 249.

79. Martin, oral interview, op. cit., p. 32.

80. Hearings, op. cit., p. 786.

81. Martin, oral interview, op. cit., p. 32.

82. Hearings, 1965, op. cit., p. 789.

83. Ibid., p. 751.

84. Ibid., p. 1042-1043.

85. Johnson Library, National Security Files—Country Files, Box 56-57, memo from McGeorge Bundy to the president dated August 12, 1965. Ambassador Bennett's two page letter is attached to Bundy's message.

86. Op. cit., p. 754, 760.

87. Johnson Library, National Security Files—National Intelligence Estimates, Box 8-9, 14 page report number 86.2-66, p. 1-2.

88. Johnson Library, National Security File, Box 75, cable from Ambassador Crimmins dated May 31, 1966, p. 3.

89. Johnson Library, National Security Files—National Security Estimates, dated June 23rd, 1996, p. 2-3.

90. Johnson Library, President's File, Box 61, memo dated June 14, 1966.

91. Johnson Library, Papers of Harry McPherson, Box 26, this one-page memo dated June 24, 1966.

92. Johnson Library, oral interview of Ralph Dungan, p. 22; for Thurston's comments see oral interview at the Kennedy Library, op. cit., p. 11-13.

93. Ibid., Thurston's oral interview, p. 17-18.

94. Ibid., p. 19, 21.

95. Ibid., p. 33, 39, 40.

96. Ibid., p. 26-27.

97. Johnson Library, National Security Files, Box 56-57, five page airgram dated February 19, 1964.

98. Ibid, especially p. 2 and 7.

99. Ibid., Box 56-57, forty page report entitled "Haiti—Proposed Plan of Action for Period Beginning May 1, 1964," p. 20, 22.
100. Ibid., p. 22.
101. Ibid., for U.S. objectives see p. 23-25.
102. Ibid., Box 56/57, "secret, special report" dated December 10, 1965; CIA analysis dated October 27, 1966.
103. Ibid., for the comment cited see the "special, secret report", p. 6.
104. Ibid., the CIA Report, p. 2.
105. On the slavery see Roger Plant, *Sugar and Modern Slavery* (London: Zed Books, 1987).

Designs for Development

1. President Richard Nixon Project, Virginia, White House Central Files, ST-51-4, Box 22, memo to Kenneth Cole dated January 5, 1973.
2. Pedro Albizu Campos, *Obras Escogidas,* Tomo 1 (San Juan: Jelofe, 1975), p. 52-53; also United States Caribbean Policy, Committee on Foreign Affairs, 96th Congress, 1st session, 1979, p. 43.
3. William Boyer, *Virgin Islands: A History of Human Rights and Wrongs* (Durham: Carolina Academic Press, 1983) p. 311-323.
4. Nixon Project, op. cit. memo cited in footnote one, dated January 5, 1973.
5. Nixon Project, WHCF, Box 21, memo for the president dated March 3, 1969.
6. Ibid., memo to Darrell Trent dated May 9, 1969.
7. Ibid., from p. 6 of an analysis labeled "Report on the Conference on the Status of Non-Citizens in the Virgin Islands."
8. Nixon Project, Whitaker Papers, Box 112, memo dated March 11, 1970, p. 3.
9. President Gerald Ford Library, Ann Arbor, Michigan, Domestic Council—Papers of James Cannon, Box 27, p. 5 of a long report dated June 11, 1975, written for President Ford by Sam Halper.
10. Congressional Record, Senate, 67th Congress, 1st session,

October 29, 1921; this fascinating debate runs from p. 6989-7003.

11. Robert Baker, Puerto Rico's Program of Industrial Tax Exemption, *The George Washington Law Review*, Volume 18, June, 1950, Number 4, p. 443-473; see p. 470 for the quoted material.

12. Tax reform Act of 1975, Hearings Before the Committee on Finance, United States Senate, 94th Congress, 2nd session, 1976, p. 1040.

13. Tax Treatment of U.S. Concerns With Puerto Rican Affiliates, Hearings Before the Select Committee on Small Business, United States Senate, 88th Congress, 2nd session, 1964, p. 84.

14. Hearings, 1964, op. cit., p. 95.

15. Milton Taylor, *Industrial Tax Exemption in Puerto Rico* (Madison: University of Wisconsin Press, 1957), p. 13; study done for Fomento, the island's economic planning organization.

16. Barton, *Puerto Rico's Industrial Development Program*, 1942-1960 (Cambridge: Center For International Affairs, 1959), p. 14-17.

17. For example, Leonardo Santana Rabell, *Planificacion y Politica* (Rio Piedras: Editorial Cultural, 1989).

18. Luis Costas Elena, I.R.C. Section 936 and Fomento Income Tax Exemptions (Part IV), *Revista Del Colegio De Abogados De Puerto Rico*, Volume 42, Noviembre, 1981, Numero 4, p. 611-668; see p. 636 for the material discussed.

19. Emilion Pantojas Garcia, *Development Strategies As Ideology: Puerto Rico's Export-Led Industrialization Experience* (Boulder: Lynne Rienner, 1990), p. 81; James Dietz, *Economic History of Puerto Rico* (Princeton: Princeton University Press, 1986), p. 275; Roberta Ann Johnson, *Puerto Rico* (New York: Praeger, 1979), p. 118.

20. Ronald Fernandez, *The Disenchanted Island: The United States and Puerto Rico in the Twentieth Century* (New York: Praeger, 1992), p. 211.

21. Nixon Project, White House Central Files, ST51-2, Box 24, memo to Ken Cole, dated April 30, 1974.

22. Response to Jamaica's Economic Crisis, U.S. Government Accounting Office, July 17, 1980, ID-80-40, p. 6.

23. Tom Barry, Beth Wood, and Deb Preusch, *The Other Side of Paradise* (New York: Grove Press, 1984), p. 102-106.
24. President Gerald Ford Library, Ann Arbor, Michigan, White House Central Files, Box 29, memo to General Scowcroft dated November 21, 1975.
25. Ibid., p. 1.
26. Ibid., see too memo from the Secretary of State dated November 19, 1975; and General Scowcroft's approval of the meeting dated November 24, 1975.
27. Michael Manley, (London: Third World Media, 1979), p. 103.
28. Overseas Private Investment Corporation, Annual Report, Washington, 1974, p. 4.
29. Ibid., p. 8–9 for OPIC's worldwide customers.
30. OPIC Authorization, Hearings Before the Subcommittee on Foreign Assistance, Committee on Foreign Relations, Senate, 95th Congress, 1st session, 1977, p. 61, 71.
31. Ibid., p. 71, 127 of the hearings.
32. Ibid., p. 67.
33. Ibid., p. 143–144 for the quotes from Church and Kissinger.
34. For example, Lester Thurow, *Head To Head* (New York: William Morrow, 1992), especially Chapters 2 and 4.
35. Ibid., p. 200–210, for complete list of OPIC's latest policy decisions.
36. Gregory K. Schoepfle and Jorge F. Perez-Lopez, Export Assembly Operations in Mexico and the Caribbean, *Journal of Interamerican Studies and World Affairs*, Volume 31, number 4, Winter, 1989, p. 134–135.
37. Alex Dupuy, *Haiti In the World Economy* (Boulder: Westview, 1988), p. 176–177.
38. Ibid., p. 179; see too Joseph Grunwald, Leslie Delatour, and Karl Voltaire, Foreign Assembly in Haiti, in Joseph Grunwald and Kenneth Flamm, editors, *The Global Factory* (Washington: Brookings Institution, 1990), p. 180–205.
39. President Ford Library, White House Central Files, Box 23, memo from Council on International Economic Policy, dated October 4, 1974.
40. On La Banda see Miriam Diaz and Martin Murphy, *The 1982 Elections in the Dominican Republic* (Rio Piedras:

Institute of Caribbean Studies, 1983), p. 25.

41. Pharmaceutical Industry, Tax Benefits of Operating in Puerto Rico, Government Accounting Office, May 1992, p. 18 and 22.

42. Luis P. Costas Elenas, I.R.C. Section 936 and Fomento Income Tax Exemption in Puerto Rico, *Revista Del Colegio De Abogados de Puerto Rico*, Volume 41, Febrero, 1980, Number 1, p. 130–131.

43. Tax Reform Act of 1975, Hearings Before the Committee on Finance, United States Senate, 94th Congress, 2nd session, March, 1976, p. 1039.

44. Thomas St. G. Bissell, The Changing Tax Structure of the United States—Puerto Rico Relationship, *Georgia Journal of International and Comparative Law*, Volume 8, 1978, p. 897–913, see p. 901.

45. Tax Hearings, 1976, op. cit., p. 1040.

46. Bissell, op. cit., p. 898.

47. On the transfer payments and a variety of other issues see President Carter Library, Atlanta, Georgia, Domestic Policy Staff, Papers of Al Stern, long analysis of the Puerto Rican economy dated June 23, 1978, see p. 1–4.

48. Ibid., especially 6–8.

49. Manuel Escobar, *The 936 Market* (San Juan, 1980), p. 21–23. Mr. Escobar then worked for Citibank.

50. The Operations and Effect of the Possessions Corporation System of Taxation, Department of the Treasury. As of 1993, the Department has issued six reports. The first four, published in 1979, 1980, 1981, and 1983 trace the flow of what the government calls Qualified Possession Source Income.

51. For example, Leo Rockas, Recent Changes in the Possessions Corporation System of Taxation, *Cornell International Law Journal*, Volume 16, 1983, p. 431–453, especially p. 443.

52. Carter Library, Staff Offices, Speech Writers, Chronological File, Box 67, speech entitled "A Caribbean Wide Partnership", quotes p. 1–2.

53. Ibid., p. 5.

54. Economic and Political Future of the Caribbean, Hearings Before the Subcommittee on Inter-American Affairs,

Notes

Committee on Foreign Affairs, House, 96th Congress, 1st session, 1979, Washington, p. 5.

55. Ibid., p. 19–20.

56. Gerald Ford Library, White House Central Files, Box 61, memo from Secretary Kissinger to the president dated November 11, 1974.

57. Hearings, 1979, op. cit., p. 27.

58. Ibid., p. 86.

59. Carter Library, White House Central Files, Box CO-23, the president's comments are quoted in letter of protest from Congressman Donald Fraser, dated November 11, 1977; quote is from p. 2 of the five page letter.

60. Diaz and Murphy, op. cit. p. 27–28; also Jan Knippers Black, *The Dominican Republic* (Boston: Allen and Unwin, 1986); Michael Kryzanek and Howard Wiarda, *The Politics of External Influence in the Dominican Republic* (New York: Praeger, 1988).

61. Ibid., p. 4.

62. Ibid., memo from Pastor to Brzezinski, dated February 3, 1978; request for no major effort appears in February 3, 1978 memo from Christine Dodson, Staff Secretary of the National Security Council.

63. Carter Library, Office of the Assistant to the President for Communications—Rafshoon, Sugar Policy, Box 7, memo dated February 12, 1979, from A.E. Kahn to Jerry Rafshoon. Mr. Rafshoon forwarded it to the president with a note of approval.

64. Carter Library, Domestic Policy Staff, Eizenstat, Box 285, memo to the president dated February 10, 1979.

65. Carter Library, Domestic Policy Staff-Eizenstat, Agriculture, Box 140, memo dated July 19, 1978, see p. 2 of the attached "talking points".

66. Ibid., p. 1 of the talking points.

67. Carter, Eizenstat, Box 285, op. cit., memo to the president dated February 9, 1979, see p. 4 of the memo.

68. Terry McCoy, U.S. Policy and the Caribbean Basin Sugar Industry: Implications For Migration, Unauthorized Migration: Addressing the Root Causes, Staff Papers of the Commission For the Study of International Migration and Cooperative Economic Development, 1987–1990,

Washington, 1990, p. 712–713.

69. Alec Wilkinson, *Big Sugar: Seasons in the Cane Fields of Florida* (New York: Vintage, 1990).

70. Carter Library, Speech, op. cit., Box 67, p. 1.

71. Carter Library, Domestic Policy Staff-White, Box 22, Foreign Affairs memo entitled the "Cuban Exodus," dated May, 1980, p. 1–2.

72. Ibid., Box 23, memo for the president from Frank Moore, et.al. dated June 6, 1980.

73. Ibid., memo to the president dated May 13, 1980.

74. Ibid., April 23, 1980 memo for Stu Eizenstat from Fran White, p. 3.

75. Ibid., "Memorandum on Status Options" dated June 5, 1980; directed to Robert Bedell, p. 1.

76. The idea for a focus on the labeling process comes from Robert L. Bach, The Cuban Exodus: Political and Economic Motivations, in Barry Levine, editor, *The Caribbean Exodus* (New York: Praeger, 1987), p. 106–130; see especially p. 107–11.

77. Memo to the President dated June 6, 1980, labeled "Congressional Consultation on the Cuban/Haitian Situation"; see p. 6 for Senator Thurmond's comments.

78. Ibid., p. 5 , 6.

79. Ibid., p. 9 of June 14, 1980 memo to the President.

80. Ibid., see, for example, a memo to the vice-president dated July 31, 1980.

Cultural Constants

1. Caribbean Basin Economic Recovery Expansion Act of 1987, Hearings Before the Subcommittee on Trade, Committee on Ways and Means, House, 100th Congress, 1st and 2nd sessions, 1987-1988, p. 83.

2. Fourth Constitution of the Virgin Islands, Hearings Before the Committee on Energy and Natural Resources, Senate, 97th Congress, 1st session, May, 1981; for the president's remarks see p. 53-57.

3. Jimmy Carter Library, Domestic Policy Staff—Stern, Box 90, 5 page letter from Jeffrey Farrow to Stuart Eizenstat, Assistant to the president For Domestic Affairs and Policy;

undated, but marked "hand delivered 8/23/78." Quote is from p. 5 of letter.

4. Ibid., p. 2 of Farrow's letter.

5. Ibid., p. 4 of Farrow's letter.

6. Ibid., document labeled "Discussion Paper—Virgin Islands Constitution, September 8, 1980. p. 1.

7. Fourth Constitution of the Virgin Islands, op. cit., p. 57.

8. Domestic Policy Staff-Stern, op. cit., comment appears on p. 1 of July 28, 1978 memo from Mr. Stern to Stuart Eizenstat.

9. Caribbean Basin Policy, 1981, op. cit., p. 134-172; for the percentages on spending see Elkanah Major, The Caribbean Basin Initiative, Unpublished Doctoral Dissertation, Atlanta University, Department of Political Science, 1990, p. 104.

10. Review of CBI Sugar Provisions, Hearing Before the Subcommittee on Cotton, Rice, and Sugar, Committee on Agriculture, 97th Congress, second session, 1982, p. 14.

11. Major, op. cit., p. 113.

12. Background on the Caribbean Basin Initiative, Special Report No. 97, Department of State, Washington, March, 1982, p. 1.

13. Caribbean Basin Policy, 1981, op. cit., p. 139-140.

14. Ibid., p. 139-140.

15. Background on the Initiative, 1982, op. cit., p. 5.

16. Review of CBI Sugar Provisions, op. cit., p. 19.

17. Nixon Project, White House Office Files, Country Files, Box 26/27, memo to the president from John Erlichman, dated June 16, 1971.

18. Review of CBI Sugar Provisions, 1982, op. cit., p. 20.

19. Caribbean Basin Economic Recovery Expansion Act of 1987, op. cit., p. 62 and 120.

20. Caribbean Basin Initiative, 1982, op. cit., p. 153.

21. Ibid., p. 154.

22. For a fine analysis see Scott McDonald and E. Joseph Demetrius, The Caribbean Sugar Crisis: Consequences and Challenges, *Journal on International Studies and World Affairs*, Volume 28, No. 1, Spring, 1986, p. 35-58, especially p. 37.

23. Caribbean Basin Economic Recovery, 1987, op. cit. p. 275.

24. United States Sugar Policy: An Analysis, U.S. Department of Commerce, International Trade Commission, Washington, 1988, p.

25. For a superb analysis see Terry McCoy, U.S. Policy and the Caribbean Basin Sugar Industry: Implications For Migration, Report of the Commission For the Study of Unauthorized Migration and Economic Development, Washington, 1990, p. 703-727.

26. Hugo Guillani Cury, *Deuda Externa: Un Proceso de Renegociacion* (Santo Domingo: Centro de Estudios Monetarios y Bancarios, 1988), p. 51.

27. Gordon Lewis, *Grenada: The Jewel Despoiled* (Baltimore: Johns Hopkins, 1988), p. 141.

28. Ibid., p. 26.

29. Carter Library, White House Central Files, Box Co-28; speech included with other material in box of Grenada documents.

30. Caribbean Basin Initiative, 1982, op. cit., p. 296 for the congressman's comment; on the cooperation of Scoon see Ewart Archer, Gairyism, Revolution and Reorganization: Three Decades of Turbulence in Grenada, *Journal of Commonwealth and Comparative Politics*, Volume 23, No. 2, July, 1985, p. 91-111, see p. 98.

31. Economic and Political Future of the Caribbean, Hearings Before the Subcommittee on Inter-American Affairs of the Committee on Foreign Affairs, House, 96th Congress, 1st session, 1979, p. 20.

32. Robert Pastor, Does the United States Push Revolutions to Cuba? The Case of Grenada, *Journal of Interamerican Studies and World Affairs*, Volume 28, No. 1, 1986, p. 1-33, see p. 5, 9 for comment of Prime Minister Adams.

33. Ibid., p. 12.

34. Inquiry Into Occupation of Haiti and Santo Domingo, Hearings Before A Select Committee on Haiti and Santo Domingo, Senate, 67th Congress, 1st session, Volume 1, 1921, p. 517.

35. Pastor, op. cit., p. 10.

36. Archer, op. cit., p. 100.

37. Robert Joseph Beck, *International Law and Urgent Fury*, Unpublished Doctoral Dissertation, Georgetown University,

Notes

1989, p. 57-58.

38. Bob Woodward, *Veil* (New York: Simon and Schuster, 1987), p. 289.

39. Beck, op. cit. p. 246.

40. Ibid., p. 295.

41. See, for example, Scott Davidson, *Grenada: A Study in Politics and the Limits of International Law* (Aldershot: Avebury, 1988), especially p. 90-91.

42. Lessons Learned As A Result of the U.S. Military Operations In Grenada, Hearing Before the Committee in Armed services, House, 98th Congress, 2nd session, 1984, p. 30.

43. Hugh O'Shaughnessy, Grenada (New York: Dodd, Mead, 1986), p. 178; for the Uriah Heep comment see Gordon Lewis, op. cit., p. 141.

44. Beck, op. cit., p. 257-258.

45. The Situation In Grenada, Hearings, 1983, op. cit., p. 24 for the remark about safety; p. 30 for the remark about Scoon's assent or approval.

46. Beck, op. cit., p. 44.

47. Dam's November 4 statement is reprinted in O'Shaughnessy, op. cit., p. 249.

48. Lyndon Johnson Library, National Security Files, Box 50, memo to the president dated October 5, 1965, p. 1, 3.

49. Harry S. Truman Library, President's Secretary's Files, Cia Report titled Cuba, dated December 23, 1948; quote is from p. 1 of the report's summary.

50. Woodward, op. cit., p. 299.

51. James Ferguson, *Grenada: Revolution In Reverse* (London: Latin American Bureau, 1990), p. 21, 43.

52. Tax Reform Proposals XXIV, Hearing Before the Committee on Finance, United States Senate, 99th Congress, 1st session, 1985, p. 53.

53. Puerto Rico's Economy, Oversight Hearing Before the Committee on Interior and Insular Affairs, House, 99th Congress, 2nd session, 1986, p. 18.

54. Ibid., p. 18-19, 60.

55. Ibid., p. 18-19.

56. Puerto Rico Business Review, Government Development Bank of Puerto Rico, Volume 13, No. 8, August 1988, p. 7.

57. Puerto Rico's Economy, 1986, op. cit., p. 130.

58. Caribbean region, Hearing Before the Subcommittee on Oversight, Committee on Ways and Means, House, 101st Congress, 2nd session, 1990, p. 201.

59. Ibid., p. 179.

60. Ibid., p. 210; for the $2 billion dollar figure see p. 43; for the tax benefit, wage comparison, p. 44.

61. Ibid., p. 49.

62. Caribbean Basin Economic Recovery Expansion Act of 1987, op. cit., p. 88.

63. Ibid., p. 83; for the figures on employment see Terry McCoy, op. cit., p. 717.

64. McCoy, Ibid., p. 714.

65. Ibid., p. 270-271; see also Ronald Fernandez, Sugar Quotas Aren't a Sweet Deal in the Caribbean, Newsday, June 4, 1992, p. 106.

66. Unauthorized Migration: Addressing the Root Causes, Hearings Before the Commission For the Study of International Migration and Cooperative Economic Development, 1987-1990, Washington, p. 95.

67. Ibid., p. 257 of the International Debt testimony.

68. See the fine article by Christine A. Bogdanowicz-Bindert, The Debt Crisis: The Baker Plan Revisited, Journal of Interamerican Studies and World Affairs, Volume 28, No. 3, Fall, 1986, p. 33-55, especially p. 39-41; also ibid., p. 209-216 for a good summary of the bankers' motives.

69. For a good analysis of the IMF see the Special IMF Issue of The Economist, October 12-18th, 1991, Sisters in the Wood, p. 1-48.

70. Richard E. Feinberg, Third World Debt: Toward a More Balanced Adjustment, Journal of Interamerican Studies and World Affairs, Volume 29, No. 1, Spring, 1987, p. 47-55, p. 49 for the quote.

71. For all the figures see Economic and Social Progress in Latin America, Inter-American Developmental Bank (Washington: Johns Hopkins University Press, 1991): Barbados, p. 36; Haiti, p. 104; Dominican Republic, p. 74; Jamaica, p. 115.

72. See, for example, John T. Cuddington and Carlos Asilis, Fiscal Policy, the Current Account and the External Debt

486

Problem in the Dominican Republic, *Journal of Latin American Studies*, Volume 22, Part 2, May, 1990, p. 331-352.

73. Caribbean Region, 1990, op. cit., p. 54; p. 159 for the discussion of interest rates.

74. Ibid., p. 213.

75. Ibid., p. 130.

76. Ibid., p. 223-225 for the Minister's report.

77. Ibid., p. 210.

78. Ibid., p. 210.

79. Political Status of Puerto Rico, Hearings Before the Committee on Energy and Natural Resources, Senate, 102 Congress, 1st session, February 1991, p. 176.

80. Carlos Romero Barcelo, *Statehood Is For the Poor* (San Juan, 1978), p. 104.

81. Political Status of Puerto Rico, op. cit., p. 219.

82. Ibid., p. 173.

83. Congressional Record, House, 101st Congress, 2nd session, May 9, 1990, p. E1439.

84. Romero Barcelo, op. cit., p. 87.

85. Ibid, p. 87.

86. Edicion de Aaron Gamaliel Ramos, *Las Ideas Anexionistas en Puerto Rico Bajo la Dominacion Norteamericana* (Rio Piedras: Huracan, 1987), p. 154.

87. Political Status of Puerto Rico, op. cit., p. 217-218.

88. Ibid., p. 227.

89. Ibid., p. 223-225.

90. Ibid., p. 217.

91. Ibid., p. 108.

92. Ibid., p. 107-108

93. Ibid., p. 103.

Index

Index

Index

Index

Index

Index